INDIAN SUMM1

1. New Delhi completed. Painting by Marjorie Shoosmith, 1931. Left to right, Lord Irwin, the Viceroy; Sir Edwin Lutyens and Sir Herbert Baker, architects; and Sir Alexander Rouse, Chief Engineer. Lady Irwin is in purdah.

# INDIAN SUMMER

*Lutyens, Baker, and Imperial Delhi*

ROBERT GRANT IRVING

YALE UNIVERSITY PRESS
NEW HAVEN AND LONDON

Designed by Caroline Williamson
and set in Monophoto Bembo.
Printed in Hong Kong.


**Library of Congress Cataloging in Publication Data**

Irving, Robert Grant, 1940–
Indian summer – Lutyens, Baker and Imperial Delhi.
Bibliography: p.
Includes index.
1. Lutyens, Edwin Landseer, Sir, 1869–1944.
2. Baker, Herbert, Sir, 1862–1946. 3. New Delhi
(India) – Buildings. 4. Architecture – India – New
Delhi – British influences. I: Title.
NA997.L817      722'.44'56      81-14648
ISBN 0-300-2422-3 (cloth)      AACR2
ISBN 0-300-03128-9 (paper)

To my parents

# CONTENTS

# PHOTOGRAPHIC ACKNOWLEDGMENTS

*Architectural Review*, 194, 215; Author, 3, 5, 28, 49, 51, 61, 62, 66, 67, 71, 75, 76, 78, 81, 87, 88, 89, 92, 98, 99, 100, 121, 122, 123, 128, 133, 134, 138, 141, 142, 143, 144, 145, 147, 148, 150, 151, 152, 153, 160, 163, 166, 167, 170, 171, 172, 176, 178, 179, 182, 183, 185, 186, 193, 196, 197, 198, 201, 202, 203, 206, 207, 212, 213, 216, 217, 218, 220, 221, 222, 223, 225, 226, 227, 228, 229, 230, 231, 235, 236, 237, 239, 240, 241, 245, 246, 247, 249, 253, 266, 267, 270, 271 (portrait of Lord Hardinge and watercolors, courtesy of Rashtrapati Bhavan, New Delhi and Government of India, Central Public Works Department); Henry Edmeades Baker, 14, 15, 26, 188, 195, 200, 209, 210, 211, 214, 234; Batsford, 30; Bettmann Archive, 7, 8; Broadlands (Romsey) Limited, 137, 139, 273; Cambridge University Library, Crewe Collection, 19, 20, 21, 22, 23, 24; Commercial Club, Chicago, 32; Constable & Co., 11; *Country Life*, 48, 68, 77, 95, 112, 114, 118, 119, 125, 132, 140, 168, 199, 224, 265, 268; *Design*, 254; Robert Freson, 57, 58, 80, 84, 85, 93, 97, 102, 103, 108, 109, 110, 111, 115, 127, 149; Earl of Halifax, 1; Rear Admiral P. N. Howes, 16, 86, 124; *Illustrated London News*, 4, 9; Government of India, Central Public Works Department, 82, 154, 155 (redrawn by Michael Beal), 174; Government of India, Press Information Bureau, 2, 12, 34, 35, 120, 173, 180, 181, 192, 205, 219, 232, 238; India Office Library and Records, 10, 13, 54, 55, 56, 104, 105, 106, 107, 113, 129, 156, 159; *India State Railways Magazine*, 90; Sean Kernan, 50, 74, 83, 94, 101, 126, 131, 161, 162, 164, 165, 175; Longmans, Green, 33; the late H. A. N Medd, 242, 243, 244, 248, 250, 251, 252; National Gallery of Art, Washington, D.C., 91; National Portrait Gallery, London, 59, 191; Princeton University Press, 9; Lord Romsey, 72, 73; Royal Geographical Society, endpapers, 6; Royal Institute of British Architects, 18, 25, 29, 52, 53, 63, 64, 65, 69, 70, 79, 96, 116, 117, 184, 187, 189, 190; Mrs. Marjorie Cartwright Shoosmith, 36, 37, 38, 39, 40, 41, 42, 43, 44, 45, 46, 47, 135, 136, 146, 157, 158, 169, 177, 204, 208, 233, 255, 256, 257, 258, 259, 260, 261, 262, 263, 264, 269, 272; Yale University Library, 27.

# ACKNOWLEDGMENTS

Many people have helped. I am particularly grateful to Vincent J. Scully for his guidance and encouragement. I am also much obliged to two other professors at Yale University, Robin W. Winks and the late Christopher Tunnard, for their interest and assistance.

For their generous financial support, I am indebted to the Yale Graduate School, the Yale Council on European and Comparative Studies, and the American Institute of Indian Studies. I am grateful for the kindness of the staff of the Yale University Library, the Avery Library of Columbia University, the Library of Congress, the Lewis Walpole Library, and the libraries of Harvard University, Trinity College, and the University of Hartford. The helpfulness of Peter J. Knapp at Trinity College, Hartford, an exemplary librarian, scholar, and friend, merits special acknowledgment.

In India I enjoyed the assistance of the staff at the American Institute of Indian Studies; the British Council Library; the National Archives of India, particularly Miss D. G. Keswani; the Delhi Public Administration Record Office; the Central Public Works Department; the New Delhi Municipal Committee; and Rashtrapati Bhavan, especially Lieutenant Colonel M. L. Bhatia, Military Secretary to the President of India. Mr. and Mrs. John L. Bissell, Dr. Ainslie T. Embree, C. S. H. Jhabvala, Ashok Nehru, B. Shiva Rao, and Khushwant Singh were generous with their time and with much practical advice. I benefited greatly from interviews with Sir Sobah Singh, a principal contractor for New Delhi, and with S. R. Deolalikar, S. K. Joglekar, and Y. A. Yardi, former Chief Architects of the Central Public Works Department, Government of India.

I wish to acknowledge the gracious permission of Her Majesty Queen Elizabeth II to use correspondence in the Royal Archives, Windsor, and I am grateful to the Librarian, Sir Robin Mackworth-Young, for his help. I am much indebted to Dr. Richard Bingle and the staff at the India Office Library and Records; David Dean, John Harris, and Mrs. Margaret Richardson of the British Architectural Library, Royal Institute of British Architects; D. H. Simpson of the Royal Commonwealth Society Library; Miss T. M. Thatcher of the Centre of South Asian Studies, Cambridge University; and members of the staffs at the University of Birmingham Library, Cambridge University Library, and Kent County Archives. I wish also to acknowledge the kindness and indispensable assistance of the Dowager Lady Hardinge of Penshurst; Lady Richard Percy; Viscount and Vicountess Ridley; the late Hope Bagenal; Mr. and Mrs. Henry Edmeades Baker; Mrs. M. H. Boyce;

James Burchell; the late Professor John Gallagher; Mrs. John Greaves and the late Mr. Greaves; Vernon Helbing; H. V. Hodson; Miss Mary Lutyens; Mrs. Robert Lutyens and the late Mr. Lutyens; Mrs. Henry Alexander Nesbitt Medd and the late Mr. Medd; the late Sir Percy Orde; Miss Jane Ridley; Mrs. Robert Tor Russell and the late Mr. Russell; Mrs. John Lewis Sale; Mrs. Arthur Gordon Shoosmith and the late Mr. Shoosmith; Dr. Percival Spear; the late Sir Basil Spence; Gavin Stamp; the Provost and Fellows of King's College, Cambridge; the President and Fellows of Magdalen College, Oxford; and the Warden of Queen Elizabeth House, Oxford. I am also obliged for his help to the late Admiral of the Fleet Earl Mountbatten of Burma, last Viceroy of India, and to former members of his Viceregal staff, Lieutenant Colonel F. J. Burnaby-Atkins, Lieutenant Colonel Sir Martin Gilliat, and Rear Admiral Peter Norris Howes. Sir Gilbert Laithwaite, Private Secretary to the Marquess of Linlithgow during his Viceroyalty, offered useful insights. I especially wish to thank John Nicoll and Caroline Williamson of the Yale University Press for their wise counsel and assistance.

   Finally, I am indebted and grateful, as always, to my parents for their support and encouragement.

Robert Grant Irving
Berkeley College
Yale University
May 24, 1981

# I

# *Durbar, 1911*

As the sun set on September 16, 1803, the torrid heat abated and immense crowds thronged the streets to watch General Gerard Lake enter Delhi in triumph at the head of a glittering cavalcade. Accompanied by Prince Mirza Akbar Shah, heir apparent to the Mughal throne, the British Commander-in-Chief made his way slowly through the packed streets of the Imperial capital until he reached the barbican and bastions of the Exalted Fort. There the octogenarian emperor Shah Alam, blind and shabbily dressed, seated beneath a small tattered canopy in the Diwan-i-Khas or Hall of Private Audience, greeted his conqueror with what dignity the ravages of time and his enemies had left him. The scene presented a pathetic contrast to the brilliance of Emperor Shah Jahan's court a century and a half before, when only the most privileged foreign potentates or ambassadors were granted admittance to the opulent splendor behind the scarlet curtains of this private apartment. Sumptuous marble piers and scalloped arches, a shimmering gilded ceiling, and the placid waters of the Nahr-i-Bihisht or Stream of Heaven provided the setting for the renowned, jewel-encrusted Peacock Throne. On the richly inlaid walls were inscribed in Persian the poet Sa'di's words: "If there be paradise on earth, it is here, oh! it is here, oh! it is here." In the ensuing 150 years, much tangible glory had been lost to a succession of invaders; the Peacock Throne itself had been plundered by the redoubtable Persian Nadir Shah in 1739. Now, in 1803, the Mughal emperor had been obliged to sue hastily for the "protection of the British government" when the defeat of the Maratha and French soldiery (whose puppet he was) seemed imminent.[1]

Ostensibly General Lake was a victorious deliverer, worthy of such traditional imperial tokens of favor as jewelry, horses, elephants, robes embroidered with gold thread, and precious gems. Material boons were beyond the means of the penurious Shah Alam, but he invoked time-honored custom in bestowing impressive titles upon Lake: Sword of the State, Hero of the Land, Lord of the Age, Victorious in War, Commander-in-Chief.[2] The emperor's grant of honors and office belied the fact that this once-proud line had become pensioners of an alien race. Lake's presence in the Diwan-i-Khas marked the fulfilment of the century-and-a-half-old prophecy of the martyred Sikh Guru Teg Bahadur, who foretold to Emperor Aurangzeb the advent of a race from across the seas to build a mightier kingdom than the Mughals'.

To the citizenry of Delhi who jostled for a glimpse of General Lake that September evening, their new masters were but the latest of a host of conquerors whose armies had tramped through the vicinity since prehistory. The Aryan invaders who entered India from the steppes of southern Russia and central Asia in the second millennium B.C. had a capital named Indraprastha, which tradition and archaeology have identified with Delhi. Dating from about 1000 B.C., or roughly contemporaneous with King David, the epic *Mahabharata* recounts in couplets the war between the Kauravas from Hastinapura on the Ganges and their hated first cousins the Pandavas, whose capital lay some eighty miles southwest at Indraprastha. In the succeeding three millennia, the city was remarkable for the number of its sites, each the quarry for the next. Reference is often made to the "seven Delhis," with the new Delhi as the eighth; but the correct count is more nearly fifteen cities, a dozen in desuetude and ruin before the first Mughal emperor occupied Delhi in 1526. [2]

The predilections of princes largely account for the changes in site. The desire to perpetuate a personal or family name, to celebrate recent victory, or to augment prestige or prominence by building new capital cities are vanities not peculiar to the Indian subcontinent. In Delhi's history these ambitions were typical of dynasties newly established through conquest. The search for security or for a position more easily defended against the challenges of marauders or aspiring rulers further contributed to the capital's mobility. Frequent alteration of the River Jumna's course similarly played a role. In addition, cities in the early Hindu era grew up beside the river for religious reasons; later, in Delhi's barren plain the Muslim conquerors from less arid climes sought the coolness and life-giving waters of the Jumna's banks with equal assiduity.

The reason for the persistence of a capital city at this particular reach of the Jumna is to be found not in its commercial or agricultural advantages but in its political and strategic importance. Set at an important ford and the most northerly navigable point of the Jumna, Delhi lies athwart the Punjab corridor which connects the northwest with the rest of India, and it is through the northwest passes from Persia and Afghanistan that many of India's invaders have come. From Delhi the whole of India lies before the would-be conqueror. Control of Delhi represented the key to Hindustan and to the fertile corn fields and rice paddies of the upper Gangeatic plain and Bengal. From Delhi pressure could be exerted on the plentiful lands of central and western India, with their access to the sea, and on Ajmer, gate to the citadels of Rajasthan. Control of Delhi offered mastery of the whole subcontinent. Small wonder, then, that for thirty centuries Delhi attracted both alien aggressors and indigenous claimants to imperial power.[3] [3]

With British possession of Delhi, the remnants of Mughal splendor became ever more tawdry, and only Shah Alam's blindness spared him the spectacle of desolation and decay which greeted visitors to the court. The British masters determined that the Emperor, whom they deigned to call simply the King of Delhi, would be no more than a crowned stipendiary. The monthly allowance doled out to him was insufficient to maintain all the palace buildings, family, and the hundreds (and later several thousands) of royal collaterals who eked out a squalid and empty existence within the confines of the Fort, entirely dependent on the King's bounty. The fountains stood silent, garden sweepings lay scattered on the marble pavements, and the dung of birds and bats stained many walls. What dignity and occasional ceremonial pomp remained was but a hollow symbol of vanished power: "the old

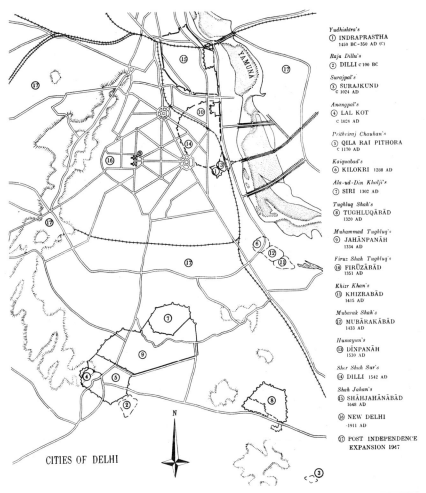

CITIES OF DELHI

N

2. The cities of Delhi from 1450 B.C.

3. The central and strategic location of Delhi.

400 miles
500 km

4. The Imperial Durbar at Delhi, 1877. The Viceroy, Lord Lytton, proclaimed Queen Victoria the Empress of India.

Mughal traditions lingered on as if in suspended animation like withered leaves on a windless autumn day."[4]

This tranquil decadence was swept away in 1857 by the bloodbath of the Mutiny, with its horrors of massacre, siege, and vengeful sack. Delhi had already been retaken from the rebels when a young British cavalry captain forced two of the King's sons and a grandson to strip at gunpoint, then summarily shot them in a bullock cart before the gates of the city. For three days their bodies were put on public display. Bahadur Shah, the aged poet-King, was spared. The last of the Great Mughals, under the benign charge of one Lieutenant E. S. Ommanney, together with twenty-nine relatives, harem women, and attendants, took his leave of the Exalted Fort at Delhi on October 7, 1858, to begin the long journey to Rangoon. There, in 1862, he died in exile.

The administration of Delhi was delegated to the Punjab, and the capital of an empire became a divisional and district center. One beautiful mosque was converted into a residence and a bakery, to be rehabilitated only under Lord Curzon. The precincts of the city's second largest mosque were sold at auction for shops, and not until the first Delhi Durbar was the whole restored.[5] Indeed Lord Lytton's selection of Delhi instead of Calcutta for the magnificent Durbar of 1877, and the vividness of the passing show, at which Queen Victoria was proclaimed Empress of India, did inspire memories of former splendor. But not until Lord Curzon's masterfully conceived Durbar on the accession of Edward VII was Delhi's proud heritage again invoked. [4]

While the preeminence of Delhi in education and culture declined, the commercial importance that the city had enjoyed under the Mughals in the cloth and grain trade increased. By the early twentieth century, moreover, its industry rivalled Cawnpore and Amritsar in north India, and its banks commanded substantial financial resources. A location equidistant from the ports of Karachi, Bombay, and Calcutta, and at the junction of major railway lines (six by 1911), helped to account for its prominence in the Punjab, United Provinces, and Rajputana. An affluent commercial class, both Hindu and Muslim, exploited these advantages. The bustling avenue of Chandni Chauk, with its cloth shops, churches, banks, cinemas, mosques, temple, and Town Hall, had a decidedly prosperous and cosmopolitan air.[6] [3]

No partisan, however, could deny that Delhi lay "on a malarial plain surrounded by melancholy vestiges of a ruined and departed alien greatness," nor could he ignore the documented evidence of unhealthy living quarters, appalling disease, and high mortality rates. Half the population of some 233,000 persons lived cramped within the city walls, while the remainder made their home in the outlying Subzimundi, Sadr Bazar, Paharganj, and Civil Lines. The Delhi Health Officer reported that the many cows who shared the city's teeming quarters were kept "in the most insanitary conditions, crowded together, in unlit, unventilated, and undrained sheds." Of all the samples of milk examined in one year by the Health Officer, not one was found uncontaminated. Every sample of the staple cereal produced an identical result. In the same year, local authorities poisoned more than 6,500 stray or pariah dogs and officially destroyed almost 70,000 rats, while the city was described as "swarming with mosquitoes and fleas." Not surprisingly, Delhi suffered repeated onslaughts of the plague and entire seasons of epidemic malaria.[7]

The city fathers of Calcutta were swift to advertise Delhi's disadvantages and deprecate its possible choice as the setting for the Durbar to mark the coronation of George V in 1911. In December 1910, shortly after the arrival in India of a new Viceroy and Governor-General, Lord Hardinge of Penshurst, a deputation from the Corporation of Calcutta called at Government House to press the claims of their city for the Durbar ceremonies. "I was very courteous and friendly," the Viceroy confided to his diary, "but firmly declined to put forward their views." He had already made up his mind. When on November 26 the Maharaja of Kashmir (a Hindu) had expressed his opposition to a Durbar in the capital of the Mughal emperors and tried to insist that the ceremony be held at Calcutta, Hardinge declared that the second largest city of the British Empire was "quite unfit for such a gathering" and had "no traditions to create any impression."[8]

The new Viceroy, whose grandfather had been Governor-General of India, had spent five years in the diplomatic service in Constantinople, Cairo, and Teheran, and he readily accepted the suggestion of his staff that "very great importance" attached in the East to "the magnificence with which such a pageant as the King-Emperor's entry into Delhi, the ceremony of the Durbar, and all other functions" were performed. Hardinge had been well schooled as a diplomat in resplendent court ceremonial, notably during his seven years in the embassy in St. Petersburg (two as

5. The first Baron Hardinge of Penshurst, Viceroy of India, 1910–16.

6. The first Marquess Curzon of Kedleston, Viceroy of India, 1899–1905.

Ambassador) and as a trusted and virtually indispensable attendant to Edward VII on royal visits to seven kings, three emperors, the French President, and the Pope. He was alive, however, to the necessity of securing and sustaining the goodwill of the Indian people and was in complete sympathy with the advice that the royal visit be "as solemn, dignified, and impressive, and still as popular" as the occasion deserved.[9]

Scarcely a month after his arrival in India, Hardinge could write to his close friend Lord Sanderson that he was already hard at work preparing for the Durbar. "The organization will be stupendous," he reported, "but I have a strong Committee running the show." A week before, the Viceroy had appointed Sir John Hewett, Lieutenant-Governor of the United Provinces, as President of the Coronation Durbar Committee. At the same time, Sir Guy Fleetwood Wilson, senior member of the Viceroy's Council, submitted to Hardinge the name of an exceptionally able young Oxford graduate as the representative of the Finance Department on the Durbar Committee. The Viceroy's appointment of Malcolm Hailey was for the youthful Indian Civil Service officer the first step in a distinguished career that would be writ large across India and the Empire for more than half a century. Hailey discharged his new financial duties with characteristic energy and accepted a host of other Durbar responsibilities, including supervision of the garden party and the

Press and Visitors' Camp. His vigor was comparable to that of Lord Curzon himself. For Hailey's chief, however, the challenge of the Durbar proved almost too much. Within three months, Hardinge was lamenting the event as "a tremendous handicap . . . during the first year of my office in India when I have so much to learn, so much to do, and so much to read." He confessed it would be "an immense relief" when the forthcoming royal visit was over.[10]

Admittedly the Coronation Durbar of 1903, under Lord Curzon's presiding genius, was a difficult act to follow. That Viceroy's dazzling and perceptive touch had extended to the most minute details, and his own person had eclipsed even the King's brother, the Duke of Connaught. Eight years later the event was still known as Curzon's Durbar. Every resource had been strained to transport, feed, and house the 173,000 persons who had descended on Delhi. The Viceroy's Committee had organized mile upon mile of roads and light railways and had made complicated arrangements for electric lighting, water supplies, sanitation facilities, medical supervision, and police, both in the city and the vast area occupied by the temporary camps. The ceremonies had lasted ten days. In addition to the Durbar itself at the amphitheater outside the city, there had been a four-mile progress or State Entry of the Viceroy and Duke and Duchess of Connaught on richly caparisoned elephants through Delhi, two investitures, a state ball, a spectacular review of the troops, and the reception of the ruling chiefs—impressive imperial ritual which proclaimed the British as legitimate successors to the Mughal court.[11]

7. The Coronation Durbar, December 12, 1911. King George V and Queen Mary at the Royal Pavilion.

Hardinge was determined that his Durbar must outshine Curzon's achievement, and throughout the elaborate preliminaries, elements of conscious rivalry were evident. "I wish you could see the Camps and all the preparations," the Viceroy wrote to Lord Sanderson. "They are on a very large scale—far larger than those of Curzon's Durbar, and the details have, I think, been more carefully looked into and controlled."[12]

The most remarkable feature of the Durbar was, of course, the unprecedented presence of the King-Emperor and Queen-Empress, an event Hardinge announced on his arrival in India on November 18. King George had himself proposed the Durbar visit to Prime Minister Herbert Asquith in early September 1910 and had pressed the suggestion in a letter to the Secretary of State for India, Lord Morley, on September 8. On November 2, Hardinge found the Prime Minister "entirely in favour" of the royal visit. Six days later the Cabinet gave its approval, although, as Asquith's Private Secretary reported, "not without a certain amount of criticism." The King announced his intended journey to India in his first speech to Parliament on February 6, 1911.[13]

The visit of a reigning British monarch to any of his overseas dominions posed questions which were at once the delight and the terror of the legalistic or bureaucratic mind. A hot debate arose, for example, over the choice of a Regent during the prolonged absence of the King from Britain. These duties would normally have devolved upon his consort, but the Queen, too, was to be in India.[14]

Even more vexing, it seemed, was the problem of a suitable crown. Tradition and security, among other factors, militated against the removal of St. Edward's Crown or any of the other regalia used at Westminster Abbey on June 22. If a special crown were to be made for the occasion, who would pay for it—the British Government or the Government of India? Or should the Indian princes be asked to finance the undertaking? Some sources suggested a public subscription in India. Should the new crown remain in India? The confidential correspondence between London and Calcutta that poured forth on the subject involved Viceroy, Prime Minister, Cabinet, and Council. Indignant at the proposal that the crown be paid for by subscription, members of the Viceroy's Council telegraphed a strongly worded protest to the India Office. Their decision, accepted unanimously by the Council of the Secretary of State, decreed that Indian revenues would pay for the Emperor's new crown. But not until some three months after the Durbar was the imperial crown's final home announced. In the official exchanges preceding this revelation, memories of the Mutiny were evident in anxious visions of armed uprisings culminating in the theft of the crown. Such fears, of course, remained unspoken when Edwin Montagu rose in the Commons to reply to a query suggesting the crown remain "housed and guarded" in India. The Under-Secretary chose instead to note the "constitutional objection" to any course construed to provide separate regalia for India or to detract from the fact that the King was crowned Emperor of India at his coronation in Westminster Abbey. At His Majesty's express command, the crown would be kept on display within the eminently secure fastness of the Tower of London.[15]

The intricate preparations for the royal visit were reaching their climax when the first of a series of ominous incidents occurred. Exhausted by a year of tremendous

8. The Coronation Durbar, 1911. The King-Emperor and Queen-Empress receiving homage.

9. King George and Queen Mary on the ramparts of the Delhi Fort, with Indian princes as pages, 1911.

exertion, Malcolm Hailey, who was later to play a pivotal role in Delhi's history, caught typhoid fever. The loss of his services was felt keenly by the Viceroy and his advisers alike. "It is dreadfully hard luck that he will miss the Durbar, for the success of which he has worked so hard," sympathized the President of the Durbar Committee. "Not only has he run our finances admirably, but he has undertaken a great deal of administrative work." [16]

The appointed day arrived. On December 2, under a fiery morning sun, the great white ship *Medina* and her four escorting cruisers dropped anchor in Bombay harbor, about two miles from shore. At four o'clock that afternoon, the heat continued sultry as the Emperor and Empress of India disembarked from the royal launch at the Apollo Bunder in Bombay, to a salute of one hundred and one guns. Two days later 26,000 schoolchildren gave the royal couple an enthusiastic reception. Colorfully arrayed groups sang the national anthem in four tongues and performed a rhythmic dance and Gujarati song, in words proclaiming fervent loyalty. [17]

The following day, the Viceroy's arrival by train at Delhi from Bombay initiated final rehearsals for the Durbar which would bring such momentous and unexpected results for the former Mughal capital. Vividly decorated horses and a legion of flags, banners, spears, and silver maces accompanied empty carriages along the route of the procession. The day, however, was not without casualties which, in a country where astrology and ancient superstitions loomed large in the public mind, were certain to be viewed as ominous portents. A generous stockpile of fireworks reserved for a popular celebration—the People's Fête—exploded spectacularly only an hour before an equally dramatic fire occurred in the Exalted Fort of the Mughals itself. An elegant red, green, yellow, and blue tent supported by silver-plated poles and enclosing more than 200,000 square yards, that was lent by the Nawab of Bhawalpur for the reception of the King-Emperor by the princes, was wholly consumed in flames. What soothsayer could have foreseen in these grim signs the reverses and rises in the fortunes of the Indian princes and common people which Delhi would witness for the next half century?

As visitors continued to pour into Delhi, the population swelled by three-quarters of a million, and the official Durbar camps alone catered for 300,000. On the morning of December 12, six years to the day after the royal couple's visit to Delhi as Prince and Princess of Wales, more than 100,000 persons filled the great arena north of the city to witness beneath a dome of azure sky what was destined to be the last and most brilliant Coronation Durbar. On top of the canopy adorning the smaller of the two amphitheaters which faced each other, the bright sunlight glinted on the gilded finials of the cupolas that recalled the imperial Mughal heritage. Among the 12,000 persons of privilege seated beneath the canopy, the colors of hundreds of turbans mingled with officers' uniforms and white helmets and with the elaborate hats and dresses of the ladies. The gold-embroidered robes of the ruling chiefs, in myriad hues of purple and scarlet, rose, pink, light blue and green, delicate orange or flamelike yellow, glittered with the ransom of many kings in diamonds, rubies, and emeralds. Facing the display was an equally colorful spectacle, yet even more imposing in its sheer numbers: the great semicircular mound covered with 70,000 lesser mortals and within this great amphitheater, 20,000 massed troops.

At the very center of this vast concourse stood the Royal Pavilion, its two thrones raised high, visible to all, beneath a gleaming golden dome. Alas, to the perceptive, the dome with its pinched neck and attenuated proportions recalled Mughal architecture in the eighteenth century—the twilight period of decadence and decline when the Emperor and his advisers, increasingly bereft of real control, struggled grimly to survive amid rapid change and tumultuous upheaval. So pointed a reminder of the transience of empires, the gilded bubble was an inauspicious ornament at a celebration of British imperial power in India. Doubtless, few harbored such dark thoughts amid the excitement and awesome beauty of the events which unfolded, punctuated by the flourish of trumpets and the roll of drums: the homage of the mightiest subjects, beneath the crimson and gold canopy of the shamiana; the procession in state to the Pavilion, Their Majesties garbed in white satin with robes of purple velvet bound in gold, preceded by fourteen mace-bearers; the enthronement; then the Coronation Durbar proclamation in English and Urdu by heralds in tabards emblazoned with the royal arms, followed by the Viceroy's announcement of the royal boons; and before the royal procession returned to the shamiana, the three cheers for sovereign and consort "that must have roused the dead Mughals in their graves." More than thirty years later, the editor of the *Times of India* was to write of the Durbar in his memoirs: "It was probably the most magnificent and dazzling spectacle of its kind that the eye of mortal has ever beheld." [18] [7, 8, 9]

But all the splendor of the ceremony could not compete with the importance of the unexpected moment yet to come. Standing once more beneath the crimson canopy of the shamiana, the King delivered an announcement which was to ring throughout the length of India:

> We are pleased to announce to Our People that on the advice of Our Ministers tendered after consultation with Our Governor-General in Council, We have decided upon the transfer of the seat of the Government of India from Calcutta to the ancient Capital of Delhi, and, simultaneously and as a consequence of that transfer, the creation at as early a date as possible of a Governorship for the Presidency of Bengal, of a new Lieutenant-Governorship in Council administering the areas of Behar, Chota Nagpur, and Orissa, and of a Chief Commissionership of Assam, with such administrative changes and redistribution of boundaries as Our Secretary of State for India in Council may in due course determine. It is Our earnest desire that these changes may conduce to the better administration of India and the greater prosperity and happiness of Our People. [19]

Later called "the best-kept secret in the history of India," the contents of the announcement had been imparted to only a self-styled "Masonic Circle," a handful of men in England and India. Given the code name of "Sesame," the project had not even been divulged to the Queen before the arrival of the royal party in India. For five months, fewer than twenty persons were privy to the scheme: the Secretary of State for India (the Marquess of Crewe), his private secretary, the Permanent Under-Secretary of State, and Crewe's predecessor, Lord Morley; and a dozen persons in India, including the Viceroy and his Councillors. Lord Crewe kept his decision secret from both the Cabinet and the Council of India until November and even then did not permit his Council any expression of opinion. The Viceroy, for his part, refrained from telling the heads of the provinces most intimately concerned, as well as the Governors of Bombay, Madras, and Bengal, until the evening before the Durbar. He even took the precaution of having his Councillors' minutes or comments on the scheme typewritten by his daughter's nurse! Both Hardinge and Crewe felt some anxiety about the King's powers of reticence, but he pledged himself to secrecy with such emphasis that Crewe was able to write, "He has so completely learned the lesson of necessary discretion since some days, not so very remote, which you and I recall, that he will be most rigid about this, I feel sure."[20]

The royal announcement, therefore, caught those few within earshot wholly unprepared. For a moment animated buzzing filled the smaller amphitheater until the whole company stood to sing the national anthem and to witness the departure of the royal carriage and escort. After the multitude of troops withdrew in seemly order there occurred, unrehearsed, one of the most moving moments of the day: crowds of the humblest spectators rushed across the arena to prostrate themselves in reverence before the empty thrones and to press their foreheads against the marble steps of the Pavilion.[21]

The King-Emperor's words burst over Delhi like tropical sun through the dark rain clouds of a monsoon. Consigned for more than half a century to provincial status, the city found itself raised at one stroke to the capital of a subcontinent. Delhi was now an Imperial capital in reality as well as in name: not simply the residence of a decadent dynasty, virtual prisoners within their palace, it boasted the seat of a powerful government whose effective authority stretched from Kashmir to Colombo, from Calcutta to Karachi.

Once the carefully kept secret had been revealed, rapid preparations were made to mark with due ceremony Delhi's new place in the sun. Two days following the Durbar, another unscheduled announcement created ripples of excitement in the Durbar camps: 500 invitations were issued to the heads of local governments, ruling chiefs, provincial representatives, and high military officers to a ceremony "inaugurating the restoration of Delhi as the Capital of India by laying foundation-stones."[22]

From the night of December 12, coolies, carpenters, and masons from the Public Works Department labored around the clock to prepare the chosen site on the avenue of the Government of India camp, where tents for members of the Viceroy's Council were pitched. On December 15, Gordon Highlanders lined the route as the King, on horseback, and the Queen, in the State carriage, arrived at a freshly erected dais, where Lord Hardinge and his Councillors conducted them to their thrones. The beginning of such a bold adventure—the creation of a new capital for India— called for brave words from the Governor-General, and he did not fail. The laying of the stones, he noted, "set a seal" upon the King's announcement:

Many capitals have been inaugurated in the neighborhood of Delhi, some of which are so ancient that their origin is lost in the mists of antiquity, but none has ever arisen under happier auspices than those which attend the ceremony which Your Imperial Majesties are about to perform, and assuredly none ever held promise of greater permanence or of a more prosperous and glorious future.

The King in his reply provided the keynote for the great project which for the next two decades was to occupy the energies of so many thousands on the plains of Delhi: "It is my desire that the planning and designing of the public buildings to be erected will be considered with the greatest deliberation and care, so that the new creation may be in every way worthy of this ancient and beautiful city." Employing ivory mallets and two silver-gilt trowels set with amethysts, the royal couple each in turn set mortar to stone, and the foundations were deemed well and truly laid.[23]

Because of the haste with which the ceremony had been contrived, two sets of dressed stones had been ordered, one from local contractors, Kunhia Lal and Sons of Kashmir Gate, and the other from the Public Works Department. The latter pair, inscribed simply with the date in gilt letters and numerals, were completed first and hence bore the honors. Before long a malicious rumor was circulated that urgency had dictated the use of a tombstone on December 15. The story gained even greater currency when repeated in the House of Commons on June 10, 1912, by the Earl of Ronaldshay, a former aide-de-camp to Curzon in India. Although wholly retracted by Ronaldshay, the story continued to recur, frequently improved by elaboration. As late as 1919, the *Indian Daily News* of Calcutta described how a piece of marble intended for a tomb, with its inscription already begun, had had to be redressed for the ceremonial foundation laying.[24]

If this tale aroused the superstitious imagination of prophets of doom, there were yet other omens. The day following the King's Durbar announcement, the Peninsular & Oriental liner *Delhi*, carrying the King's sister, Princess Louise, and her husband, the Duke of Fife, together with their daughters, foundered in the Straits of Gibraltar in heavy seas. Although the ducal family were rescued, the shock and exposure left their mark: by the end of January the Duke was dead. In India the incident was widely reported. "The popular mind," one Member of the Bengal Legislative Council told Curzon, saw in the wreck of the *Delhi* signs "of grave danger to the British Raj."[25]

In one of the Durbar week's most spectacular events, the King-Emperor reviewed the parade of 50,000 British and Indian soldiers, whose formations stretched in a line nearly four miles long. The Nawab of Bahawalpur's exotic Camel Corps, the Maharaja of Jodhpur's lancers, and four Highland regiments, bagpipes skirling, were among the most striking elements in a display of apparently invincible might. But could it be thought portentous that during one climactic moment the Commander-in-Chief's Indian horse almost threw his imperial master, scattering medals and decorations on the Delhi plain?[26]

On December 14, at an investiture held by the King-Emperor at Delhi, in which the Queen was created Knight Grand Commander of the Order of the Star of India, fire alarm whistles echoed through the royal reception tent and electric lights flickered. A nearby tent was consumed by fire—this time the quarters of Lord Crewe's private secretary. But prompt action prevented further calamity, so that the Viceroy was able to write to Lord Sanderson and Sir John Hewett that the Durbar "passed off without a hitch of any kind."[27]

The Maharaja of Alwar, in a private letter, presented a more jaundiced view of the proceedings: "The organization and arrangements at almost all the functions was— well! we wanted Lord Curzon out here." Such appraisals of the Durbar evidently

10. Their Majesties leave India, January 10, 1912. Ceremony at the Apollo Bunder, Bombay.

escaped the ears of Hardinge, who told Sanderson, "everybody considers that it has been an unprecedented success, and I have not heard complaints or grumbling from any side. The actual Durbar was, I should imagine, the biggest and most wonderful show that has ever been seen." His sentiments were soon echoed in the House of Lords by a former Governor of Bombay, Lord Reay, who called the ceremony "an unprecedented event in the brilliant annals of India." On January 10, when the King and Queen sailed from India, Hardinge recorded with satisfaction in his diary, "There has never been such a successful visit."[28]

The King was overcome with emotion during his final address to his Indian subjects. "I actually broke down in reading my farewell speech in Bombay," he told his mother, Queen Alexandra. Hardinge reported that the royal couple wept as the launch took them to their ship. While dusk gathered, the *Medina* and her escort steamed out of Bombay harbor in a single line, and the Viceroy "gave a sigh of welcome relief."[29] [10]

From early in his reign the King had felt his own presence in India might inspire and consolidate the loyalty of the Indian masses and act as a counterbalance to the growing power of the nationalists. Richard Barry, a correspondent for the *New*

*York Times*, put his analysis of the visit's purpose more bluntly: "that the native hordes may be properly impressed with the might of Great Britain." The Durbar provided an appropriate excuse for the marshalling of India's fearsome native army, which, together with a comparative handful of British civil servants and British troops, maintained the fiction of white supremacy on the subcontinent. The King-Emperor's passage through India was swift but "flashing with the facets of concentrated power," to the end that the Imperial name might "lie upon the land like a mighty threat concealed in the soft robe of a shining benediction." Already the perceptive recognized that Britain's days in India were numbered; the royal visit was seen as a desperate bid to salvage supremacy, the playing of the chief trump card at a critical juncture.[30] The monarch at his Durbar, the incarnation of benevolent despotism, was meant both to soothe and terrify the Oriental imagination, to impress upon the Indian people that they possessed an Emperor whose civil service was efficient and whose army still stood ready.

As the *Medina* sailed steadily westward into the twilight toward Suez with its royal passengers, its bright lights growing faint on the horizon, night descended over Bombay. In Delhi a breeze whispered softly across the empty Durbar amphitheater, and the moon's rays played on the shimmering domes of the tombs which gave the plain its title, "the graveyard of dynasties." Beneath the most majestic dome, one which inspired the Taj Mahal, the simple sarcophagus of the Mughal Emperor Humayun lay enveloped in darkness—its chill, small slab a silent testimony to the common end of all earthly splendor and imperial glory.

# 2

# Transfer of the Capital

Calcutta's position as the premier city of India had been firmly established since 1774. In that year, a Regulating Act had made the celebrated and controversial Warren Hastings Governor-General of Bengal, with supervisory powers over Bombay and Madras, and had provided for a Supreme Court of Judicature in Calcutta. But proposals to remove the seat of British Government in India from Calcutta had a respectably long lineage. In a minute written in 1782, Hastings cited Calcutta's defects, especially its climate and remote situation, and expressed his "decided opinion" that the permanence of British dominion in India could not be ensured with such a capital. He urged changing the seat of authority to the healthier and more central Colgong district "or to any other that shall be judged more eligible." Lord William Bentinck, during his tenure as Governor-General from 1828 to 1835, had contemplated transfer of the capital to Meerut, later the scene of the outbreak of the Mutiny. In 1844 serious suggestions to move the Government of India up-country to Agra had occupied the attention of the British Cabinet. The fifth Earl Stanhope recorded that in October 1844 the Duke of Wellington declared himself strongly opposed to such an action for strategic reasons: he believed it indispensable that the capital be readily accessible to the superior might of the British navy in the event of indigenous uprising or external threat.[1]

When the Mutiny swept across India in 1857, the Governor-General, Viscount Canning, felt keenly the inconvenience and difficulty of ruling the subcontinent from its southeast corner. In the course of restoring the north of India to normality, "Clemency" Canning moved his government up the Gangeatic plain to the more centrally positioned Allahabad. There in 1858 Canning held an historic Durbar at which he read Queen Victoria's proclamation of November 1, announcing the transfer of the governance of the subcontinent from the East India Company to the Crown. Allahabad thereupon relinquished primacy to Calcutta and once again became the headquarters of a merely provincial administration.

Delhi's claims to replace Calcutta as the focus of British rule in India were promptly discredited by her role in the Mutiny. Sir John Lawrence, the Chief Commissioner of the Punjab who had besieged the Mughal capital for four months, bore it no love and was determined to prevent its ever achieving greatness. Consequently he altered the route of the main railway line then under construction so as to avoid Delhi, with the result that until 1889 Allahabad remained the center of rail communication in northern India. Not long after his appointment as Governor-General in 1863, Lawrence initiated the annual migration of the senior government officials to Simla for the hot weather, a change he considered preferable to permanent removal of the capital from Calcutta.[2]

In the latter part of Lawrence's Viceroyalty, during the interval 1867 to 1868, the Secretary of State, Sir Stafford Northcote, and the Government of India thoroughly discussed permanent transfer of the capital as well as raising Bengal from a Lieutenant-Governorship to a Governorship. Promotion to a Governorship would have conferred upon the provincial administration the rights of direct correspondence with the Secretary of State, of appeal to him against the orders of the Government of India, and of full discretion in filling major posts in Bengal. Northcote favored such a change and established a committee to consider the possibility, and the question was the subject of a learned memorandum by the eminent jurist Sir Henry Maine, who was at the time Legal Member of the Viceroy's Council. But Lawrence's opposition seems to have been conclusive in defeating the proposal. A decision to create a Governorship very likely would have precipitated a transfer of the capital, for there appeared to be agreement that the presence of a Governor in Calcutta would be incompatible with the continued domicile of the Viceroy and Government of India in the same city.[3]

On January 1, 1877, with Lord Lytton presiding at Delhi amid great pomp, Queen Victoria was proclaimed Kaisar-i-Hind, Empress of India, and saluted by the Indian princes as Shah-in-Shah Padshah, Monarch of Monarchs, effective heir to the Mughal throne, titles, and feudal system of honors and homage. In the same year Lytton revived the proposal for removing the capital from Calcutta, but the Prime Minister, the Earl of Beaconsfield, rejected the Viceroy's suggestion on strategic grounds, preferring a capital promptly accessible to the navy.[4] Disraeli's veto was tinged with irony: thirty years earlier, in his novel *Tancred*, he had depicted the transfer of the capital of the British Empire from London to the heart of India!

The question of a change of capital city never really died. Curzon's Durbar of 1903 renewed interest in the discussion, but the Viceroy this time demurred, certainly in part because of his keen personal interest in Calcutta's Victoria Memorial Hall, a museum he conceived as a monument to British rule. Evidently, however, he did give consideration to the claims of Ranchi, Agra, and Delhi. Walter Lawrence, Curzon's highly capable private secretary during his Viceroyalty, afterward expressed disappointment over his master's reluctance: "I wish with all my heart that I could have persuaded Lord Curzon to make the move." Curzon's successor as Viceroy, the Earl of Minto, made no move to desert Calcutta for Delhi during his term of office from 1905 to 1910, although he later admitted he found much that was attractive in the idea and confessed to having "often discussed the possibility of such a change."[5]

Toward the end of Minto's Viceroyalty, the Finance Member of the Viceroy's Council, Sir Guy Fleetwood Wilson, confided to Lord Kitchener, then Commander-in-Chief in India, his ardent belief in the necessity of a Governorship for Bengal and the transfer of the capital to Delhi. He was evidently persuasive, and found the General "extraordinarily receptive." Kitchener fully expected to be named successor to Minto, and he indicated to Fleetwood Wilson that if he became Viceroy "the capital of India would be on the ridge at Delhi." He even discussed with the Finance Member the cost such a project would entail.[6]

The change of capital to Delhi had been pressed upon the King during his visit in the winter of 1905–6 as Prince of Wales. Several Indian princes, including the Regent of Jodhpur, General Sir Pertab Singh, who accompanied the royal party as an aide-de-camp, strongly supported Delhi "as being in every way more convenient and on account of its historical associations with the ancient Government of India."[7] The memory of this advocacy helps account for the King's enthusiasm for the idea.

In February 1910, almost two years before the Durbar, the Lieutenant-Governor of the Punjab, Sir Louis Dane, had boldly predicted that one day Delhi would be restored to her former splendor and pride of place. Standing once again in the Exalted Fort of the Mughals on December 23, 1912, Dane had occasion to recall his prophetic words there, as with great ceremony he relinquished the administration of the city to the Government of India.

Hardinge's proposal to change the capital, made to his Council in June 1911, six months before the Durbar, was thus not a revolutionary suggestion but in reality the culmination of more than half a century of discussion and agitation. Who, then, were the actors who had had the audacity and the vision to place the project upon the stage? How had they contrived to initiate what others had merely discussed?

The great scheme received its original impetus, astoundingly, from the King-Emperor himself. "It was entirely my own idea to hold the Coronation Durbar at Delhi in person," King George wrote in his diary. Ever since his visit as Prince of Wales, he had been impressed with the advantages which might result from a visit to India by the sovereign.[8] With characteristic persistence or indeed obstinacy, therefore, he promoted his plan until he secured his Ministers' approval, then promptly advanced an even more controversial proposal. Indian tradition dictated that a Durbar of such importance should be commemorated by boons or marks of special favor. The unique occasion of the King-Emperor's presence raised the event to an altogether transcendent level, and any boons conferred would have to be necessarily proportionate.

The "seditious spirit" which the King acknowledged to exist in India distressed him. Like many others he saw its genesis in the partition of Bengal devised by Lord Curzon in 1905. This well-meant attempt by the Viceroy to reduce the increasingly ungovernable size of Bengal, which numbered 78 million persons, had provoked violent and sustained agitation from Bengali nationalists. For not only was the Bengali-speaking area split in half, but the division also corresponded with communal boundaries. The result was that Eastern Bengal became a preponderantly Muslim province, while Biharis and Oriyas outnumbered the Hindu Bengalis in the province of Bengal itself. Protest meetings and resolutions left Curzon unmoved. His own authoritarian instincts (typified by his alleged motto, "Never apologize, never explain") suited well the independence he enjoyed as head of a distant and far-flung autocracy, with even the right to overrule a majority of his Council. The Government of India adhered fixedly to the doctrine of efficiency and reasoned that concession to popular outcry could be interpreted as weakness.

The King deplored the continued unrest in his Indian Empire, especially Bengal. At forty-six years of age he had experienced the prerogatives of kingship only since May 1910, but he dreamed of playing a constructive role in allaying the discontent. Had not his father by personal intervention and diplomacy helped mitigate the differences among the Great Powers and earned the title of "Peacemaker of Europe"?

In November 1910, the monarch not only conferred the Grand Crosses of the Star of India and of the Indian Empire upon a new Viceroy but also presented the seals of office to a new Secretary of State for India. The Earl of Crewe succeeded Viscount Morley at the India Office. As early as the summer of 1910, at a time when Crewe had no expectation of India Office responsibilities, the King had spoken to him about the partition of Bengal. The King had asked whether there was not some action that the Government could take to satisfy those who opposed the division of the province, something which he could possibly announce at a Durbar. He himself had always disagreed with the change and had found support for his opinion from numerous persons, including Sir Walter Lawrence, a trusted friend and adviser who had been chosen to accompany the royal couple to the subcontinent five years before. Lawrence told the King that although he had been Curzon's private secretary in India, he had been against the partition from the outset. In the late autumn of 1910, therefore, buttressed by such authority, the King proposed to Lord Crewe raising a united Bengal to the status of a Presidency with a Governor, and on December 16 Crewe transmitted this suggestion to the new Viceroy.[9]

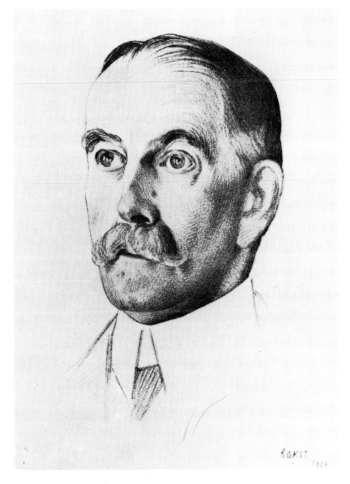

11. The first Earl (later first Marquess) of Crewe. Drawing by Leon Bakst, 1921.

At the age of fifty-two, Robert Offley Ashburton Crewe-Milnes, first Earl of Crewe, had already had a distinguished record of service in the public domain before his appointment as Secretary of State for India in 1910: he was created Viceroy of Ireland in 1892, Lord President of the Council in 1905, and Lord Privy Seal, Colonial Secretary, and Liberal Leader in the House of Lords in 1908. Moreover he was one of the royal family's most trusted friends and advisers: he had been a Lord in Waiting in 1886 and created a Knight of the Garter in 1908; King Edward VII as Prince of Wales had been present at his wedding to his second wife; and King George V was shortly to be the sponsor, in person, at the baptism of his fifth child. There was general agreement among his contemporaries that he was a man of high cultivation and attractive personality, a wealthy aristocrat with a classical education who devoted himself to politics as well as to racing, breeding cattle, and his library. He was not a born orator and had a quiet, even hesitant, delivery, which evinced solid reflection and disappointed those who looked for radiant flashes of wit. Edwin Lutyens, for example, who was shortly to play such a central role in directing the shape of architecture in twentieth-century India, met Crewe for the first time in 1912 and reported that he was, "though slow and non-brilliant, a gentleman." [10]

The Viceroy, Charles Hardinge, first Baron Hardinge of Penshurst, born the same year as Lord Crewe, shared an equally aristocratic education (Harrow and Trinity College, Cambridge) and distinguished record of achievement, but in the diplomatic service rather than practical politics. He had held posts in Constantinople, Berlin, Washington, Sofia, Bucharest, Paris, and Teheran, and had been Ambassador at St. Petersburg as well as Permanent Under-Secretary for Foreign Affairs. His loyal and much valued attendance upon Edward VII in many personal capacities had earned him the gratitude of his sovereign's heir, the new King.

Hardinge never seems to have gained a reputation as an orator, and public speaking was a task he confessed he disliked. Indeed, by several estimates, he was afflicted with a certain shyness, a characteristic which expressed itself in a reserved manner, concealing his sense of humor and giving many persons an impression of austerity. With such a personality Hardinge found the strain of the royal visit and the Durbar "almost unbearable," a sentiment which would scarcely have escaped from Curzon. He was nevertheless determined, ambitious, and hard-working. By his own estimate he spent nine or ten hours a day fulfilling his "never-ending" duties, earning himself a reputation for thoroughness and "an unequalled capacity for work." [11]

Hardinge was not without his detractors, however, and his ambition produced charges of opportunism. Having never acquired that thick skin which is a product of the political arena, he was hypersensitive to such unfavorable judgments, and indeed to all censure. Lord Curzon's criticisms of his Indian administration elicited not merely Hardinge's wrath, but provoked an enmity which grew in intensity with the passage of time. For support, Hardinge relied heavily on a very few trusted colleagues and above all upon his wife Winifred, daughter of the first Lord Alington. After some observation close at hand as Member of the Viceroy's Council, Sir Harcourt Butler was prompted to remark that "Hardinge has Crewe in his pocket, and Lady Hardinge has Hardinge." [12]

Although long in public service, neither Crewe nor Hardinge had had any previous responsibility for Indian affairs. Hardinge's grandfather had been Governor-General, but the new Viceroy and the Secretary of State had no direct experience of India or her governance. Necessarily, therefore, they relied upon the members of their respective Councils for advice, especially in the case of Hardinge, who lacked the political experience of Crewe.[13]

During his Viceroyalty, Hardinge often looked for direction to the Member of his Council responsible for finance, Sir Guy Fleetwood Wilson. The senior Member of the Governor-General's Council, he had been in India only since 1908, but his long acquaintance with military and financial affairs (he had been Director-General of Army Finance) gave his words authority on many questions which were to arise. As Fleetwood Wilson himself admitted, he was "always a bit of a red flag" to his "bullish colleagues." He was, Hardinge recorded, "a perpetual source of irritation" to the other Members of Council; there were "few men so disliked." His sympathetic attitude toward moderate reforms and aspirations, however, endeared him to educated Indians. At the end of his term, no less than eighteen Indian Members spoke warmly, even affectionately in the Legislative Council of his personality and ability; six took the unusual step of asking that his appointment be extended. Furthermore he was very loyal to the Viceroy, and this counted for much.[14] Such devotion in a vital post, combined with an aging bachelor's nose both for detail and for current public and private opinion, made him a more than ordinarily useful source of counsel.

Next most senior of Hardinge's advisers was John Lewis Jenkins, who was to be knighted at the Durbar. Proficient in the Gujarati, Baluchi, Sindhi, and Persian languages and Hindustani dialect, Jenkins had been in India more than thirty years when he was appointed to the Governor-General's Council in 1910. He had the additional advantage of having served in the Legislative Council of Bombay in the previous decade. He was, Hardinge acknowledged, a very masterful man, honest and straightforward, but with that flaw which Hardinge failed to recognize in himself: he resented opposition.[15]

The incumbent Lieutenant-Governor of Bengal, Sir Edward Norman Baker, was similarly a man with experience valuable to the new Viceroy: he had been Financial Secretary to the Governments both of Bengal and India, had served in the Bengal Legislative Council, and had been a member of the Governor-General's Council. His jurisdiction, moreover, encompassed the most populous province in India and the largest city after London in the British Empire, and his residence in Calcutta made his advice readily accessible to Hardinge.

The new Viceroy's reliance on the knowledge of men about him was amply evident when he was confronted with Crewe's proposal (initiated by the King) of a Presidency for Bengal, with the capital at Dacca and Commissioners for the different geographical divisions. Crewe also suggested on his own initiative the creation of an imperial enclave consisting of the city of Calcutta and a small surrounding district administered by officers directly responsible to the Viceroy. Hardinge later confessed that "having been barely two months in the country, I was hardly in a position to give a definite opinion of my own." As a result, before replying to Crewe, the Viceroy "consulted two or three people," including "some of the Members of my Council."[16]

The Viceroy relied in particular on the Lieutenant-Governors of Bengal and the province of East Bengal and Assam and, within his Council, on John Jenkins. Sir Lancelot Hare, Lieutenant-Governor of the new province of East Bengal and Assam and Member of the Governor-General's Council in 1905–6, wrote at length in defense of the status quo, arguing that "a strong feeling of provincial pride" had now grown up not only among the partisans of partition but even among its previous opponents. Sir Edward Baker declared that the idea of altering the partition of Bengal filled him "with something like despair," and was a step which "would be fraught with disaster" for India. Jenkins was equally emphatic. He commented on Crewe's letter that "what India requires above everything at the present moment is peace and quiet. We do not want fireworks, or grand coups, however artfully designed to produce an effect." Confronted with such a unanimity of opinion, it is not surprising that Hardinge replied in the negative to the India Office, rejecting the proposals of the King and the Secretary of State as "impracticable." Without further ado Lord Crewe accepted the Viceroy's initial suggestion to allow the scheme "to quietly drop altogether."[17]

Four months later, by June 1911, preparations were rapidly progressing for the forthcoming Durbar in December, and the question of financing a special Durbar crown for the King-Emperor had yet to be resolved. In his diary on Sunday, June 16, Lord Hardinge recorded: "Received a letter from Crewe urging the raising of subscriptions for the purchase of the Crown. A very tiresome idea." The next lines were, however, pregnant with consequence: "also received a bomb shell from Jenkins. A big idea. Will talk to Jenkins tomorrow." The following day the die was cast for an event of real moment. That evening the Viceroy wrote in his diary, "Saw Jenkins and intend to take up his idea." Later Hardinge was to call it the most important decision of his tenure in India.[18]

Jenkins's idea was contained in a memorandum to the Viceroy dated June 17. The Home Member of the Viceroy's Council called for revision of the partition of Bengal, a revision whose central point was the creation of an Imperial capital at Delhi. Jenkins appealed to Hardinge's sense of his place in the long story of India: such a scheme "would be a bold stroke of statesmanship, which would give universal satisfaction, and mark a new era in history." The Home Member argued that the holding of the Durbar at Delhi recognized that city as the true capital, and he pleaded that when a King or Prince of Wales again visited India he might be received not in a city of canvas tents but in a capital worthy of the Empire.[19]

Jenkins's suggestion fell on fertile ground. Since the beginning of the year, when he had declared a modification of partition as impracticable, Hardinge had witnessed the continued turmoil in Bengal with increasing anxiety and the realization that if nothing were done there would inevitably be even more serious trouble. If there was to be peace, the Viceroy reasoned, something must be done to remove "the cause of all the anarchical agitation in Bengal." After seven months spent mastering the intricacies of his office, the Viceroy was ready to act. He was sensitive to the implication of a policy of drift which Jenkins himself raised the previous month. The Home Member had disseminated a printed minute throughout his Department in which he said he was ignorant of the Government's policy, if indeed it had one. In a scathing personal interview on May 23, Hardinge branded his Councillor's attitude as disloyal.[20] Jenkins had been properly penitent, and his scheme, which may have been motivated in part by a desire to win anew the Viceroy's favor, contained a formula for action, a recipe he clearly felt both Hardinge and India needed.

Both the scheme and the source were a surprise, for in February, as Hardinge commented, the Home Member had provided "powder and shot" to refute Crewe's proposals. At the time Jenkins had been emphatic in his hope that the partition "not be touched in any way," for a reversal would have inflamed the Muslim majority in East Bengal by submerging them once again in a Hindu province. Jenkins had, however, been equally forcible in asserting that it was "a most unfortunate thing" that Calcutta should be the headquarters for the Government of India. There ought to be an Imperial capital, he had declared, just as there were federal capitals in the United States, Canada, South Africa, and Australia, and it should not be in one of the great commercial cities. Jenkins's new scheme was devised to conciliate all parties and overcome previous objections. He envisioned a magical effect when the plan was announced at the Delhi Durbar; for as the masses had associated Delhi and Empire in their minds from earliest history, the changes would touch their imagination "indescribably."[21]

After long consultation with the Home Member on June 19, therefore, Hardinge was in full agreement, and drafted a secret memorandum on June 20 for the opinions of the Members of his Council. The principal intentions were: (1) to restore the Chief Commissionership of Assam, (2) to make Bihar and Orissa into a Lieutenant-Governorship with a Legislative Council and an entirely new capital at Patna, (3) to create a unified Bengal as a Presidency with a Governor in Council (normally a peer) appointed from England, and (4) to create an Imperial capital at Delhi, with the city and neighboring district under the direct administration of the Government of India. The transfer of capital was, Hardinge told his Councillors, "the keystone of the whole scheme," on whose acceptance the entire proposal must depend.[22]

From the printed correspondence on the subject, from Lord Hardinge's diary, and from his memoirs (written decades after his Viceroyalty), it would appear the idea of the transfer was very much that of the Home Member, John Jenkins. As Hardinge wrote in *My Indian Years*, Jenkins's memorandum of June 17 caused his views "to materialize into a definite policy."[23]

But if Jenkins's note proved the catalyst, the unprinted correspondence of Sir Guy Fleetwood Wilson indicates that the Finance Member had discussed the whole issue with the Viceroy nearly two weeks previously. Fleetwood Wilson was shown Crewe's correspondence on the subject for the first time, and he suggested a line of action which Jenkins's later memorandum duplicated, with the exception of certain geographical demarcations. Any reversal of the partition, he emphasized, was "absolutely dependent upon the removal of the Government of India to Delhi or some other suitable centre, which should be created into an enclave on the lines of Washington." Although such mention is absent from his memoirs, the Viceroy early acknowledged Sir Guy's important role in the formulation of the proposals. On June 21 he wrote to Fleetwood Wilson, "I send you first of my Council a scheme from the responsibility for which I cannot entirely absolve you. I have little doubt of your approval." The Viceroy asked his Finance Member to state the political and financial sides of the question in a note, then discuss it with him before the secret memorandum was sent to the other Councillors.[24] In this way, Hardinge clearly realized, he could ensure that a strong supporting statement from the senior member of his Council would be seen by the others before they appended their comments.

In a memorandum dated January 1, 1912, inscribed "India: Transfer of the Capital to Delhi (which I and I alone initiated)," and placed on record in his personal papers, Fleetwood Wilson described for posterity the extent of his role. He recalled that Jenkins originally sent the Viceroy a strongly worded opinion adverse to the whole suggestion (apparently his letter of February 14), but that he subsequently "became a convert to and an enthusiastic supporter of the policy I advocated." The Viceroy's communication with Fleetwood Wilson in the first week of June, with details of Lord Crewe's proposals, was crucial. "I saw my chance and I took it," the Finance Member recorded; the policy he suggested apparently appealed to the Viceroy "at once."[25]

Fleetwood Wilson had felt earlier in 1911 that he would have great difficulty in getting Jenkins not to oppose absolutely any change in partition. Possibly some prompting from the shrewd senior Member of Council, at a point when Jenkins was seeking to recover the esteem of the Viceroy, may have inspired the catalytic memorandum of June 17. The Finance Member was politician enough to sacrifice short-term plaudits in order to win support for the scheme from Jenkins, "who, if violently opposed to it, would have presented an almost insuperable obstacle." Fleetwood Wilson was content to await the judgment of history: "In regard to myself, it matters little what I did or did not do: but for the sake of historical accuracy, I should like to place on record that I was the only member of the Government of India, at the time, who initiated the consideration of the question and who advocated the transfer of the capital since carried into effect."[26]

In his note or minute of June on the Viceroy's scheme, Fleetwood Wilson recounted that as early as the beginning of 1909 he had concluded it would be necessary to modify partition and to remove the Government of India from Calcutta. Thus his strong support for the transfer of the capital to Delhi and the creation of a Governorship for Bengal was not a decision of the moment but a view he had held for several years. In the same note, the Finance Member abandoned his customary caution to say that he could not conceive that more than five million pounds would be necessary for the new capital city.[27] This bald guess, which Fleetwood Wilson acknowledged was made without adequate information, was later reduced in a published despatch to four million, a figure destined to plague the new Delhi for years to come.

The other Members of Council agreed to the scheme in principle, but were careful to point out the possible difficulties and their own reservations. Jenkins in his note gave the policy his "heartiest support" and discreetly avoided any appearance of authorship.

Given this strong approval by his colleagues, Hardinge proceeded with the utmost secrecy on July 6 to send to the India Office proposals which bore a remarkable resemblance to those of Lord Crewe seven months before. "It is a bold scheme and a big scheme, but I believe it to be a good scheme," he wrote, and then added at the end of his missive, "This letter is rather a bombshell, is it not?" On July 13, when forwarding the unedited minutes of his Council on the proposals, the

Viceroy asserted that though there might be differences over the means, there was unanimity on the ends: the transfer of the capital to Delhi and the revision of the partition. For assistance with the lengthy covering letter of explanation, Hardinge called upon Fleetwood Wilson, whose emendations and improvements he adopted gratefully. The Viceroy indicated to Crewe that he regarded the question as one of such great secrecy that he had copied his letters himself, and his Councillors' minutes had been typewritten by his little girl's nurse.[28]

A "very satisfactory telegram" approving the scheme "on general lines" was on Hardinge's desk in Simla by July 26. Then on August 7, full authority to proceed came over the wires. "You have my entire support," the Secretary of State telegraphed from halfway around the world, and with those words the future destiny of Delhi was sealed. The following day, amid the Victorian splendor of Viceregal Lodge at Simla, Lord Hardinge regarded the contents of the deciphered telegram with gratification. Only four days before he had written Crewe that he felt "greatly exhilarated at the thought of pushing the scheme through." In his diary, however, his customary restraint did not fail him, and his laconic entry did not betray his emotions: "Had a satisfactory telegram from Crewe about my scheme."[29]

Crewe's telegram asked for a formal despatch on the subject, to be sent as a private letter to ensure privacy and prepared for ultimate publication in its entirety. Hardinge had already completed a draft despatch on the evening of August 4, and in a midnight letter (signed "Yours very sleepily") he had solicited Fleetwood Wilson's suggestions, which were subsequently accepted en bloc. A fresh despatch was prepared following Crewe's telegram; the first version contained certain reflections on the Bengalis which the Viceroy felt would not bear publication.[30]

John Jenkins drafted an important passage in the despatch: Section 3, forecasting increasing devolution to the provincial governments without impairment of the supreme authority of the Government of India. The Home Member, when in the Bombay Government, had discussed with the Governor, Lord Sydenham, plans for releasing the provinces from the detailed control of the Governor-General in Council. His minute of June 24 on Hardinge's scheme dealt with the prospect of provincial autonomy in language almost identical to that of the despatch.

Notwithstanding the concert of opinion among the scheme's authors, unanimity did not prevail in the Viceroy's Council. Members suggested certain alterations of the draft despatch, with the most persistent reservations being expressed by R. W. Carlyle and Harcourt Butler. Fleetwood Wilson was deputed to apply pressure on Butler, and Jenkins on Carlyle.[31]

In Britain, the tempo of events began to increase. Lord Crewe, map in hand, explained the scheme fully to the King and his private secretary, Sir Arthur Bigge (later Lord Stamfordham), on August 11. The King was excited about the new arrangements for both Bengal and Delhi, and the following day Crewe telegraphed that His Majesty entirely approved and would make the announcement himself at the Durbar. With royal support, Hardinge regarded the plan as "practically secure" and allowed himself to confess "great pleasure." Four days after confiding the plan to the King, Crewe broke it to Prime Minister H. H. Asquith and Viscount Morley, the previous Secretary of State for India, now in the Cabinet as Lord President of the

Council. Both were favorably impressed, and John Morley's acquiescence was especially gratifying to Crewe because, as he remarked, "J.M. is particularly apt to tear his hair and scatter ashes when a novel scheme is afoot." The Prime Minister was struck by the bigness of the idea and considered its merits to outweigh the hostile arguments. Hardinge himself uncharacteristically admitted that he was "thrilled" by the whole idea, and Crewe replied that the Viceroy could "hardly be more thrilled and absorbed" than he was at the thought of the project.[32]

On Friday morning, August 25, the Viceroy and his Council assembled in Simla to set their signatures to the secret despatch. In the succeeding months the Council discussed in secrecy the legislative and statutory measures necessary to execution of the scheme. Meanwhile in London, in order to ensure that leakage of details would be kept to a minimum, Lord Crewe did not inform his own Council until the last two days in October, securing their agreement on November 1, and shortly thereafter that of the British Cabinet.[33] The stage was set for the King's dramatic Durbar announcement.

King George, in announcing the changes contemplated for Delhi, Bengal, Bihar, Chota Nagpur, Orissa, and Assam, emphasized that the end sought was "the better administration of India," as well as the increased prosperity and happiness of her people. A cardinal feature of the scheme, as originally proposed by Lord Crewe and as ultimately sanctioned, was the severance of the entangled operations of the Governments of India and Bengal by the removal of one from Calcutta. Both Sir Guy Fleetwood Wilson and John Jenkins, writing in support of the suggested transfer of capital, agreed that the location of the two governments in the same city was most unfortunate. The presence of the Imperial Government in Calcutta lent the persistent Calcutta and Bengali grievances and agitation "a factitious importance," while responsibility for events in Bengal was often mistakenly attributed by the public to the Governor-General in Council.[34]

Hardinge and his colleagues felt it imperative that the central or supreme Legislative Council (thirty-two of whose sixty-eight members were Indians following the reforms of 1909) should not be subjected to the direct and daily influence of Calcutta public opinion, considered "the worst in India." Jenkins described the Europeans in the capital as "conservative and prejudiced," while the Indians were "flighty and running into extremes." Clearly the contentious atmosphere of Calcutta was detrimental to the impartiality of the central government, while the actions of the Bengal Government were subjected to criticisms and impediments from which other local governments were exempt. With the increasing political autonomy of the provinces, forecast in the Viceroy's despatch of August 25, it was deemed more urgent than ever that the central Government be dissociated from any single local government.[35]

The creation of a Governorship for Bengal, a gesture calculated to flatter the self-importance of all Bengalis, would, however, run the risk of an unfortunate consequence: an antagonism or rivalry between Viceroy and Governor, both men prominent in British public life and both rulers resident within the confines of the same city. This question, Hardinge recalled, had been fully considered as early as 1867 and 1868 by the Secretary of State and the Government of India, respectively, who had concluded that a Governorship would necessitate consideration of the transfer of the Imperial capital from Calcutta.[36] The new plan resolved these dilemmas by removing the Imperial capital to Delhi. This bold proposal also found support from those who urged a capital city separate and independent from the influence of the great commercial cities, an enclave in the manner of Washington, Ottawa, Pretoria, and Canberra.

Delhi, however, had an advantage that those new capitals could never match: a site with deep-rooted historic associations. Lord Hardinge's germinal despatch of August 25 declared that Delhi's traditions as an Imperial capital, from the ancient Indraprastha to the Mughal Shahjahanabad, should find favor with Hindu and Muslim alike. Its Hindu heritage, however, was remote compared to its prominent role as an Islamic capital from the thirteenth to the nineteenth centuries. Its revived importance, therefore, appealed chiefly to Muslim sentiment and was intended to play an essential role in placating disgruntled East Bengal Muslims, now part of a reunited province dominated by a rich and well-educated Hindu elite in Calcutta. As one experienced "India hand" told Parliament, "the idea of Delhi" clung "to the Mohammedan mind in India," and establishing the seat of British power at the ancient Imperial capital should have "a powerful effect" on Indian Muslims. Lord Crewe agreed with Hardinge that erecting a new capital would be taken as "an unfaltering determination to maintain British rule in India"; Delhi's imperial associations would not only assert a sense of historical continuity but would promise as well "the permanency of British sovereign rule over the length and breadth of the country."[37]

Its central location also argued on behalf of Delhi as capital of the Indian Empire. Proponents of the transfer were swift to point out that it was equidistant from the merchants of Bombay and Calcutta, not tucked away in a corner of the subcontinent. Although representatives to the Legislative Council from Madras, Bengal, and Burma would have further to travel, Allahabad and the major port of Karachi were closer. In addition, Delhi was on the frontier of two important areas, the Punjab and the United Provinces. Delhi's convenience of access, moreover, would please the loyal Rajput princes and the numerous other ruling chiefs to be found principally in northern India. Since 1889 the city had been the junction of a great railway system, served by no fewer than six lines; from this point of view it was described as "ideal." Apart from its central location and fine communications, Delhi was appreciably closer than Calcutta to Simla, with the result that the annual migration to the hills would consume far less time and be much less costly. The city's other qualities, its champions asserted, included a comparatively good climate, enabling the Government of India to remain in the capital for a longer sojourn of some seven months, from October 1 to May 1.[38]

Calcutta's climate seems to have played no little part in inspiring the transfer of the capital. Lord Curzon admitted in Parliament that Bengal did not possess "a single healthy district," and Lord Hardinge apparently found the heat intolerable. After four months in India, the Viceroy complained of the March temperatures in Calcutta, which were daily ninety-five degrees Fahrenheit in the shade. Delhi, he told the King, has "a far better climate than Calcutta." In mid-March 1912, he wrote to Lord Sanderson from Calcutta, "We are all suffering terribly with a temperature of 98 in the shade, while at Delhi one was able to be out all day long and the nights

are extremely cold. . . . Here at the present moment it is an effort to do anything."
Defending his estimate of the Delhi climate to Lord Crewe, the Viceroy compared
Calcutta to Hell itself; he had found the climate in Delhi at the end of March
"perfectly delightful," while the previous six weeks in Calcutta had been "like the
infernal regions." As the annual migration to the hills commenced, Hardinge
expressed great satisfaction in leaving Calcutta: "One is able to take a much broader
view of life when one is well away from that very hot and mosquitoish place." The
Viceroy anticipated no less advantage in quitting Calcutta permanently; in a
revealing line, he emphasized he was looking forward to the change of climate that
the transfer of the capital would bring.[39]

Gratification of the personal vanity of those in power played its part in Delhi's
new destiny. Highly sensitive to criticism, Hardinge was no less susceptible to
flattery, and an experienced figure like Fleetwood Wilson realized the irresistibility
of such blandishments when he wrote: "I believe that if this change is effected it will
make Your Excellency the 'biggest' Viceroy who ever came to India. You will have
added a page to the history not of England, not of India, but of the world." By July 2
the Viceroy was writing with some pride that he had "always thought Delhi must be
the capital some day."[40]

Such contributions to the decision to transfer the capital could hardly be expected
to find expression in published despatches or public documents. But that limitation
made them no less real, as private correspondence confirmed. One contributing
ingredient was the very natural desire by officials in Britain and India to mark the
royal visit and Durbar by some outstanding or dramatic act. By June 1911,
Fleetwood Wilson later recalled, "everyone was casting about for something which
would appeal to the public imagination." A certain air of expectancy prevailed, and
articles in the Bengali press expressed hope that the Durbar would be used as an
opportunity to modify the partition. Lord Crewe later said he felt there would have
been bitter disappointment in India had the Durbar been simply an occasion for
spectacular pageantry. Already articles had appeared disparaging the forthcoming
tour by stating that the King had no sovereign powers, and that his visit to India
would be profitless. It was not surprising, therefore, that when in mid-June the
Home Member proposed the creation of an Imperial capital at Delhi to the Viceroy,
he emphasized it would also be regarded as "an exercise of Sovereign power, such as
oriental peoples expect and admire."[41]

Among British officialdom there was a growing conviction in 1911 that both the
situation in Bengal and that of the Government of India at Calcutta were "daily
becoming more impossible," and that prompt, purposeful action was imperative.
At the *Times*, Valentine Chirol felt that the outbreak of sedition following partition
made removal of the capital from "that mephitic atmosphere" supremely urgent.
Fleetwood Wilson had harbored such sentiments from his first winter in Calcutta in
1908–9, when he had observed a situation so tense that leading merchants feared an
imminent uprising by the Bengalis, Europeans were often deliberately pushed off
the pavement, and ladies were jeered at by the student population. Having decided
that some revision of the partition was essential, Fleetwood Wilson concluded
privately that any modification must be based on another readjustment so important
that it overshadowed the actual partition rearrangement. The transfer of the capital

neatly fitted the bill. Hardinge reasoned that it was preferable anyway to combine the two inevitable events than to carry them out separately. An announcement by the King at the Durbar, the Viceroy told Lord Crewe confidentially, would be such a powerful asset in popularizing the decision that "it would be a fatal mistake to neglect such a golden opportunity."[42]

The months of discussion and preparation culminated on December 12. The historic despatch of August 25 from Simla and Lord Crewe's reply of November 1 were made public directly following the Durbar. Both the Viceroy and the Secretary of State displayed a vision of things to be and benefits to come that did not ignore the perspectives of the past. Though much criticized in the days ahead, their brave words rang with a rhetorical eloquence that struck an appropriate note on an occasion which itself invoked the sanction of tradition.

"Delhi," the Viceroy had written, "is still a name to conjure with. It is intimately associated in the minds of the Hindus with sacred legends which go back even beyond the dawn of history. . . . To the Mohammedans it would be a source of unbounded gratification to see the ancient capital of the Moguls restored to its proud position as the seat of the Empire." The scheme which Hardinge and his colleagues outlined would assuredly bring, they believed, "a new era in the history of India." The Secretary of State was, in his approval of the changes envisioned, no less grandiloquent. He agreed that the site of the new capital was rich in meaning and significance: "the ancient walls of Delhi enshrine an Imperial tradition comparable with that of Constantinople, or with that of Rome itself." In granting his imprimatur, Lord Crewe wrote that the administrative changes and transfer of the main seat of Government would prove of little detriment to any class of the community, while assisting the efficiency of the Government, removing widely felt grievances, and "satisfying the historic sense of millions."[43]

The momentous announcements on Durbar Day had scarcely issued from the King's lips before they drew fire. From the outset the Viceroy had quite correctly predicted the resentment of the European community in Calcutta over the transfer of capital and had considered postponing announcement of the change until after the King's visit. As if in anticipation, the Calcutta Corporation, on December 16, 1910, had urged the fitness of their city and deprecated Delhi's claims as the site of the Durbar. As early as June 1911, a Member of the Viceroy's own Council, Harcourt Butler, had expressed reservations about the transfer, citing (with good reason) the considerable European opposition that could be expected.

> The trade of Calcutta will perhaps not suffer much, but it is the only European town in India, all our associations are with Calcutta, our institutions have grown up, the High Court, the Museum, the Victoria Memorial, etc., will be stranded. The *Statesman* will become a purely local paper. The clubs will suffer and so on. Powerful influences will be worked at home.[44]

Butler's forebodings proved absolutely correct. The vehemence of the reaction by the Calcutta Europeans caught by surprise not only the Viceroy, but those of longer experience in India, such as the newly knighted Home Member. Three days after the Durbar, Sir John Jenkins admitted he was "afraid we must expect some trouble," and reported that not only were the principal British newspapers in

Calcutta waxing rancorous, but altogether "a big row" was brewing. Bitter feelings over the removal of the Imperial Government and its Viceregal appurtenances were expressed not only by sportsmen and socialites (especially female), but by leaders in the mercantile and trades communities. The protest gathered in strength despite Hardinge's concerted efforts to "keep things quiet" by using the good offices of friendly businessmen of influence. For the rest of his tenure the Viceroy was subjected to what he called "vulgar abuse." Seven months after the announcement at Delhi, he commented with no little bitterness of his own that "the Calcutta people are making a dead set at me and would like me to be sacrificed upon their altar." He was even treated to a leading editorial entitled "H.M.G.," which he discovered meant "Hardinge Must Go."[45]

Calcutta's mercantile community complained that the transfer would necessarily mean the isolation of the Imperial Government (and especially its Department of Commerce and Industry) from commercial opinion and indeed all public opinion. Already the annual sojourn in Himalayan Simla meant seven months of detachment. Their plaints were echoed by the Lieutenant-Governor of the United Provinces, who doubted whether India's rulers would benefit from being so far "from criticism and rubbing of shoulders with others." In these sentiments he was joined by Bhupendranath Basu, a leader of the Indian National Congress, who said that the Imperial Government, distant from any center of opinion, would come to be seen as "a secret conclave, screened by long-stretching partitions of time and space, and issuing its edicts through the cold pages of lifeless official publications." The privation, Basu later lamented, was mutual: Calcutta would miss the cosmopolitan influence of the Legislative Councillors and the "inestimable benefit" of personal contact with the Viceroy. The Raja of Dighapatia, a Bengali ruling chief, in deploring the change in capital, echoed this sorrow for the historic city so "intimately associated with the foundations of the British Empire in India."[46]

Vernacular Bengali newspapers, while far less strident than the *Statesman* and the *Englishman*, were generally outspoken in their regret at losing the "privilege, advantage and distinction" of an Imperial capital in their midst. The *Hindoo Patriot* and the *Dainik Chandrika* thought the transfer "a serious blow" to Bengal's dignity and prestige which would deeply affect both social and political life; the *Hitavadi* and the *Muhammadi* agreed that the loss would deprive the province of its political supremacy. Two other journals, the *Amrita Bazar Patrika* and the *Pallivarta*, predicted the change would hurt Calcutta's commercial importance.[47]

Furthermore, there was widespread resentment that normal channels had been altogether ignored in the very decision to transfer the capital. The Bengal Chamber of Commerce remonstrated that no recognized organs of public opinion, professional or commercial, European or Indian, had been given an opportunity to consider the scheme; nor had the Provincial Legislative Councils or the Imperial Legislative Council, the Lieutenant-Governors or Governors of the provinces, or even Parliament itself been told the project was contemplated. The European and Anglo-Indian Defence Association similarly protested against the secretive manner of the decision, and the *Statesman*'s editors deplored the failure to consult "the large interests affected." Half a year before, the Viceroy's most trenchant critic within his Council, Robert Carlyle, had warned his colleagues of "well-founded discontent" should they adopt the scheme without giving those affected a chance to be heard or without attempting to ascertain that such a plan accorded with popular feeling. Instead the Viceroy had heeded John Jenkins's advice that the administrative changes contemplated would require exceptional procedures. The Home Member had urged that there be "no reports, no consultation of public opinion, everything to be settled by a small Committee across a table in consultation with the local offices." Now the result was an outcry in which the Viceroy's actions were compared to the autocratic rule of the Russian Czar.[48]

One Bengali Legislator complained of the "cowardly device" of using the King-Emperor to make the announcement, thus effectively muzzling voices of objection, lest they be thought disloyal to the monarch. In the initial discussion of the scheme in June, Robert Carlyle had cautioned against the King announcing the changes: "Nothing could be more unfortunate than to allow the King to proclaim as a boon anything likely to be a matter of bitter controversy." After the Durbar, Carlyle's words were echoed by the *Madras Mail*, which, while approving the annulment of the partition, disparaged the judgment of Ministers who associated the King directly with changes distinctly political and controversial. The President of the Durbar Committee, while admitting that the King's surprise speech had had a dramatic effect, reported to Lord Curzon that there was "much criticism" of the attempt to stifle discussion by announcing the changes through the person of the King-Emperor himself. Despite such censure, Hardinge nevertheless further cemented the King's association with the transfer in a speech marking the State Entry into Delhi of the Imperial Government in December 1912. Referring twice to "His Majesty's decision" to alter the capital, the Viceroy's speech proclaimed the proposed new Delhi as "a permanent memorial to His Majesty's visit."[49]

Coupling the King's name with the transfer proved unsuccessful, however, in stemming the tide of criticism, including attacks on the cost of the new capital. The Carlton House Terrace residence of Lord Curzon, author of the original partition of Bengal in 1905 and a partisan of Calcutta, became the focus of dissent from the Durbar changes—"a sort of receipt for grievances bureau." Letters to the former Viceroy from India decried "the waste of money" as "appalling" and asked how the Government could "view without apprehension" the expenditure which the new Delhi would entail. The public protests of the Bengal Chamber of Commerce, deprecating the lavishing of public funds raised from taxation "on the swamps and plains of Delhi," reached the floor of the House of Commons. The proposal to finance construction of the new city partly by loan and partly out of spare revenue (which critics asserted might otherwise be used for Indian railways) came under specific attack.[50]

The *Englishman*, one of Calcutta's leading newspapers, dwelt at length on Delhi's indefensible location and her lack of security relative to Calcutta. Quoting as eminent an authority as the Duke of Wellington, the paper pointed out that a capital accessible to the sea had the might of the British navy at her call. Delhi, on the other hand, had the traditional menace of the nearby Afghans and the Russians, with the imminent threat of a Russian occupation of northern Persia.[51]

Delhi's Indian critics were not at a loss to enumerate the full gamut of her disadvantages. Details of her unsanitary and unhealthy reputation were circulated, and one Calcutta partisan recalled that "at the Durbar everyone got fever." Even Delhi's historical associations, which the Viceroy and Lord Crewe had been so careful to emphasize, were disparaged. One official wrote with feeling that the "miles and miles of ruins" ought to give the Government pause before raising yet another city. The influential *Pioneer* agreed that the city's past did not contribute to its fitness as a capital, remarking that Delhi's story had been one of "intermittent splendor, of careless luxury, of a ruling power which did not look very far ahead even when its own permanence was concerned." The vernacular journal *Nayak* in turn repeatedly reminded its readers of the city's unlucky reputation as the graveyard of dynasties. Delhi, the editors asserted, would never rival Calcutta; it would take a century to transform a near-desert site into a city. Similarly, at Bombay, the *Phoenix* disparaged the new capital as an "almost lifeless" backwater of the "benighted" Punjab, scarcely touched by progress.[52]

In the House of Lords, Curzon's incisive rhetoric played on similar themes. "The less we say about the history of Delhi the better. . . . It was only the capital of the Moguls in the expiring years of their regime." The environs of Delhi, the former Viceroy told the House, were strewn with ruins and graves, a poignant picture of the mutability of human greatness. In a lengthy, scathing, and impressive attack on the entire scheme, he expressed wonder that shifting the capital from Calcutta, with its century and a half of British traditions, to the dead seat of Muslim kings could signify a determination to maintain British rule in India. Small wonder, with such stinging provocation, that he was like "a red rag to a bull to Hardinge."[53]

As early as August 1911 Hardinge had forecast the violence of Curzon's reaction to the transfer. The former Viceroy's opposition, Hardinge remarked sardonically, would in large part derive from his founding role in Calcutta's Victoria Memorial Museum, "in which his own statue is going to have a place." Hardinge also later correctly predicted resentment and controversy in Britain over the Durbar proposals. Dissenting voices came from the Secretary of State's own Council: Sir Hugh Barnes pronounced the scheme "an act of stupendous folly" and on December 12 told Curzon the impending storm of protest would prevent its execution. Curzon was further emboldened in his antagonism by Sir John Hewett, President of the Durbar Committee, who urged resistance and suggested that Parliamentary objections could make it difficult to carry through the proposals.[54]

Many of the same objections to Delhi that were raised in India were indeed voiced at Westminster during the course of 1912. Curzon posed the apprehension that in Delhi the Government might become aloof from public opinion, shut off from the main currents of public life. The Marquess of Lansdowne, one of Curzon's predecessors as Viceroy, expressed fears of the Government's divorce from outside influences, "shut up at Simla" and in "an equally bureaucratic and remote society" at Delhi. In the Commons one Unionist Member expressed his hope that the Department of Industry and Commerce would not be removed to the isolation of Delhi but instead would be kept at Calcutta.[55]

Curzon was no less biting in his denunciation of the Government's secrecy and lack of consultation. He charged that the Liberals' conduct had been unconstitutional, their actions carried out "behind the back of Parliament," and that they had sought to shelter themselves behind the person of the Sovereign. Lord

Lansdowne in turn declared that a wholly undesirable precedent had been set for changes of immense importance, while another former Viceroy, the Earl of Minto, criticized the Government's "unconstitutional secrecy," which ignored their responsibility to the public in both India and Britain. In the Commons, Bonar Law, destined to be Prime Minister ten years later, accused the opposite benches of autocratic, unconstitutional action in exploiting the prerogative of the Crown. Criticism outside the public forum was equally acerbic. In a private letter to Curzon, one ex-Lieutenant-Governor of Bengal wrote with some sense of personal injury that the Government had acted "without any enquiry from those who could have informed them."[56]

As for financing the new capital, Sir Hugh Barnes predicted privately that New Delhi could require eight years to complete and not the three publicly announced, while Lord Curzon said it could not be done in ten years and for less than twelve million pounds. He called it a financial millstone around the neck of the Indian taxpayer, money spent on purely unproductive works.[57]

Delhi's "advanced position," her strategic exposure compared to Calcutta, drew comment not only in the Lords from Curzon, but also in the Commons from Sir John Rees and Colonel C. E. Yate. Already some months before at the India Office, Sir Hugh Barnes had warned that locating the Government of India so far inland would be "a source of grave anxiety and alarm" in the case of any serious disturbance.[58]

Both Lord Lansdowne and Lord Curzon queried the good climate and healthiness attributed to Delhi by the Government's published despatches. Curzon remembered from personal observation the fever and malaria prevalent in October and May, while his colleague described in detail the ulcerous malady known as the Delhi boil and called the city's sanitary conditions markedly inferior to those of Calcutta. Delhi had long had such a reputation. The French physician François Bernier, visiting the Mughal seat in the seventeenth century, recorded, "I may hope, too, for better water than that of the capital, the impurities of which exceed my power of description." Curzon's estimate of the climate was to be confirmed by a later Viceroy, Lord Reading, who told his own successor that Delhi had five months of delightful weather, but toward the end of March it got hot and became so unpleasant that he would be "glad enough to leave."[59]

The ignorance of the Government of India regarding local conditions in Delhi was easily explicable, as Lord Curzon was swift to point out. The scheme was undertaken on the initiative of a Viceroy who had been in India only a few months and a Secretary of State "who had not enjoyed his great position for a longer period." The Viceroy's Council, Curzon asserted, had less experience of India than any Council in modern times, and the Parliamentary Under-Secretary for India, Edwin Montagu, who claimed that the majority of Indians favored the proposal, had never been in India at all.[60]

As for the argument that the coexistence of the Imperial and Bengal Governments in the same city was a serious anomaly, Curzon declared that, on the contrary, during his Viceroyalty the two Governments found their association mutually advantageous. He pointed out the much more anomalous juxtaposition of the Imperial and Punjab Governments on the narrow ridge of Simla for seven months of the year. Sir Hugh Barnes, for his part, did not believe that the creation of a Governorship in Bengal must inevitably lead to the removal of the Imperial Government from Calcutta. Barnes reminded his colleagues at the India Office that the Government of India was not federal and that analogies with Washington, Ottawa, or Canberra were false; he saw no incongruity with the Supreme Government of India holding its legislative sessions in a clearly subordinate province.[61]

If, on the other hand, as the despatch of August 25 indicated, the principle of increasing provincial autonomy was adopted and coupled with the isolation of the Imperial Government at Delhi, Curzon feared future disaster. The central Government would then soon weaken, and the Viceroy in Delhi would become a puppet like the decadent Mughals before their overthrow.[62]

Perhaps most alarming to British observers and critics of the Indian scene was the impression the reversal of partition would create in India itself. Lord Lansdowne felt many persons would regard the scheme as the triumph of sedition, and Lord Minto said that the overthrow of a policy which had been repeatedly declared a settled fact since 1905 would assuredly depreciate the reputation of British rule in India. As Sir James Bourdillon remarked to Lord Curzon, every agitator would now be convinced of the susceptibility of the Imperial Government to persistent pressure.[63] Such portentous prophecies and criticisms were to haunt British rule in India to the very end.

The newly announced scheme, the subject of so much censure, was hotly defended by its proponents and their allies. In a letter on New Year's Day to Lord Sanderson (who later showed it to Lord Lansdowne), Hardinge asserted emphatically that India was "absolutely enthusiastic" over the Durbar changes except for "a few commercial people" and the "racing and smart set" of Calcutta. As for the discontent which the leaders of Bengal's twenty-five million Muslims had expressed to Curzon, the Viceroy wrote in late January that "a perfect calm" prevailed and the native population were "enchanted" by the proposals.[64]

Hardinge replied to the charges of lack of prior consultation with the retort that Parliament had nothing to do with discussion of administrative changes in India that did not require legislation and added, rather lamely, that there would be discussion later when legislation for the changes was required. The Lieutenant-Governor of East Bengal and Assam admitted that had the transfer scheme been published for public consideration, rival claims would have been urged with great bitterness, and much heat and bad feeling engendered. In Parliament Lord Crewe confessed that if the question had been opened to public discussion, the British residents and papers in Calcutta, and the East Bengal Muslims, would doubtless have engaged in an agitation of some violence and length. Such agitation over a series of "purely administrative acts," he declared, would have produced much ill-feeling while availing nothing.[65]

Hardinge bridled at condemnation of his scheme in Parliament. Trained as a diplomat, Hardinge could not comprehend the opposition inherent in the political process and resented such censure. Curzon's and Minto's arguments, he claimed, represented only the views of a small body of British malcontents in Calcutta. Their criticism, he asserted, undermined the King's position in India and in Curzon's case he dismissed the objections as attributable to "personal egotism." He labelled the agitation over the Durbar changes as "fictitious," and cited a highly successful Government loan, negotiated in July, as evidence of the Indian confidence in his regime.[66]

The Viceroy staunchly maintained that the removal of the Government in India from daily contact with Calcutta's commercial community was a distinct advantage rather than a cause for lament. The capital's merchants were renowned as the most reactionary in India, and a central position in Delhi enabled the Imperial administration to develop closer relations with the more progressive mercantile interests of Bombay and Karachi. Furthermore, the severance of the direct association in Calcutta of the Bengal Government with the central Government, Lord Crewe asserted in Parliament, had been a primary motive in the framing of the Durbar changes. He emphasized that the increasing turbulence since Lord Curzon's tenure had brought to the fore the difficulties inherent in ill-defined and overlapping responsibilities. Even the *Statesman*, he told the Lords, a paper which had expressed general opposition to the Durbar announcements, had called the coexistence of the two Governments in Calcutta a bad arrangement, rendering provincial autonomy for Bengal impossible.[67]

The much-criticized cost of the new capital "need not necessarily be formidable," the Viceroy confided to Lord Sanderson in February with remarkable unconcern. "We can easily supply one million sterling per annum out of revenue for the next two years." Nine days later Lord Crewe confessed in Parliament that the new capital could not be completed in the intended three years. Furthermore he was considerably less sanguine about the expense than Hardinge; he restricted himself to the hope that the cost might "not largely exceed" the announced sum of four million. In a speech to the Legislative Council in March, the Viceroy sought to counteract the mounting furor over the cost of the new city; denouncing "irresponsible critics," he stressed the cheapness of land at Delhi and the ready availability of lime, bricks, stone, and marble. In October the preliminary engineering estimates for Delhi were forwarded by the special officer in charge with the comment that it was impossible for the full cost ever to exceed "some figure between 4 and 5 million pounds." He dismissed Lord Curzon's prophecy of twelve million as belonging to "the limbo of hasty and hyperbolean criticism."[68]

The strategic question, Hardinge assured Lord Sanderson, presented "no difficulties," with many soldiers stationed only forty miles away at Meerut and with the advances in railway communication and wireless telegraphy. Sir George Birdwood suggested that a guardship in the major ports and a gunboat or two on the Jumna would make Delhi "as safe as Clapham Common," and Lord Harris noted with approval Delhi's equidistance from Bombay, Calcutta, and Karachi, should reinforcements be required.[69]

As eminent a figure as Lord Roberts, former Commander-in-Chief in India and veteran of the Mutiny, indicated that in the event of another uprising, he much preferred Delhi's centrality to Calcutta's location. Were Delhi to be captured in an external invasion from the northwest, it would be equally disastrous, he reasoned, whether the Viceroy had to bolt from that capital or lived in Calcutta. The Imperial Government, he pointed out, already spent nearly seven months at Simla, a site no more nor less defensible than Delhi.[70]

The Viceroy bade the timid to be stout of heart in the face of bloodcurdling rumors that Delhi was afflicted with the ten plagues of Egypt. In defending the healthiness of the city, he reminded his Legislative Councillors (who would be obliged to assemble there) that Delhi's death rate did not exceed Lucknow's and that her increase in population for the past twenty years had been steady.[71]

The Viceroy and Lord Crewe could count important allies in their camp. G. E. Buckle, editor of the *Times*, told Curzon privately that the whole scheme seemed to him to be both a marked advance in administration and "a powerful appeal to the Indian imagination." As anticipated, the Rajput princes, among the most loyal supporters of the British in India, endorsed the announced changes, which placed the Imperial Government virtually in their midst. The Maharaja of Alwar, for example, characterized the transfer as "great" and "good" and attested to its popularity in Rajputana. Another prince praised the change in capital as "beneficial and advantageous to the public interest" and thought it would improve communication between the Provincial and Imperial Governments of India. Unquestionably, as one Member remarked in the Legislative Council, the new capital's central location ensured closer touch between the Government and "the great body of Feudatory Chiefs." Small wonder, then, that these rulers received the King's announcement "with open arms."[72]

Other Indians of varying political persuasions commended the change of capital. Editors of a native paper, the *Cochin Argus*, called transfer of the seat of government "from a flank, once a marsh, to a central position," a wise and "daring act," while other native journals, the *Oriental Review* and the *Indian Social Reformer*, praised British statesmanship and constructive genius. The *Indu Prakash* warmly welcomed removal of the capital from Bengal's extremist atmosphere. The Maharajadhiraja of Burdwan, accepting the Government's arguments in favor of Delhi, urged the erection of a truly imperial capital, a city which would exhibit the best principles of British rule and ultimately win the endorsement of its current critics. The celebrated Gokhale, unofficial Leader of the Opposition in the Legislative Council, waxed sentimental about his associations with Calcutta but affirmed his faith that the Durbar changes would eventually benefit both Bengal and the entire subcontinent. Another former President of the Indian National Congress, Pandit Madan Mohan Malaviya judged the conception of New Delhi to be a happy event of great importance, one that had elicited expressions of approval from the whole country except, of course, Calcutta.[73]

Most Members of the Legislative Council applauded the removal from Calcutta. Rama Rayaningar said that the transfer would free India's rulers from pervasive commercial influence, and that Delhi's ancient heritage would inspire a more catholic temper and a fresh architectural impulse. Madhusudan Das, a Christian Liberal from Orissa, felt that the new city embodied a concept of empire which rose above "all parochial, commercial, or communal interests." Another Member acclaimed Delhi (in contrast to Calcutta) as a "truly Indian capital."[74]

On several occasions Council Members reiterated their belief that the transfer enjoyed widespread approbation. Rai Sri Ram Bahadur, a taluqdar from Oudh, thought the change a welcome measure "to the great majority of the Indian people," and Khan Bahadur Mir Asad Ali Khan asserted that the restoration of Delhi to its historic preeminence had given "supreme satisfaction" to both Hindus and Muslims. Nyapati Subba Rao Pantulu, another leader of the Congress, reminded the Legislative Council that Lord Crewe's famous despatch of August 25, 1911 had anticipated the gradual growth of a federal system for India in which the central government must "not be associated with any particular Provincial Government." To remove the Government of India from the capital of Bengal, Crewe had concluded, would promote the development of local, popular autonomy "on sound and safe lines." Given these assurances, Subba Rao declared, the intelligent public across India interpreted the move to Delhi as "a first and necessary step" toward self-government. Consequently, despite its costliness and disadvantages, the people at large welcomed the transfer. Thirteen prominent Bengali leaders, moreover, signed an open letter on December 14 which likewise hailed the change of capital as a "necessary adjunct to the establishment of provincial autonomy in Bengal" and expressed confidence that the King's announcements would inspire gratitude in "the hearts of all Indians."[75]

Bengal's vernacular newspapers generally regarded the loss of the seat of government with regret but resignation. The *Nayak* and the *Hitavadi* felt the province "must consent" to the transfer in exchange for the benefits of reunion under a Governor appointed from Britain; the *Murshidabad Hitaishi*, the *Bangavasi*, and the *Dnyan Prakash* agreed that annulment of Lord Curzon's partition was "a more than ample compensation" for removal of the capital. Other native papers assumed an altruistic tone. The *Indian Mirror* accepted the change as necessary to the better governance of India, and the *Hindoo Patriot* remarked that Bengal must abide by its fate, which was for the common national good. The *Hitavarta*, in roundly defending the transfer, condemned "the selfish attitude" of Calcutta's Europeans in opposing an act which would "benefit the entire country."[76]

According to the *Hindoo Patriot*, "the general body of the Bengali population" was in fact indifferent to the shift of capital. The absence of any organized protest meetings, furthermore, confirmed that "popular leaders throughout Bengal" viewed the loss "with equanimity." Vernacular papers claimed that the rest of India, Hindu and Muslim alike, favored the transfer to Delhi. Because of their proximity, the Punjab and the United Provinces in particular were "jubilant over the restoration of the Rome of India to its old position of political importance." Elsewhere in the subcontinent, public opinion approved the change of capital with more detachment, but often "with considerable satisfaction" and even enthusiasm.[77]

For Lord Hardinge, such evidence of Indian support was heartening. But in his opinion, the best response of all to the critics of the Durbar changes was the unusual peace which prevailed following the King's announcements. Political murders, which for several years had averaged one every two weeks, ceased entirely, and the Viceroy's extensive autumn tour was undertaken without detectives or any special police precautions.[78] As India experienced a tranquillity unknown for years, Delhi prepared for the State Entry of the Viceroy, the official assumption of residence by the Government of India in its new capital. Among the many factors which had made that event possible, the vision and faith of a handful of men loomed large. A generous measure of these qualities would be required in the decades ahead before the shining dream of a new capital would be finally realized.

# 3

# *Choice of the Site*

The Durbar fanfares were scarcely silenced, and the King-Emperor and Queen Mary were still in their eastern Empire, when planning for the new capital of India began. The newly knighted Home Member of the Viceroy's Council, Sir John Jenkins, and the Lieutenant-Governor of the Punjab, Sir Louis Dane, met on December 17 in the Durbar tents of the Punjab Government to make initial preparations for the new home of the Government of India.

In his notes on this important conference, sent to the Viceroy, Jenkins proposed three names for appointment to the town planning committee which would shortly be constituted. The duties of the committee—including temporary accommodation of the Government, demarcation and acquisition of the enclave, and planning and building the city—the Home Member outlined in a very matter-of-fact manner: there was little to suggest that this was to be the Imperial capital for a subcontinent, the culmination of the dreams of British rulers for a century. Proposed for responsibility over this historic undertaking were the Deputy Commissioner of the Punjab, the Superintending Engineer of the Jumna Canal, and the Consulting Architect to the Government of Bombay. Two days before Christmas, the harassed Viceroy (whose royal charges were to stay in India another two weeks) wrote that he was prepared to accept Sir John's proposed committee upon the concurrence of his Council.[1]

Members of the Viceroy's Council had ideas different from Sir John's, however, and more important, they had a vision of the building of a grand capital beside the Jumna. Sir Guy Fleetwood Wilson, the senior Member of the Council, wrote most forcefully of all: "I feel very strongly that this is an opportunity which has never yet occurred, and which will probably never recur, for laying the foundations of one of the finest cities in the world, and certainly the finest city in the East. To hand over the planning of such a city to three nonentities . . . seems to me to court disaster and discredit." Harcourt Butler agreed that the names proposed by Jenkins did not inspire him with confidence, and Carlyle, who had named five candidates of his own for the Committee, belittled the experience and training of Jenkins's nominees. The Commander-in-Chief urged that town planning and sanitation experts be brought from England; in this he was supported by the sole Indian member of the Council, Syed Ali Imam, who thought it necessary to go outside India to secure the services of proper experts.[2]

His schedule now less hectic with the departure of the royal party on January 10, the Viceroy moved to find experts in Britain adequate to his Council's wishes and his own intentions. The Local Government Board, when consulted regarding an engineer, suggested the municipal engineers of Liverpool and Birmingham. John A. Brodie was interviewed by the India Office and recommended, and the town fathers of Liverpool reluctantly surrendered the services of their Borough Engineer for three months.[3]

Selecting a member of the Committee who combined the abilities of architect and town planner proved more difficult. The Local Government Board in London suggested Stanley Davenport Adshead, founder of *Town Planning Review* and Professor of Civic Design at the University of Liverpool, School of Architecture, as the one architect in England who had made a systematic study of town planning. The President of the Royal Institute of British Architects, Leonard Stokes, told the India Office he regarded Adshead as provincial, and theoretical rather than practical, while Sir Lawrence Gomme, Clerk to the London County Council, labelled him a theorist who carried no weight. J. A. Brodie, partly responsible for Adshead's appointment at Liverpool, gave a lukewarm appraisal and remarked that the tall, gaunt professor did not have a convincing manner. As a result, Sir Thomas Holderness at the India Office concluded that Adshead might not be "a quite big enough man for the job." Adshead did receive serious consideration, however, and the Viceroy asked the architect H. V. Lanchester if he would be agreeable to serving with Adshead and Brodie. Reservations on the part of the influential Holderness appear to have been decisive, however, for on February 28, Lord Crewe wired to Calcutta his conclusion that Adshead was "not good enough for such responsible work."[4]

The India Office did not lack for suggestions for the post. The editor of the *Times of India*, Stanley Reed, proposed George Wittet, the young Consulting Architect to the Government of Bombay who had worked in England under Sir Thomas Graham Jackson. Professor Patrick Geddes, Director of the Cities and Town Planning Exhibition of 1911, suggested himself, and secured a warm testimonial from the Secretary of State for Scotland, Lord Pentland. The names of Leonard Stokes, Reginald Blomfield, Sir Robert Lorimer, and Cecil Brewer were all recommended to the India Office for consideration. At the India Office itself, Lord Crewe initially proposed Raymond Unwin, the principal planner of the Hampstead Garden Suburb, but the Local Government Board did not favor his nomination.[5]

Gradually, two names emerged: Henry Vaughan Lanchester and Edwin Landseer Lutyens. The President of the Royal Institute of British Architects suggested both architects, and the name of John William Simpson as well. The Local Government Board noted with approval that Lanchester and Simpson were very competent architects, each with a large practice, but thought Lutyens too much an expensive country house specialist. The Clerk of the London County Council, when sounded by Sir Thomas Holderness, reported Lanchester to be capable, but brusque and irritable, and judged Lutyens very able as a domestic architect.[6]

The Viceroy at first professed ignorance of Lutyens's work but letters by the artist Reginald Barratt, forwarded by the influential writer Sir Valentine Chirol, proved helpful and even convincing. Calling Lutyens "a very exceptional man," Chirol named Lutyens as the British architect "most suited in his talents and temperament" to formulate and initiate the new scheme. Lord Derby's suggestion of Lutyens for the post, together with Crewe's acquaintance with the architect from the Hampstead Garden Suburb and the Committee for the "Shakespeare's England" Exhibition at Earl's Court, were no doubt useful in persuading the Secretary of State of the candidate's fitness. Ultimately it was Crewe's word that was conclusive; the Viceroy remarked that the question was difficult to consider from such a great distance and he must necessarily "leave the matter a great deal in the hands of Crewe."[7]

Thus it was that a telegram of fifteen sentences, which arrived in Calcutta at six o'clock on the morning of February 29, 1912, proved crucial. The Secretary of State indicated Lutyens's availability, then added decisively that he recommended him "in preference to Lanchester and Adshead." The Viceroy could hardly reject this suggestion. Crewe added immediately that if Lutyens were engaged in the town planning committee, this involved no understanding whatsoever to employ him on the actual erection of buildings. Crewe closed this important telegram by proposing the appointment of Captain George Swinton, Chairman of the London County Council, as third adviser or nonprofessional head of the committee.[8]

Swinton was eager for the position, and had begun lobbying in January. He had useful allies. He secured support for his candidacy from the Clerk, the Chief Engineer, and the Chief Architect of the London County Council, and from Lord Montagu of Beaulieu, a recognized authority on highways and transport. He elicited a letter on his behalf from Lord Lansdowne, the ex-Viceroy whom he had served as aide-de-camp in India, and he came to an interview at the India Office armed with a letter of introduction from a former Secretary of State for India, Viscount Midleton. He impressed both Crewe's Private Secretary and Sir Thomas Holderness with his personality, his practicality, and his experience gained serving on the foremost municipal body in Britain. They found him agreeable and full of character and possessed of a cautious enthusiasm about town planning, together with knowledge of traffic problems, space design, and finance, derived from London improvement projects. Swinton followed up this successful interview by a letter to Holderness with his views on the planning of the new Delhi, stating quite baldly that he was one of the few already in training for the position of planner, and adding that he heard from every side that Adshead was "hopeless." Within two weeks Adshead was no longer a candidate, and Crewe had recommended Swinton to the Viceroy. On March 3, Lord Hardinge cabled his acceptance of the proposed committee of Brodie, Lutyens, and Swinton and, in addition, advised employing H. V. Lanchester as a consulting expert for one month, as the India Office had suggested on February 2. On March 12, the Committee's composition won the King's commendation as "excellent." and their fees and departure date were set.[9]

It remained only for the Viceroy to engage Lanchester, whom he had interviewed in India. Lanchester had meanwhile returned to London, apparently under the mistaken impression that he would be appointed a full member of the Committee. Upon publication of the Committee's appointment, he complained that a mere temporary consultancy would put him in a "useless and false position." The Viceroy was unmoved, however, cabling that Lanchester's services would not be needed except as a consulting expert at a moderate fee for a month. Confronted with such firmness, Lanchester accepted the Viceroy's terms with alacrity, and arranged to leave on May 31 for India.[10] Announcement of the Committee's appointment appeared in the press on March 13. Lutyens wrote exultantly to Herbert Baker, his close friend since student days twenty years before: "Delhi is all right!! I start on 27th March!!! It is a wonderful chance." Shortly before their departure, the Committee were summoned to Buckingham Palace for an interview lasting three-quarters of an hour. There the King instructed them not to consider themselves committed to the site of the foundation stones he and the Queen had laid and to regard the Ridge at Delhi, with its heroic memories of the Indian Mutiny, as sacred.[11]

With this caveat from their sovereign, the Committee boarded ship for the East at Marseilles on March 28. In addition to the three experts, the entourage included Brodie's plump spouse and a young assistant for both Brodie and Lutyens. The Committee were remarkably ill prepared. Of the three, only Swinton had been in India. Holderness at the India Office had referred them to certain standard guide books and gazetteers, but as Lutyens confessed to his wife, they had been given "very little information to work on—only an incomplete map with a few contours every fifty feet."[12]

Bombay, for Lutyens and Brodie, was their first impression of British civilization in India and its architectural tradition. The city's towering High Victorian and Edwardian public buildings, [12] where features derived from twelfth- to fifteenth-century English, French, and Venetian Gothic jousted with elements of the native Indo-Saracenic style, could scarcely have found a less sympathetic critic than Lutyens, whose work reflected new directions in British architecture: broad, simplified designs freely developed from Elizabethan and Jacobean sources or inspired by the restrained English classicism of Inigo Jones and Wren. Similarly, Herbert Baker, his colleague at the office of Ernest George and Peto twenty years before, characterized Bombay's Victorian architecture as "a nightmare" on his first visit to India in 1913, and in 1931 the critic Robert Byron denounced the "hideous chaos" of High Victorian buildings in India, "in which Hindu ornament and Moslem domes fought for the possession of Gothic substructure." Lutyens had occasion to meet George Wittet, the Consulting Architect to the Government of Bombay whom Sir John Jenkins had originally suggested for the Delhi project. The central block of Wittet's Prince of Wales Museum of Western India, based on Indian architecture of the sixteenth century in the Bombay district, was nearing completion. [13] A lavish, effervescent compound of domes, pinnacles, finials, pendants, brackets, balconies, and polychrome pointed arches, it must have been anathema to Lutyens. Even before his arrival in the subcontinent, his opinion of the indigenous architecture had been adverse: the buildings of the Mughals, for example, he pronounced to be "piffle." Later he belittled contemporary hybrid or Eurasian buildings, with their eclectic Indian details, as "half-caste."[13]

Enveloped in "a perpetual bath of sweat," the Committee were shown the achievements of the Bombay Improvement Trust, which Lutyens characterized as the "same old story of blind committees and half measures and eventual waste and loss." He concluded that none of it was worth seeing, and, as in England, every job was rendered forty times more difficult by previous errors, false economies, and lack

12. Bombay, Victoria Terminus, completed 1888.

13. Bombay, Prince of Wales Museum, completed 1914. George Wittet, architect.

of imagination. The French and Germans, he felt, were far ahead of the British in town planning.[14]

Lutyens soon developed a genuine affection and respect for his portly colleague Brodie. He early referred to him as "apple-shaped," and described him as "a dear broad matter-of-fact Midland middle-class thing," but he professed admiration for the engineer's sensible, practical nature. With Swinton, it was otherwise. Lutyens found him an exceedingly garrulous dilettante, "talkative and speechful." Hardinge first met this triumvirate after they had been on the spot for two weeks. The "Delhi experts," as they were universally called, "favorably impressed" the Viceroy. He told them he was keen to have them settle on a site without delay, as their decision affected the location of the temporary Delhi to be occupied until the new capital was complete.[15]

The Committee's task was to advise the Viceroy and his Government on two main points, which Hardinge wished to deal with separately: first, the selection of a site for the future capital, and second, the general planning of the city on the chosen site. A host of questions were to be considered, including health, security, room for expansion, cost, sites for principal buildings, water supply, sanitation, drainage, railways, roads, electric power, parks, existing buildings, and the relationship of the new city to the old Delhi and the cantonments. The Delhi experts' responsibilities in sum were to study and report on "such matters as affect the convenience and comfort of the inhabitants, whether for purposes of residence, business or inter-communication, together with, of course, dignity, beauty and a due consideration of amenities."[16]

The Committee's daily schedule was rigorous. Up at 5:15 with a cold bath and a cup of tea at the Maiden's Hotel, they left to see the terrain either in two or three Ford Landaulette and De Dion cars or, frequently, perched on elephants. When the heat became too intense, about 9:30, the experts and accompanying engineers and staff returned "sweatful" for another bath and breakfast, then worked at a house given them for an office from 11:00 until 2:00, adjourning for lunch until 3:00, with discussion and correspondence until 5:00, then out in the cars until 8:00, with a third bath and dinner at 8:30. After dinner, more discussion or an evening at the Club until 11:30. "We are so busy," Lutyens complained, "that there seems to be no time for anything."[17] [14, 15]

Their journeys north and south of Shahjahanabad and to the east bank of the Jumna encompassed much wild and rugged country. Fauna of every description abounded, Lutyens wrote: "buck of all sorts, baboons, monkeys, jackals, hare, porcupine, water snakes, great fish, great tortoises which eat babies, snake, bats, flying fox, vultures, weird birds and many lovely ones, a lizard of sorts, yellow and dry and three feet long. The elephant. Tigers at Jeypore, fresh caught and angry, a black panther, hyena, and then a host of tame birds and animals."[18]

By mid-May the Committee had covered a wide territory and had had an opportunity to discuss many details with local officers. The heat, however, became so intense that it was difficult to work outside, which was "all dust & death & the middens of ages blowing about." Tempers often flared. In particular Swinton's verbosity—"gas bag nonsense" Lutyens called it—grated on the others. All three experts, moreover, were anxious to begin their preliminary report on the choice of

14. The Delhi Town Planning Committee, February 1913. Center row, left to right: Herbert Baker, John A. Brodie, George S. C. Swinton, and Edwin L. Lutyens. Top row: second from left, Thomas Ward; extreme right, Geoffrey de Montmorency.

15. The Delhi Town Planning Committee at work. Left to right: mahout, George S. C. Swinton, Edwin L. Lutyens, and Herbert Baker.

site in consultation with the senior officials of the Government of India at Simla.[19]

Immortalized by Kipling, that fabled hill station, with its corrugated tin-roofed and half-timbered gingerbread cottages and incongruous Jacobean-style Viceregal Lodge crowded together on a knife-edge ridge more than 7,000 feet high, stirred mixed emotions in Lutyens. The snowy Himalayan peaks on the horizon and the deep valleys—"sheer giddymaking drops"—impressed and even moved him. He found inspiration in the magic of God's work, the natural landscape. But man's work was so vile it depressed him. Simla (he later wrote) was "a pure piece of folly such as only Englishmen can achieve." Its buildings looked as though the omnipresent monkeys had built them, and he concluded that the creatures "must be shot in case they do it again."[20] [16]

Already by May 2 in Delhi, Lutyens had been able to write that the Committee were gradually agreeing on a site south of Shah Jahan's city. By June 9, he could declare that the site was settled: "south of Delhi, near Malcha." It was right in all respects: "aspect, altitude, water, health, virgin soil," and not least, "views across old Delhi to that wilderness of ruined tombs that form the remains of the 7 older Delhis." In their first report, written by Swinton and Brodie and issued on June 13, the Committee revealed that after consideration they had rejected three alternative sites: the east bank of the Jumna, unhealthy and subject to flooding; the Durbar area, north of Delhi, costly to acquire, involving expensive sanitation and drainage and difficult realignment of road, canal, and railway routes as well as possessing inadequate good land for expansion; and the western side of the hills or ridge south of city, destitute of historical associations and lacking any view of Delhi. The Committee recorded that they had "no hesitation" in advising selection of the southern site.[21]

Originally the Viceroy had intended the Committee to stay until the monsoon rains began to pelt India, in order to see the prospective sites under wet conditions. But by June, the Committee were impatient to leave. The resident engineers, moreover, who had proved admirably efficient, were deemed capable of gathering any necessary wet weather information, especially as the southern site did not become waterlogged. The experts would come out again in December, it was decided, when the Government had settled in Delhi. For the moment Lutyens radiated satisfaction. "I have got all my points," he crowed, "& scored over Brodie & Swinton in everything I wanted: site, location, & general lines, etc."[22]

There remained, however, the awkward problem of H. V. Lanchester, who had been engaged as an extra consultant. Lutyens had hoped to avoid him entirely, but the Viceroy arranged for them to meet on June 25 in Delhi, when Lanchester would be briefed on the Committee's findings and make any suggestions. Lanchester loomed as an aggressive rival. The Town Planning Committee was not to design the new Delhi's buildings. That plum attracted many aspirants, not the least Lutyens, who wrote to his friend Baker that he hoped to "rope him in" as well. Experienced as a planner and architect in India and editor of the *Builder*, Lanchester was a candidate to be reckoned with. Would Lord Crewe support Lanchester to design the buildings? Lutyens's anxiety mounted throughout the spring. Admittedly, at the Committee's interview at Buckingham Palace, the King had said, "You are going to do the buildings," to which Lutyens had promptly replied, "Yes, sir!" But this was

16. Simla, Viceregal Lodge, completed 1888.

far from the final word on the appointment, and Lutyens anticipated Lanchester would "pull for it like the deuce."[23]

By June, Lanchester seemed less formidable. The Viceroy explained that Lanchester's appointment was really the result of a misunderstanding, and Lady Hardinge had said she and her husband would just have to "be tactful with Lanchester for a month." More important, Lutyens was able to write to his wife, Lady Emily, "Hardinge has practically given me Govt. House and the big Place." By the third week in July, back in England, he could write triumphantly to Baker that "on the ground that the Viceroy can do what he likes with his own," Hardinge had "definitely" given him the task of designing Government House and its estate as well as the new Durbar plaza and its adjacent building. Moreover, he reported, the site had been approved and the three experts directed to produce a town planning scheme to take out to India in December.[24]

The Committee heard no more until the Viceroy loosed a veritable thunderbolt in August. As the result of a visit to Delhi at the end of July, Hardinge announced that the Ridge must be reconsidered as a site for Government House. All decisions respecting the town plan were consequently postponed until the Committee's return to India in December, but Lutyens proceeded with the designs for the Viceregal residence on the shaky assumption that it would be unaffected by an altered location.[25]

Meanwhile the Committee's membership and mandate had not escaped public criticism. Within six days of the experts' appointment, the Parliamentary Under-Secretary for India was being queried in the Commons on Swinton's competence as a town planning consultant. A wide-ranging attack on the new Delhi project was made during a debate in the Commons on December 20, 1912, just as the Town Planning Committee had reassembled in India to complete their assignment. An effective broadside was launched by Joseph King, Liberal Member for Somerset North, whose incisive questions on the new capital had increased in number and specificity in 1912, and constituted a source of some embarrassment to the Asquith Ministry. Later it was disclosed that the source of his information, as had been suspected, was the disaffected Consulting Architect to the Government of India, John Begg, whose residence in Delhi gave him convenient access to both rumor and fact concerning the project. Begg's grievance was that the Government had failed to consult him, their duly constituted adviser, on the planning and design of the new Delhi, and had thus cast a slur on his professional reputation. He felt strongly that his training and attainments entitled him to some part in the one truly big architectural opportunity which had occurred in India for many years. Upon receiving no redress, Begg resorted to a covert campaign in the press and Parliament that highlighted any inadequacies or deficiencies of the project, particularly in those areas where he possessed some experience himself.[26]

In the Commons King questioned the qualifications of both Swinton and Lutyens for their appointments, asserting that neither had experience in town planning, and asked why it had been thought necessary to send Lanchester to India. Furthermore, he complained, there had been a singular lack of available information; no committee report or plans had been yet forthcoming. He made a strong plea for Indian craftsmen and artists and for buildings which would give expression to Indian tradition, and he objected to any plan to design the new Council chamber as a mere annex to Government House. Then he touched on a question which was destined to consume the energies of the Committee in the months ahead: the recent and highly publicized suggestion that damming the River Jumna might greatly improve the healthiness of Delhi.[27]

As the clamor of debate rose at home, an impatient Committee assembled in Delhi, anxious to settle the location of Government House and prepare a suitable town plan. The Viceroy had examined the sites on December 8 with Swinton, who had arrived before Lutyens and Brodie. But the question was still unresolved and the Viceroy absent from Delhi until two days before Christmas, when a ceremonial State Entry would mark the formal occupation by the central Government of the city which the King had proclaimed India's capital a year before.

December 23 dawned perfectly cloudless and the scene was brilliant with color when the Viceregal party arrived at the railway station at eleven in the morning. The Viceroy and his wife seated themselves in the silver howdah atop a gigantic and richly caparisoned elephant, the biggest beast Hardinge thought he had ever seen. Never again would a procession of such striking splendor be seen in India: jewel-bedecked ruling princes of the Punjab, officials of the military headquarters and the Government of India, and Viceregal staff began to make their way to the Red Fort mounted on elaborately decorated elephants. They were preceded by an impressive cavalry band on gray chargers, kettle drums glittering in the sun. The pageant conjured up visions of the Mughal Empire at the summit of its rule. As this cavalcade neared the center of Shah Jahan's imperial city, the Viceroy had "an unaccountable presentiment of evil" and told his wife that he felt certain "something dreadful" was going to happen. Moments later the procession entered the principal avenue, Chandni Chauk, "a street of sinister memories." There in 1659, Aurangzeb's popular brother Dara Shikoh was paraded in the clothes of a beggar on a small dirty elephant, the crowds bewailing his imminent death at the order of his unmerciful brother. There, too, in 1739 the Persian ruler Nadir Shah, the most hated man of his age, had seated himself to witness the sack of the capital and the bloodthirsty massacre of its residents.[28]

An enthusiastic, deafening cheer greeted Lord and Lady Hardinge as their elephant entered the "Silver Street." Then, some 300 yards later, there was a tremendous report and a cloud of smoke as a bomb exploded. The elephant halted, but the Viceroy gave the order to proceed until his wife noticed that the chobdar standing behind them holding the State Umbrella had been killed outright. His mangled body, "precious little left," hung head downward from the ropes of the howdah. Hardinge, himself wounded in the neck, shoulder, and back, stopped the procession and promptly fainted from loss of blood. With the greatest difficulty he was removed from the battered howdah in an unconscious state and borne away in a very small motorcar. His wife, who was beside him in the howdah, was miraculously unhurt.

In a moment of consciousness, the Viceroy had directed the ceremonies to continue as scheduled and his speech to be read by the senior Member of his Council, Sir Guy Fleetwood Wilson, who was to perform many of Hardinge's functions in the weeks ahead. The Viceroy's wish, in his own words, was "that India should realize that nothing could deflect the British Government and the Government of India from their declared intention."[29]

Whatever his intention, in his weakened condition the Viceroy could not conduct the affairs of state with anything resembling his normal powers. The planning of the new Delhi, by choice Lord Hardinge's personal business, was inevitably delayed. Initially even his Military Secretary and his Private Secretary refrained from seeing the Viceroy lest they suggest work to him by their presence. "Until the Viceroy is up and about again," Lutyens wrote Lady Emily, "everything in the way of initiation in the country stops, and as he is doing the new Delhi himself, everything as far as I am concerned waits."[30]

As Lord Hardinge lay recuperating, a copy of a lecture entitled "Delhi, the Metropolis of India," delivered in London on the afternoon of Thursday, December 12, arrived from the India Office. The speech had been given to the Royal Society of Arts by Sir Bradford Leslie, an engineer associated with projects in India since 1857. Sir Bradford's proposal to create a lake by damming the Jumna just south of Delhi had been the subject of discussion in the House of Commons on December 20 and had received much publicity in the press. By building a weir to hold surplus flood water, Leslie hoped to improve public health and sanitation by transforming the swampy, malarious dry-season bed of the Jumna into a sparkling amenity dotted with bathing ghats to encourage the personal ablution necessary to the prevention of plague. Electric power developed at the weir would be first used in land reclamation, then later for street lighting and transportation. A tree-lined boulevard and park would adorn the margin of the lake, the whole an appropriate ornament to the new capital.[31]

As he later readily admitted, the press publicity given the Leslie proposal, plus "the interested motives" of many persons who possessed land north of Delhi, convinced the convalescent Viceroy that the whole question of a northern site for the city once more should be thoroughly examined. First, Brodie was summoned to the Viceroy's side briefly to discuss "water effects," and then in an interview on January 18, Hardinge asked Swinton to have the Committee prepare an alternative layout north of the city in the area comprising the Civil Lines, the Ridge, the cantonments, and land further to the northwest. Finally, two days later, the Viceroy sent Sir Bradford Leslie's paper to Swinton for consideration "before any final decision" was taken on the site of the capital.[32]

Lutyens's reaction was bitter. Hardinge's order to reconsider the area north of Delhi, he noted, came after months of work expended on the south site and after both the India Office and the Government of India had agreed on the southern location. Lutyens correctly attributed the reversal to adverse press coverage, especially "letters to the editor." He took comfort that the Parliamentary Under-Secretary for India, E. S. Montagu, shared his anxiety, deploring the weakness of the Government volte-face as pandering to an ignorant public. Lutyens lamented that the invalid Viceroy seemed to have lost his nerve. Hardinge appeared unwilling or unable to depute authority except to his wife, who was "practically running India" but was understandably fearful of decisions. His vacillation was patent; he asked Fleetwood Wilson to deny authoritatively any suggestion that he might be an adherent of the southern site. "I see the advantages and disadvantages of both sites," he wrote, "and I endeavour to keep an open mind on the subject." Proponents of the northern site, sufficiently vociferous to force a reconsideration of the Town Planning Committee's decision, advanced a number of pertinent arguments. The Committee was obliged to acknowledge the strength of some of these in its three reports.[33]

There was, of course, the fact that the foundation stones of the new city had been laid on December 15, 1911 by the King-Emperor and Queen Mary on the Durbar site. At that ceremony Lord Hardinge had referred to the new city "we hope to rear around the spot where these stones are laid," and King George had spoken of "the Imperial Capital which will arise from where we now stand." Then, too, there were the historic and sentimental associations of three Durbars: the proclamation of Queen Victoria as Empress of India, commemoration of Edward VII's accession, and the visit in person of George V and his consort. Furthermore the area was hallowed by the memory of British sacrifice during the Mutiny of 1857, "the heroic efforts of the Army before Delhi." Finally, the ruins of previous Delhis did not encumber the ground.[34]

The northern site had great scenic and architectural possibilities, and initially the Committee had been drawn to it for that reason. It was close to the river, which might be used to good effect, and the commanding height of the most historic part of the Ridge afforded an extensive panorama, especially beautiful in the evening and before summer foliage restricted the view.

There were economic considerations, too. The area between the Ridge and the river comprised about one and a quarter square miles, including Civil Lines (with some 120 attractive bungalows), the Metcalfe Estate, and a tongue of land along the river. Adaptation to the capital city might be achieved without excessive expenditure, it was claimed, by the preservation of existing residences and gardens and the addition of necessary government buildings. Amenities such as polo grounds and shops at Kashmir Gate and Chandni Chauk were conveniently at hand, and roads, railways, and canals provided adequate communication.[35]

In their report of June 13, 1912 on the choice of a site for the new city, however, the Committee had concluded that a healthy capital laid out on a large scale and occupied for seven months was impossible on the north site except at vast expense; the arguments against the area were "overwhelming." In their report of March 11, 1913 the Committee came to the same judgment again. They concluded that the northern area was too cramped for a worthy city, and inadequately supplied with ground for expansion without incurring inordinate costs to acquire the land and make it fit for habitation, if indeed it could ever be. To build on the northern site "could hardly produce a city which would give a capital, evolved under the guidance of British rule, as a pattern and inspiration to the East."[36]

As for Sir Bradford Leslie's project, a detailed discussion by the Committee, appended to their report of March 11, convincingly refuted his proposals, remarking that the scheme had evidently been based on "very little accurate information with regard to the site." Two additional reports on the healthiness of the north and south sites and on the location of the new Delhi cantonment both rejected the northern site. A committee chaired by Sir Pardey Lukis, Surgeon-General of India and Director of the Indian Medical Service, concluded that "no doubt" could exist about the superior healthfulness of the southern site. Another committee of seven military officers raised objections to the Pitampura tableland, the only area to the north and in the vicinity of the city, as unhealthy and too restricted in size for a cantonment. In a confidential memorandum to his Council, the Viceroy declared the medical report on the north site to be "conclusive." The insanitary condition of the area around the site was to his mind an "absolutely overwhelming" objection, quite aside from the cost of acquiring and developing the site, and the lack of room for a cantonment and for later expansion.[37]

Hardinge had favored the southern site as early as March 1912, when he sought a view of it by climbing the monumental eighteenth-century observatory built by a Maharaja of Jaipur. The site had struck him as "distinctly good." By May 25, 1912 the Viceroy could report with satisfaction that the Committee, who at first had been attracted to the scenic potential of the northern site, were "coming round" to his views in favor of the southern site. In their first report in June 1912, the experts noted that the southern area had a number of advantages: there was good natural drainage, the plain was not manworn or cumbered with ruins, railway communications could be easily effected, the land could be acquired at moderate prices without displacing any business or manufacturing center and there was plentiful land for future expansion. The Committee recorded that they had no hesitation in advising the selection of the southern site. In their second report, which compared the northern and southern sites, the experts confirmed their earlier conclusion that the latter area was a "better, cheaper, and healthier site conveniently at hand."[38]

The Viceroy and members of his Council had originally chosen a committee of British experts in an effort to secure knowledge and a breadth of vision absent in Indian officialdom. Given this mandate, the Committee made it clear that the simple addition of a few buildings to the suburb of Civil Lines would not create a worthy capital; rather it would be a complete abandonment of the transcendent ideals of the initial conception. Delhi, they felt, must be a truly Imperial city that absorbed the heritage of the many ancient capitals. As the seat of the Government for the entire subcontinent, it had to "convey the idea of peaceful domination and dignified rule over the traditions and life of India by the British Raj." The principal features and buildings of the new city ought to be as interesting after the passage of centuries as the older buildings that now adorned the Delhi plain.[39]

The Viceroy welcomed this breadth of view. A constricted city on the northern site would dampen the enthusiasm felt throughout India about the transfer of the capital, a capital which must be "a model and an example." In raising a new city, he told his Councillors, they must look far beyond the next decade. It was imperative to extend their horizon to envisage Imperial Delhi half a century hence, a Delhi that none of them would live to see.[40]

# 4

## *Evolution of a City Plan*

From the beginning, the mission of the committee of "Delhi experts" had been twofold. Lutyens, Swinton, and Brodie were charged with advising the Government of India not only on a site for the new capital but also on a city plan for the selected site. Deciding upon the appropriate tract for the new Delhi was an agonizing process. Establishing the outline of the plan, especially the location of Government House, was no less fraught with anguish and conflicting crosscurrents.

By the end of May 1912, the Committee had agreed on a site south of Shah Jahan's seventeenth-century Delhi, but for Lutyens, the work of planning the city had only just begun. As early as May 5, he wrote to his wife, "I have made up my mind as regards site, but not how to treat it yet." Within three weeks, however, he had produced his first rough plan to show Hardinge. Because the whole question posed so many difficulties, the Viceroy was discreetly noncommittal; Lutyens, nevertheless, was encouraged that Hardinge did not simply single out thorny details but instead took a wise, broad view and seemed to like the embryonic design.[1]

The canvas on which Lutyens was to exercise his genius comprised the slopes and plain between the Ridge and the Jumna River. While the eastern and southern margins of the area were studded with the monuments of vanished empires, the area from the Qutb road west to the Ridge was less accessible to the river and hence historically neglected. Unencumbered and convenient to the existing metropolis, this well-drained site offered virtually unlimited room for new buildings of all types, with the additional attraction of vistas over landmarks encompassing the entire sweep of Indian history. In their report of June 13, 1912, the Committee described the historic landscape as seen from a prospect at the foot of the Ridge, just northeast of Malcha, "almost in the center of the site": a broad crescent from Shahjahanabad and Kotla Firoz Shah south to Tughlaqabad and the Qutb, with the tombs of both Safdar Jang and the Lodis as well as the Jantar Mantar observatory in the foreground.[2] This panorama, then, was the setting for the Committee's tentative layout, while the Committee's vantage point northeast of Malcha became the first site proposed for Viceregal Lodge or Government House. [17]

By June 14, Lutyens could sketch the rough quadrilateral lines that the Viceroy's residence had taken in his mind. A hasty drawing sent to Herbert Baker showed the seeds of a fairytale palace and piazza that would rival the splendor of the Mughals. In succeeding years, the site and orientation of Government House would alter considerably, but the forms penned on that $8\frac{1}{2}$-by-10-inch stationery changed remarkably little. The forms were those of a British Palladian country house on a

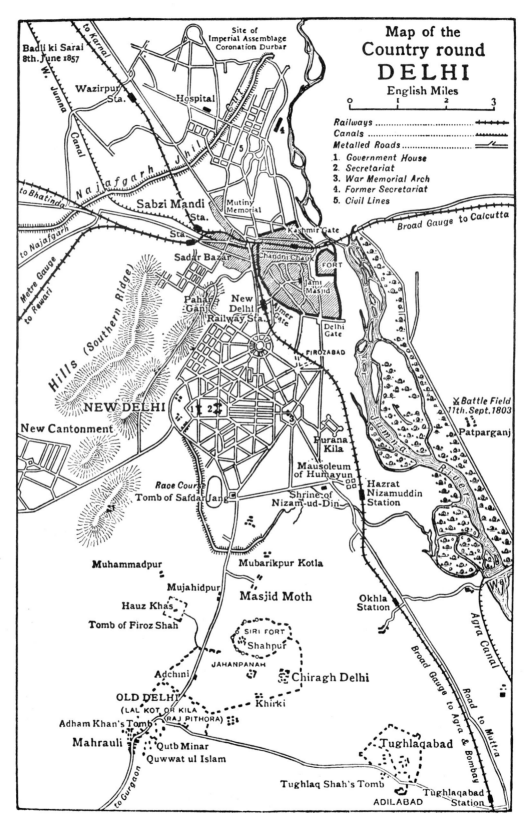

17. Delhi and region.

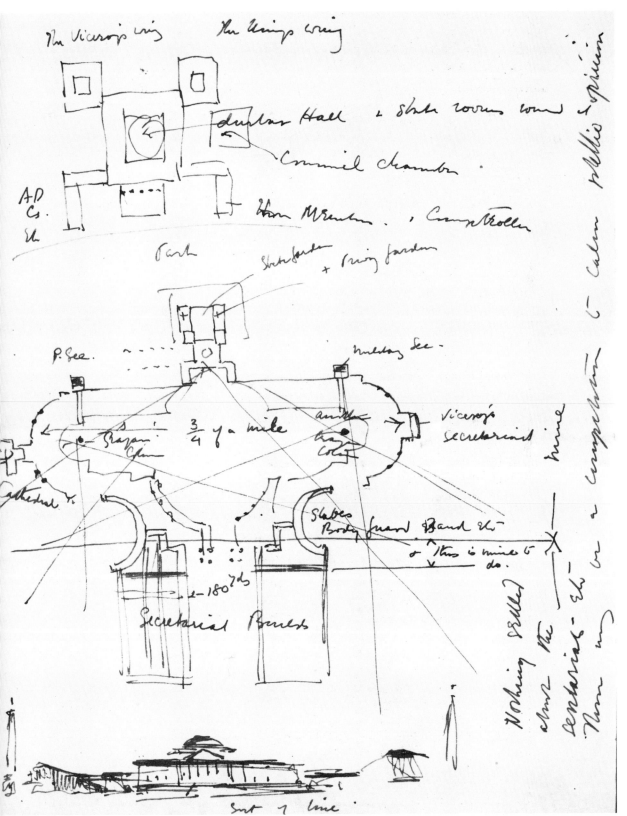

8. New Delhi, germinal sketch plan and elevation of Government House (later named Viceroy's House) and plan of the capitol complex, by E. L. Lutyens, June 14, 1912.

palatial scale, one whose majestic forecourt, flanked by imposing edifices, was the climax of a grand processional axis.[3] These, then, were the broad outlines of the heart of the Imperial city destined to rise fitfully over twenty years. Even the most imaginative guest at the inaugural ceremonies for the new Delhi nearly two decades later could scarcely have dreamed how much was owed to a few rough designs for a rejected site near Malcha. [18]

The origins of the new Delhi of 1931, in its general plan, lay in a tentative layout of the Delhi Town Planning Committee, a design in which the north Malcha site served as a crucial anchor for the central axis of the plan. This principal avenue, designated AB on the tentative layout, ran due northeast from Government House, its long uninterrupted vista crowned by the white domes and spiky minarets of the Jama Masjid, the largest mosque in India. The road followed the inclination of the ground, so that the avenue assumed a slightly concave form in a longitudinal direction, rising by easy gradients to the terminal features, "somewhat," the Committee noted, "on the lines of the Champs Elysées in Paris." (This was not to be the only time a comparison with that famed boulevard would be invoked at Delhi.) At the point where the main avenue was intersected by a line due north from the Jantar Mantar observatory, a low summit served to emphasize a circus introduced at that juncture, a direct antecedent of the present Connaught Place. This vista from Government House to the great Mughal mosque, integral to the earliest conception of the new capital, was preserved in all succeeding plans.[4]

Not retained, however, was Lutyens's original scheme for dressing the main avenue with the palaces of Indian rajas, with impressive gateways on the frontages. The Viceroy thought it undesirable that the ruling chiefs should spend time and money away from their states in this way, perhaps recalling the sycophantic, absentee nobles who had clustered around the royal presence at Versailles. Possibly more important, he was opposed to the idea of the rajas' "numerous and motley followers" in close proximity to Government House and the Government buildings.[5]

For the rest, the tentative layout was characterized by some nine long, perfectly straight roads, closely spaced, with frequent right-angle intersections. This feature prompted anxiety on Hardinge's part. Visually perceptive, the Viceroy concluded (doubtless correctly) that only "extraordinary efforts" of architectural elaboration could save such a checkerboard plan from monotony. If left unaltered, the tentative layout would be simply one more addition to the already lengthy list of grid-pattern cantonments and civil stations in India.[6]

By the end of June, the Town Planning Committee had departed from their Himalayan mountaintop retreat at Simla and sailed for home: first Brodie, then Lutyens and Swinton after conferring with Lanchester. Newly arrived from England on June 21, Lanchester had visited Delhi earlier in the year and now went over the ground in detail, assisted by thorough explanations from Lutyens and Swinton of the principal features of the tentative layout. Lanchester sensibly accepted his position as consulting expert rather than member of the Committee, although his disappointment was obvious. He said at once he did not wish to criticize or modify the principal portion of the tentative layout, including and bordering the main avenue AB, but he felt he might make helpful suggestions for more effective treatment of side roads and the outer limits of the layout. The Viceroy agreed that Lanchester should submit proposals for improvements and extensions of Shahjahanabad which would unite the old and the new cities in a harmonious whole.[7]

Lanchester's initial layout, incorporating his suggested alterations to the Committee's plan, accompanied the first of five reports prepared for the Viceroy.[8] [19] The report began by affirming the Committee's choice of site for the new city, enumerated the areas of Lanchester's specific concern, and discussed the aesthetic principles governing his philosophy of urban planning. A city's impressiveness, he felt, was dependent on the excitement of interest throughout: "As in a symphony or a drama, one should be able to pass from point to point ever finding new aspects and fresh developments." The civic designer should reveal his conception by degrees to create a cumulative effect. Practical necessities, furthermore, could assist rather than hinder in giving an imaginative quality to a city scheme.

With the Committee's principal axis AB clearly in mind, Lanchester suggested that such inventive treatment was essential to avoid monotony in main avenues of considerable length. He cited the Champs Elysées and Regent Street to illustrate the successful use of unfolding variety to maintain aesthetic interest. Thus, while not quarreling with the Committee's basic concept of route AB, Lanchester proposed breaking the long line of closely packed buildings by a cross-axial plaza on which two Secretariat blocks would stand recessed to provide subsidiary interest and terminal vistas for other roads—a compositional device which was ultimately incorporated in the plan as executed.

Hardinge had criticized the Committee's numerous long straight roads and multitude of angular intersections as lacking visual interest. He had moreover predicted that the hot premonsoon winds, sweeping dust down their long stretches, would make such roads insufferable, and he suggested hedges and trees along curved routes to mitigate this local nuisance.[9] Not surprisingly, therefore, Lanchester's layout deviated from the Committee's axial symmetry, so typical of Ecole des Beaux Arts planning, to introduce curves. New views of the historic Indrapat fortress further augmented vistas of Humayan's and Safdar Jang's tombs to heighten the scheme's aesthetic appeal. Realignment of the Committee's avenue FG, from the Qutb Minar to the Delhi Gate of Shahjahanabad, provided additional visual variety by avoiding the monotony of three closely parallel roads. This alteration, moreover, preserved large areas rich in landmarks for a proposed Archaeological Park.

The Viceroy especially commended Lanchester's design within the walls of Shahjahanabad, between the Fort, the Jama Masjid, and Delhi Gate. In his report Lanchester deprecated the Committee's view that from the existing railway station a road could be thrust through the Victoria Gardens parkland and a densely populated area of the old city to the point where their main avenue reached the city wall, near Ajmer Gate. Lanchester's criticism reflected his essential philosophy of urban improvement, which, like that of his friend Patrick Geddes, evinced a preference for corrective surgery on existing fabric, rather than for wholesale redevelopment. This is apparent, for example, in a report on the city of Lashkar in Gwalior, which Lanchester forwarded to Lord Hardinge in February 1912. In it he urged that "every necessary improvement should maintain the general character of the city" and recommended against widening the narrow bazaars to facilitate traffic, lest the remedy destroy good buildings, disturb business unnecessarily, and alter "the characteristic picturesque quality of the city."[10]

Instead of the Committee's disruptive route over valuable property, Lanchester suggested as an alternative a new ceremonial railway station from which Lothian Road, much enlarged, would lead south to an extensive square with the Jama Masjid on the right and the Fort and a rebuilt Daryaganj quarter on the left. From the square the avenue would continue directly south to pierce the city wall, while an east–west cross road from the mosque to a bathing ghat would secure a view of the water. The Jumna, Lanchester felt, was an essential factor in the city's total effect, and he advocated conversion of its margin into an attractive public park with a river drive, bridle paths, and playing fields.

Study of projected population increases, plus the urgent need to provide land for persons ousted from villages on the site of the new Delhi, dictated a suburban extension of the old city. The Committee and Lanchester urged that territory to the west and southwest of the existing city be reserved for this purpose. As proposed by Lanchester, the extensions would develop from existing roads in the Sadr Bazar, with the central avenue on an alignment due west from the Jama Masjid and with easy connections to the suburb Sabzi Mandi, the Durbar area, and the Grand Trunk Road.

Lanchester's scheme, elaborated in his second report to the Viceroy under the heading, "The Extension of the Indian City," provided for wholesale markets for grain and wood, factories and godowns or warehouses on land adjoining the railway lines, and bazaars conveniently close to the residential quarters. The plans incorporated several classes of dwellings, from 3,000-square-foot houses to ten-foot-square one-room adobe units for the poor. Lanchester, by his own admission, accepted existing Indian traditions. His designs denoted sanitary rather than social reforms: sweepers, leatherworkers, brickmakers, and limeburners—the pariahs or untouchable caste—were placed on the outskirts of town, while weavers, cotton stampers, washermen, daily laborers, and keepers of cattle plying for hire were considered "respectable neighbors." A progressive feature of the layout was the reservation of open spaces throughout the various districts, to furnish "adequate aeration" for the more compactly built residences. Sites were set aside for mosques, temples, and a thana or police station. The gridiron pattern of the contemplated extension comprised five grades of road: a few wide avenues for aesthetic and utilitarian reasons, with the remaining subsidiary streets in proportion to the actual requirements of traffic, lest initial costs and, especially, later maintenance be unnecessarily extravagant.[11]

In a subsequent version, which was known as Lanchester's "revised layout," the grid of the extensions was altered by introducing more open space, judiciously including eight curved streets, and reducing individual blocks in size. [20] No fundamental alteration was made to his first layout, but Lanchester attempted to improve the approach of the ceremonial route from Shahjahanabad into the main avenue, which the Viceroy had criticized as "too abrupt." More important, the circus at the end of the main avenue of the Imperial city was considerably enlarged to provide an island treatment for two temples in the hamlet of Jaisingpura. Of modern vintage, the temples had nevertheless been erected by an important sect of rich Hindu bankers, and the Viceroy deemed their preservation a politic gesture to Hindu sensibilities. Lanchester's solution obviated removal of the structures, while retaining the center line of the avenue and the center point of the circus. The larger circus shortened the avenue's straight portion, reducing the distance between the Secretariats and altering the point of the medial break.[12]

In his fourth report to the Viceroy, Lanchester prepared a sketch plan showing a carefully considered arrangement of the Secretariats on the main avenue and central square. The area allocated for these buildings was relatively large in relation to existing departmental requirements, so that a unified phased development was suggested, with the first instalments disposed in a manner to fill up the frontages. A more compact treatment, the architect admitted, would have been more economical but would have left much of the principal avenue void.[13]

While Lanchester was bent over his drafting board, energetic young engineers tramped across the terrain, gathering information pertinent to irrigation, drainage, roads, parks, buildings, and the acquisition of land for the new Delhi. Within the area designated by the experts for acquisition, the insanitary village of Paharganj, the sole settlement of any size to mark the site, stood athwart the grand avenue which led straight to the white domes of the Jama Masjid. Only 126 of the 290 acres comprising the suburb belonged to the Government, and the estimated cost of the remainder was more than twenty-seven lakhs of rupees or about £180,000. This figure did not include the expense of transplanting the 15,000 inhabitants. The village had the additional difficulty of being full of shrines and temples whose disposition would inevitably be a sensitive and controversial issue.[14]

The Viceroy was plainly alarmed. In a note which he conceded might be "a severe shock," Hardinge wrote the Committee on August 1 that it would be too expensive to expropriate the householders of Paharganj. Ten days later he telegraphed Lord Crewe that the high cost would require modifying the main avenue of the Committee's proposed layout to avoid the suburb. Using Government House as a pivot, the axis of the plan would have to be pointed not toward the Jama Masjid but a few degrees southwest toward the Delhi Gate of the old city. More radically, the axis could be turned about forty-five degrees southeast toward the river and the ancient fortress of Indrapat, the direction Hardinge had initially and instinctively preferred on viewing the site in March. In either case, the main avenue would more nearly bisect the new Imperial city, and Government House and the Secretariats would become the focal element rather than merely the western flank. The site of Government House might be changed, but he emphasized that "the House should face towards the river."[15]

News of the Viceroy's volte-face did not generate enthusiasm in Whitehall. At the upper echelons of the India Office, Sir Richmond Ritchie, Sir Thomas Holderness, and F. H. Lucas studied maps of Delhi in the light of Hardinge's telegram of August 11 and found the new development "far from promising." Turning the axis south and east, Lucas told Lord Crewe, would bring the city down onto lower, man-worn ground that the Delhi experts were committed to oppose. Details of Hardinge's proposals, he felt sure, promised to be "rather a thunderbolt" to the Committee. Events proved him correct.[16]

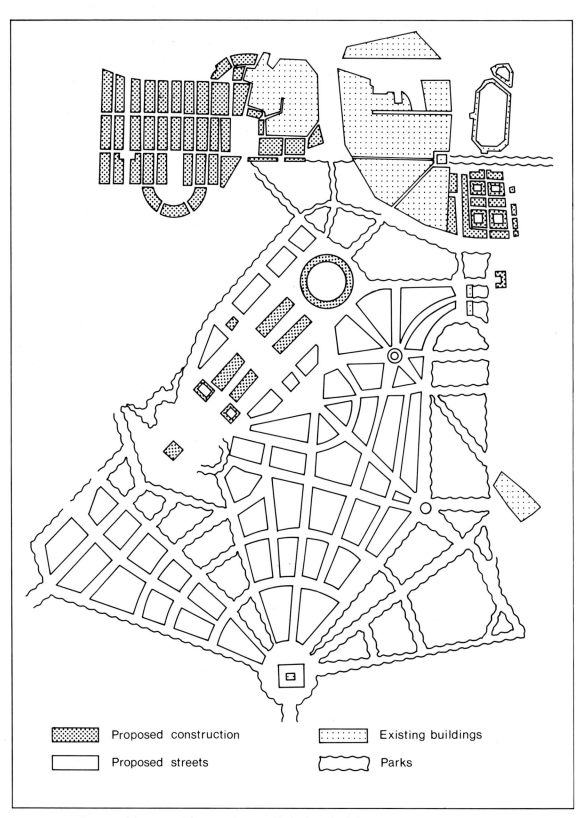

19. New Delhi, initial layout, with extensions to Shahjahanabad, by Henry Vaughan Lanchester, July 1912.

News reached Swinton on vacation in the north of England. Not surprisingly, he called the Viceroy's suggestions "drastic" and summoned Lutyens and Brodie by telegraph to an immediate conference. Lutyens, told of Hardinge's wishes by the India Office the day previously, had said that rather than change the aspect of Government House, he would prefer to terminate the main avenue before reaching Paharganj and to design the connecting road to enter Shahjahanabad by the Delhi Gate. The cost of acquiring Paharganj he thought doubtless exaggerated, and he felt in any event the suburb's insanitary state, so close to the old and new cities alike, required acquisition and reform.[17]

In Delhi, instructed to prepare a "second revised layout," Lanchester worked with a speed Hardinge called "really somewhat remarkable" and a later partner, Thomas Arthur Lodge, described as "tremendous." First impressions of him might be unfavorable, "owing to the roughness of his manners," but the Viceroy found

20. New Delhi, "Revised Layout", by H. V. Lanchester, July 1912.

Lanchester "by far the most practical and sensible" of all the town planners. Hardinge credited him with "some excellent ideas," and felt that in a month in India he had accomplished much more than the Committee had done in over nine weeks.[18]

Lanchester's third scheme, known as the "second revised layout," proposed three avenues radiating from Government House, all of equal size, rather than the single gigantic avenue of the earlier plans: one with a vista of the Jama Masjid, as before; a second to Indrapat; and a central processional avenue toward the Delhi Gate, meeting in that neighborhood the ceremonial route from the railway station, Lothian Road.[19] Lanchester intended these radial avenues, with two subsidiary ones to Safdar Jang's and Humayan's tombs, to make Government House a more effectively dominant feature, its focal quality particularly enhanced by a ceremonial avenue that bisected rather than skirted the new city. The more easterly orientation of the Viceroy's house, moreover, not only improved its aspect, but rendered possible a more direct route to the military cantonment north of the Delhi Gate.

The arrangement of the radial avenues furnished six sites for Secretariat buildings, in close proximity to Government House and to each other, with ample room for later extension. To the east of these offices were four blocks of land, one occupied by Raisina Hill, another by several temples, and the two others reserved for future buildings of importance.

Lanchester's third layout, however, prepared on the eve of his departure, did not fulfil all Hardinge's scrupulous standards "of taste and convenience." Earlier Hardinge had deprecated the monotony of the Committee's checkerboard, but Lanchester prompted the identical criticism with too many curving roads. While the Viceroy had thought the Committee's arrangement of Secretariats on the main avenue too extended, he felt Lanchester's "somewhat too compressed." Furthermore, uniformly facing Government House, the six buildings proposed gave "undue publicity" to activities in front of the Viceregal residence. Perhaps more important, the contraction of the spacious avenue to Indrapat through a hundred-foot-wide cut in Raisina Hill would doubtless snarl traffic, and the rocky eminence would still mask the notable vista to Indrapat.[20]

In his final report Lanchester had confidently voiced his belief that while details might be modified in the future, his second revised layout "could be accepted as determining the general lines of the proposed Imperial City." Scarcely had the architect sailed for England than the Viceroy sought an independent appraisal of both Lanchester's scheme and the tentative layout of the Committee from two senior Government engineers. The report of this pair, Michael Nethersole and C. E. V. Goument, proposed a fundamental change: adaptation of Lanchester's layout to a new site for Government House on the Ridge, dominating the entire city. The Committee's site for Viceregal Lodge, the report indicated, lay too low for a dominant or commanding position in the new city. Shut in on the northwest, west, and southwest by the Ridge and on the east by Raisina Hill, the projected residence would boast only limited views and would suffer from "a depressing sense of confinement." The two engineers believed that with irrigation and artificial soil improvement, necessary afforestation of the Ridge might prove possible, and they urged the selection of a Forest officer to examine the question. Hardinge agreed at once. He appointed a Forest officer and the same day gave the Town Planning Committee notice that if afforestation proved possible, the site of Government House would have to be reconsidered.[21]

P. H. Clutterbuck, whom Hardinge described as "the most distinguished Forest officer that we have in Northern India," reported on August 18 that the afforestation of the Ridge was "decidedly possible," its difficulty proportionate to the water available. He listed seventy-two species of trees suitable for the Ridge. The afforestation could be done either slowly without regular irrigation or quite easily with unlimited water.[22]

T. R. J. Ward, an Engineer officer attached to the Town Planning Committee, reported independently that conservation and arboreal skill would produce "a fine growth of trees on the Ridge," which would be attractive in ten or fifteen years. But he declared himself strongly opposed to placing the Viceroy's residence and grounds on the Ridge; Ward's own instincts favored preservation of the range as a people's park for riding and driving. The initial cost of improving the site and the expense of future maintenance militated against its choice for Government House. Furthermore, Ward demonstrated that buildings on the Ridge site suggested by Nethersole and Goument would not be seen to advantage from a number of places in the plain nor would they enjoy some of the best views of the seven older Delhis, being screened by Raisina Hill, some parts of the Ridge itself, and, ironically, the proposed afforestation. He did admit that the vista to the north gave a fine impression of the Mutiny Memorial. Geoffrey de Montmorency, an indefatigable young Indian Civil Service officer assigned to the new capital project, agreed that the Nethersole-Goument site could be improved upon and recommended that if the Ridge were to be used then the Committee should try to secure "the best site available."[23]

On receiving Clutterbuck's afforestation report, the Viceroy wrote to Swinton that the location of Government House had to be completely reconsidered. He confessed that a ridgetop siting, with magnificent views over the whole plain, had great attractions for him personally, and he felt it would appeal to Indians as well, who would be able to identify it "from miles away" as the residence of Lord Sahib. To Lord Crewe he cabled that until their return in December the experts should consider an alternative layout with Government House either on the Ridge or three-quarters up the Ridge on the slope near the Talkatora Garden, not far from Raisina. His own inclination was to place the residence just at the top of the slope above Talkatora Garden, with level space for gardens behind.[24]

There was no lack of opinion regarding the site for the Viceroy's house. The King told Lutyens he was strongly against any proposal to put Government House on the Ridge, and Lutyens in turn expressed his own reservations to Hardinge. One Member of the Viceroy's Council, with twenty-eight years' experience in India, argued that the top of such a rocky ridge could be bleak in cold weather while in hot weather it would be even more uncomfortable than the plains below. Swinton repeatedly emphasized his preference for a site "absolutely on Malcha village," but Lutyens and Brodie both had qualms about its distance from the existing Delhi.[25]

Most important among all these opinions was the Viceroy's emphatic statement that as the result of his visit to Delhi at the end of July, there was one position he "liked immensely" and considered "the most beautiful site of all": Raisina Hill. Further, he had been struck "very forcibly" with the effect of facing Government House east toward the river rather than northeast to Old Delhi. Lanchester had thought the Raisina spur posed too many engineering problems, but Hardinge had been encouraged by rough estimates of the cost of clearing rocks at the site. His inspection in July showed that the hillock had many advantages over alternative locations, such as Swinton's choice, Malcha. Raisina was surrounded by splendid soil, was not too distant from the great landmarks, and was so central that the main avenues would be short enough to fill easily with buildings.[26]

The Viceroy notified Swinton that the Committee was to consider the site in December. Swinton replied that Brodie had in fact at one time favored Raisina and the Committee had discussed its potential but that he personally had felt it lacked adequate height for "command." He assured the Viceroy it would be given careful reconsideration. Lutyens in turn wrote that if the Committee's tentative site between Malcha and Raisina were abandoned, he would side with Swinton in favoring Malcha over Brodie's preference for Raisina.[27]

In reply to Swinton's persistent advocacy of Malcha over Raisina, the Viceroy finally wrote from Kashmir, "I do not go into the question of Raisina Hill as a site for Government House until I have again seen it." Within two weeks, Hardinge was in Delhi. The afternoon of Monday, November 4, was crucial. Accompanied by three engineers, T. R. J. Ward, C. E. V. Goument, and W. B. Gordon, the Viceroy visited all the proposed sites in the southern area, and, in his own words, "came to the conclusion that Raisina was the best for Government House." The engineers agreed unanimously. The top of the hill could be removed, giving a level space of five acres and a commanding position. Water could be pumped there more easily than to the Ridge, and the park below would have some of the best soil near Delhi. The engineers believed there would be little difference between the costs of preparing Raisina and of the tentative site picked by the Committee. As for the Ridge sites Hardinge had once espoused so warmly, they now appeared to him "impracticable, since it would be a continual struggle against nature, and nature is generally likely to win in the long run." Moreover the Malcha site, he wrote Lutyens, was similarly stony and was definitely too far away.[28]

Swinton arrived in Delhi on Monday morning, November 25, in advance of his two colleagues on the Committee. That afternoon Sir Guy Fleetwood Wilson marched him over the various sites under consideration. "I left him blind and choking with dust and feebly protesting that he had only just arrived," chortled the Finance Member. Thirteen days later, on December 8, Swinton accompanied the Viceroy, together with Sir Valentine Chirol and Malcolm Hailey, on an inspection of the possible sites for Government House. Hardinge recorded that he "liked Raisina more than ever and Chirol had no doubt as to his preference of that site"— much to Swinton's very evident disappointment. The visit appeared decisive, for the Viceroy resolutely recorded in his diary the elimination of Raisina's only serious competitor: "I will not listen to any suggestion of Malcha, [which] is far too distant."[29]

With the arrival of Lutyens and Brodie, the full Committee began reconsideration of their tentative layout and site for Government House. The attempted assassination of Lord Hardinge, which shattered the pomp of the State Entry on

December 23, brought the Committee's activities to an abrupt halt. As the Viceroy struggled to recover from his grave wounds, Sir Bradford Leslie's proposals for Shahjahanabad and its immediate environs prompted a new press campaign in Britain and India for selection of a northern site. Bombarded by this publicity and in receipt of a crucial message from Lord Crewe suggesting that Sir Bradford's scheme might be examined, the invalid Viceroy capitulated: on January 18 he asked Swinton to have the Committee prepare an alternative layout north and northwest of Old Delhi. Stunned by this news, the Delhi experts hastily set about fulfilling their new mandate in the short time before they must leave India again.[30]

The previous day, in an interview with Sir Thomas Holderness at the India Office rooms in Whitehall, Herbert Baker had declared his willingness to collaborate at Delhi with Lutyens, his friend of many years. Discussions and negotiations about this arrangement had been underway for months. Now events moved rapidly. The India Office telegraphed news of Baker's assent on Friday evening, and on Sunday evening, January 19, the Viceroy's Council, chaired by Sir Guy Fleetwood Wilson, gave its approval. Lord Crewe engaged Baker on January 22, and the architect sailed aboard the steamship *Egypt* on January 25.[31]

When he met Baker on February 7 in Bombay, aboard the Governor's launch, Lutyens had already "been working very hard with Brodie" on layouts for the northern site. Baker, accustomed for two decades to designing with success on sites atop a rocky eminence or kopje in South Africa, threw himself with enthusiasm into these schemes for the Ridge on the northern site. He envisioned great architectural possibilities, with Government House and the Secretariats sited to dramatic effect on an impressive "Via Sacra" along the Ridge. As a result Lutyens wrote home in despair that Baker was "exactly where we were when we first came out: tremendously pro-North." Not surprisingly for a recent visitor to classical sites in the Mediterranean, Baker referred to his plans for the Ridge as an acropolis; for his text he adopted Matthew 5:14, "A city that is set on an hill cannot be hid." He visited both north and south sites on horseback repeatedly, held lengthy discussions with pertinent officials, and spent long hours on designs for the northern site.[32]

Hardinge's only instructions to Swinton on January 17 had been to examine the rejected area again in the light of Sir Bradford's paper and of publicly and privately expressed opinion, "in order to see whether under modified conditions a city could be fitted on to the north site." The modified conditions were not specified, but the Committee discussed these with the Chief Commissioner of Delhi, the Commanding Officer at Delhi, and the Chief Engineer, and accepted their views as a working basis.[33]

By the third week in February the Committee had concluded that a small, closely built city, occupied for only five months annually, could be placed on the north site at considerable expense—provided that there was no subsequent expansion. On Tuesday, February 25, the Delhi experts showed the Viceroy how, under those conditions, the north site could be used in either of two ways.[34]

The first of the plans shown the Viceroy, labelled "Layout A," [21] made provision for Government House, six Secretariats, buildings for the Viceregal staff and bodyguard and two companies of infantry, a hospital and schools, a Free Church and an Anglican cathedral, a hotel, shops, a bathing ghat on the Jumna, parks, a polo ground, and an amphitheater on the Durbar site. The main avenue was aligned generally northwest to southeast, with Government House facing the river. There were echoes of the Committee's tentative plan from June 1912 and of Lanchester's three layouts, especially his last. The nine straight roads, closely spaced, of the tentative plan were retained, only the outermost two having been realigned to conform to the topography and scenic possibilities of the northern site. The new layout, avoiding both the checkerboard pattern and excess of curved streets the Viceroy so disliked, duplicated the radial avenues, central ceremonial route, and thirty- and sixty-degree angles of Lanchester's third plan. The vistas were of course no longer aligned on the Jama Masjid, Delhi Gate, Indrapat, and Humayan's and Safdar Jang's tombs but instead on a hexagonal park area, the river, a proposed bathing ghat, and a projected church and cathedral. The focus of these radii, Government House, became the focus of the site, as Lanchester had intended, with a handsome prospect terminating at a riverside ghat. The center of this main avenue, as in Lanchester's second layout, was punctuated by four large, tightly-knit government office buildings and a cross axis closed by two edifices, forming an impressive forum or *place*. Betwen this plaza and the river, an oval ring of buildings constituted the focus for another series of radial avenues, in a pattern that would later find parallels at Princes' Park in the completed city.

The Committee had an alternative, simplified plan for the northern site to show

21. New Delhi, "Layout A" for a site north of Shahjahanabad, by the Delhi Town Planning Committee, February 1913.

22. New Delhi, "Layout B" for a site north of Shahjahanabad, by the Delhi Town Planning Committee, February 1913.

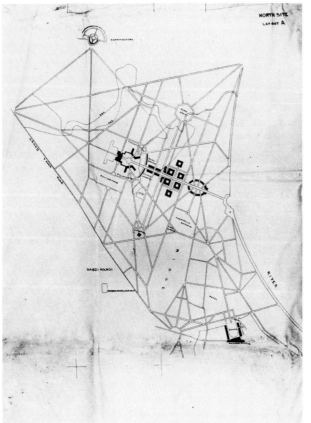

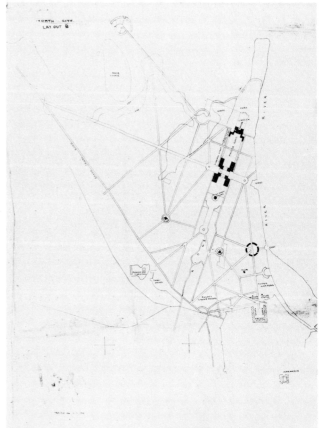

Hardinge on February 25. [22] The grand axis of "Layout B" was aligned in a north-east-to-southwest direction along the Ridge, with the Flagstaff Tower one of its principal features. A broad cross axis ran from the northwest to the southeast, on the precise route of the main avenue of "Layout A," terminating at a ghat on the Jumna. The design accommodated Government House and four Secretariats, quarters for the Viceregal staff and body guard, a cathedral and church, parks and ghats, a racecourse, and that essential component of British colonial society, a club. The forecourt of the Viceroy's residence was labelled, with a degree of pretension, a "piazza"; indeed the designs for the Ridge envisaged a formal, dignified presence, sanctified by history, but not without an alertness to the dramatic use of natural features. To the west, radial avenues emanating from the cathedral site and a large circus (the hexagonal park of "Layout A") formed two giant triangles whose stark geometric simplicity reflected the primacy of axial Beaux Arts planning principles over concessions to an uneven topography. The layout was composed for the most part of a network of such thirty- and sixty-degree angles, intermeshed with a central grid bounding the focal capitoline hill.

The Committee's new report on the southern site, at that stage in draft form, embodied a more concentrated layout than that of the previous June. The Viceroy requested several copies of this "rough idea for the southern site" on February 27, together with those for the northern area. The Viceroy had already directed Lutyens on November 5 to prepare a layout with Government House on Raisina Hill, and in early January Lutyens had shown the convalescent Hardinge two plans, one with an east–northeast aspect for Government House and the second with the residence facing Indrapat. As evidence mounted of serious sanitary and military objections to reconsidering the northern site, Raisina once again assumed the preeminence it had enjoyed in early November when the Viceroy and Gordon, Goument, and Ward had been unanimous in considering the hill "by far the best site" for Government House.[35]

Lutyens produced a carefully ordered but compact layout centered on Raisina, its southern terminus at Safdar Jang's tomb rather than the distant Qutb Minar.[23] The route from Government House to the Jama Masjid was retained, but only as a subsidiary road. There were instead three large terminal vistas: one from the Viceroy's house to Indrapat; a second ceremonial route, emanating from a new railway station and plaza at Jaisingpura, crossing the Indrapat avenue at right angles and closed on the south by a cathedral; and last, an avenue leading south–southeast from the railway plaza until it turned to a north–south alignment on Government House. The Viceregal residence commanded the city in solitary splendor on top of Raisina Hill, its forecourt below ringed by large and small quarters for staff and troops. Substantial buildings lined the Indrapat vista, four especially impressive edifices ornamenting the junction of the two major ceremonial cross axes. The banks of the Jumna were decoratively landscaped, with a riverside drive from Shahjahanabad, and a weir at Indrapat formed a shimmering lake to frame dramatic reflections of the ancient fortress.

The layout of the new city was rapidly approaching its ultimate form, as appended to the Committee's final report in March. The penultimate stage was reached when, at the initiative of Herbert Baker, Government House was moved westward from its exclusive situation, and the Secretariat buildings joined the Viceroy's house on a broad platform on the crest of Raisina Hill. Baker's success in designing on the South African kopje made him insistent that the Secretariats, for which he alone was responsible, should share the elevated and dominant position. He cited as a precedent Darius the Great's "stupendous platform" at Persepolis, and he argued the symbolic value of such an arrangement, expressing the unity of the Viceroy with his Government. Lutyens pointed out the great difficulty and cost entailed, but as he later reminded Baker, "I met you at once." [36]

Hardinge's idea had always been that the Viceroy's house alone should crown Raisina so that it was visible without obstruction from every part of the new Delhi, but the architects pressed him to accept their platform scheme. Despite the obvious disadvantage that views of Government House from the city would be frequently blocked by intervening Secretariats, Hardinge at the time thought the acropolis a fine architectural conception. On February 26, he gave his assent, conditional on a design of more modest proportions than initially proposed. [37]

By the first week in March, the architects had conceived two alternative plans for

23. New Delhi, layout with Government House alone on Raisina Hill, by E. L. Lutyens.

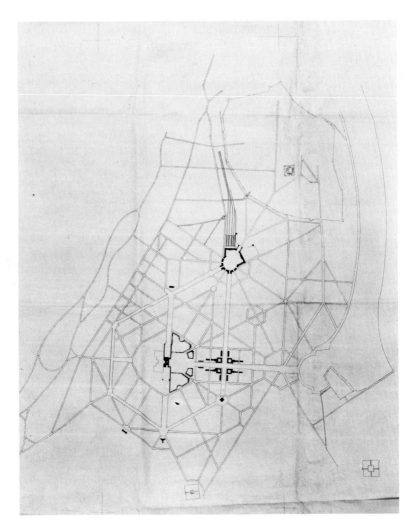

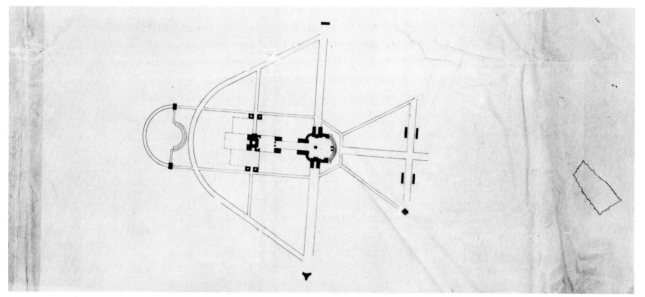

24. New Delhi, layout with Government House and Secretariat buildings sharing Raisina Hill, by E. L. Lutyens, with Herbert Baker, 1913.

25. New Delhi, sketch of the Raisina acropolis, in relation to the entire city, by E. L. Lutyens, March 6, 1913, and marked, "Seen and approved by H. Ex. March 11. 13 with bigger Place in front."

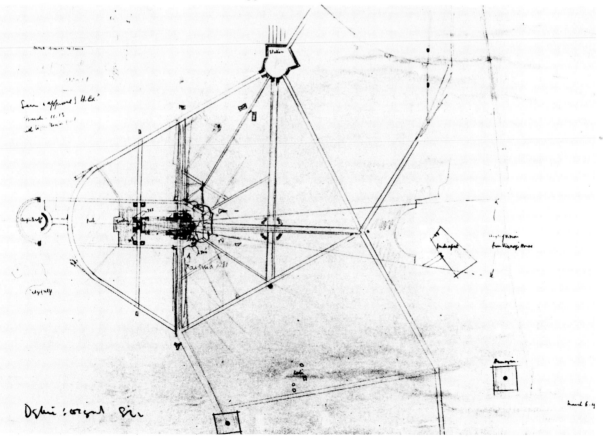

the acropolis. The first showed Government House displaced by two pairs of Secretariat blocks, linked around a grand oval court, a place of privilege raised above the streets which skirted its eastern flank. Another pair of buildings framed, with Beaux Arts symmetry, the main gateway to the Viceregal precincts while two further pairs stood sentinel at the north and south entrances. A giant Durbar amphitheater, at Baker's suggestion, climaxed the western end of the Indrapat axis.[38] [24]

Anxious that the four separate blocks might "not be conducive to efficiency," the architects furnished an alternative plan in which the focal buildings were compressed and their relationship to the rest of the city resolved in a sketchy manner.[39] [25] The Secretariats were brought forward into alignment with the Indrapat avenue and the wings of Government House. This alteration reduced the prominence of the Secretariats by contracting the generous oval court to a rectilinear plaza bordered by two pairs of hyphenated back-to-back L-shaped blocks and bounded on the east by a compact semicircular terrace. The gateway buildings at the principal entrance to the Viceroy's enclosure were omitted, while the wings of Government House were extended eastward. The large amphitheater planned for the Viceregal park was shifted further westward, where its huge bowl, hewn from the quartzite Ridge,

26. New Delhi, diary entry by Herbert Baker, March 11, 1913, showing (right to left) amphitheater, capitol, plaza, and the cultural edifices at the intersection of King's Way and Queen's Way.

would mirror the outlines of the distant Indrapat lake. Four tripartite buildings highlighted the geographical centerpoint of the composition where the juncture of two main routes bisected the city.

Hardinge was shown these layouts during an hour-and-a-half interview with Lutyens, Baker, Swinton, and Hailey on Monday afternoon, March 10. The Viceroy expressed general approbation. He liked Baker's amphitheater and he agreed that the ceremonial route should proceed from the new railway station. But anxious about the altered position of Government House, which he thought "a difficult problem," he asked for time to consider. At a meeting with the architects the following day, he approved the raised platform (although apprehensive about its cost) with a less constricted plaza east of the Secretariats.[40] Lutyens hastily pencilled in an amplified plaza to scale on the second layout, and scribbled across one corner: "Seen and approved by H. Ex. March 11. 13 with bigger Place in front," while Baker sketched the new "large open Place," as he described it, in his diary. [26] Six surviving versions of this expanded plaza bear witness to Lutyens's intense, inventive struggle to accommodate vehicular traffic and, especially, the geometric alignment of terminal vistas to an altered capitol design, one which embodied not only his own ideas but Baker's and Hardinge's conceptions as well.

After lunching on St. Patrick's Day at the Viceregal Lodge in Civil Lines, the architects had their final interview with the Viceroy before leaving India. Baker, who presented perspectives showing the eastern front of the Secretariats framing Government House, recorded in his diary that Hardinge registered broad approval of all the plans shown him. Increasingly perturbed by the delays, the Viceroy emphasized his hope that construction would begin by the end of the year.[41]

Ten days before, the Viceroy's Council had met to discuss the reports on the northern site by the town planners and by specially appointed medical and military committees. The military authorities concluded that the site lacked sufficient healthy land for a cantonment, posing grave problems for protection of a city already haunted by specters of the Mutiny massacres. Another important committee, headed by the Director-General of the Indian Medical Service, warned that selection of the damp northern area would risk excessive respiratory sickness, especially tuberculosis; they also quoted a survey showing a rate of endemic malaria nearly three times that of the southern site.[42]

The town planners, in their own report on the north site, conceded the possibility of designing a reduced, closely built layout of five square miles, rather than the ten square miles originally proposed for a new capital of 30,000 to 57,000 persons. But the planners reiterated the serious sanitary and military objections to the northern area and emphasized, above all, the lack of room for expansion in a city destined to prosper and grow. To build a capital sufficient only for present requirements, Lutyens had written his wife, "would indeed be laying a dead hand on the future."[43]

Such unanimity from specialists and experts was persuasive, and at a meeting on March 7 the Viceroy and his Council expressed their accord. The Chief Engineer for Delhi later recounted that it was the report on comparative medical and sanitary conditions, north and south, which had "finally tipped the balance." On March 8, Hardinge telegraphed the India Office that "the southern site selected by the experts must be adhered to," underscoring the decision with his personal opinion that the location had "very great advantages." If the Viceroy felt any anxiety about Lord Crewe's reaction, it was dispelled by a telegram he received on March 11: "I am glad of your decision in favour of south site, which I am sure is right."[44]

It remained for Lutyens and Swinton to finish the Town Planning Committee's third and last report. Before departing in February, Brodie had drafted his contributions and authorized his signature on the completed document. Both his colleagues worked feverishly, and on March 20, Swinton delivered signed copies of the final report to Viceregal Lodge. Only two days later, he and Lutyens, together with Baker, sailed from Bombay. In a parting letter as Chairman, Swinton admitted that the Committee's task had not always been easy, but he told the Viceroy that the ultimate plan pleased him more than any of its predecessors, for it was compact yet elastic enough to meet future needs. "I believe in the future of Delhi," he concluded poignantly, "and I hope that Your Excellency will live to be very proud of your child."[45]

The final report made it plain that the Committee did not consider town planning as simply street layout but as a three-dimensional problem in design that encompassed numerous physical elements.[46] Besides the pattern of streets and plazas and traffic circles, the "Delhi experts" exhibited concern for such diverse elements of the plan as water supply, drainage, sewage systems, refuse destruction, railway facilities for passengers and freight, tram and bus transit, river training, arboriculture, and parks and open spaces for ornament and recreation. While the Committee were certainly much concerned with the visual impact of monumental arrangements of public buildings, their report showed a genuine awareness of the social implications and consequences of town planning.

Certain general principles, the Committee asserted, must obtain in all good planning. A well designed city must, with due regard to economy, have beauty, comfort, and convenience. Foresight could ensure that prime requisite, healthiness, as well as adequate room for a flexible expansion. Special heed should be given the presentation of natural beauties and the architectural splendors of monuments both ancient and modern. No class of inhabitant should be neglected in providing recreation space.

The Committee also recognized the particularity of every site, the special principles governing each individual plan. For Delhi the planners acknowledged specific physical conditions and the necessity of realizing the concept of an Imperial city, embodying peaceful domination and dignified rule. As the Committee had said before, the British capital for India had to uphold a venerable tradition of Imperial governance, weaving the strands of many centuries and empires into a new whole. Swinton had noted in December that the Committee labored under the onus of comparison: the British Raj would now be ranged in tangible form beside the monuments of past rulers, and it was essential that it "quietly dominate them all." The King's Private Secretary, Lord Stamfordham, had struck this very note three months before. He wrote Lord Crewe that King George felt Government House must be "conspicuous and commanding." The Viceregal residence, flying the British flag, should be the first object in view when approaching the capital, and it must not "be dominated by the Jumma Masjid and the Fort nor dwarfed by the Ridge." Every effort should be made to create a city representative of the British

Raj and worthy of the King-Emperor. The Indian was of a critical mind, fully aware of what Hindu and Mughal builders had accomplished. "We must now let him see for the first time," Lord Stamfordham declared, "the power of Western science, art, and civilization."[47]

Delhi had distinct physical circumstances the Committee felt commanded attention in a city intended for seven months' residence annually. Most notable were the endemic malaria and the wide variations in rainfall, river levels, and temperature (from 105 in the shade to near freezing). Irrigation was necessary for the trees and grass required to combat characteristic local dust, glare, and barrenness.

The layout which accompanies the Committee's final report includes the area bounded on the north by Shahjahanabad, on the east by the Jumna, and on the west by the Ridge. The southern boundary no longer encompasses the Qutb Minar as in earlier designs; a line drawn from a point on the Ridge west of Talkatora to Safdar Jang's tomb and then due east to the river marks the planned city's southern limit. The tract between the line and the Qutb, eminently suitable for building, is designated for further expansion. [27]

The plan exhibits numerous features common to earlier versions. The focal point is the Raisina acropolis, comprising Government House (with an integral Council Chamber) and the large Secretariat blocks that house the individual departments administered by Members of the Viceroy's Council. The Government complex is not simply the heart of the new city, but it is meant to be, as the report declares, "the keystone of the rule over the Empire of India; this is the place of Government in its highest expression." The visitor normally approaches the raised platform or forum from the east and reaches the wide steps, portico, and dome of Government House after passing between the massive Secretariats. This progress is deliberately symbolic: "The imagination is led from the machinery to the prime moving power itself." East of this forum lies a spacious forecourt defined by trees, from which the principal parkway—King's Way—leads to Indrapat, site of the oldest Delhi of all, Indraprastha. North and south of the forecourt, avenues radiate in a tripartite pattern, linking empires past and present, and uniting the business and lives of the new Delhi's people with the Government of India.[48]

Crossing the 440-foot parkway at right angles is a north–south avenue, the Queen's Way, terminating in a new railway station on the north and the Anglican cathedral on the south. Around a grand plaza at the railway station are grouped municipal offices, banks, shops, and hotels; the post office is symmetrically juxtaposed to the station. The intended ceremonial or processional route leads due south from the railway to the intersection of the Queen's Way and King's Way and thence west to Government House. At the junction of the two avenues, four large buildings are placed within the central vista or mall, forming a cultural or intellectual plaza: the Oriental Institute, National Museum, National Library, and Imperial Record Office. A long, alternative processional route extends south from the Delhi Gate of the Fort and Shahjahanabad past the houses of the Indian rajas and nobles and affords handsome views of the Jumna and the artificial lake proposed for the environs of Indrapat. Halfway from the old city, the route is inflected southwest toward a commemorative column at the east end of the King's Way. Seven main roads converge on this column, just as seven roads converge on the forecourt of the

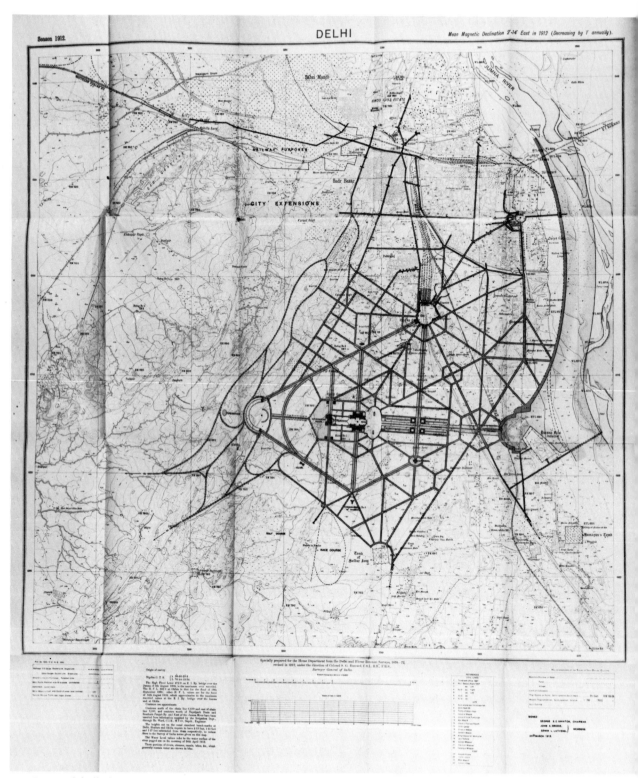

27. Layout labelled "Accompaniment to the Final Report of the Delhi Town Planning Committee on the Town Planning of the New Imperial Capital." Signed and dated, George S. C. Swinton, Chairman; John A. Brodie and Edwin L. Lutyens, Members; 20th March 1913.

Government acropolis at the opposite end of the central vista. With the exception of the central parkway, the city's avenues range in width from sixty to 300 feet.[49]

The axis leading northeast from the Secretariats to the railway plaza, in the direction of the Jama Masjid, forms the city's main business avenue. In this area southwest of the station lie the houses of the local administrators and the European clerks' residences. Segregated to the west, by income if not race, between Talkatora Gardens and the unattractive Paharganj, are the residences of the Indian clerks. Land is allocated in the immediate vicinity of the Raisina acropolis for housing Members of Council and the other highest officials. The Commander-in-Chief's residence lies directly south of the Secretariats.

The Committee placed the club, an indispensable fixture of the colonial scene, southwest of the Viceroy's house, easily accessible from European residences in the city and the military cantonment, itself located southwest of Malcha on the other side of the Ridge. The town planners judged the land adjoining the club on their layout to be well suited for golf and that absolutely essential feature, a racecourse. Parks were projected for the area of Safdar Jang's Makhbara and the Lodi tombs on the new city's southern margin, while other parks separated Imperial Delhi from Shahjahanabad and encompassed the Ridge and riverside, forming a green belt that virtually ringed the capital.

The avenue from the new railway station aligned on the Jama Masjid connects the new city and Shahjahanabad on the layout. Inside the city walls this route divides: one branch thrusts its way through densely packed quarters to the King Edward VII Memorial near the Fort; the other pushes through the center of the old city, across its principal artery, Chandni Chauk, and the Victoria Gardens to terminate at St. James's Church. Broad roads straight through the heart of the crowded Sadr Bazar connect the new Delhi with Civil Lines.

To ameliorate Delhi's particular physical problems, the planners recommended wide grass strips and lines of well-irrigated trees to temper the glare and give rest to the eyes as well as to dissipate heat radiation. For control of the omnipresent dust, the Committee proposed lowering the margin of roadways and footpaths to enable the grass to be wholly covered by irrigation water, thus trapping the dust and adding it to the soil.[50]

The planners recognized that theirs was not a detailed layout. They urged that when that stage was reached, care should be taken to provide "ample air space and playing grounds for children" near the residences of minor officials and the less privileged. The Committee underlined this progressive social attitude by advising a minimum proportion of one acre of open space for every ten acres throughout the city, especially in the Indian extensions to Shahjahanabad and the quarters of the large railway staff, housed by necessity close to the railway yards.

While the proposed routes through the old city seemed notably oversimplified and insensitive to existing urban patterns, the Committee's report showed the planners were only too aware of the complexities involved. They admitted that "months of patient investigation" into property values and conflicting interests would be required before improvements to Shahjahanabad or the Sadr Bazar could be properly defined. Compulsory reforms in crowded neighborhoods, the planners noted, were costly, unpopular, and produced a more insanitary congestion as the dispossessed huddled even closer in the side streets. A few wide through-traffic routes, however, would furnish easy access and adequate connection to virgin land and better conditions in the nearby western extensions. In this way the Committee felt the Indian populace in the old city might be induced to move. The planners again emphasized matters of social conscience: in all future improvements, responsible authorities must recognize "the paramount need for open spaces, not only for large parks, but for small play grounds." Such considerations, the Committee declared, were "the essence of town planning."

The disposition of the various residences and institutions on the layout had in fact been largely the work of the engineer Thomas Ward and of Geoffrey de Montmorency, now Secretary of the Imperial Delhi Committee, the body constituted on March 25, 1913 to execute and administer the new city. De Montmorency had submitted a note or report on August 24, 1912, based on Government of India departmental calculations of areas required for their personnel. The two officers attempted to fit these estimated acreages to Lanchester's second revised layout with its three radial avenues pointed to the Jama Masjid, Delhi Gate, and Indrapat. The need for such an action was highlighted by the town planners' discovery that there were not enough blocks of Secretariats of sufficient size to dress even half the principal ceremonial avenue.[51]

The allocations of residential space in the de Montmorency report strike a discordant note today, when it is customary (even in planned cities like Brasília) to find the poor and less privileged housed in the urban inner core, with the most prestigious quarters on the city's suburban margin. De Montmorency's scheme acknowledged and reinforced the inherent hierarchy in a city of civil servants. Houses of the high officials "such as Members of the Viceroy's Council" would be "the most costly and imposing" of the official Government of India residences, and he recommended that they should line the main ceremonial avenue near the concentrated grouping of Secretariats. "By virtue of their position," the heads of Government departments should also be "within the inner ring in the finer parts of the town" near their work at the Secretariats.

Fanning out from this core along the radial avenues at an increasing distance were the residences of Deputy Secretaries, Under-Secretaries, Registrars, Superintendents, and then the higher ranks of European and Indian clerks, admittedly already at a "considerable distance" from their offices. The report confessed that some involved juggling would be necessary to spare the petty clerks and menials (least able to provide their own transport) from traveling too far to their work. The Indian clerks' quarters were situated beyond those of the European clerks, segregated at the end of the radial avenues aligned toward Indrapat and Humayan's and Safdar Jang's tombs, and near Paharganj on the route to the Jama Masjid. A leading Calcutta newspaper later quite rightly queried this arrangement whereby the houses of the lesser officials in the capital were the furthest removed from the Secretariats. "Would it not be kinder," one reporter asked pointedly, "to put the senior and richer men who can afford plenteous petrol and tyres on the outskirts, while their subordinates walk to work?"[52]

At Balmoral, less than a month after de Montmorency's report, Lutyens drew a diagram for the King's Private Secretary in which the pattern of seniority housing

28. Layout plan of New Delhi, 1931.

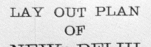

# LAY OUT PLAN
## OF
## NEW DELHI

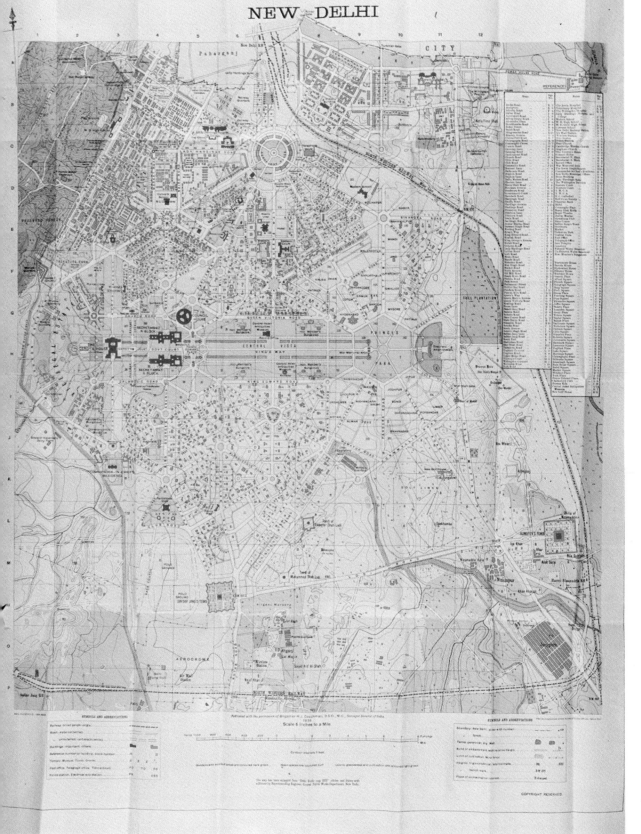

clearly reinforced racial distinctions, and segregation was made even more emphatic by placing bungalows of junior European officials on rising ground above junior Indians (labelled "thin white" and "thin black"), with the residences of senior officers ("rich white") still higher. [29] The summit of the "line of climax" was the dome of Government House. This "elementary idea" of segregating "the native clerks in one spot, Indian chiefs in another, and white people elsewhere" earned brickbats from the editors of the *Town Planning Review*. Furthermore they voiced the criticism often made of Beaux Arts planning (sometimes unjustly), that eagerness for "the attainment of fine architectural effects" had precluded adequate study of "the growth of the city as an organization of social units." Evidently, the editors concluded, the Town Planning Committee had designed the city "to captivate the imagination of the Indian with the glories of architectural display."[53]

De Montmorency suggested in his report that the Indian ruling chiefs, aristocrats, and plutocrats be placed in prominent positions, but he noted that nothing required their proximity to the Secretariats. Similarly, shopkeepers—European and Indian—did not need residences in the center of town, but instead close to such businesses as the new city attracted. Business, however, was intended to strike but a minor note. Both the Viceroy and the influential senior Member of his Council were agreed in their opposition to commercial or industrial development in Imperial Delhi. "We do not want factory chimneys on every side," Hardinge wrote Sir Guy Fleetwood Wilson; there were "already too many of them" close to the new city. The Viceroy saw no advantage in having a large commercial center in the capital of India. As Swinton remarked, "The motive of the new city is Governmental."[54]

De Montmorency's proposals for allocation of space had been circulated to the Viceroy's Council. Sir Robert Carlyle and W. H. Clark doubted the necessity or desirability of concentrating the Secretariat buildings. But Sir Harcourt Butler, whose ideas frequently reflected those of his good friend Lutyens, was emphatic that rows of small residences in the center of the layout and the scattering of the large buildings would simply duplicate the haphazard appearance of the ordinary civil station in India. What was wanted instead, he stressed, was a truly modern city with

29. New Delhi, pencil sketch showing the relative heights of the proposed buildings and the Ridge, by E. L. Lutyens, September 1912.

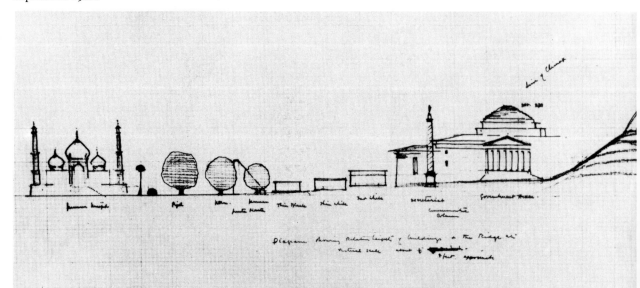

big buildings massed together, a busy heart, and the smaller private residences screened by parks which would serve as lungs. Butler's astute comments (possibly the result of direct prompting from Lutyens) received support from Sir Reginald Craddock, head of the Government department responsible for the city. The important Home Member of the Viceroy's Council concluded pessimistically, however, that it would be impossible to achieve much more than a glorified civil station. "All we can do," Craddock lamented, "is to concentrate on certain fine and striking features." Contradictory and paradoxical juxtapositions of Beaux Arts features and garden city environs, of monumental axial boulevards lined with one-story bungalows, were not so much the desired effect as the inevitable result of the realities of a stringent budget and the needs of a government bureaucracy of modest proportions. During the Delhi town planners' second visit, Craddock admitted with a mixture of resignation and despair that the Government could not hope to achieve impressive "European street effects" in the new Delhi.[55]

Twenty years later, in speaking of Lord Hardinge's founding role, Lutyens declared, "His command that one Avenue should lead to Purana Kila, and another to the Jumma Masjid, was the father of the equilateral and hexagonal plan."[56] Certainly Lord Hardinge's partiality to vistas of both the Jama Masjid and Indrapat (Purana Qila), married to Lutyens's transcendent fervor for geometric symmetry, was a vital factor in determining Imperial Delhi's distinctive pattern of equilateral triangles and hexagons. The Secretariats (Point A) and the commemorative column (later the War Memorial Arch) on the central vista each became the focal points for seven axial routes, while ten roads radiate from the proposed railway plaza. Virtually all roads make an angle of thirty or sixty degrees with the lines between these three main foci. In the resultant multiplicity of intersecting polygons, the importance of each of the city's principal monuments—Government House, Secretariats, cultural plaza, commemorative column, cathedral, and railway plaza—is underlined by location at the center of a hexagon, at one of its six angles, or in the middle of one of its sides. The chief exceptions (no less geometric) to this pattern of thirty- or sixty-degree intersections are the right-angle crossings along the two main ceremonial avenues plus the rectilinear clerks' quarters on the city's northwest periphery. This interlocked duality of contradictory grid and radial diagonals heightens the visual impact of each element and gives the entire plan a complex and creative tension not otherwise possible.

The passion for order and symmetry exhibited in the new Delhi's layout had an honorable ancestry in India: it was one of the Mughals' chief gifts to the subcontinent. The first Mughal emperor, Babur, had early bemoaned the confusion manifest in North India, and the order he and his successors cherished was reflected in court ceremonial, imperial administration, and, more tangibly, the geometric regularity of their gardens and palaces. The processional routes which distinguished the layout of seventeenth-century Shahjahanabad gave it claim to be the first example of modern city planning in India, as imposing as its Persian contemporary, Shah Abbas's nobly conceived capital of Isfahan.[57]

But the inflexible rigidity with which the Town Planning Committee enforced symmetry precluded the King's Way from focusing on the center of the Indrapat fortress; strict adherence to a sixty-degree angle on the Committee's map meant the vista was aligned only on the qila's northern tip. Lanchester later publicly criticized this "prepossession in favour of the equilateral triangle" which produced several vistas awkwardly aligned on the principal buildings or other terminal features. Beginning in 1913, detailed layouts by the newly constituted Imperial Delhi Committee, charged with constructing the city, would show minor distortions of the hexagonal pattern. Such departures, sometimes expressed in picturesquely curving secondary roads, were commonly the result of the "endless features"— mosques and tombs—whose copious numbers Lutyens compared to motor cars in London.[58]

Lutyens found major historic monuments useful to terminate the main axes of Imperial Delhi and to provide strong visual accents emphasizing his street pattern, in the fashion of contemporary Beaux Arts or City Beautiful planners. He enthroned these sacred landmarks in open spaces, approached directly and without subtlety, albeit with formal dignity, precisely as he was to do thirty years later in the Royal Academy reconstruction proposals for a devastated London. Mughal architecture might be "piffle," but such edifices had their uses, and Lutyens thought that Curzon, "with all his ignorance," had done much good in having the Taj Mahal and other buildings restored. As centerpieces in the elaborately landscaped park system envisioned by the Archaeological Survey, such monuments called to mind pavilions or gazebos set amidst the greenery of an English garden. They added variety and interest to Imperial Delhi, creating an antique setting for the new jewel, if not making it (as one official predicted) among "the most unique and attractive cities of the world."[59]

Lutyens had less use for monuments lacking a major reputation. He had reduced the elements of his plan to a simple, unified hexagonal pattern, an exclusive plan with no room for the historic fragment that did not fit a grandiose terminal vista. Existing monuments which did not conform to his predominant hexagonal order Lutyens pronounced to be awkwardly situated and "a nuisance." His instinct for preservation did not extend to the minor tombs dotting the site, relics he deplored as "nameless uncared-for erections" which would "interfere everywhere," spoiling avenues and building sites. "Imagine the Place de la Concorde in Paris," he wrote his wife, "with tombs anywhere or everywhere about it, in the middle of the road, half on & half off pavements."[60]

A similar reluctance to accommodate complexity three decades later prompted one critic to label aspects of Lutyens's brainchild, the Royal Academy plan for London, as "severe," "inflexible," and reflective of an "imposed rigidity" recalling the town planning of earlier, autocratic eras. He queried the wisdom of pulling down half a main metropolitan thoroughfare in order to widen it. Might not a compromise be possible, he asked, such as cutting through less vital and more timeworn quarters? In short, might not the plan permit inconsistencies?[61]

This argument was familiar to those who sought to ensure reconstruction of London on geometric lines following the Great Fire in 1666. Never officially adopted, Christopher Wren's plan for rebuilding London, [30] together with three proposed schemes by John Evelyn, [31] would have required the radical suppression of inconsistent or contradictory elements in the manner of fashionable Continental Baroque urban patterns. These English designs incorporated piazzas as elegant as any

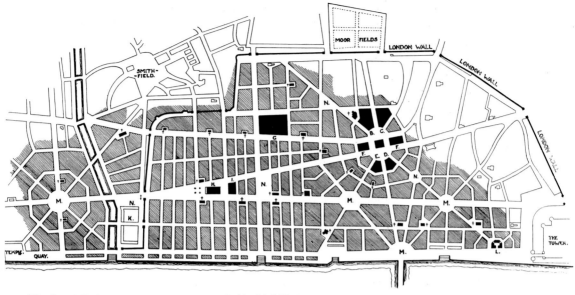

| A | The Royal Exchange | F | Goldsmiths' Hall | M | Piazzas |
|---|---|---|---|---|---|
| B | Post Office | G | Guildhall | N | Market |
| C | Excise Office | H | St. Paul's | † | Churches |
| D | Mint | I | Doctors' Commons | ‡ | Continuation of London Wall |
| E | Insurance Office | K | Wood Market | | |

30. London, plan for rebuilding the city after the Great Fire, by Christopher Wren, 1666.

31. London, plan for rebuilding the city, by John Evelyn, 1666.

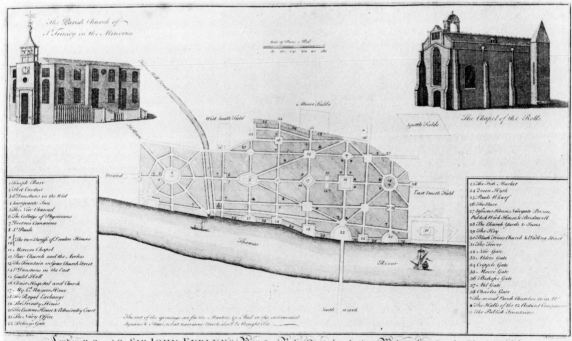

from the pages of *I Quattro Libre dell'Architettura* by Palladio, Lutyens's principal deity other than Wren and Inigo Jones. Major monuments were isolated in great plazas from which radiated multiple avenues connected by circumferentials, creating a spiderweb polygon that Lutyens was to employ in his New Delhi layout at both the railway station and proposed commemorative column. As at Delhi, each of Wren's and Evelyn's projects combined contradictory grid and radial systems in a supremely ordered yet complex pattern. Evelyn's spider web, monumental cross axes, and diagonal terminal vistas forming a hexagon, all well known through publication, bore certain striking resemblances to features of the layout in the Delhi Town Planning Committee's final report.

Lutyens was acquainted at first hand with major achievements in Continental town planning. Appointed Consulting Architect to the Royal Commission responsible for British participation in the Rome Exhibition of 1911, he had visited the Eternal City in October 1909. For the first time he had been able to experience that network of ordered vistas which Domenico Fontana had developed for Pope Sixtus V and which had given Rome an enduring framework of design since the sixteenth century. The tall obelisks accenting key foci and the three bold avenues issuing from the imposing Piazza del Popolo in a patte-d'oie were later to find their echoes in the plans for Imperial Delhi. Discussion of Lutyens's plans for the new British School had taken him to meetings with the municipal authorities at the capitoline acropolis, with its steeply inclined axial approach and tripartite arrangement of central buildings. Both Lutyens and Baker would later cite the Roman Capitol in their successful argument that the Secretariats and Government House should share the top of Raisina Hill: "The old buildings which have perhaps made most impression on the imagination of mankind are those which are raised up on an eminence, even as those of the old Greek cities and the Capitol at Rome."[62] When Lutyens first sailed for India, he was (like Baker a year later) fresh from a visit to these Roman splendors only weeks before.

Responsible for the British Pavilion at the Paris Exhibition of 1900, Lutyens was familiar, from frequent visits, with Haussmann's boulevards as well as the Avenue des Champs Elysées, whose monumental sweep terminated in the Place de l'Etoile, Jacques-Ange Gabriel's Place de la Concorde, and Andre Le Nôtre's Tuileries Gardens. Equally important, he knew the fanlike town plan of Versailles as well as the intricate palace parterres and great royal park which shared features common to civic design.

Pierre Charles L'Enfant had also known at first hand the gardens and town of Versailles (his father had been a court painter) and the avenues of the capital city, where he had been a student at the Royal Academy of Painting and Sculpture. Doubtless, too, he was familiar with architect Pierre Patte's influential ideas on town planning, especially as expounded in his treatises of 1765 and 1769. In the earlier work, Patte had combined several proposed layouts for a monument to Louis XV into one master plan of Paris, creating an archetypal city of multiple foci. Diagonal avenues, rond-points, axial arrangements of buildings and open spaces, and terminal vistas were all integral parts of L'Enfant's design vocabulary when he drew a capital city for the fledgling American republic that envisioned itself heir to Rome's greatness.[63] [32]

Had L'Enfant's layout (or its twentieth-century revival) influenced the Delhi planners in 1913? Certainly Herbert Baker, so closely involved in the Delhi Town Planning Committee's deliberations over a layout in 1913, had four years earlier expressed his estimate of L'Enfant's scheme as "at once original, practical, and beautiful," and had lamented that it had not been adopted by the American Government, to serve as "an ideal and stimulus" for all future efforts. Washington's layout, with its "wonderful vistas," had "greatly impressed" Lord Hardinge while posted there (1885–86) as a young diplomat. Nearly thirty years later, during the conception of New Delhi, "the first thing" he did, in his words, "was to send for plans of Washington and Paris." Lutyens had himself explicitly linked the American and Indian cities when he described Delhi's hexagonal plan as "a sorry nuisance" to those persons whose minds could not "embrace the intelligence of L'Enfant at Washington." On visiting the American capital in 1925, Lutyens told his wife frankly and without false modesty that he thought the plan "not as good as Delhi or as fine," but he confessed that the buildings, the bulk of them in marble, were "far better."[64]

Unquestionably there are remarkable correspondences between the plans of Washington and New Delhi: a system of grand diagonal avenues and rond-points delineating giant hexagons, interlocked with a grid pattern; a commanding capitoline acropolis from which radiates a patte-d'oie, including a broad two-mile parkway terminating at a monument at the river's edge; and a bold axis crossing the center of this leafy mall, one end crowned by a church intended for national ceremonies. If the American plan is viewed from the north, the correlations with the Indian capital are even more obvious. Evidently these similarities did not escape

32. Washington, D.C., the Pierre Charles L'Enfant plan as developed by the Senate Park Commission, 1902.

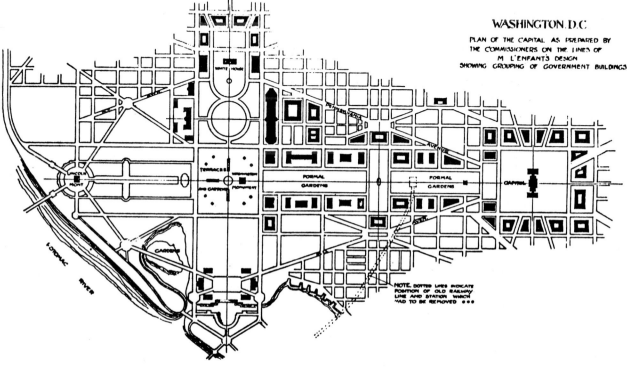

CAPITOL TO RIVER—ABOUT TWO MILES.

Herbert Baker: in 1930 he characterized New Delhi's "ingenious" layout as "a noble development of the germ of L'Enfant's plan of Washington and Wren's rejected design for the City of London."[65]

The centenary of Washington as the seat of the national government in December 1900 prompted the American Institute of Architects and the Senate Committee on the District of Colombia to collaborate in securing appointment of a genuinely distinguished Park Commission, charged with the improvement of the capital city. Headed by Charles McKim, the body included Daniel H. Burnham, whom Lutyens was later to meet at a town planning conference in October 1910, a year and a half before the Delhi planners went to India. The Commission visited Europe (including Rome and Paris) to study parks in their relation to public buildings, then fashioned a scheme with emphasis on visual impression—on diagonal boulevards and concentration of monumental classical edifices in a grandiose civic center. Herbert Baker gave this plan of 1902, reviving L'Enfant's ideas, prominent treatment in a 1909 article on South African architectural needs. Four years later Baker's counsels were to play a part in molding the new Delhi.[66]

The Senate Commission's design for Washington reflected the principal preoccupations of the City Beautiful movement in America in the early twentieth century. The more complex economic and social problems of a planned, unified neighborhood environment received earlier and closer attention in England than America through the medium of the Garden City theorists and developers. But even the early Garden City layouts, Letchworth and the revised plan for Port Sunlight, as well as Ebenezer Howard's model itself, had centers with a distinct urban flavor, carefully composed groupings of public buildings whose arrangement was the result of both practical and visual considerations.

Financial difficulties long hindered the growth of Letchworth, designed in 1903 by Barry Parker and Raymond Unwin. As a result, the Hampstead Garden Suburb, while not a self-sufficient town, may be said to mark the first genuine fulfilment of Unwin's design principles, to which Lutyens owed much. Enunciated at a town planning conference in 1901, the plan of Unwin's ideal Garden City took cognizance of natural configurations and sited public buildings in conspicuously dominant locations, with wide avenues furnishing vistas of these edifices and glimpses of open country in the other direction. Much was to be learned, Unwin later declared, from "the scale and breadth of treatment" in American planning schemes. In his influential *Town Planning in Practice* (a book Lutyens would have known), Unwin chose designs for Fairmount parkway in Philadelphia with its classical acropolis to illustrate the contemporary American penchant for what he called "the French treatment" of terminal vistas and symmetrical radial diagonals. Unwin's volume included as well an illustration of the Wren plan for London and also of the layout of Washington, D.C., with the caption, "The basis of this plan is a rectangular system of streets relieved by numerous diagonals radiating at angles of 30 degrees or 60 degrees."[67]

By contrast with the vast American projects, Unwin and Parker's first Hampstead plan, dated February 22, 1905, was simply for a dormitory suburb. But their intentions from the beginning were "to secure some good centre for the estate," one which would dominate the development (in accord with Unwin's principles) and lend it a certain unity of character.[68] Lutyens was appointed consulting architect upon the organization of the Hampstead Garden Suburb Trust in 1906, with direct responsibility for the Central Square. Here was an opportunity to create a dramatic hilltop ensemble of churches and an institute in the Beaux Arts manner, and he seized it. Mrs. (later Dame) Henrietta Barnett, the suburb's real author and fairy godmother, found Lutyens's initial monumental effects at variance with her homely village conceptions, however, with the result that he rendered his intentions on a more domestic scale, lowering the cornice lines of both churches. Nevertheless the elevated site, the elaborate style of the Institute, and the axial vistas along Heath Gate, upper Erskine Hill, and the patte-d'oie formed by Northway, Middleway, and Southway, all combined to help give the Central Square a distinct air of dignified formality.

Half a world away, contemporary planning principles directly affected the design of the new Australian Federal Capital, Canberra, in the person of the American architect Walter Burley Griffin. The Australian Government issued information on the site characteristics and planning requirements in April 1911 and appointed a board of Assessors in March 1912. The Minister of State for Home Affairs adjudicated a split decision by the Board and awarded Griffin the first premium on May 23, 1912—just at the moment the Delhi Town Planning Committee were preparing their initial layout. The plans of the two capitals were destined to be curiously interwoven.

Canberra's scale was monumental, befitting the national capital of a country which encompassed a continent. [33] While New Delhi was intended for 30,000 to 57,000 persons in ten square miles, Griffin's Canberra covered an area of twenty-five square miles, with provision for an immediate population of 75,000. Despite its size, however, the proposed plan was distinguished by its attention to detail. The two giant cross axes were specifically related to the topography.[69] The "land axis" aligned conical Mount Ainslie to the northeast with the perpetually snow-capped

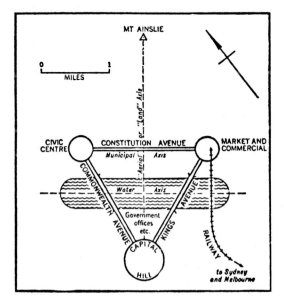

33. Canberra, Australia, schematic diagram of central city, showing the water axis, the land axis, and the three principal avenues.

Mount Bimberi thirty miles away and crossed two minor eminences destined to become Parliament Hill and Capital Hill. The "water axis" led from Black Mountain, at its western extremity, along a sequence of formal waterways to a large informal lake created by damming the Molonglo River.

The central district was bounded by an equilateral triangle formed by three nodes from which boulevards and streets radiated: the Federal Government center, the municipal center, and the mercantile center. The outlying area boasted another five functionally zoned centers: three for agriculture, one for manufacturing, and a fifth for suburban residences. Residential streets connecting the great axial arteries were designed to enjoy quiet and parklike seclusion.

A *New York Times* reporter noted at once the currently fashionable Beaux Arts character of the Canberra design: "In planning the Australian capital, with centres and radial avenues, Mr. Griffin has followed the plan generally held by architects to be the ideal one for cities of the future." The reporter described Daniel Burnham as "among the foremost advocates of such a plan," and cited two cities he had planned "along these lines"—Chicago and San Francisco.[70] The radial pattern of the primary streets does recall Burnham's proposals for those two cities or L'Enfant's for Washington, but the spider webs formed by straight feeder streets at right angles to the diagonals resemble features from Wren's and Evelyn's London designs and the plan accompanying the Delhi Town Planning Committee's final report.

The dominant architectural feature of Canberra was the Capitol, enthroned in a sea of open park space atop an eminently visible, centrally located hill, some eighty feet above the Parliament House. Like the acropolis at Raisina, Capital Hill was intended to be profoundly symbolic: although not meant to house the mechanism of government, its building was to serve as a ceremonial and archival center, commemorating Australian achievements and representing an emotional and spiritual focus of national life.

Municipal activities were to be situated on a subordinate axis, parallel to and northeast of the water axis. At the eastern end, in a natural bowl at the foot of Mount Pleasant, Griffin placed the mercantile and railway center, and a mile and a half to the west on the connecting avenue was the urban administrative center. Designed around City Hill, this municipal core contained echoes of Ebenezer Howard's Garden City center with its town hall and other public buildings disposed around a circular garden from which axial boulevards led to outlying residential, manufacturing, and agricultural districts.

Its insistent symmetry and geometry gave Griffin's design an atmosphere of dignity and power appropriate to a commonwealth in the full vigor of youth and believed destined for greatness. Griffin was fully aware, however, that he was planning for a democracy. The social organization of the city was, Griffin said, "planned on the British model, which means a federation of smaller groups of people"; neighborhood units had their own local civic centers with shops, offices, and town halls. While Griffin hoped for unity in plan and a measure of control over architectural relationships and scale, he believed that under popular government little unity of style could be imposed by decree. Indeed he welcomed the diversity as a complement to the unified plan. Quite unlike Lutyens and Baker, who exercised supervisory control over all building within Imperial Delhi, Griffin favored "all forms of aesthetic endeavor to express themselves, so adding incident and variety to a consistent whole."[71]

The first-prize scheme for Canberra, and explanatory remarks by Griffin, were widely published not only in America but in Britain as well. Some two months after Griffin's success in the competition, Lord Hardinge telegraphed to the Australian Governor-General, Lord Denman, requesting a copy or photograph of the Canberra plan. Ultimately, in December, as the Town Planning Committee assembled in Delhi, Griffin's design and seven other principal plans were forwarded to India, followed a month later by a potpourri scheme by a Departmental Board "incorporating the salient features of the promulgated and purchased designs." Hardinge acknowledged both despatches on March 11, 1913. The eight principal designs, sent a month before the Departmental Board's scheme, should have arrived by early or mid-February, in the very midst of the Delhi Town Planning Committee's deliberations over a choice between the north and the south sites and probably at least two weeks before a very rough preliminary design for the Raisina acropolis was shown to the Viceroy on February 25. By coincidence, the day after Hardinge acknowledged Lord Denman's despatches, the Australian Governor-General mentioned Imperial Delhi at official ceremonies announcing the name of the new capital, Canberra. In referring to the Viceregal request for plans, Denman said it was "interesting to note that those engaged in the building of the capital of one of the oldest of civilized countries are apparently not above accepting ideas from this, one of the youngest countries in the world."[72]

What role Griffin's plan might have played at New Delhi in, for example, influencing the spiderweb street pattern at the railway plaza and on the King's Way, is impossible to determine. What is certain is that by 1913 Lutyens was fully acquainted, in both theory and practice, with Garden City and City Beautiful planning principles.

Granted the contributions of many other persons, the plan of New Delhi is primarily the fruit of the mind and heart of Edwin Lutyens. Possessed of a genuine historical perspective, he was at the same time keenly sensitive to the newest developments in the art and science of town planning. The examples of Ebenezer Howard, of Prestwich and Mawson at Port Sunlight, and of Parker and Unwin, underlay his Delhi scheme no less than precedents from the hands of Palladio, Domenico Fontana, Wren, Evelyn, Gabriel, Le Nôtre, L'Enfant, Haussmann, Burnham, and Griffin.

The British vision of the new Delhi had from the first been as eclectic as the assortment of individuals involved, ranging from urban grandeur to rural greenery. The King-Emperor's wishes had embraced an imposing city expressive of "the power of Western science, art, and civilization," while the Chairman of the Town Planning Committee had declared it essential for the capital of the British Raj to dominate the monuments of India's earlier empires. On the other hand, the less monumental inspiration of Ebenezer Howard might be discerned behind Sir Louis Dane's remark, a month after the Durbar, that he had been examining possible sites "for a large and spacious garden city, such as I presume the new Government Capital should be."[73]

Lutyens's own idea of the city exhibited a shifting pattern. Initially, in April 1912, he and his colleagues on the Town Planning Committee had been drawn to the Ridge north of Shahjahanabad, where a dramatic, compact urban environment could have been created on a constricted site. On the healthier southern site eventually selected, the ample available land had spawned a plan in May 1912 for an Imperial city as grandiose as any European capital, with an imposing center and a ceremonial avenue with Secretariat buildings ranged along its two-mile length.[74]

In the summer of 1912, the Viceroy and certain colleagues suggested paring the generous size of bungalow compounds and other areas. Hardinge concluded that the Town Planning Committee's tentative layout was "far too spacious." The broad streets proposed would only be attractive if lined with five-storied buildings like those "in the Champs Elysées or Bombay"—which he knew his announced four-million-pound budget and the Government's requirements made impossible. Indeed, the revelation that departmental needs projected insufficient buildings to dress even one avenue, plus the Viceroy's veto in July of rajas' palaces along the processional route, sharply reduced the Town Planning Committee's bold dreams of monumentality. By October, as senior a member of the Viceroy's Council as Sir Reginald Craddock was resigned to concentrating on certain "striking features" amongst a sea of trees—the scheme destined to be embodied later in the Committee's final report.[75]

On Lutyens's return to Delhi, exasperated by the reduction of acreages previously requested by the Government Departments and agreed upon, he wrote to Lady Emily, "Now they want, apparently, a town rather than a Garden City." But the prospect of a more tightly knit, urban arrangement met with his approval: "I agree to this and am glad if they do it."[76] Both then and again thirty years later in the Royal Academy scheme for London, the impulse of grandeur and heroic pretensions outweighed the alternatives.

Force of circumstances, and persons other than Lutyens, determined that the new capital should be a contradiction in terms, both Garden City and City Beautiful, rus in urbe. Air and light and greenery, those nineteenth-century symbols of progress, abounded, and town and country were interwoven. Certain natural features of the site, particularly Raisina Hill and the Jumna River, were employed to advantage. Buildings were arranged in a discontinuous pattern, zoned according to function as Ebenezer Howard would have wished; housing was separated from recreation and business. The Delhi Town Planning Committee's reports gave serious, if all too fleeting, attention to the economic and social foundations of the new capital. While the planners recognized the city to be primarily a governmental center, industrial and commercial development and its area of future expansion were discussed. The Committee duly acknowledged hygiene and traffic circulation as priority considerations.

Aesthetic effects were not neglected. Amid the symphony of garden city greenery, the predominant notes of American Beaux Arts city planning were struck: the grouping of public buildings in a monumental center as well as radiating axial vistas, terminating in polygons, ovals, and circles of open space which enthroned monuments and buildings as imposing visual accents.

But was a garden city punctuated by urban oases truly suitable for an imperial capital? Indeed, was it a fit expression of British genius? "Little dwellings crouching separately under trees on either side of a great space—how can they look other than mean and contemptible?" the critic Thomas Sharp was to ask two decades later in examining the very basis of the garden city itself:

> We want something to reflect our achievement, our great over-topping of nature: something that is a worthy symbol of civilization, "of society, of broad expanding sympathies, of science, art and culture." That we can only get through pure medium, the town. Town-country, garden-city will never give it. Only sheer, triumphant, unadulterated urbanity will.[77]

Strong voices, however, were raised in 1912 for a garden city at Delhi, even at the risk of having large bare spaces for the forseeable future. "In India we must have space," Sir Harcourt Butler told the Viceroy. "We could not breathe with a Champs Elysées." If the right trees were planted, Butler felt that buildings with intervening lawns would not look small. Furthermore, he argued, inevitable expansion and periodic Durbar ceremonies necessitated broad avenues if future generations were to be adequately served.[78]

The new Delhi which ultimately arose was decidedly not "unadulterated urbanity." At the inauguration eighteen years later, a *Daily Telegraph* correspondent would note the hybrid features of the new city, its official buildings an impressive urban centerpiece, the rest "developed on the most spacious garden-city lines," the great avenues decorated with classical buildings "embowered in trees." This Fleet Street emissary had no qualms, however: the leafy capital that had arisen on the banks of the Jumna was a monument altogether worthy of British rule in India.[79]

If, as the *Daily Telegraph* reported, New Delhi's buildings embodied "classic purity of design," its layout was certainly an expression of the classical conviction that man through his own reason can discern the world's basic order, can determine a framework for human behavior, and can control his environment. The enlightened planning and homogeneous clarity of the new Delhi formed, to British eyes, a symbolic contrast with the heterogeneous confusion and narrow, twisted byways of the existing city. The capital India's rulers planned in 1912 and 1913 now stands as a monument to their belief in ordered governance and that elusive but keenly sought goal, progress. New Delhi testifies to the founders' faith that art and life as they ought to be can be realized in this world, that ideals can be translated into practice.

Intended to express the achievements possible under British dominion, Imperial Delhi, as it was initially called, was also meant to be an appropriate backdrop for an autocracy as mighty as Rome of the Caesars. The capital's imperial flavor—emphasized by processional avenues, imposing plazas, and impressive facades—moved one critic to remark that the city suggested "a setting for a perpetual Durbar." Certainly the inclusion of King's Way and Queen's Way, triumphal avenues where a resplendent army could troop with awesome effect on the native spectator, was an inevitable part of the planning of the new city. Symbolically, these boulevards asserted the fact of British rule; practically, such wide avenues helped make authority without affectionate consent possible, expediting control in the event of disorder or uprising. The city's sweeping avenues embodied Curzon's doctrine of efficiency, which he had acknowledged as the gospel and keynote of his administration. Almost a dozen imposing axes led toward Raisina Hill, focussing on the Viceroy and the machinery of his rule. That great palatine acropolis bound to itself the broad boulevards as the Viceroy himself gathered the power once dispersed among a multitude of feudal rajas and warrior chieftains.[80]

Union under one Emperor was Britain's gift to the diverse peoples of India. The geometry of the new capital, invariable and relentlessly exclusive, linking in a single pattern many diverse parts, seemed symbolic of the Imperial attempt to impose unity and even uniformity on India's institutions.

New Delhi's authors, like the Beaux Arts and Baroque planners before them, assumed without question that the order they created was eternal. Their scale was enormous, for they built for the ages. Ruskin had contended that the glory of a building was its antiquity; how much more so a city! "It is not a cantonment we have to lay out at Delhi," declared Sir George Birdwood, "but an Imperial City— the symbol of the British Raj in India—and it must like Rome be built for eternity."[81]

Lord Curzon, while Viceroy, had affirmed Britons' deepest convictions when he declared, "To me the message is carved in granite, it is hewn out of the rock of doom—that our work is righteous and that it shall endure." Herbert Baker envisioned British influence measured in millennia: "In 20,000 years there must be an Imperial Lutyens tradition in Indian architecture, as there now clings a memory of Alexander." Such sentiments still came easily. This generation, British and American alike, aspired to bind the past and present; confidently they sought to dictate the future. The sheer boldness of the visionaries captured mens' imagination and inspired their support. Armed with the newest powers of technology, they set out to create the greatest cities the world had known. Daniel Burnham's ringing words epitomized their spirit: "Make no little plans; they have no magic to stir men's blood and probably themselves will not be realized. Make big plans; aim high in hope and work, remembering that a noble, logical diagram once recorded will never die."[82]

For Herbert Baker one February afternoon in 1913, the self-assurance so often characteristic of those years faltered momentarily. Seated atop Raisina Hill, he surveyed a scene strewn with the ruins of previous empires, what Curzon had called "the deserted cities of dreary and disconsolate tombs." Together with his companions, H. A. L. Fisher and Ramsay MacDonald, he wondered how beauty could be nurtured in such unpromising environs, when the sun, setting beneath the dark rainclouds, formed a perfect rainbow over the future King's Way. At once all doubts vanished, and the three men—architect, scholar, and statesman—acclaimed the omen, bright with promise.[83]

# 5

## Rush to Begin

The progress of the new Delhi from the triumphant Durbar of 1911 until the week of inauguration festivities in 1931 was by no means smooth. From its conception, the Imperial city was dogged by constant discord, its development impeded by adverse circumstances which the founders could scarcely have foreseen.

Responsibility for architectural design, while not causing a major conflict of interests, was a critical question and beset with difficulties. The Home Member of the Viceroy's Council, Sir John Jenkins, initially proposed that the preparation of plans and estimates "for all the more important buildings" be entrusted to a committee consisting of a canal engineer, a Bombay architect, and a Deputy Commissioner from the Punjab. This suggestion was promptly denounced by his colleagues in a Council meeting on December 28, scarcely two weeks after the Durbar, and in subsequent notes. Jenkins noted a "general feeling" in favor of competitive designs and estimates, but in a subsequent memorandum he presumed this sentiment applied only to Government House, the Council Hall, and other important construction; for ordinary residences and minor offices he thought it preferable to employ the Government of India's own salaried architect and engineer.[1]

With the appointment of the Delhi Town Planning Committee in March 1912 and the realization that a site must be selected before buildings could be designed, the Viceroy and his Council seem to have taken no further action. Then on June 7 Hardinge telegraphed the India Office to obtain "full information" on the "usual terms for competitions in architectural designs for public buildings," with the time limits generally permitted for their preparation. Four days later the Permanent Under-Secretary of State for India, Sir Richmond Ritchie, addressed the President of the Royal Institute of British Architects in a letter which virtually duplicated the wording of Hardinge's telegram. Leonard Stokes's prompt reply enclosed the Institute's regulations and outlined the various types of competition, but included a caveat about competitions in general. A competition, Stokes conceded, gave young men an opportunity, but architects of standing often avoided such ventures, and the New Delhi project was best put in the hands of men of experience. Of course a competition restricted to invited architects, he noted, would help achieve this object. Later, in an interview at the India Office, Stokes suggested that an open competition was probably not expedient. But even a limited competition obviously involved considerable expense: in addition to providing fees for the assessors, the Government of India would be required to compensate architects for their costs, including an obligatory trip to India. If the buildings were likely to be large and numerous, Stokes advised dividing responsibility for their design and instituting separate competitions, which would necessitate further subsidies. For a Viceroy pledged to economy, this was not acceptable.[2]

In a perceptive analysis for Lord Crewe of the major points to be considered, Sir Richmond Ritchie acknowledged that designs for Government House were the personal province of the Viceroy, who would "choose his own architect." The Viceregal residence, which would "stand apart" from the rest of the city, need not determine the design of the Secretariats and municipal offices and a possible Legislative Council House—perhaps each one entrusted to a different architect. But these public buildings would doubtless influence the architectural lines of the city's minor buildings. The problem, Ritchie realized, would be to ensure unity and coherence of design throughout.[3]

Following the departure of the Delhi Town Planning Committee, Hardinge asked Lanchester, newly arrived, to suggest terms of competition for designs of two blocks of large Secretariat buildings. Lanchester submitted draft proofs dated July 15 and July 20, 1912; the final draft reached the Viceroy's Private Secretary on August 6. Lanchester suggested that one or more of the Secretariat buildings should be offered for open competition to all architects who were British subjects residing in Britain, India, or the colonies; in his final draft he stipulated four office blocks of nearly equal size. A Committee of Adjudication would make their final decision some five months after issuing the conditions. The successful designer would travel to Delhi, visit the site, and confer with the Consulting Architect to the Government of India before making the fair drawings and carrying out the construction.[4]

Discussion of Lanchester's proposals produced several modifications. Percy Hawkins, Under-Secretary to the Public Works Department, urged that the Government of India first decide the city's layout and prepare a complete plan before dividing the buildings into suitable groups for competition. This opinion found support from Hawkins's superior, Michael Nethersole, who insisted that the Town Planning Committee be told the competition was "simply to admit of selection of architects to deal with the Secretariat designs" after the layout had been approved and the site selected.[5]

The Government's principal salaried architect, John Begg, when consulted for his opinions, proved only too anxious to be given a role. "There is only one way in which Home architects can be successfully employed," he asserted, "—that is that they should collaborate with an architect of sufficient Indian experience in the preparation of the fair drawings and details, that is, in effect, with me." Begg was even more insistent in a note on September 9, when he raised the problem of reconciling architects' interests and methods with the personnel and methods of the Public Works Department. This problem had been his exclusive concern for twelve years—"how to adjust matters so as to produce the best possible results architecturally without unduly dislocating the existing Indian works system." Only he, Begg claimed, had had an opportunity "of observing the working of the problem in so many different parts of India." The Consulting Architect's self-advertisement was somewhat counterproductive; Nethersole remarked with heavy irony that "Mr. Begg is too diffident as to his ability to manage the work in India."[6]

Begg and Nethersole were both sufficiently persuasive, however, that by September the Viceroy had incorporated their suggestions into Lanchester's draft conditions for competitions. Most important, the initial competition was limited to one Secretariat block; echoing Nethersole's recommendation, Hardinge made it clear that, as the final layout had not been determined, the first competition was only a means of selecting architects "likely to design what is required to suit Indian conditions." In order that Indian feeling and requirements be well preserved, the Viceroy suggested that the Committee of Adjudication have but one English architect, together with Begg and a senior member from both the Indian Civil Service and the Indian Public Works Department. Furthermore, the Public Works Department of the Government of India, and not an English architect unfamiliar with the local scene, should carry out the eventual erection of the buildings. Hardinge laid "great stress on the Indian tradition": besides his own personal feelings, he declared, the public life in India and for the most part in Britain, expected such emphasis. As for Indian architects, the Viceroy did not anticipate any would send in a satisfactory plan, but he did feel strongly that "the door must not be shut in their faces." After all, he noted, "it satisfies their vanity and can do no harm."[7]

At Simla on September 19, the Viceroy and his Council issued an important despatch, forwarding competition conditions for the New Delhi Secretariats to the India Office "with a view to the early selection of an architect or architects competent to be entrusted with the preparation of the final designs as soon as the general lay-out has been approved." The despatch suggested premia of 300, 200, and 100 pounds, and the competition conditions proposed that the first prize winner and possibly others be given the task of designing the various Secretariat offices. The wording of the competition terms also reflected Lord Hardinge's resolute bias: "the general character of the architecture, while meeting modern requirements of convenience, should harmonize externally with the monuments of old Delhi and with the traditions of Indian art."[8]

The despatch was issued without the signature of one Member of the Viceroy's Council, Sir Harcourt Butler, whose opinions often coincided with those of his friend Lutyens. Butler made it clear that he did not favor competitions of the sort envisaged nor did the proposed Committee of Adjudication inspire his confidence. "I believe," he wrote, "that the best men may be unwilling to compete and especially to submit their plans to such a committee." In the Commons, Arthur Soames, the Liberal Member for South Norfolk, echoed these sentiments: he felt certain that "every architect worth his salt" would agree that a public competition never produced the best work.[9] Butler's opposition, from within the highest Council in the Indian Empire, and Soames's statement in Parliament, were indicative of the controversy that from the outset attended the selection of New Delhi's architects.

Lutyens made no secret of his eagerness to be the architect for the new Delhi; at the same time, he fully realized that his appointment to the Town Planning Committee was not a commitment to select him for the post. From the outset of his career he had been alive to the necessity of actively seeking influential supporters. Indeed, when once asked at an Architectural Association dinner what were the chances of a promising architect without wires to pull, he replied characteristically that he would probably, like the sculptor Alfred Stevens, "drink himself to death."[10] Lutyens's extremely solicitous behaviour toward Lady Hardinge, his prospective client's wife, was but one tactic among a battery which ambition and economic necessity had in years past driven him to perfect. Throughout 1912 he mounted a continuing campaign to secure his appointment to design not only Government House but as much as possible besides. He complained bitterly of "enemies" when others employed similar devices, while the apparent ascendancy of Lanchester for a brief time, as well as the prospect of an open competition, predictably produced in him an exaggerated anxiety.

His first visit to India as a town planner he used to advantage over possible competitors: within two months of his arrival he had won not only commendation from the Viceroy and Vicereine for the rough sketches he prepared of the projected Government House, but orders for more. When Lutyens pressed Lady Hardinge for an indication about his possible appointment to do Government House, she replied, "Yes, of course! Who else?" By the second week in June, the Viceroy had recommended him to Lord Crewe as architect of Government House and the Great Place before it. Hardinge intended to commit the Secretariats to competition, but Lutyens was to be allowed as many buildings as necessary to complete the Durbar Place; such an arrangement, Lutyens felt, clearly included a handsome portion of the Secretariats—and he so marked his sketch to Baker on June 14: "This is mine to do." Five days later, a lunch with the Viceregal couple appeared to have settled the matter: a jubilant Lutyens wrote home that he was to design the Foreign and Legal Secretariats "to complete my big square or place."[11]

Lutyens failed to win such favor in all eyes, however. Lionel Earle, who had been Lord Crewe's Private Secretary at the Colonial Office, wrote emphatically that it would be difficult if not impossible for the India Office and Government of India to keep a job of such magnitude outside any sort of competition. The Parliamentary Under-Secretary of State for India, Edwin Montagu, wrote to Lord Crewe even more strongly that Government House and the other buildings in Imperial Delhi should all be thrown open to competition. Lutyens, he felt, while the author of much meritorious work and "somewhat fortunate in being well pushed," was not of such preeminence to entitle him to triumph without contest over all possible rivals.[12]

Such opposition from intimate and influential colleagues was persuasive. Crewe confessed to the Viceroy that he admired Lutyens's work, but he feared public outcry and difficulty with his Council at the India Office in authorizing an expenditure on "an outlay privately incurred, but to be publicly defrayed." He urged Hardinge not to commit Government House to Lutyens.[13]

Unhappy with this response, but undaunted, the Viceroy continued to press for Lutyens as the architect of Government House, while admitting that other Government buildings must be subject to competition. Anxious to make rapid progress and keep costs to a minimum, Hardinge favored the selection of the man on the spot, a skilled practitioner in the design of domestic architecture to whom every Viceregal necessity had already been explained. "It was only after frequent interviews with me, my wife, my Military Secretary and my Comptroller that

Lutyens was able to arrive at an idea of our requirements and to draw plans accordingly,'' wrote Hardinge. "How then are we to put the designs for Government House up to competition?'' Any other architect of distinction whom Lord Crewe might name would have to come to India to grasp what Lutyens now knew. The Viceroy was adamant that his choice was correct and he argued forcefully for "a certain liberty of action,'' for it was assuredly neither Crewe nor his Council but Hardinge who would "receive credit or blame at the hands of Indian as well as of English opinion.''[14]

Impatient as he was, Hardinge knew from his years as a diplomat the value of waiting for what he wanted. Two months later, he confided to Captain Swinton that he still hoped to get the Government House commission for Lutyens, but he was "going steady about pressing it,'' as the moment was not propitious.

Lutyens meanwhile proceeded with vigor through the summer on the drawings for Government House, working rapidly to complete as much as possible before his next visit to Delhi in December. At the India Office, Sir Richmond Ritchie greeted him cordially and appeared pleased that Hardinge had taken the initiative to entrust him with Government House and its precincts. Everyone seemed to take it for granted that Lutyens was to do the work. But Lord Crewe remained uncommitted.[15]

Realizing that his appointment still hung in the balance, Lutyens intensified his persuasive techniques: he told Baker that Geoffrey Robinson, appointed editor of the *Times* the previous month, was "being worked'' on their mutual behalf.[16] Throughout 1912, Lutyens's interest in Baker's collaboration noticeably increased as it became apparent such association might help him secure the jobs he eagerly sought at Delhi.

Since Baker's departure for South Africa in 1892, the two friends had kept up an enthusiastic correspondence. Upon his appointment to the Delhi Town Planning Committee, Lutyens had written Baker that the selection of architects for the buildings remained problematical; clearly there would be more than one man could do. "Oh, what fun if we could come together over it,'' he exclaimed. "I hope H.B. and E.L.L. may *build* the city,'' he emphasized on the eve of his first visit to the East. Not long afterward, as his ship steamed toward Aden, Lutyens revealed he had been at work at the game he knew so well: "I have been pushing a bit to get the buildings done by you and me.'' He made certain that Swinton saw photographs of the important buildings at Pretoria and that Hardinge also was "primed up properly'' about Baker. "I have got people working for you in London too,'' Lutyens reported. By May Lutyens could announce, "I guess I am in the running and so are you.'' When Lanchester's prospects for appointment seemed especially threatening, Lutyens was prompted to try to erase any of Baker's doubts about accepting work in India. Clearly he infinitely preferred cooperation with his friend Baker to any association with Lanchester.[17]

By July, with the Viceroy's promise of Government House and assurance that Lanchester's star was only a temporary fixture, Lutyens's anxiety centered on the possibility of a competition for the Secretariats, which he decidedly opposed. "I want you and me to do them!'' he wrote Baker, "and I think when they realize the time they will save, something will come of it.''[18] Summoned to a royal interview at Balmoral, Lutyens reiterated his support for Baker as an associate. The King, on Crewe's advice, was wholly noncommittal.

Apart from Lutyens's crucial advocacy, Baker had other important partisans and champions. Sir Guy Fleetwood Wilson had mentioned his name to Hardinge less then three weeks after the Durbar, noting that his work in South Africa (especially at Pretoria) was "the admiration of all who have seen it." W. B. Gordon, Secretary to the Public Works Department in India, and Member of the Imperial Legislative Council, had met Baker while Director of Irrigation Works in the Cape Colony from 1903 to 1907, and his support was crucial, if not decisive. Baker himself believed that James Meston, Secretary of the Finance Department in India in 1912, first suggested his name to Hardinge; Meston had been an adviser to the Governments of the Cape Colony and the Transvaal on civil service reform from 1904 to 1906 and later told Baker he had brought the Union Buildings in Pretoria to the Viceroy's attention. Baker was fortunate in having still another friend on the spot: William Marris, former Civil Service Commissioner in the Transvaal, who had been a member of the Coronation Durbar Executive Committee and in 1913 became Acting Secretary to the Home Department of the Government of India.[19]

In London support came from the artist Reginald Barratt, who specialized in scenes of Oriental life and architecture, had studied architecture under Richard Norman Shaw, and perhaps most important, counted Lord Hardinge as a friend. Barratt had twice painted for Edward VII and had earned the future Viceroy's respect for his opinions. He had already urged Lutyens's fitness upon Lord Crewe, emphasizing that able architects, engineers, intellectuals, and at least seven major journals and newspapers had all voiced high estimates of his ability. To Hardinge Barratt repeated his "very sincere hope" that Lutyens and Baker might be jointly commissioned as architects for the principal buildings and to oversee the entire scheme. The two men, he was convinced, would be an ideal combination. When the appointment of New Delhi's architects was ultimately confirmed, Barratt privately claimed credit for having "pulled it off."[20]

At this critical juncture, Baker in effect spoke up for himself: he wrote to the *Times*. Ostensibly his eloquent article on October 3 was a carefully considered discussion of the architectural style appropriate for Imperial Delhi.[21] As its author doubtless anticipated, however, one important side effect was to place his name before the *Times*'s influential readers as a serious candidate for a part in designing the new city.

Baker's "very thoughtful" letter inspired Swinton to write at once to the Viceroy with the enthusiastic words, "Here we have a man who *is* a successful architect and speaks not only like a poet, but like a statesman." Swinton had scarcely heard of Baker until then, but within a week he wrote Hardinge that he had examined photographs of the architect's South African buildings and heard much of him from "heartfelt admirers." He noted that Baker was accustomed in South Africa to using high rocky ground as a setting for his architectural effects, and added that he was "the one man" with whom Lutyens had said he could work.[22]

A week later, another even more influential ally joined the swelling chorus. Viscount Gladstone, youngest son of the great Prime Minister, had been Governor-General of South Africa since 1910 and had an intimate knowledge of Baker's work there. On October 17 he addressed a forceful letter to his Liberal colleague and friend, Lord Crewe, supporting the association of Baker with Lutyens at Delhi. He recognized Baker's genius in adapting his buildings to the local landscape, both mountain and plain, and he remarked that Lutyens's idealism and Baker's practicality would make "the best combination possible." While taking care not to commit himself, Crewe agreed that such an alliance might well be both "brilliant and efficient," and he endorsed Lord Gladstone's opinion when forwarding his letter to the Viceroy. The two architects' supporters had succeeded in making themselves heard: Crewe indicated to Hardinge that the idea of associating Baker with Lutyens at Delhi had "gained a good deal of currency" among persons whose judgment he valued. By October 21 Lord Crewe's Private Secretary could write that the principal organs of opinion were "clamoring for this very conjunction of men"; the *Morning Post* added its voice to that of the *Times* and the Northcliffe and Garvin newspapers.[23] The weeks of wire-pulling were proving worthwhile.

Lutyens's meetings on October 26 with Sir Thomas Holderness, the new Permanent Under-Secretary at the India Office, was pivotal. Assuring Lutyens that it reflected no want of confidence in him, Holderness asked him if he would collaborate with Baker, as it would strengthen Lord Crewe's hands in dealing with inevitable criticism. Fully aware of the difficulties in obtaining the appointment for himself alone (as he frankly confessed to Swinton), Lutyens agreed at once and telegraphed Baker with alacrity. The answer came on the evening of October 29: "willingly collaborate."[24]

The Viceroy's attitude remained the unknown factor. "I hope it is all right," Lutyens wrote Baker anxiously, "and we shall be created partners by force majeure." The India Office was still ignorant of Lord Hardinge's views on the proposed partnership when Holderness, with Crewe's approval, drafted a telegram in late November that effectively placed the question of architectural appointments in the Viceroy's hands.[25]

Lutyens sought to reassure Baker, who was a somewhat reluctant debutante, cognizant of his own shortcomings and alert to the difficulties of the projected association. Lutyens now realized he could afford to be generous: as he told his proposed collaborator, there was more work than two men could do. Earlier he had written that Hardinge had nominated him to do Government House and two or three of the Secretariat blocks; now he wrote soothingly, "I should like to do Government House, you the Secretariats," with each helping the other by discussion of his work. The lap of Fate, he said, he pictured as a Christmas pie from which he had hopes of pulling out plums for the two of them![26]

Shortly after Lutyens's arrival in India for the second time, the attempted assassination of the Viceroy threw all anticipated schedules into confusion. But Lady Hardinge, unscathed by the attack, dropped a bombshell of her own when she told Lutyens that he and Baker were to be the architectural overlords of Imperial Delhi, advising the Viceroy on the whole capital and arranging and assessing a competition for some single part of the city. Sir Swinton Jacob was to be associated with them as a "walking dictionary" of advice on Indian materials and details.[27]

On January 5 the Viceroy telegraphed to the India Office his confirmation that Lutyens would accept collaboration with Baker and Jacob and had agreed to adapt his designs to official requirements, climatic conditions, and Indian sentiment. Three days later Sir Thomas Holderness wrote Baker (then in Rome) offering him an appointment, and on January 10 Lord Crewe sent a telegram to the Viceroy approving the proposed triumvirate and promising to communicate the project to his Council for final sanction.[28]

From the Palace Hotel in Rome Baker responded that he was "rather overwhelmed at the honour suggested," and cabled to settle a date in London to discuss the offer, especially the difficulties posed by his intended return to Pretoria to supervise completion of the Union Buildings and their landscaping. The reply to a private telegram to his friend General Jan Smuts advised him to accept the offer. Thus January 17 found him at the India Office awaiting an interview. Realizing that acceptance would mean severance from his work in South Africa, he found his conscience pulling against "the glamour of the great Imperial Quest." But as he gazed upon the India Office portraits, the enduring example of Warren Hastings, the eighteenth-century Governor-General who had confronted far greater difficulties, dissolved his doubts, and any lingering irresolution was dispelled by Holderness and Lord Crewe.[29]

General Louis Botha, Prime Minister of South Africa, confirmed that his Government had no objections to extending Baker's absence. Baker accepted a four-week engagement to advise the Indian Government at Delhi, and promptly left England on January 24, bound for Brindisi and Bombay.[30]

Sir Swinton Jacob's association with Lutyens and Baker had been at the insistence of the Viceroy, who admitted Jacob was "no architect," but had been included in order to ensure "that there should be no doubt as to the introduction of Indian traditions in the new buildings." Jacob, aged seventy-one, had retired from the Public Works Department in 1896 and had only recently retired from active work as an engineer and architect to several leading Indian princes in Rajputana. Even before the India Office had solicited Jacob's services, however, Lutyens had been outspoken in belittling his ability: the Jaipur Museum he thought "shoddy" and Daly College at Indore he described as "very elaborate, cheap, and oh! absolutely in want of all that Haldane has described as clear thinking." On learning of the projected appointment, Lutyens commented despairingly that Jacob's buildings were "all made up of tit-bits culled from various buildings of various dates, put together with no sense of relation or of scale."[31]

The India Office invitation to Sir Swinton explained that his role would be to assist Lutyens and Baker with advice on Indian architectural details and materials, probably by a visit to the subcontinent in the autumn. Jacob's prompt reply from the Grand Hotel in Biarritz indicated he would be willing to go to India in the forthcoming cold weather season. He had no desire, he wrote later to Lord Hardinge, "to put on harness of any kind" after fifty-three years of service in India, but he was mindful of the honor of being part of such a momentous undertaking.[32]

Other architects, indeed, coveted a part in the birth of Imperial Delhi. H. V. Lanchester had favorably impressed the Viceroy with his industry and imagination during his brief period as a consultant to the Town Planning Committee. But reports reached the Viceroy following Lanchester's departure that he had been conveying the impression in England of having overturned the Committee's plan and having "succeeded in upsetting Lutyens's apple-cart." Annoyed, Hardinge told Captain Swinton angrily that he thought Lanchester's remarks "petty puerilities." Swinton replied with evident surprise that Lanchester seemed anxious to be helpful and not the least self-serving. Whether truthful or without foundation, however, the rumors from London had damaged Lanchester's standing with the Viceroy. When Lord Crewe cabled Hardinge in October that Lanchester did not expect reemployment, but wished to know for certain, and had offered assistance or advice at any time, the Viceroy's reply was unequivocal: he would not require Mr. Lanchester's services.[33]

As Lutyens well knew and aptly remarked, there was "a good deal of crosspulling." Lord Crewe's former Private Secretary, Lionel Earle, wrote strongly to the India Office on behalf of Sir Herbert Jekyll, brother of Lutyens's early patron and client, Gertrude Jekyll. Sir Herbert had been an effective Secretary to the Royal Commission which organized the British sector of the Paris Exhibition of 1900, and Lionel Earle envisioned him as a planning czar and watchdog of taste for the new Delhi. But despite Earle's helping hand, and Lutyens's expressed desire "to rope in" his friend, Jekyll was never really a candidate.[34]

Sir Brumwell Thomas, architect of the Belfast Town Hall and a keen aspirant, was likewise not given serious consideration as a candidate. Thomas elicited a testimonial letter from the Earl of Aberdeen, Lord-Lieutenant of Ireland, and went to India in December in hope of winning a commission from Lord Hardinge, but all to no avail. Hardinge's injuries sustained at the State Entry precluded even an interview.[35]

Sir Reginald Blomfield's candidacy is a less straightforward tale. An elegant, Oxford-educated social lion and prolific author whose public buildings epitomized the currently fashionable classicism in the Grand Manner, Blomfield had succeeded Leonard Stokes in 1912 as President of the Royal Institute of British Architects. In Lutyens's voluminous correspondence at this time with his own wife and with Baker, Blomfield appears scarcely at all—and then only as a figure whom Lutyens thought Crewe might have mentioned to Hardinge. Lutyens had in fact submitted Blomfield's name along with others in response to an India Office query, and when questioned by the Viceroy's Secretary had described Sir Reginald as "a good chap" and "a good Architect," adding "What can you say more of any man?" But Lutyens was clearly wary of any colleague in addition to Baker; a third man might prove difficult to handle, and his position would have to be quite strictly defined. As Sir Reginald's opportunity receded, Major-General C. J. Blomfield, stationed at Peshawar on the Afghan frontier, addressed a rather pathetically desperate appeal to the Viceroy on behalf of his brother ("a very able man, as his various distinctions show").[36] But by December 23, when the testimonial was penned, the Viceroy had already decided to employ Baker, Lutyens, and Jacob, and he himself lay savagely wounded by an assassin's bomb, which effectively prevented further discussion.

For thirty years Blomfield nurtured a grievance against Lutyens, who he said had originally asked him to be his collaborator at Delhi, but had then thrown him over. Baker, on whom this formidable figure later vented his wrath, felt Blomfield would actually have been unsuitable: he would never have compromised his strict French classicism to meet the Viceroy's desire for an expression of Indian tradition, and he would not have accepted the arduous work that Lutyens required of a collaborator.[37]

John Begg was equally vexed not to have a part in designing the new Delhi. As Consulting Architect to the Government of India, he interpreted the failure to confer with him or to include him on the Town Planning Committee as a slur on his professional reputation, and he asked for posting to a Government department in Britain. The Government of India remarked in reply that Begg's present job was simply too demanding to permit his employ on New Delhi; any omission to consult him constituted no reflection upon his competence. Government of India proposals in September to give Begg a major role in organizing and judging the competition for the New Delhi Secretariats may be seen at least in part as a sop to the Consulting Architect's feelings.[38] But the engagement of Lutyens and Baker extinguished even this consolatory gesture.

In a despatch on May 8, 1913, the Viceroy and his Council submitted a memorandum intended as the basis of a formal agreement between Crewe and the two architects. The document provided for annual visits to Delhi, the appointment of assistants as representatives on the site during their absence, remuneration of five per cent of the cost of completed works, and additional compensation for services as general advisers. The architects would receive their instructions directly from the newly established Imperial Delhi Committee. The Council designated Lutyens and Baker as principal architectural advisers to "ensure unity of artistic treatment." In addition they were to be assessors should there be any competition for buildings. The projected Secretariat contest, which in February Lord Crewe had asked to be delayed for reconsideration, was cancelled with the circumlocutory phrase, "competitive designs are not being called for."[39]

The architects' appointment, published on January 29, 1913, provoked immediate attack. Joseph King redoubled the campaign he had for weeks mounted in the Commons, fueled by information which the embittered John Begg furnished to his brother-in-law, a Parliamentary reporter. King's biggest salvoes, launched the day after the announcement of the architects' selection, assailed the evident abandonment of the pledge to seek competitive designs, a principle reiterated as recently as December 20 on the floor of the House. The Government's lame rejoinder laid responsibility for the appointments at the feet of the Viceroy. "Practical difficulties" were said to stand in the way of competition, but the Government spokesman promised, rather rashly, that as far as was possible, design of the city except for Government House and the Secretariats would be competitive.[40]

A competition for designs for bungalows at Imperial Delhi had in fact been launched in 1912. Lutyens had drawn up the draft conditions which were then overhauled by the Indian Public Works Department to meet indigenous requirements. Advertisements were placed in important English and vernacular newspapers in British India and the native states with the object both of obtaining designs for possible use as well as ascertaining if there existed any talent in India fit to devise suitable bungalows. The competition was a signal failure. Begg, who helped judge the entries, reported that only two men (from about 140) showed they had the capacity to provide what was wanted—and even they would require close supervision.[41]

Not surprisingly, therefore, in February 1913 the Government of India assigned responsibility for the new Delhi's buildings, except those entrusted to Lutyens and Baker, to William Henry Nicholls, the Architect Member of the Imperial Delhi Committee. In October 1914 this policy, with its concomitant abandonment of the principle of open competition for the capital's public buildings, was officially clarified. In a despatch to Lord Crewe, the Governor-General in Council noted that the standard of entries in the contest for bungalow designs had been "distinctly disappointing," and declared that the design of public buildings necessitated frequent consultation with pertinent Departments, a process impossible to adapt to a competition.[42]

Controversy over the principle of competitive designs for Imperial Delhi was mild compared with the emotion that surrounded the issue of an appropriate architectural style—Indian or European—for the new capital. As early as June 1912, while still simply a member of the Town Planning Committee, Lutyens had observed that already "a fearful battle" was brewing over the question of style.[43]

Lutyens's own outspoken opinions helped fan the flames of debate. His pronouncements about indigenous Indian architecture grew increasingly derogatory with time and exposure. The Mughal buildings scattered throughout north India he thought cumbersome, poorly constructed, and tiresome to the Western mind. Some of the detail he found attractive enough, but then he felt its beauty attributable to outside influences, possibly Italian. To be fit for such architecture, he told his wife, "you must squat on your haunches covered with jewels and little else in the way of clothing." For Baker he reduced Mughal architecture to a formula:

> Build a vasty mass of rough concrete, elephant-wise on a very simple rectangular-cum-octagon plan, dome in space anyhow. Cut off square. Overlay with a veneer of stone patterns, like laying a vertical tile floor, & get Italians to help you. Inlay jewels & cornelians if you can afford it, & rob someone if you can't.
>
> And then on the top of the mass, put on 3 turnips in concrete & overlay with stone or marble as before. Be very careful not to bond anything in, & don't care a damn if it all comes to pieces.

The recipe he devised for Hindu construction was equally caustic:

> Set square stones & build childwise . . . before you erect, carve every stone differently & independently, with lace patterns & terrifying shapes. On the top, build over trabeated pendentives an onion.[44]

Lutyens felt India had no real architecture: the buildings were just tents in stone and little more. Architecture that seemed to be "all pattern," "veneered joinery," and profuse stone carving without evident purpose offended his Ruskinian ethic of simple, grand massing and honestly expressed materials. Equally deplorable to one who built for perpetuity, nothing Indian was constructed to last, "not even the Taj." The entire debate over architectural style distressed Lutyens as useless "tongue-wagging." He did not believe there existed any great architectural tradition in India, but simply spurts by various mushroom dynasties, episodes with as little intellect in them "as any other art nouveau." As for the hybrid Eurasian style whose multiplicity of Saracenic domes surmounted the public buildings of Madras, he later roundly condemned "that particular form of vulgarity" that British rule had for its monument.[45]

But, as Lutyens recognized, the question was not simply one of taste, but also of high politics. The Viceroy was quite clear on this point: he felt it would be a "grave political blunder" to place a purely Western town on the Delhi plain. The public in India, he claimed, was very emphatic that the capital's principal buildings should have an Indian motif. He could not disregard this opinion, lest Indians justly complain he had ignored their tastes while asking them to underwrite the cost. Hardinge reminded his architects that it was not a solely British administration that was raising the new city, as when Calcutta was built, but a joint British-Indian administration. It must be their aim to achieve a style symbolic of twentieth-century India, a composite civilization both Hindu and Muslim, British and Indian. Year by year Indian influence and experience in the administration of government was increasing, making ever more necessary an architecture expressive of the new reciprocity between East and West.[46]

Less than four months after the Durbar, Hardinge had announced in the Legislative Council his inclination toward an Oriental style of architecture suited to the climate and local surroundings at Delhi. But while political opinion (including the King's wishes) was the major influence in his partiality, Hardinge was not devoid of artistic judgment, as he told Lutyens rather defensively: he was himself a keen watercolorist, and his father, a friend of Sir Francis Grant and Sir Edwin Landseer, had exhibited at the Royal Academy for twenty-six years. Moreover, Hardinge felt that his years as a diplomat in Constantinople and Teheran helped him understand "the whisperings of the east" and the language of Eastern buildings. The Mughal buildings of Agra and Fatehpur Sikri, Hindu monuments at Elephanta, and Buddhist remains at Sarnath, for example, had struck a responsive chord in him during visits in 1911 and early 1912.[47]

By the summer of 1912, opponents of Eastern architecture for Delhi had made themselves heard, and the Viceroy's initial inclinations toward an Indian style, as expressed in the Legislative Council, had crystallized into an eminently British compromise solution: "Western architecture with an Oriental motif." Hardinge acknowledged a strong sentiment against Indian architecture among the Europeans in India, an attitude Lutyens evidently encouraged while at Simla. Pure Western or pure Oriental architecture both had their detractors. The solution, therefore, as the Viceroy outlined it to Lutyens and the India Office, lay in the integration of Palladian and Pathan principles. Lutyens's British School at Rome, which Hardinge had studied in photographs, could be "most successfully orientalized" with elements from the period preceding the Mughals, although doubtless some persons would call the result "a bastard form of architecture." But the Viceroy felt confident that the Pathan style "with its rectangular or hexagonal columns, its breadth of treatment with big walls, buttresses, flat domes and few windows would lend itself to a composition with Italian architecture that would inspire beauty, solidity and originality."[48]

Hardinge's description of the European component he sought betrayed his uncertainty in the face of shifting tides of opinion from many quarters: "Western architecture" in July 1912 became "Italian" in August, "some form of Renaissance" and "a good broad Classic style" in October. By August 1913 the Viceroy waxed eloquent in favor of a blend of Indian sentiment and symbolism "with English (not Italian) traditions."[49]

Opinion among the European community in India, with rare exceptions, favored an Occidental style for Imperial Delhi. Similarly in Britain important voices during 1912 and 1913 espoused a Western architecture qualified only by allowance for local climate and available materials. Another equally passionate group advocated construction in the indigenous styles of India, while a third group adopted the supremely British, "sensible" middle course: a compromise Indian form of European Renaissance architecture, with Indian detail and executed by Indian craftsmen.

Influential architectural journals in Britain supported selection of the Renaissance style. The *British Architect* argued that European architecture had both a venerable tradition and a continuing, vital dynamism that justified its use. The editors pronounced it unthinkable that Indian architecture, with its dependence on applied forms and ornament, should be preferred to the proportions, outlines, and dignified spaces that distinguished Western building. S. D. Adshead, in an editorial in the *Architects' and Builders' Journal*, stated explicitly that New Delhi should be Hellenistic Greek—"the Greek of the Alexandrian period, with its rich ornament borrowed more than 2,000 years ago from India herself." The later, more monumental phases of Charles McKim's work exemplified an achievement worthy of emulation; native Indian architecture was wholly unfit for large-scale modern buildings. The editors of the *Builder* declared that the "classic Renaissance" style—Britain's "natural means of expression"—should serve India's necessities; illustrations of Mughal architecture were reproduced as proof of that style's unsuitability for the needs of modern India. In Allahabad, a lead editorial in the prestigious *Pioneer* suggested that an appropriate style would emerge from the requirements of the site, as yet undetermined, and from the projected functions; the paper inveighed against those whose chief concern seemed to be exterior decoration with Indian details.[50]

Such sentiments were not confined to journalists. On the floor of the Commons, Arthur Soames, the Member for South Norfolk, pleaded for Italian Renaissance, a style designed for brilliant sunshine and hence particularly appropriate to India. Modern Indian buildings were "trumpery affairs," he declared, which failed utterly to reproduce the admirable features of Agra's monuments. Reginald Barratt, whose access to Hardinge was useful to both Lutyens and Baker, confessed that his travels in India had not made him sympathetic to its art; he advised Baker not to let "claptrap" from its proponents affect him. Delhi needed a simple, beautifully proportioned classic design—"as McKim would do in America." Sir George Birdwood, a former Sheriff of Bombay, sometime special assistant to the India Office, and a well known "India hand," urged the Viceroy to ensure that the Government buildings were distinctly English. Amid the Hindu and Mughal cities which littered the Jumna riverain, the new capital must be unmistakably "the Delhi of the English."[51]

Indian architecture, however, was not without its champions. Even before Lutyens's first visit to India, the King had told him that Mughal was the style for

India "if it was not so dreadfully expensive." Some six months later Lutyens told Lady Emily that the King's preference for Mughal buildings still distressed him: "Fancy Shakespeare being asked by Elizabeth to write an ode in Chaucerian meter." Not only the British monarch but also India's ruling princes (Hardinge and Sir Valentine Chirol reported) were nearly all in favor of an Indian style of architecture at Delhi, while in the Legislative Council, Sir Gangadhar Chitnavis suggested feeling was widespread throughout the subcontinent that "the dominating feature" of the new city should be Oriental in appearance.[52]

Authoritative professional opinion rallied to the support of Indian architecture. H. V. Lanchester, reflecting preferences later shown in his own buildings in India, recommended that all buildings in the residential extensions of Shahjahanabad should be in the vernacular style; "intrusion of any in the European manner" he felt would be detrimental to Delhi's visual harmony. In his preliminary report on Lashkar in Gwalior, prepared before his engagement with the Delhi Town Planning Committee, he eschewed forcing "European ideals on those possessing such well-defined artistic traditions of their own." Years later, Lanchester castigated his fellow Britons for what he considered their obsession in India with Western architecture, which he said had been not only destructive of indigenous artistic traditions and craftsmanship, but more expensive than any of the local vernacular styles.[53]

The noted writer on Indian art E. B. Havell, in a letter to the *Times* shortly after the Durbar, denounced the "bastard Gothic and emasculated Italian Renaissance" edifices of Calcutta, suggesting to the Public Works Department as models the Mughal works of Delhi, Agra, and Fatehpur Sikri. In 1912 Havell pressed his attack. In a lecture before the East India Association at Caxton Hall, Westminster, on October 21, later published in the *British Architect* and circulated privately to persons of importance, he excoriated the *Times* and other proponents of Renaissance architecture. If adopted for Delhi, he protested, it was a style which spelled "the ruin of Indian craftsmanship, the intellectual impoverishment of the educated classes, and the strangling of Indian art." The public buildings of the Government of India exercised a potent influence for good or evil, for Indian craftsmen and aristocratic Indian patrons alike looked to them for models of taste and fashion. In 1913 Havell reserved the entire last chapter of his monumental volume, *Indian Architecture*, for an impassioned polemic against a "make-believe" capital city of Renaissance or, equally, British-designed Indo-Saracenic architecture. He suggested that intelligent patronage of the indigenous heritage of India, following the example of Akbar, could prove a bridge between the cultures, "a means of reconciling racial and religious differences."[54]

Other leaders of opinion commended Havell for his views. C. F. A. Voysey deplored the advocacy of English Renaissance architecture, and other "claptrap" about styles, as "positively disgusting." Consideration of local conditions, especially climate and traditional character, were the premises for fine buildings. Following Havell's speech in Caxton Hall, Sir Bradford Leslie had risen to lend his support, decrying the projected imposition on the Indian people of pretentious Renaissance buildings. Two months later, in a widely reported speech of his own before the Royal Society of Arts, Leslie warned that adoption of a pseudo-Renaissance style, quite divorced from contemporary structural methods, would mark the final separation of architecture from its roots in the builder's art. Robert Chisholm, an architect with long experience of India, endorsed Sir Bradford's address with the comment that Renaissance architecture was as inappropriate for the new Delhi as ancient Greek would be "on the poster of a kinematic peep-show." Another architect with lengthy service in the subcontinent, F. O. Oertel, both wrote and spoke in favor of adoption of an Indian architecture suited to climatic and local conditions; while resigned to European architecture for Government House, he recommended the crossbred Hindu–Muslim style of Fatehpur Sikri for the majority of Imperial Delhi's buildings. The Consulting Architect to the Government of India, John Begg, agitated publicly and privately for architecture of an indigenous character, inspired by the past yet not "purely antiquarian," fully recognizing modern requirements and means of construction in the manner of his own works in the fashionable hybrid Indo-Saracenic style.[55]

In Parliament, Joseph King was quick to take up the cudgels. Characterizing himself as a lover of art and of justice, he asked the Commons if it was fair that Indians, with their own proud heritage, should pay for the construction of "palaces of Italian art" in the new capital. Such a prospect, of buildings which might as well be built in New York or Rio, was "absurd and unjust"; furthermore it effectively precluded use of India's native craftsmen and artists.[56]

The Viceroy's projected compromise of Western architecture "imbued with a spirit of the East" was a solution which attracted a wide spectrum of adherents. Herbert Baker, some four months before his appointment to Delhi, had (in the *Times*) called for a new style of architecture that would reflect the new civilization in India under British rule, "a blend of the best elements of East and West." Rejecting Gothic and Mughal prototypes for both functional and symbolic reasons, he envisioned a style that would adapt the work of Inigo Jones, Wren, and their eighteenth-century disciples to both a tropical climate and the requirements of the Government. Southern European classicism and the "nobler features" of Indian architecture could provide the necessary elements for such an alchemy: the dome, the colonnade and the arcade, the open court of audience, the deep portal arch or exedra, and formal site planning in the grand manner. Use of the column, Baker later told the Viceroy, was "the crux." He assured Hardinge he would fully recognize Indian sentiment, but "balconies, oriels, turrets, and domelets in picturesque confusion" would be unsuitable for a practical Secretariat building, and in Government House they would detract from the intended effect of "awe and majesty."[57]

In contrast, the editors of the *Town Planning Review*, among the principal spokesmen for Beaux Arts design in Britain, thought admiration for Palladio, translated through Jones and Wren, was misplaced. With marble accessible, a "less vernacular," more refined classicism was possible. What was needed was a building fully modern in function, its appearance "inspired by the rich delicacy of Hellenistic Greece"—a style which would admit the assimilation of "the gorgeous decoration of the East."[58]

Lord Curzon's advocacy of a composite Indo-European architecture for the new city came as no surprise to those familiar with the plans for the Victoria Memorial in Calcutta. That monumental museum edifice of polished Indian marble owed its conception to the former Viceroy, and it represented just the combination of "a good broad Classic style with an Indian 'motif'" that Hardinge favored at Delhi. After Curzon's vociferous opposition to the transfer of the capital, Hardinge gratefully acknowledged the correspondence of opinions on this issue as "a great support" in his struggle against proponents of a purely Occidental city. Later, when Curzon saw Lutyens's sketches in the autumn of 1913, he expressed his delight that the introduction of Indian elements "met the requirements of Eastern sentiment."[59]

The Secretary of State's attitude was of considerable consequence. Crewe emphasized in an address on town planning that New Delhi would not "be hostile in appearance or in spirit to the Mohammedan ideals of the past." He found the integration of Moorish and Renaissance elements in southern Spain, which Curzon cited as a successful admixture, to be a persuasive illustration of the possibilities; he in turn used it when impressing upon Lutyens the importance of giving "an Eastern flavor to a Western design in India." In acknowledging Lord Brassey's note of April 1913, which suggested the Oriental character of the great hall at the hotel in Heliopolis near Cairo as a successful model, Crewe assured his Liberal colleague that it seemed "quite likely" Delhi's new buildings would "combine Eastern feeling with the satisfaction of European needs and habits."[60]

This proposed compromise echoed the very goals of British tutelage itself: at the Legislative Council in Delhi, Srijut Ghanasyam Barua recalled the King-Emperor's expressed desire for a "union and fusion" of the culture and aspirations of European and Indian subjects alike. Indians, for their part, the representative from Assam suggested, must "imbibe and assimilate" all that was good from the West while conserving the best from their own ancient civilization. Malcolm Hailey, whom Hardinge had handpicked to be first Chief Commissioner of Delhi and President of the Imperial Delhi Committee, agreed with the Viceroy that "breadth of treatment, and sympathy with Indian sentiment," much more than simply Indian decorative detail, should be their concern. From Madras, the English Theosophist leader, Mrs. Annie Besant—an old friend—wrote Lutyens suggesting he use Western architecture to "modify & enrich" the Indian tradition, rather than planting a completely alien style (however noble) on the subcontinent. Major L. B. Keith, a former conservator of monuments in Central India and member of the Archaeological Survey, expounded his views at length in the columns of the Allahabad *Pioneer*. He condemned the exclusive use of European Renaissance architecture as inappropriate in the vicinity of Shahjahanabad's Oriental heritage, and he asserted that Akbar's blend of Hindu and Mughal styles, despite its beauty, had not survived. Modern Indian architecture was chiefly Hindu; the present goal should be to "unite the finer qualities of the Hindu and the European," appealing to Hindu sentiments and "doing justice to Hindu architecture and the native craftsman."[61]

Major Keith's polemics touched on a question inextricably intertwined with the battle of the styles, and an issue fiercely debated in connection with the new Delhi: the employment of Indian architects and craftsmen. Much of the interest in this subject originated with the India Society, founded in 1910 to promote the study and appreciation of Indian culture. In November 1910, more than a year before the

Durbar, the Society appealed to the India Office to assist it in investigating the principles and practices of traditional Indian art and architecture, information valuable not only to the archaeologist but to any scheme for promoting technical and art education. As a consequence, the Government of India deputed a young architect with the Archaeological Survey, Gordon Sanderson, to collect material pertinent to the Society's request. In a sketchy survey of Rajputana, the Central Provinces, and some Punjab districts, Sanderson amassed photographs and much data illustrating the work of large numbers of Indian masons, carvers, and mistri, or supervisory master builder-architects. Upon the announcement of the transfer of the capital to Delhi, the Government of India ordered Sanderson to present his findings without delay, and John Begg penned an introduction in December 1912. The report, published in 1913, added fuel to the fire lit by numerous partisans of the Indian arts.[62]

The growing agitation coalesced in a petition from 175 influential men and women presented to the India Office on February 6, 1913. Signatories included Members from both Houses of Parliament, persons with relevant interests in India, and distinguished representatives of the world of the arts and letters. Together they urged the employment at Imperial Delhi of the master builder with his craftsmen, "working in accustomed materials upon the site, from simple instructions as to accommodation and arrangement" that a medieval king might have given a master mason. Such a course, the petitioners argued, was financially economical, and would have the desirable political effect of tying Indians ever more closely to Britain herself.[63]

The prominence of the petitioners, ranging from Thomas Hardy, George Bernard Shaw, Laurence Housman, and Sir Arthur Evans to the Duke of Newcastle, Lord Napier of Magdala, and Adeline, Duchess of Bedford, ensured that the petition was not ignored. Read in the Council of India, it was forwarded to the Government of India, where the Consulting Architect, John Begg, drafted a despatch made public on April 24. In this reply, the Viceroy's Council remarked that while they were sympathetic to the petitioners' aims, the methods advocated were no longer applicable when confronted with the complex requirements of modern civilization. The Government emphasized their hope, however, that the work at New Delhi would encourage the best craftsmen in India and afford ample outlet for skills in the decorative arts.[64]

Lutyens might growl that no one in India knew "any sort of craftsmanship except accountancy," and the editors of the *British Architect* might call it unthinkable that the new capital be "handed over" to "the combined efforts of a race of native craftsmen." But few persons seriously disputed that employment of Indian craftsmen was desirable or even necessary. The King-Emperor himself regarded Imperial Delhi as a "splendid opportunity" to encourage Indian artists and artisans. The editors of the *Town Planning Review* advised against ignoring "the wealth of native talent" in India, and the *Builder*'s editors felt that even Renaissance architecture could offer "ample scope for employing native craftsmen" and for the display of their skill in devising and carrying out handsome detail. The *Builder*'s prediction proved to be an understatement. As Herbert Baker acknowledged in 1930, the construction of the new city, under the direction of the Imperial Delhi

Committee, was "executed entirely by Indian workmen," except for a handful of British foremen.[65]

The question was the method. Given the fundamental principle which required fully prepared plans and estimates before the expenditure of any funds, it is not difficult to understand the Government's resistance to adopting the traditional, unstructured methods of the mistri. These master builders normally began work with only a general elevation drawing, no detailed working drawings, and without any estimate of the cost. Details were worked out as the construction proceeded, often by the workmen themselves; no schedules of rates or quantities were prepared.[66] Such a procedure was inconceivable at Raisina.

The Government of India's views, communicated to the petitioners by the India Office, simply initiated another round of debate. A. Randall Wells, on behalf of the signatories, called attention to the "unimpeachable" evidence in Gordon Sanderson's report on modern Indian architecture that there existed numerous master builders possessing a "free mastery of construction and design" and capable of erecting works "both of magnitude and of utilitarian purpose." Casting about for "an easy and satisfactory solution" to the employment of Indian designers, Malcolm Hailey, as President of the Imperial Delhi Committee, suggested selecting certain portions of the principal buildings (he mentioned the Durbar Hall and the Secretariat conference room) for an Indian designer. Certain lesser buildings, such as the Oriental Institute, might also be given to an Indian designer; the Imperial Delhi Committee would work out "engineering and other details." Furthermore, the Government might create a studio or workshop of native craftsmen, directed by an Indian. Only this latter suggestion appears to have gained any official acceptance, and even then in a much modified form, primarily as a gesture to public relations. Lanchester, in his second report at Delhi in July 1912, had proposed a workshop for stone and wood carving, with an Indian director. Three months later, the Principal of the Government School of Art at Calcutta had suggested a similar studio for Indian sculptors whose task would be the architectural decoration of the new city.[67]

Lord Hardinge's attitude was cool, at best. "I do not believe in this studio," he told Hailey in August 1913. "It strikes me as eye-wash." He thought the Principal of the Lahore School of Art, an Indian, might be put in charge of the decorative work connected with the New Delhi Government buildings, but he displayed no haste in making the appointment. Repeated badgering of the India Office in Parliament and in the press obliged the Government of India in 1914 to crystallize a policy in response to the critics. Hailey's suggested formula was adopted: the Viceroy told London that his Government had engaged Indian craftsmen to carry out the decorative work on the main buildings, and that within two years he hoped to have assembled "an organized body of these craftsmen under charge of an Indian Master craftsman." Use of the word "studio," and especially the term "school," was scrupulously avoided. As Hailey hastened to note, the Government intended to select experienced workmen who would need no training. The duties of the man in charge, to be called the "master craftsman" for public consumption, would be simply to "direct and supervise" the workmen's efforts.[68] Then, the following month, on June 28, 1914, events at Sarajevo triggered a war destined to engulf Britain and her Indian empire. The financial burdens of that cataclysm, coupled with the Viceroy's attitude, effectively precluded establishment of anything resembling either a studio for aspiring students or a workshop for experienced decorative artists.

Coincident with the debate over methods of executing the new permanent capital, the Government of India hastily sought to provide interim winter quarters for its staff and for the Legislative Council. Not only the cost, but even the very existence of this accommodation, generally known as "Temporary Delhi" or (to Lutyens) "Tin Delhi," increasingly became a focus for controversy. The completion of this temporary city was kept distinctly separate from Imperial Delhi and its executive committee. Scarcely was the Durbar announcement made when Sir Robert Carlyle, the Member of the Viceroy's Council for the Public Works Department, initiated the first arrangements. Carlyle secured prompt approval of his nominee for the post of Director of Temporary Works: Lieutenant-Colonel H. W. G. Cole, who had successfully administered the East Bengal Camp at the Durbar. A small staff of engineers assisted Cole.[69]

Between the beginning of January and May 1912, no fewer than three complete schemes were submitted to the Government of India before a final plan was approved. The first proposals, ready on January 3, assumed that the Durbar area west of the Ridge would comprise the permanent city site. Consequently, Metcalfe House, an historic mansion in the Civil Lines area east of the Ridge, was chosen as the temporary Viceregal Lodge, and other mansions and bungalows in the civil station were listed for acquisition. The suggestion to use either the Diwan-i-Khas or the barracks in the Fort for offices was rejected.

With the Viceroy's selection in the second week of January of the Circuit House west of the Ridge as his residence, Colonel Cole's staff were ready to prepare preliminary estimates for buildings. No sooner were these estimates submitted, however, than Cole was directed to consider using some part of the Durbar area. In a week a new layout was completed for a site near Kingsway Station, which the Viceroy provisionally approved on March 7. The plans for residences under canvas and for offices in tin sheds and buildings habitable only in the cold weather were abandoned. Among other reasons, the seclusion of Indian women accustomed to purdah conditions could not be properly ensured in tents! Most important, spacious brick buildings suitable for year-round occupation would find a ready market when the Government moved to its permanent site. Large-scale site plans, elevation drawings, and detailed estimates were prepared, with a more elaborate Council Chamber and Secretariat than originally contemplated. When objections were raised to the use of sites west of the Mall (a principal artery), still another alternative site plan was devised.

On April 30, after an inspection of the various sites with members of the Delhi Town Planning Committee, the Viceroy abandoned the Kingsway scheme. For Cole and his staff, this was a bitter blow after their arduous labors to create an effective and coherent layout. Within three days, however, the mass of figures and drawings were adapted to a final scheme comprising the Metcalfe House estate in Civil Lines, part of the existing cantonments, and a small part of the Durbar area near the Circuit House. Private houses and hotels in Delhi were leased and others were acquired and altered. The foundation stone of the Council Chamber and Imperial Secretariat, designed by E. Montague Thomas, was laid on May 25. At the height of the work some 13,000 men and women, principally imported from Jaipur, were employed. The work was completed with despatch: the Auditor-General and his staff occupied the temporary Secretariat on October 1, and other accommodation was finished by January 1913. The total cost was 5,933,889 rupees, or nearly £400,000.[70] [34]

As early as April 1912, Members of the Viceroy's Council had anticipated the censure which "Temporary Delhi" would arouse. The Finance Member noted that the architect's plans depicted buildings of a "decidedly ambitious" character, and foresaw "very hostile criticism" if the Government embarked on heavy expenditure on temporary arrangements, especially for Members' houses. Harcourt Butler, the Education Member, echoed these views, holding that it would be preferable to use tents than to incur large sums for construction. He could imagine nothing more prejudicial to Imperial Delhi than £500,000 or even £200,000 hastily spent on temporary buildings.[71]

The most trenchant of the critics, predictably, was Lord Curzon, who rose in Parliament to decry the expense incurred in building "this temporary evanescent capital on the plains." The Viceroy and many ranking officials would be on tour for much of the winter anyway; could the Government not simply stay at Simla until the permanent city was completed? He had no doubt that money was being "foolishly and lavishly spent" on a needless temporary city. In the Commons Sir John Rees peppered the Parliamentary Under-Secretary with questions about the interim arrangements. How much would the temporary accommodation cost? How did the Government propose to recover part of this expense? When would the buildings be ready? Would it not be better to stay in Calcutta until Imperial Delhi was complete?[72]

Stung by such attacks, Hardinge telegraphed the India Office that "the greatest care and economy" were being exercised. Further questions should be met with an authoritative statement that nothing would be wasted: after the permanent city was finished, the Postal Audit Office and Indian Treasury would occupy the Secretariat on Alipur Road, and even more clerks' quarters would be required in the future than were now under construction. Colonel Cole, in a memorandum prompted by criticism of the project, emphasized that all the temporary accommodation could later be put to "some useful purpose," and the valuable properties recently acquired would, if necessary, find a ready market. He felt it highly likely that in any sale the Government would realize the full value of their outlay, or would receive the equivalent value from their own use of the property.[73]

The criticism which "Temporary Delhi" provoked was short-lived, however, compared with the continuing outcry over the cost of the permanent city. Much of the initial attack was levied against the four-million-pound figure that had been announced in the now-famous despatch of August 25, 1911, as the maximum expenditure that the transfer from Calcutta would entail. Originally the Viceroy's Finance Member had named a figure of five million, then just before the issue of the despatch two months later had suggested substituting a top estimate of four million. This very rough estimate had been based on the cost of capitals in various Indian provinces, multiplied by a certain factor to compensate for the greater size and importance of the new Delhi.[74] Local information had been necessarily scanty because the Government could not gather data prior to the Durbar without jeopardizing the secrecy surrounding the project.

Lord Curzon kept public silence for more than two months after the Durbar announcement. Then at the end of February, he launched a detailed, spirited onslaught in the Lords of several hours' length. Of the many able authorities he had consulted, he asserted, not one estimated the cost of the transfer (including the new capital at Patna in Bihar) at less than eight million pounds. The majority calculated ten million, and others, among them Curzon himself, predicted a minimum cost of twelve million. Returning to the lists once again four months later, the former Viceroy assailed the new projects as "a financial millstone" around the Indian taxpayer's neck, an experiment which, undertaken without any proper estimates, constituted a "most gigantic leap in the dark."[75]

In March, chastened by Curzon's opening salvoes in February, and sobered by belated research into water and drainage costs for Bombay and Calcutta, Sir Guy Fleetwood Wilson returned to his original maximum figure of five million pounds. The Viceroy, although admitting that the estimate of four million might eventually be exceeded, chose "for the present" to adhere to it. Clearly angered by attacks in Parliament on his scheme, he prepared a Budget Speech whose bluster was designed "to scotch the idea" that New Delhi would cost twelve or more million pounds, a belief he felt had gained acceptance simply on Curzon's word. But time seemed only to make that prediction more reliable: in December, Lutyens condemned Fleetwood Wilson's "mistake," and asserted unhesitatingly that "Curzon was much more correct in saying 12,000,000." A year later, however, the Town Planning Committee unwittingly furnished the Viceroy and his Finance Member with a

34. The Imperial Secretariat in "Temporary Delhi," completed 1912. E. Montague Thomas, architect.

perfect alibi for any estimate exceeding that first wild guess. The selection of a site south of Shahjahanabad, Fleetwood Wilson wrote, appeared to vitiate the basis for the calculation of four million pounds: the assumed use on a northern site of existing railway facilities, roads, water supply, lighting, and drainage would now be impossible.[76]

In March 1912, during the week before the Viceroy's Budget Speech, the Public Works Department and the Army Department had hastily put together some figures that confirmed the original four million estimate—if the new cantonments, temporary works, and improvements in Shahjahanabad and Civil Lines were excluded and if receipts from the sale of buildings in Calcutta and land in Delhi were deducted from expenditures. Survey of the sites and collection of information for the Town Planning Committee began in April, and Thomas Ward and his staff began a concentrated two-month effort to prepare a complete set of preliminary estimates in early August, based on H. V. Lanchester's second revised layout. The Viceroy received Ward's report and estimates on October 2, and while recording with satisfaction that the projected cost was under four million, noted that the Public Works Department had still to examine and check the figures. In a note on Ward's report, Geoffrey de Montmorency declared the estimates for Government House, the Secretariats, and other public buildings to be too low to produce buildings worthy of the Government's intentions. Nevertheless, two months later Hardinge wrote to Lord Sanderson privately that the preliminary estimates sent to England had amounted to less than four million "without any cheeseparing." Conceding the possibility that expenses might exceed these preliminary calculations, he expressed confidence that "the whole thing" would cost less than five million.[77]

The Town Planning Committee issued its final report in March 1913, and by December 18 the Chief Engineer's staff had prepared massive, detailed project estimates totalling £6,072,533—with contingency funds, £6,820,600. Scrutiny by the Public Works Department, under pressure from the Viceroy, succeeded in materially reducing the total estimate to £5,113,620, or with contingency reserves, £6,113,260—the figures which Hardinge announced to the Legislative Council on March 24, 1914 and which the Secretary of State sanctioned on June 15. Part of this sum, the Viceroy told the Council Members, would be recouped from rents, the sale of leases, general taxes, and indirect receipts. Hardinge frankly admitted that many items had been excluded from the estimates: the cantonment, diversion of railway routes, and sanitary reforms and urban improvements in Shahjahanabad—needs which would have "inevitably" been met in the normal course of the old Delhi's expansion and improvement. Nor did the estimates include the temporary Delhi or such buildings as museums, institutes, and additional hospitals which the future would doubtless bring. While clearly the initial figure of four million pounds would be exceeded, the Viceroy believed a capital worthy of India could be built without excessive expenditure. Responding to repeated criticism that emanated from Parliament and the European community in Calcutta, the Viceroy asserted that provision of funds, spread over eight years from New Delhi's inception in 1912, would be carefully arranged to cause "no embarrassment" to India's development.[78]

The usual practice in India when Government buildings were required had been to find necessary funds from current revenue, meeting the expenditure from the proceeds of ordinary taxation. But the magnitude of the Delhi scheme precluded such a method. Instead the money was raised partly by ordinary loan and partly from accumulated balances or revenue surpluses as they arose. A proposal to finance the new city by a special loan was seriously contemplated, and won favor from Lord Crewe, Sir Thomas Holderness, and Sir Harcourt Butler, among others, but was ultimately considered impracticable and rejected on the strong recommendation of Fleetwood Wilson's successor as Finance Member, Sir William Meyer. Holderness calculated privately at the India Office that the true cost of the transfer, including the cantonments and other expenses not charged to the Imperial Delhi account, was some seven million pounds, four million of it to be borrowed.[79] The figures did not yet approximate Lord Curzon's dire predictions in 1912 but in two years the cost had swiftly and inexorably climbed much closer to fulfilling his prophecy.

Curzon underscored this fact in the Lords with his customary eloquence and thoroughness, highlighting every item excluded from the estimates. Moreover he confidently revised his estimate of the total cost of the transfer from twelve million pounds to fifteen or sixteen, and scoffed at the idea that the works would be completed in 1920, the Government's newest target date. Altogether he was, as often, infuriatingly and devastatingly on the mark. The thin-skinned Hardinge took it badly. "What does he want?" the Viceroy wrote home angrily, his blood boiling. "Is it all due to spite or does he simply want to embarrass his successor?"[80]

Curzon was not alone. The European community in Calcutta remained highly vocal in its criticism. The unanimous resolution of the Bengal Chamber of Commerce on February 27, protesting "the excessive outlay of public funds on a new capital city at Delhi" that might better be expended on industrial, commercial, and railway development, was sent not only to the Viceroy but also to the India Office, the Governor of Bengal, all Members of both Houses of Parliament, and all Chambers of Commerce in the British Empire. One member of the Bengal Chamber, in seconding the resolution, compared Lord Hardinge's Government to a man who deserts his wife for a more attractive mate on whom he lavishes all, relegating his wife and family to penury! The Calcutta newspapers were equally vituperative: the *Statesman* spoke scornfully of a brazen extravagance in the face of imminent famine and decried "a useless, heart-breaking prodigality of expenditure" reminiscent of Mughal finance rather than "the great traditions of British rule."[81]

Not all voices called for economy. The King expressed anxiety that Hardinge would limit expenditure simply to keep within his original four-million-pound estimate, which he realized could only have been conjecture. Doubtless Lionel Abrahams, Secretary to the Finance Department at the India Office, bore this in mind when inspecting the plans and estimates on a visit to Delhi five months later; he made it plain he opposed construction with a cheap appearance. Lutyens himself commented privately that Hardinge's adherence to the initial estimate was producing "mad folly"; Fleetwood Wilson's guess was like a witch's curse in its effect on future generations. The Government was estimating the scheme at half its value to make it fit "random political statements," and the result was cursing engineers, depressed architects, and a city that might best be called Bedlampur![82]

Influential Indian opinion, spanning the representative spectrum of the Imperial

Legislative Council, furnished Lutyens with additional support in his battle for adequate financing. In the Council's budget debate on March 24 1914, nearly a dozen Indians urged construction of a capital worthy of India, her Emperor, and of the British Empire. Two Members, Sir Fazulbhoy Currimbhoy Ebrahim and Sir Gangadhur Chitnavis, both magnates, tempered their advocacy with the hope that costs "should not cause a severe and sharp strain upon the general revenues." But others showed less restraint. Sardar Daljit Singh asked the Government not to allow its few critics to deter creation of a capital of "magnificence and beauty," consonant with "the grandeur of the mighty Empire," while Raja Kushal Pal Singh asked that "no money should be grudged" for the construction. The projected expenditures were both justifiable and necessary, Raja Saiyid Abu Jafar of Pirpur declared; the new city, surrounded by the "glorious memories" of earlier Delhis, must be a fitting tribute to British rule in India. How appropriate, Sir Ibrahim Rahimtoola noted, that the nonofficial Members of the Council, who could "well claim to represent the taxpayers" of the country, should express their unanimous opinion in favor of an Imperial capital of global pretensions, "befitting not only the great Indian Empire, but the dignity of the vast British Empire."[83]

Worthy of an Empire! Hardinge moved swiftly to assemble a staff to construct this Imperial capital. The Member for Public Works, Sir Robert Carlyle, displayed an eagerness to have the entire scheme placed under his own authority, but the Viceroy's trusted confidant, Sir John Jenkins, thought that Department quite "unfit to deal with great administrative schemes." Furthermore, Carlyle's dilatory and indecisive character would cause endless disputes and delays. Hardinge agreed that the new Delhi was not a project for either Carlyle or his Department, and he declared his preference for "a small, but strong Committee" to deal with all aspects of the planning and execution of the capital.[84] Jenkins promptly recommended in a note circulated among the Viceroy's Council the creation of an executive Committee with "an able officer" on special duty to transact all business directly with Lord Hardinge. He suggested for the post an outstanding young member of the Finance Department who had recently distinguished himself during the preparations for the Durbar only to be struck down with enteric fever virtually on the eve of the event: William Malcolm Hailey.

Jenkins made it plain he was not angling to have the Delhi project placed under the Home Department: he had "more than enough to do." They were practically his last words to the Viceroy: by January 13 he was dead. In February, Hardinge did actually designate the Home Department, whose concerns traditionally included public policy and general administration, as the agency responsible for coordinating all the activities connected with New Delhi.[85]

Even before Jenkins's suggestion on New Year's Day, the Viceroy had been mulling over the appointment of Malcolm Hailey to head the Delhi project and had broached the subject with Sir Guy Fleetwood Wilson on December 24. Hardinge, it happened, could not have asked for a more ardent supporter of Hailey. Austere, sometimes petty and disagreeable, Fleetwood Wilson could be generous and even sentimental, and in word and deed he showed great admiration and affection for Hailey, whose appointment to the Delhi Durbar Committee he had secured. He knew no one, he told Hardinge, who could more loyally and successfully carry out the Viceregal wishes, and he urged Hailey's appointment as "Commissioner of the new Delhi." To Hailey, he in turn painted the prospect of a role in a great historic event, a part in creating what he envisioned would be "the finest capital in the world." On receiving a favorable response, Sir Guy went to the Viceroy, and on January 7 he wrote Hailey that Hardinge intended to make him (his health permitting) the principal officer of the small committee responsible for the creation of the new Delhi.[86]

The new Home Member, Sir Reginald Craddock, had serious misgivings about the possible public and official reaction to entrusting such a major post to so junior an officer as Hailey. But the Viceroy's clear preference, coupled with strong support from Sir John Hewett, the former President of the Durbar Committee, succeeded in reversing even this opposition. The enclave of Delhi, independent of any local or provincial government, was duly created on October 1, 1912, and Hailey was appointed the first Chief Commissioner. The Viceroy told Fleetwood Wilson with satisfaction that, thanks to his advice, he had given Hailey "a good kick upstairs" and he knew he would be "perfectly invaluable." Six years later the retired Viceroy would have occasion to congratulate his appointee on his "splendid work" with the words: "Both Old and New Delhi will be a monument to you owing to the improvements and progress that you have inspired."[87]

Hailey, as Chief Commissioner, became President of the Imperial Delhi Committee, which was constituted by a resolution of the Government of India on March 25, 1913, and assumed charge of its duties on April 1. The other committee members included H. T. Keeling, Chief Engineer, previously Superintending Engineer of the Madras Public Works Department, who had been in charge of the new capital works since November 29, 1912; H. G. Stokes, Financial Member, formerly Deputy-Secretary to the Government of India, Financial Department; and W. H. Nicholls, Architect Member, previously Consulting Architect to the Government of Madras after service as an archaeologist for the Government of India. Geoffrey de Montmorency acted as Secretary to the Committee.

The Member for Public Works had recommended Keeling as a man with experience in the construction of large buildings and the design and control of important sanitary works, with a reputation for being personable and enormously energetic. The Architect Member was placed under the Chief Engineer on his staff (to avoid any conflict of authority) as Consulting Architect to the Government of India for Imperial Delhi, with responsibility for designing all the buildings not assigned to Lutyens and Baker. Nicholls, a former pupil of Sir Thomas Jackson, had proven ability, a knowledge of Indian conditions, and the sympathetic attitude that was deemed essential to the delicate task of advising the English architects and often carrying out their ideas. After Nicholls's appointment, Hardinge directed that papers relating to the new capital need no longer be sent to John Begg, the Government's principal salaried architect. At one stroke the Viceroy effectively stifled the prime source of information for Joseph King, Imperial Delhi's severest critic in the House of Commons.[88]

Over the entire administrative structure in India, of course, hovered the Viceroy, and Lord Hardinge was in a hurry. The new Delhi's architects and engineers were beset not only by his insistent demands for economy, but also by continued pressure for speed. Three weeks after the Durbar, Sir John Jenkins had urged the Viceroy to take personal charge in order to expedite construction of the capital, for delays would occasion scorn from many critics. By May 1912, as the Delhi experts explored the terrain, Hardinge grew impatient for a decision on the site; he explained that although wishing to avoid the appearance of indecent haste, he was "simply itching" to begin work on the new city. The King's Private Secretary perceived that Hardinge was keen to finish Government House during his term of office, which would normally end in 1915. But Lord Stamfordham felt there need be no undue hurry and was anxious lest the Viceroy rush the undertaking and stamp his own personal predilections too much on a city which after all would be forever associated with King George's name. Nevertheless Captain Ward's preliminary report and estimate in October 1912, prepared in extraordinary haste and in the absence of designs for the principal buildings, held to Hardinge's timetable. Work would begin in 1913–14, and the report predicted that with energetic prosecution, Government House and sufficient Secretariats and bungalows would be ready for occupation in October 1915. Virtually all construction would be finished during 1917, and accounts would be closed in 1918.[89]

Altogether Hardinge was a remarkable client, whose contributions as His Majesty's "man on the spot" had from the very first helped to determine the shape of things to be. He had early preferred what it took others weeks to perceive as the only possible site for the capital. His daily attention to minute details in Imperial Delhi's infancy had much to do with the project's ultimate success. Except for his persistent prodding of even his most reliable subordinates, there might have been little tangible sign of progress before the economies induced by the guns of August 1914 slowed and even threatened to end forever the project so courageously begun.

"Delay would be fatal," the Viceroy told Herbert Baker bluntly on New Year's Day in 1914, and he stressed his hope that the foundations for the major buildings could be started promptly. Under such pressure, architects and engineers alike worked with unaccustomed haste. The Chief Engineer had produced his four-volume project estimate in December 1913. Lutyens, "fearfully busy," toiled every day until midnight trying to bring his designs within the budget, while Baker worked at a white heat with his partner Francis Fleming to reduce his plans to their ultimate form. With a barrage of letters and repeated personal visits to the site, the Viceroy cajoled and exhorted the Public Works Department and the Imperial Delhi Committee to greater activity. Even the India Office did not escape: unsigned articles by Hailey in May issues of the *Times* and the *Times of India*, written at Hardinge's request, declared pointedly that only the sanction of the Secretary of State was needed to begin construction. When approval of the project estimate reached the Ridge at Simla in mid-June, the Viceroy wrote Hailey jubilantly that their motto should henceforth be, "Full speed ahead."[90]

# 6

## A City Rises

When His Britannic Majesty's Government declared war on the German Empire on August 4, 1914 and on the Austro-Hungarian Empire eight days later, few persons could have foretold that this would ultimately destroy these three empires, and indeed an entire way of life. Only by the narrowest of escapes did the new imperial city rising on the Delhi plain elude extinction or catastrophic mutilation.

Even before the Great War, the vision of an Indian capital more splendid than any predecessor had been tempered by political and economic realities; these had impelled the Viceroy to seek every device to restrict expenditure to the announced cost of four million pounds. Early evidence that this hasty estimate was woefully inaccurate had proved highly embarrassing to Lord Hardinge and had redoubled his determination to effect all possible economies compatible with a venture worthy of the sovereign's mandate. At Hardinge's behest, the Imperial Delhi Committee curtailed the town planners' layout, reducing the size of individual residential compounds, restricting the southern boundary of the city, abandoning the elaborate scheme for riverside parks and drives, and proposing an alternate site for extension of Shahjahanabad which would have eliminated another projected park. The magnificent marble facades envisaged for the principal edifices were quickly transformed to stone, and even plaster was contemplated. Lutyens lamented that promises from Sir William Meyer, Finance Member of the Viceroy's Council, to be "lavish" with funds for Imperial Delhi, had as yet proved empty. "So it all wags," he despaired. "Oh! for the greatness and help of a Wren & Newton is my everlasting prayer."[1]

Despite Hardinge's economies, detailed estimates derived from newly collected data and from actual experience of construction costs, as well as sanction of additional works not included in the project estimate, obliged the Viceroy to abandon altogether his much-publicized budget of four million pounds. Four months before the outbreak of war, he sought the Secretary of State's approval for expenditure on Delhi of £6,113,600 over a six-year period. By this time the history of such estimates aroused skepticism about even these more generous figures: the King's Private Secretary anticipated completion of the city ten years after the expiry of Hardinge's term in 1915. The previous year the Education Member of the Viceroy's Council had made a similar prophecy. In 1914 Lord Curzon reiterated his earlier prediction of ten years to conclude the scheme.[2]

Pessimistic forecasts served only to spur Hardinge to greater endeavors. Although wounded by the criticism that attended the transfer of the capital, the former diplomat exhibited a perspicacity worthy of a seasoned politician: he told Hailey he attached "enormous importance" to having some tangible evidence of construction during the winter of 1914–15. "The more that we are able to show," he concluded, "the better will be the political effect." Without visible progress, Hardinge anticipated embarrassing questions during the Budget debate in March.[3]

When the Viceroy discovered that slow delivery of stone from quarries in Bharatpur was causing construction delays, a whirlwind of action ensued. The wires fairly hummed with telegrams, and Hardinge and the Chief Engineer of Delhi had personal interviews with the State Engineer at Bharatpur. The Imperial Delhi Committee promptly undertook to work one of the quarries with its own staff and to conclude negotiations with Dholpur State for supply of stone from its Barauli quarries on a light railway line that the Committee would itself build.[4]

The war was scarcely two weeks old before the Finance Member of Hardinge's Council raised the specter of serious economic dislocation in India should the hostilities be prolonged. This prospect goaded the Viceroy to yet more efforts to expedite Delhi. From his palace on Simla's empyreal heights, he wrote to Hailey that he hoped for "a considerable advance" in construction at Delhi since his departure three months previous; he urged him to overspend the annual budget by a million rupees to achieve "a real step forward." He remained pledged to economy in the total cost, even obdurate about "an extra penny" for Government House, as Lutyens complained, but he was equally committed to speed. His Viceroyalty had been extended to March 1916, but its end would come all too soon, and Hardinge prodded Lutyens to "push things on fast this winter." With a hint of apology, he added, "I am like the old man in a hurry."[5]

The war, inevitably, had its effect. The marked rise in the cost of imported articles paralleled general wartime price rises, but it was augmented by increases in insurance and freight rates. Electrical and sanitary work on Government House, and major municipal sanitation, waterworks, and drainage projects—all requiring imported materials—were postponed until the war had ended. With the diversion of available funds to the military effort, expenditure on Delhi during the fiscal year 1914–15 declined one-fifth from that of the previous twelve months, and grants sanctioned for the two successive years likewise fell substantially. The four million rupees allocated for 1916–17 represented only sixty per cent of the annual budget three years before. The Government of India considered the sum merely sufficient to prevent deterioration of materials and machinery and to preclude disbanding an engineering staff already depleted by military transfers and enlistments.[6]

As a result of the war, Hardinge acknowledged on the eve of his departure, spending had been reduced to "the lowest possible limit consistent with the avoidance of loss." By March 1916, the project outlay amounted to only £1.25 million out of the more than six million sanctioned. The number of workers, including masons, stonecutters, engineers, and coolies, dropped to 8,000, or about one-third those employed in the winter of 1913–14. Consequently the period of construction was destined to be much protracted; Delhi's Cassandra, Lord Curzon, had once again been proved correct. Anxious lest building be suspended entirely, or the original bold conception mutilated, Hardinge implored his Legislative Council to oppose any "petty ideas of parsimony" which might curtail Imperial Delhi's "future glory and beauty." For those who sought equality for India among the British Dominions, he added shrewdly, the new capital was "an integral and essential part" of the subcontinent's political self-development.[7]

The financial stringency deeply worried Lutyens: to get adequate funds "to avoid base nastiness" in Delhi's architecture seemed an impossible task. Painful illness, added to this concern, induced depression. The motto of his youth—"As faith wills, so fate fulfills"—now seemed to him "a very empty boast."[8]

While changes brought by the war distressed the Viceroy and Delhi's architects alike, the delays were not without their positive feature. At the India Office, Holderness discerned that the retarded activity might not be "an unmixed drawback": Baker and Lutyens would have more time "to think and plan." Lutyens himself confessed that a slower pace was "a good thing," allowing proposals to "get digested and thought out better."[9]

Given the grave wartime crisis, the drastically reduced budget for Delhi was still vulnerable to attack. Among the city's most adamant opponents was Lord Islington, who had served as Chairman of the Royal Commission on the Indian Public Services and who in 1915 became Parliamentary Under-Secretary for India. He did not mince words. Declaring that "what is only an unjustifiable luxury in time of peace may be wanton extravagance today," Islington warned that visions of Imperial Delhi must be squared with wartime facts, and the whole scheme reconsidered. He wrote forcefully to the new Secretary of State for India, Austen Chamberlain, urging abandonment of an enterprise that was (he later told Curzon) fatuous, useless, and absurd.[10]

Chamberlain's own view was that the original decision to move to Delhi was a mistake, and early in 1916 he had drafted a despatch to Hardinge's successor, Lord Chelmsford, inviting reconsideration of the Delhi scheme as a result of "the altered financial conditions brought about by the war." Chamberlain withheld the despatch on receiving a formidable memorandum from Lord Curzon, who called the new capital a "costly but futile bauble," an "unpardonable" peacetime extravagance which had become a wartime "incubus." The former Viceroy declared that a further ten million pounds would be required to complete the new Delhi; indeed the total cost of the transfer, including the collateral arrangements in Bengal and Bihar, would be at least eighteen million pounds! No wonder that Curzon urged "peaceful extinction" of the Raisina scheme. The temporary Delhi north of Shahjahanabad had already cost nearly half a million pounds and he suggested that with some improvements it could suffice for the brief cold weather visit of senior officialdom. Simla, already the residence of the Government of India for seven months annually, should be recognized as the principal center. The Secretariat staff could easily remain there throughout the year.[11]

Lord Hardinge's reaction to the Curzon memorandum and to Chamberlain's proposal to reconsider the Delhi scheme was predictably charged with emotion. Hardinge clearly regarded himself as the city's founder, and he had promised on his departure that his interest in the new Delhi would "never wane." Tradition dictated that former Viceroys did not return to India, but he was determined, he had told Hailey, to see the new capital on its inauguration. Early in July, word had leaked to Hardinge of Curzon's memorandum. Obtaining a copy from Chamberlain, he bridled at its "animus and misrepresentation" and moved swiftly to oppose its effect. To alter the plans, he told the Secretary of State, would be "incredible," and any reduction would be widely viewed in India as an act of irresolution, implying the impermanence of British rule. He hastily furnished Crewe (now Lord President of the Council) with lengthy notes for a counterblast. Completion of Imperial Delhi as approved, he underlined, would assert to the world that Britain's position in India was "firm and durable." To his successor at Delhi, Hardinge directed letters and memoranda designed to stiffen his will.[12]

At Buckingham Palace, discovery of Curzon's newest proposals ignited the royal wrath, as its author had rightly foreseen. "Perfectly furious" on reading the document in early August, King George told Hardinge he would never consent to any diminution of the original program, so inextricably associated with his own person. A breach of the Durbar pledges, the King emphasized to Chelmsford, would be disastrous to British prestige among Indians, and he expected his new Viceroy to resist such folly.[13]

The Queen, who inspected the plans in Lutyens's Delhi office in London at 7 Apple Tree Yard (a mews behind St. James's Square), was "horribly shocked" to find designs for Government House had been reduced since their display at Balmoral three years before. She hastily summoned Austen Chamberlain to the Palace. Alterations initiated by financial stringency or the whims of successive Viceroys, she feared, might compromise the original completeness and convenience of the buildings.[14]

Hardinge deliberately fanned the flames of royal discontent, forwarding to the Palace photographs of Raisina taken in July. The King's Private Secretary sent a "most satisfactory" reply. Their Majesties, wrote Lord Stamfordham, were anxious that "nothing should be done in any way to reduce the work from its original design, even if it takes twenty years to complete." Shortly after returning Hardinge's photographs, the King sent a strongly worded letter to Chelmsford. New Delhi and its public buildings, he exhorted, should be "a landmark for all time" in the annals of the British Raj. He acknowledged that the war necessarily restricted available resources and caused long and inconvenient residence in temporary buildings. But he hoped a farsighted vision would inspire the incumbent Viceroys to carry out the original plans, without regard for the time needed. "For the honour of British rule in India," the completed scheme must be a noble one. At Hardinge's insistence, the Queen received Baker before his departure for India, expressly to demonstrate the royal couple's very real interest in Delhi. The King had already met with Lutyens at the Palace early in November.[15]

Chelmsford had made clear his attitude from the outset of his appointment. Even before leaving England, he had written Hailey that only the King could reverse the transfer, and although the war entailed reduced expenditure, he intended to see the project executed as well as was humanly possible. Once in India, he again impressed on Hailey the need to limit further annual spending on Delhi while at the same time preventing dispersal of expert staff and safeguarding extant work from deterioration. Sensitive to the importance of symbolic acts, Chelmsford pointedly visited Delhi first, then Calcutta, where he firmly told the plaintive Corporation that the change of capital was an accomplished fact.[16]

Curzon's memoranda did not shake the new Viceroy's convictions. He and his Council were unanimous: the move to Raisina could not be reversed. Completion would be postponed, Chelmsford told the King, but he did not propose amending the original plans "in any shape or form."[17]

Chamberlain's request for an opinion on future policy regarding Delhi elicited a militant, uncompromising reply from the Government of India, drafted by the tireless Hailey. Acknowledging the effects of the war, the Viceroy's Council declared (far too confidently) that even the transfer's most consistent critics now accepted Delhi as the winter capital of India. This fact effectively narrowed the discussion to the necessity and manner of modifying the arrangements approved in the project estimate. Despite the uncertain course of the war, the Council felt certain that Indian resources were adequate for execution of the initial scheme by 1924–25.

Members of the Viceroy's Council found the alternatives to completing the original designs to be unacceptable. To reduce the sanctioned accommodation at Raisina would mean sacrificing expenditure already incurred on the principal buildings as well as limiting the number of officers brought annually from Simla, thereby perpetually hampering the work of administration. The second, more drastic, option entailed wholesale abandonment of Raisina and the new cantonment for restricted quarters in the existing Civil Lines. Such a solution, the Viceroy's Council emphasized, could not fulfil the King's Durbar pledge of an Imperial city worthy of India. Instead Delhi would be "a mere temporary encampment," with Simla the real capital. Indians would judge the unfinished city at Raisina as humiliating testimony to British weakness: the forsaken foundations and thirty-six miles of desolate roads would be "a permanent monument of unstable policy and halting resolution."[18]

On February 13, 1917 at the India Office, Deputy Clerk James H. Seabrooke stamped "Approved Council," then neatly inscribed his initials on a draft of Public Works Despatch number seven, addressed to the Viceroy. The document represented a critical milestone: the Secretary of State had authorized continued construction of Imperial Delhi on the bold lines Lord Hardinge had early envisioned. A subsequent Secretary might be convinced of "the awful penalties of the migration to the hills" and label Delhi "a mistaken capital," but he would not resolve the question of how to "undo the city" the King-Emperor had founded. No man wished to leave as his legacy an unfinished capital on the Delhi plain.[19]

Nearly two years later, the sky over the new city blazed and crackled with bursts of fireworks, casting into relief the unfinished capital, whose edifices resembled the hoary remains of a moldering acropolis. Countless earthenware saucer lamps flickered and shone with magic effect, outlining prominent landmarks. A pair of huge bonfires, the work of officers from the Public Works Department and two Punjabi battalions, crowned Raisina, pillars of flame consuming the winter darkness.[20] After more than four years of unprecedented horrors, the Great War had ended.

By the end of the century's second decade, India was almost unrecognizable to those who had known her before the European hostilities. In 1913 Sir Guy Fleetwood Wilson had pictured Delhi as "the capital of a contented empire, the abode of peace and prosperity, of wise and prudent counsels." The same year, an

Indian representative in the Legislative Council had declared that his countrymen universally desired the appointment of a royal Viceroy. Another Councillor, Babu Surendra Nath Banerjee, had urged Government of India officials to discharge their duties in such a manner that all might feel, whether English, Scottish, Irish, or Indian, that they were *British*: "fellow citizens, participating in the privileges and also in the obligations of a common Empire," the greatest the world had ever seen.[21]

By the twenties, such sentiments seemed almost quaint, certainly singular, possibly obsequious. The prolonged war had made Britain appear less awesome in Indian eyes and the West much less a model for emulation. Exasperated by restrictions and wartime scarcity, impressed by the rhetoric and fact of the Russian Revolution as well as by Woodrow Wilson's call for democratic freedoms and self-determination, Indians had grown restive and expectant. Voluntary suspension of political criticism in India, coupled with fervent expressions of allegiance, had marked the outbreak of the war. But within seven months, a growing body of Legislative Councillors gave notice that the war's end must bring progress toward self-government and direct representation in the councils of the British Empire. Indians would anticipate "a substantial concession" of their demands, not as a reward for loyalty, but as a requirement of justice, a right owed to free citizens.[22]

By 1916 the moratorium was over; newly founded Home Rule Leagues had begun agitation and the Lucknow Pact signified Hindu-Muslim agreement on the goal of self-government. The considerable reforms proposed in the Montagu-Chelmsford report of April 1918 marked a genuine, if belated, Government response to mounting political pressure. But its salutary effect was undercut by the repressive Rowlatt bills, which crystallized anti-Government sentiment and propelled a forty-nine-year-old lawyer, Mohandas Karamchand Gandhi, to national prominence. Tension was running high in the Punjab, when in April 1919 General Reginald Dyer ordered troops to fire 1,605 rounds into an illegally assembled crowd at Amritsar, killing at least 379 persons and wounding over 1,200. The incident became as conspicuous a watershed in relations between Indians and Britons as the Mutiny of 1857. The aftermath, with its widespread racial bitterness, dissolved the assumptions and trust that had bound together the disparate civilizations of Britain's empire in India.

New voices in the legislative chamber, ever more strident in tenor, signalled difficult times for Imperial Delhi. The most trenchant opposition to the new city now came not from disgruntled ex-Viceroys or Europeans in Calcutta or British proponents of Indian arts, but from Indians themselves. Curzon's cannonry might be silent, but, as Chelmsford told the King, an attack had developed from a different quarter, a movement by "Indian politicals" to transfer the capital from Delhi back to Calcutta or to a suitable year-round site.

The Imperial Secretariat, intended as a temporary building in Old Delhi, provided the backdrop for lengthy discussions in the Legislative Council on February 11 and 18, 1920, initiated by Rao Bahadur B. N. Sarma's resolution that Government headquarters be "permanently located in one place" and that "a suitable centre . . . if necessary, be selected for the purpose." Members reiterated arguments familiar from the transfer controversy of 1912–13, but enactment of the Montagu-Chelmsford proposals as statute only weeks before in December cast the deliberations in a new light. In 1911, Sarma pointed out, parliamentary forms of government were considered outside the range of practical politics. Now the representative bodies created by the Act of 1919—a Legislative Assembly and a Council of State—were likely to have long, continuous sessions; they could not be distant from major centers of public opinion, and for reasons of convenience and expense they should no longer be nomadic. Declaring that the reforms had ushered in a new era, one Muslim Member supporting the resolution quoted James Russell Lowell's words to a well-known hymn: "New occasions teach new duties, time makes ancient good uncouth."[23]

Two days of largely repetitive speeches revealed substantial sentiment hostile to the expensive annual trek to Simla's Himalayan isolation as well as considerable annoyance with the new capital's defects. Delhi's critics were not limited to Calcutta: a Member from Madras moved the initial resolution, and support for the motion came from representatives of widely separated localities, including Assam and Bombay. Equally diverse, however, were the alternate sites advanced; there was no unanimity on that subject. Members suggested no less than fourteen: Calcutta, Bombay, Karachi, Ranchi, Allahabad, Poona, Dehra Dun, Mussoorie, Pachmarhi, Nasik, Jubbulpore, Betul, Chikalda, and the island of Salsette near Bombay. One speaker proposed permanent establishment of three or four capitals! Lutyens himself judged the Government's coming to Delhi, and keeping Simla, "a great mistake," but as he correctly perceived, no one would ever agree on another locality. As for the sanctity of the royal word, given at the Durbar, Members pointed out that the King-Emperor was a constitutional monarch who had simply been the victim of poor counsel from his advisers. An announcement by the Prince of Wales during his forthcoming visit to India could make right the mistake.[24]

Both European and Indian Members rose to oppose the resolution. Many of the complaints directed against Delhi, Sir Claude Hill suggested, derived from an understandable impatience with the discomforts of dusty tents after the "fleshpots of Calcutta." He reminded his colleagues that such conditions were but a temporary purgatory before realizing their long-awaited vision. Furthermore, Members had proposed a plethora of different locations, but Delhi was the only city whose historic traditions endowed it with a truly national character. Indeed one Muslim Councillor saw Delhi as a symbol of Hindu–Muslim unity.[25]

Sir Zulfikar Ali Khan chastised fellow Members for "floating in the airy regions of political romanticism." How could any responsible person, he asked, ignore the sums already spent on both Delhi and Simla, or those that would be required for yet another capital? Sir Dinshaw Wacha echoed this query. He, too, underlined the difficulty of getting all parties to agree about a perfect location. Even a dozen Diogeneses tramping all corners of India would never find it! Sachchidananda Sinha deemed an ideal twelve-month capital to be beyond "the range of practical politics." This conclusion, the Home Member hastened to affirm, possessed "great force."[26]

The King-Emperor was "almost appalled" to learn of Indian agitation to "disestablish" Delhi as capital, and he commended the Viceroy for his resolute adherence to the Durbar pronouncement. Chelmsford perceived no real alternative to Delhi and Simla, but he was equally certain that the attack on both capitals would be resumed in the legislative councils created by the Act of 1919.[27] His prophecy was to prove correct, but the preponderant sentiments in the ensuing debates must surely have surprised him.

Despite a boycott by the powerful Congress Party, elections in November 1920 sent 106 Members to the Legislative Assembly; the full complement comprised a further forty nominated Members, including twenty-five officials. The Council of State, a new upper house of sixty-one "elder statesmen" representing a limited electorate of major landowners, was designed to review and revise the Assembly's acts.

On the morning of February 9, 1921, in the temporary Secretariat built north of Shahjahanabad, the Duke of Connaught inaugurated the first session of these two assemblies, heralding "the awakening of a great nation to the power of its nationhood." Three days later, in laying the foundation stone of the legislative chambers, [35] the King-Emperor's seventy-year-old uncle emphasized the symbolic importance of the occasion: it marked India's entry on the path of responsible government with an edifice destined to be as noble and imposing as the Dominion Parliament Houses, the Viceregal residence and Secretariats on top of Raisina Hill, or indeed any historic monument on the subcontinent. The Duke's text, attractive to the vanity as well as the generous spirit of Indians, was the work of Herbert Baker and Sir Valentine Chirol, both keenly aware of the agitation to abandon Imperial Delhi or economize in its construction. The speech conjured visions of the Athenian acropolis, the Capitol at Rome, and proud Oriental cities of antiquity, asserting that every great civilization had created its enduring and tangible records. His Royal Highness was hopeful the new city might become worthy of India's "future greatness," one of the splendid national capitals that would link peoples of the farflung Empire under the aegis of the British Crown.[28]

As Lord Chelmsford had predicted, Members of the first Legislative Assembly were quick to propose reducing expenditure on the new Delhi. The prompt introduction on March 16 of a motion for retrenchment, however, abruptly encountered determined Indian opposition, with European support. One Indian representative deplored the slow progress made during "seven weary years" and bluntly asked for "more speed." Another urged completion "as early as possible." The Bombay Parsi magnate, Sir Jamsetjee Jeejeebhoy, declared that "no expense should be spared" to create a truly Imperial capital, while Chaudhuri Shabab-ud-Din told his compatriots that they should, "like true Indians, contribute liberally" to finishing the city. Concluding the debate, Sir Sydney Crookshank, Secretary to the

35. Foundation stone of the Council House or Indian legislative chambers, laid February 12, 1921. Inscription in Hindi, English, and Urdu.

Public Works Department, painted a picture for Members of a city equal to any in the world, admired by all, the symbol of India's position as "the head partner" in the greatest empire in history. Given increased financing, the work could be completed in five rather than eight years. Repeated official appeals to Indian pride, plus the continued discomfort of tents and temporary offices, evidently had a persuasive effect: the motion to reduce funds for the new Delhi failed.[29]

One week later, a resolution by J. K. N. Kabraji to expedite execution of the new capital "in the interests of economy and of general convenience" was adopted after relatively little discussion. Chaudhuri Wajid Hussain expressed a near-unanimous opinion: the capital of an empire embracing one-fifth of the human race, he declared, should not be an assemblage of unfinished buildings. An accelerated program won general acceptance; debate principally concerned the means of financing construction, whether from revenue surpluses, or a lottery, or loans, the method Lutyens himself preferred. The motion's swift adoption by the predominantly Indian Assembly furnished encouragement and useful ammunition to supporters of the new Delhi for the battles ahead. The Secretary of State, Edwin Montagu, who frankly regarded the Delhi project "with the gravest possible misgiving," was obliged to acknowledge the scheme's important popularity with the Indian legislature. Malcolm Hailey, now Finance Member in the Viceroy's Council and normally an apostle of austerity, was emboldened to consider a regular program of more rapid construction. He confessed to Herbert Baker that he had deliberately avoided prompting the Assembly, letting it "whip itself into excitement" because of his stringency—thereby strengthening his position when compelled to foot the bill.[30]

By March 1921, Government House was nearly one-third finished, the Secretariat blocks roughly two-fifths, and residences about three-fifths completed. The Central Vista or King's Way, planted and cleaned, looked "imperially spacious," and the Great Place, the plaza at the foot of Raisina Hill, was well advanced. Construction of the Secretariat facades had been rushed to make an impressive showing for the Duke of Connaught, and except for the scaffolding, the simple mass loomed on top of its hill like the ruins at Persepolis, colored red. This attempt to create an illusion of greater accomplishment than actually existed Lutyens found disgusting. Such a policy he thought ungentlemanly and not likely to produce sound building. Money should be spent only "for the good of the work," to improve it, "not to make fools of the public." Postwar architecture on the subcontinent, Lutyens had astutely observed a year earlier, was the British "swan song," and he prayed it might be "a good tune, well sung," a tribute to the dignity both of Britain and India. He could not help noting the parallels with another imperial saga: he was engrossed nightly now in Edward Gibbon's *Decline and Fall of the Roman Empire*.[31]

Despite the brave show for the Duke's visit, the architects found the work on their buildings in early 1921 "practically stopped" and "very behindhand," with funds spent principally on bungalows and hostels for the numerous legislators. Baker lamented the "cold fit," with the Government apparently afraid of the new councils and their Members in turn afraid of taking responsibility. His designs for the Council House had been ready for a year, yet only the ceremonial stone had been laid. To both architects' dismay, plans had even been suggested to effect economies by finishing the capitol buildings in plaster rather than stone.[32]

Postwar prices of labor, materials, equipment, and freight continued the spiral begun in 1914–18. The Chief Engineer for Delhi, Hugh Keeling, submitted a revised project estimate in January 1921, amounting to 129,180,000 rupees or nearly Rs. 1,292 lakhs, some forty per cent more than his prewar estimate of Rs. 917 lakhs. Expansion of the building program, in order to house the new legislatures and provide their Members with residences, added to the effect of rising costs, compelled this substantial revision. Keeling warned of variables that could alter the estimates yet again, such as a protracted construction period, further price increases, and continued political unrest.[33]

By the next year the Government of India had already introduced changes raising the estimate to Rs. 1,307 lakhs. Of this amount, Rs. 223 lakhs represented increases in the cost of labor and materials brought by the war; Rs. 141 lakhs, additions to the building program required by the political reforms; and Rs. 26 lakhs (less than three per cent of the initial estimate), items not foreseen in 1913. From the outset, the Government's aim was not to create a fully equipped city in the widest sense, but to confine the scope of estimates to those offices and houses, plus services and public amenities, deemed necessary to the effective occupation of new headquarters. Further construction, commercial and residential, and institutions not critical to the function of the Government, such as a university or central research institute, were left to private enterprise.

Eighty-five lakhs of rupees were spent by the end of 1913–14, but during the six years 1914–15 to 1919–20, expenditure was severely restricted, varying between Rs. 39 and Rs. 54 lakhs per annum. Following postwar reorganization, spending rose to Rs. 129.5 lakhs in 1920–21 and Rs. 142.5 in 1921–22, and the Government allocated Rs. 204 lakhs for 1922–23.[34]

Inevitably, given its costliness, the new capital project drew criticism throughout its long construction. Even the Prince of Wales voiced his censure. On February 16, 1922, the future sovereign of British India concluded a three-month tour of the subcontinent to the flourish of trumpets and roll of drums. From beneath a golden canopy in Shah Jahan's Diwan-i-Am at Delhi, the young heir apparent acknowledged greetings and homage of some fifty bejewelled princes and chiefs and 5,000 other notables, including both the Council of State and Legislative Assembly. A mellow sunset, then wintry twilight, illuminated this splendid Imperial Durbar, fated to be the last in India's long history.[35]

King George's triumphant Coronation Durbar had ended amid the blaze of high noon; now the red orb of the sun which sank quickly in the evening sky seemed a harbinger of a different destiny. Rousing and often touching outbursts of loyalty had marked the King-Emperor's progress a decade before. By contrast his son's arrival in Bombay was the focus of Indian National Congress demonstrations that provoked serious rioting and produced fifty-three deaths.

Accompanied by the Viceroy and Vicereine and principal architects, and apparently nervous, self-conscious, and bored, the Prince toured India's new capital privately. Baker thought he evinced "little imagination or interest" concerning the design of the Secretariats, and his only remark on being shown a model of

Government House was an exclamatory "Good God!" But there was a flash of that independence of mind which would one day stun the world: he told Baker that the Delhi project, so dear to King George's heart, was a waste of money—and should be stopped. Afterward, Lutyens remarked wryly that the Prince was "pleasant to look at."[36]

Attacks on the new capital scheme in the press, both Indian and English, continued with vehemence, even vituperation. In London the well-known author and correspondent, Edmund Candler, wrote in the *Observer* of his astonishment that the "sinful" and "frivolous" outlay on New Delhi was so rarely condemned as a crime against the sumptuary laws. Sir Krishna Gupta, who had been a Member of the Council of India in London from 1907 to 1915, redoubled the offensive in the *Observer*'s columns. Delhi's purported climatic advantage over Calcutta, he asserted, had proved unfounded, and he favored designating Simla as the year-round capital. Gupta's attitude toward the new city was not surprising, given his birth in Dacca and his distinguished career in Bengal, but his recent and important service at the India Office lent weight to his remarks. Another noteworthy foe of the Delhi scheme, Dr. Hari Singh Gour, had quickly earned a reputation as a persistent financial watchdog in the Legislative Assembly. His appointment as the first Vice-Chancellor of Delhi University did not mute his criticism of expenditure on an arid site he considered wholly unsuitable for a permanent capital. Delhi's historic associations, he declared in May 1922, were insuffient to compensate for its disadvantages, particularly its notorious unhealthiness and isolation from public opinion. Nor was it more central than many other places in India. As he had suggested to the Legislative Assembly the previous year, at least five plateaus (two of them at 4,000 feet) were both accessible and habitable. But he thought Calcutta was the natural capital; should no better site be agreed upon, he urged the Government's return to its former seat. These theses had an air of déja vu a decade after the Coronation Durbar announcements, but their proponents seemed, if anything, even more obdurate, especially as India's serious postwar economic plight worsened.[37]

An unprecedented financial situation confronted the subcontinent, reflected in five successive budget deficits and the scant success accorded Indian loans on the London market. Then, in March 1921, the Earl of Reading, whose remarkable career spanned a gamut from ship's cabin boy to Lord Chief Justice, succeeded Chelmsford as Viceroy. Frustrated in his initial attempts to reduce military expenditure, Reading welcomed the Secretary of State's appointment of a committee for Indian retrenchment headed by his friend Lord Inchcape. Chairman of the Peninsular and Oriental Steam Navigation Company, the famed P&O, Inchcape had been Lord Morley's candidate to succeed Minto as Viceroy. For thirteen years he had played a pivotal role on the Council of India in London. The Indian Government at the same time directed another committee to prepare an independent report on changes in the New Delhi project that might reduce its cost and expedite its completion. The model for both enquiries, the "axe committee," chaired by Sir Eric Geddes from August 1921 to February 1922, had proposed drastic economies in British national expenditure, eventually totalling £120 million. Lord Inchcape had been a member.

While Baker thought the Viceroy and his wife seemed "keen on Delhi," Lord

Reading in fact always thought the change in capital a decision of dubious wisdom, and he scanned expenditure on the city (his son recorded) "with a jealous and critical eye, alert to seize any opportunity to reduce it." The New Capital Enquiry Committee, over which the recently knighted Malcolm Hailey presided from November 1 to 12, 1922, concluded that total spending need not exceed Rs. 1,292 lakhs, including Rs. 42 lakhs for loss from currency exchange. This was a substantial reduction when compared with the most recent project estimate of Rs. 1,307 lakhs, which included no allowance for loss by exchange. Economy and expedition were considered virtually synonymous. To speed up the work, the Committee recommended increasing the capacity of the Raisina stoneyard, hastening the architects' production of detailed plans, enlarging the powers of their representatives when the architects were absent, and avoiding the lapse of unspent grants by their automatic reappropriation the following year—a system Lutyens had advocated for a decade. These suggestions, if accepted, would have insured completion of the bulk of the work by October 1925 and the remaining work a year later.[38]

The "Delhi axe committee" had left him "fairly well alone," Lutyens told his wife with relief after the investigation, and he paid tribute to the Public Works Member, B. N. Sarma, for his defense of the new capital scheme. The unanimous report did not tell the whole story, however, for evidently the committee had been sharply divided, with four Indians opposing four Britons. The latter, Lutyens wrote home, gave sympathetic support to the Chief Engineer, acknowledging that they could not seriously criticize a project in ten days that had cost millions of pounds over ten years. But one Member divulged that, before falling into line, the four Indians had proposed giving Baker's Council House commission to several Indian architects, each responsible for a portion. Furthermore, they had suggested a moratorium on Delhi until a handful of Indian architects could tour the world—beginning with the parkways of Kansas City—to report to the Government of India on international city planning![39]

The Inchcape Committee, whose deliberations followed directly on the heels of the Hailey inquiry, posed a more serious threat to the Delhi project. A former President of the Bengal Chamber of Commerce, Lord Inchcape thought (predictably) the transfer from Calcutta was "a consummate blunder," the new city itself "monstrous," "a veritable white elephant," deserted seven months a year and maintained only at colossal cost. On the subject of expense, he agreed with the Commander-in-Chief, General Lord Rawlinson, who was "tempted to curse and swear" when he passed the huge palace being built for the Viceroy. Small wonder Lord Hardinge was "rather frightened about the Inchcape axe." But the King-Emperor had personally intervened to warn that there must be "no lopping" of New Delhi's budget. And despite his adamant dislike of the scheme, Inchcape realized that by March 1923 the gross outlay on the city totaled Rs. 841 lakhs, or nearly nine crores (£6 million), while Rs. 531 lakhs (£3·5 million), or less than forty percent of the project estimate, remained still to be spent. He confessed to Lord Curzon that the Government of India had "gone too far" for him to suggest abandonment.[40] Cries for economy would persist, but serious challenges to New Delhi's actual existence were now history.

Repeated suggestions to abandon the capital, however, had created an understandable timorousness among private real estate developers and prospective retail merchants. Even those Delhiwallahs who worked at Raisina preferred to return nightly to familiar alleys behind Shahjahanabad's protective walls. A few reluctantly agreed to purchase land in order to please their official superiors. The first general store, opened by an ambitious Parsi, closed several months later for lack of customers. Early houses and communal "chummeries" stood amid haunts of jackals and wild pigs. A solitary theater, the Regal Cinema, seemed but the newest of Delhi's countless mausolea, often with less than a half-dozen patrons, whom the proprietors begged to accept a refund and leave. Freehold sites in the principal shopping district, Connaught Circus, carved out of a forest of kikar trees, sold for two rupees a square yard. Forty years later the price for leasehold was two hundred times that amount. As Lord Curzon had predicted, the capitol at Raisina retained an artificial, isolated appearance, much like the Summer Palace of the Chinese Emperor some six miles from the walls of Peking.[41]

Responsibility for building the new city throughout its checkered career was vested in a sequence of bodies. After the Secretary of State sanctioned the Imperial Delhi Committee's project estimate on June 15, 1914, financial and technical control over each part of the large program lay not with the Government of India but with the five committee members. Although nominally large, their powers were in practice restricted because piecemeal construction required previous reference to the Government of India on all major points. This fact, plus the preaudit of all expenditure on the new city, rendered a financial officer superfluous. Accordingly on December 8, 1916, the Secretary of State approved a request of the Governor-General in Council to dissolve the Committee and delegate its powers (with some restrictions) to the Chief Commissioner of Delhi, effective April 1, 1917. At this juncture, W. H. Nicholls, the Architect Member, sought and received permission to return to the Government post he had vacated in Madras nearly four years before. Although Nicholls had been anxious to do the right thing and willing to learn, Lutyens felt he had perpetrated blunders and "ugly errors," largely by his loyal and literal adherence to Government orders. Lutyens was hopeful about the replacement, E. Montague Thomas, architect of the temporary Secretariat in Civil Lines, whom he judged to be "able" and tending "to the *grande* manner" he himself now favored.[42]

After the war, proposals to revive the Imperial Delhi Committee and simplify its procedures and correspondence led to the official creation of a "New Capital Committee" during the winter of 1919–20. Organized for more expeditious despatch of work, and exercising powers equivalent to the Government of India, the new body's functions exceeded those of its predecessor. Moreover, inclusion of the Member and Secretary for Public Works (later Industries and Labor), in addition to an officer of the Finance Department, gave the central Government a direct and more representative voice on the Committee. Assignment of certain powers of sanction to the Chief Commissioner of Delhi saved the Committee from many petty details. Responsible for both the engineering and construction at Raisina, the Chief Engineer exercised administrative control over budgets and furnished the Committee with explanatory notes about all items requiring their approval. Furthermore he dealt directly with Lutyens and Baker as the agent of their client, the

Government of India. Within the Chief Engineer's office, an Architectural Branch held responsibility for designing all Government buildings not specifically entrusted to the two English architects.[43]

In a rare moment of approbation, Lutyens pronounced the new arrangements "much more sensible," with adequate discussion so that matters were brought to committee only for formal resolution. Even the files were reduced! Altogether he felt "in better heart," particularly as he began to discern a new respect at Raisina for his architectural judgment.[44]

As first Chief Engineer of Delhi, Hugh Keeling grew to be, in Lutyens's words, the "veritable mother" of the new city and of "all who worked for it." Able, experienced, and adept at handling people, he exacted as professional a performance as feasible from his subordinates. Public Works officers organized the provision of materials, transport, and equipment, while Indian contractors supplied thousands of laborers. Hindu, Sikh, and Muslim, this remarkable fraternity of contractors for the most part had only modest means, little education, and no acquaintance with construction. Shrewd and industrious, they quickly learned both pidgin English and the building trade, and their bold investments in desolate land at Raisina made them millionaires.[45]

Among the first of these pioneers were Sindhis from northwest India. Seth Haroun helped to build Government House. Lachman Das, who took a major part in constructing the legislative chambers, was renowned for his honesty: he used good materials, paid his workers promptly, and did not even cheat on his income tax. Aggressive Punjabis early shared the initiative. The peasant Narain Singh, active in the Coronation Durbar arrangements, subsequently built most roads at the new Delhi, many bureaucrats' bungalows, and foundations for the Viceregal residence. Baisakha Singh, who came from an obscure village in the Amritsar district, rose from overseer to become contractor for the North Block of the Secretariats and a host of official bungalows. Similarly, a humble beginning as an overseer proved no impediment to Dharam Singh Sethi, whose wealth (and munificence) at his death had few equals among Delhi's builders. Two Punjabi Muslims also attained eminence at Raisina: Akbar Ali from Jhelum, who built the National Archives, and Nawab Ali of Rohtak, who had a principal role in creating the Viceroy's Mughal Garden.

Conspicuous among the successful were Sujan Singh and his son Sobha Singh, from a family already exceptional among builders when they came to Delhi, by virtue of both their wealth and experience. They owned land and a camel transport business in the Punjab and had helped construct the state's railways. Sobha Singh acted as contractor for the South Block, Viceroy's Court and the Great Place, the War Memorial Arch, Baroda Palace, and innumerable residences. Like other farsighted pioneers, he acquired unpromising wilderness land at open auction and later reaped handsome rewards. He gave loyal service to both the New Delhi Municipal Committee and the Council of State. As the last bittersweet flourishes sounded for British rule, a knighthood crowned his remarkable career.[46]

For thousands of other Indians, the new Delhi spelled neither fortune nor renown but at least gave eagerly sought employment. When a maund of wheat

36. Seth Haroun-al-Rashid, contractor for most of Government House, New Delhi.

37. At Government House, peasants toiling to build a palace.

38. An army of coolies at work on Government House, New Delhi.

39. Men and women working shoulder to shoulder to build New Delhi.

41. Workers on the site of the Government House gardens and tennis courts.

42. An Indian infant awaiting his meal on the construction site among the baskets and shoes of his elders.

(about twenty-five pounds) sold for four rupees, male coolies received eight annas (half a rupee) a day, women six annas, and boys four annas. Housed in Government camps, these unskilled workers, bagris from Rajasthan and the more robust bandhanis from the Punjab, were provided with good water, latrines, and free medical care. Nearly two decades of building never witnessed a single strike. Once during a "labor famine" in the germinal stages of the project in 1913, when local Delhi coolies demanded two to three times the normal wage, the Salvation Army suggested importing "thousands of 'Crims'" to meet the need. Their tasks completed, the convicts would be removed at once to an existing site designated "Crim Canaan" in remote Assam. The proposal was not approved.[47]

At the outset of construction before the war, the Public Works Department employed an army of 29,000 workers. But during wartime, and as the project neared completion, their numbers dwindled dramatically: in 1916 there were 8,000, and in 1925, 15,000. Mostly cultivators by profession, they often disappeared to their homes at planting and harvest time. All day their monotonous chant—"haisa, haisa"—mingled with the pit, pit, pit, of the stonecutters and the background roar of the stoneyard ara-masheen or power saws. Workers by the score scrambled up primitive ladders with as many as thirteen bricks on their heads, then received a given number of cowrie shells per load for later redemption. When darkness fell, the songs of Rajasthani women returning to their camps filled the tranquil evening air. Tiny infants, who began existence tied to a brick at the building site, grew to take part in raising the city. In turn they, too, labored in the ancient manner of their forebears who built capitals for Akbar and Shah Jahan.[48]

40. Primitive ladders and scaffolding adorning the half-built Garden Loggia at Government House.

The sangtarash or stonecutters, from Agra, Mirzapur, and Bharatpur, could likewise often claim descent from those who had built the Mughal monuments. In the busiest years, over 2,500 masons sat on their haunches in the Indian fashion, dressing and carving stone and marble, while thirteen horizontal saws, four diamond saws, twelve planers, and seven lathes worked around the clock in a stoneyard reputed to be the world's largest. W. B. Cairns, a Scot who had been foreman on Baker's Pretoria buildings, together with a handful of other British stonemasons, supervised the work of the vast yard (its buildings alone covered twenty-two acres) from its inception in July 1915.[49]

In such other trades as joinery or plumbing or electrical wiring, a few foremen, selected from among the best in Britain, trained and guided thousands of Indian workmen. Lutyens, for one, depended heavily on these foremen, and in gratitude he gave an annual dinner in their honor. But he grieved that there were so few such men. As Government House neared completion, he complained angrily that there was "not near enough skilled supervision" and that he hated to leave the palace to "hooligans" to finish in the summer of 1929. He bemoaned the Public Works Department methods and "want of decent knowledge": everyone was "all thumbs & wits of dough." Haste at the last moment had given Indians their "chance to do shoddy work." "They smash 50% of what they do," he growled, citing 3,000 broken panes of glass in the Viceroy's residence alone. No one could achieve good work in India "without power of life and death" over the workers. It was, he fumed, "a heartbreaking country." His bitterness lingered. Years later he continued to tell the tale of an Indian mason who tried to alter his template to fit a badly cut stone: the man had been rehired shortly after discharge because he had exhibited that rare commodity, "a dawning intelligence."[50]

Output at the quarries and Raisina stoneyard was crucial, for the rate of supply was a major determinant of the rate of construction, as Lord Hardinge had early discovered. Government House and the other capital buildings were constructed of Vindhyan stone from the upper Bhandar strata. The red as well as the whitish-buff sandstone selected by the architects had been used by Akbar and Shah Jahan in their buildings and came from Dholpur, Bharatpur, and Agra quarries. Akbar's sixteenth-century methods were still standard procedure, and efforts to cut stone in larger quantities by opening deep-faced pits proved fruitless. Although the supply of sandstone was more than ample, there was no consistent color or quality within even short distances. In Dholpur, trial-and-error quarrying to locate satisfactory stone took place over a radius of six miles from Barauli. Broad-gauge railways eventually transported about six million cubic feet of stone some 115 miles to the new Delhi for preparation at the stoneyard.[51]

Altogether, 100,000 cubic feet of handsome Indian marble were used to decorate the central or capital buildings. White marble came from Shah Jahan's quarries at Makrana in Jodhpur and from Alwar, green marble from Baroda and Ajmer, black from Bhaislana and Gaya, gray from Marwar, and pink from Alwar, Makrana, and Haripur. Yellow marble from Jaisalmer had to be transported for forty miles over trackless desert, which limited the size of each block to a camel's capacity. Red Italian marble in the Durbar Hall was the only stone imported. Local Delhi quartzite, which was to have been dug extensively behind Government House,

43. The east portico of Government House rising amid an array of derricks and dressed stone.

44. Stonecutters preparing the plinth of the Jaipur Column in the forecourt of Government House.

46. Coolies loading their bricks.

proved very difficult to work and was used only for concrete and for road paving.[52]

Indigenous woods as well as marbles were prominent in the decoration of the central buildings. Teak from the Central Provinces and Burma, durable and elegant, was widely used, but others employed with effect were Bombay blackwood, a rich red padauk, and shisham. For furniture, Indian cabinetmakers used these same woods, as well as ainee, poon, koko, Kashmiri walnut, and ebony, and about ten other varieties in small quantities. Antique English furniture imported as an experiment deteriorated rapidly in the extremes of Indian temperatures and humidity.[53]

South of the city, suitable clay was found for bricks, which ranked second in use to stone as a building material at Raisina. Construction of the project used about 700 million, nearly all of them from the twenty-two Government kilns. The brickfields connected directly to the thirty-inch-gauge Imperial Delhi Railway that traversed the capital site. A freight station at Barakhamba linked this sixty-mile system with the Great Indian Peninsula broad-gauge railway from the distant quarries. In all, the tiny Delhi transport division carried five million tons of material, not only stone and bricks but also sand from the Jumna, manure from the city dumping grounds, and fertile earth for splendid new gardens. As they chugged and squealed their way ceaselessly around the city, day and night, the I.D.R. locomotives were a visible link with the vast network of rails which sprawled over the subcontinent as proudly as Rome's highways had once crossed Europe. Yet by uniting Indians as never before, railways helped hasten the momentum of change destined to end British rule.[54]

For over a dozen years, during the terms of three Viceroys, Hugh Keeling was the stage manager of Imperial Delhi's complex production. His post as Chief Engineer crowned nearly four decades' service in India, the last five years after his retirement in 1920, when he was deemed indispensable and reengaged. Small wonder that farewell entertainment, organized in his honor at Raisina's Great Place by admiring colleagues, inspired comparison with royal Durbar receptions at Delhi Fort. Fireworks showering overhead reflected in the Central Vista's waterways, filled for the first time, while myriad lights suffused the fountains with color and sparkled in the trees and shrubbery. Brightly floodlit against the darkened sky, the Secretariat buildings towered above the scene, a grandiose theatrical set of imperial proportions. For the new Delhi, a happy outcome seemed within reach: the first occupation of Secretariat offices had begun in October 1924, five months before.[55]

Alexander Rouse, Keeling's successor as Chief Engineer and Member of the New Capital Committee, had been Superintending Engineer of the new city. He promptly submitted the draft of a second revised project estimate in May 1926. The completed estimate, presented in July, amounted to Rs. 1,419 lakhs, some Rs. 127 lakhs more than the first revision in 1921. Official causes given for this excess fell in three categories: supplementary items, underestimates or cost increases (particularly in rates for stone), and protracted building time. Supplements to the first revised estimate had already been approved for marble interiors and a Mughal garden at Government House, for portions of the Secretariats not originally intended for use, for additional housing for Government employees, and for preparing further sites for the ruling princes. Other added expenses included insurance against delays in completion, an extended water supply system, and loss on currency exchange. Cost increases, compounded with underestimates, accounted for further spending on Government House and the Secretariats, notably for stone but also for electrical and sanitary services. The prolonged construction period, moreover, effected a larger commission for the principal architects as well as unexpected outlays for Public Works Department staff and equipment.[56]

In February 1916, by his authority as Chief Commissioner, Malcolm Hailey had created the Raisina Municipal Committee. At first that entity had few activities beyond distributing Government educational grants and collecting a trifling income from such sources as tonga licenses and cattle trespass fines. But a full-fledged Imperial Delhi Municipal Committee of ten appointed Members, established by the Chief Commissioner in April 1925, hastily widened its sphere of responsibility. Both the New Capital Committee and Public Works Department rapidly transferred many administrative functions to the civic body, whose income and spending grew markedly. Imposition of a house tax, effective from January 1, 1926, and appointment of a full-time Secretary, were measures of both practical and symbolic importance: the new municipality had come of age.[57]

Of equal symbolic importance was the capital's new name. On November 9, 1926, officers charged with administering the city met to consider details of its future governance. Suggestions for a suitable designation included Raisina, New Delhi, and Delhi South, but the conference came to no agreement. Action in London, however, was decisive. Fifteen years after announcing a fresh capital for his Indian Empire, the King-Emperor approved a formal change in the city's name: Imperial

Delhi officially became New Delhi. The act was a measure of the real distance from 1911.[58]

Three years later, King George decreed yet another new name, to Lutyens's rapturous delight. Government House became Viceroy's House, making it unique among residences for Britain's imperial proconsuls. Immensely pleased, Lutyens wrote to his wife of the King's edict four different times![59]

This gratifying sign of royal approbation capped growing public approval of the capital project. As early as 1920, Lutyens recorded that Delhi had come alive and begun "to interest everybody." By 1925 the unfinished Viceroy's palace was "beginning to have a success," with many persons asking to see it. Distinguished visitors, when shown over the building three years later, appeared "overwhelmed with its beauty." Then finally, in February 1929, ten months before its occupation, Lutyens wrote contentedly that "everyone seems to like Viceroy's House."[60]

Reading's successor, Lord Irwin, and his wife [48] were among the most appreciative. From the outset, Lutyens found them a joy to work with; they were simple and unaffected, genuinely interested, and even deferential! Irwin showed great ability, and his extraordinary spiritual qualities and highly charming manner appealed to Briton and Indian alike. "One can say anything!" Lutyens noted with

47. Laying the last stone of the dome, Government House, April 6, 1929. Center row, left to right, Teja Singh Malik, Public Works Department; Sir Alexander Rouse, Chief Engineer; Lord Irwin (wearing hat); Sir John Simon; and Arthur Gordon Shoosmith, Lutyens's resident representative.

46. Hoisted to the dome of Government House, April 6, 1929. Back row, extreme left and center, Sir John (later first Viscount) Simon and Lady Irwin.

48. Dorothy Evelyn Augusta Wood, first Lady Irwin (later first Countess of Halifax), Vicereine of India, 1926–31.

astonishment, adding "I feel happier than I have ever been with Delhi." This remarkable harmony increased with time. Eventually either the Viceroy or Vicereine visited the building site every day, full of support and eager to take up residence. On one occasion, Irwin said "splendid" seven times in the Durbar Hall, and described the Mughal Garden as "too lovely for words." He told Lutyens the more he saw of the great house, the more he liked it.[61]

At this final, critical stage, the Irwins' imaginative vision and creative assistance were an enormous boon to New Delhi, and especially to the Viceregal palace. The Vicereine labored continuously to help design the furnishings and order materials in both Britain and India. Lord Irwin's attentiveness proved constantly useful, for, not surprisingly, there was "a better spirit" at the Public Works Department when His Excellency personally wanted a task done! Even in Lutyens's battle against economy, the Viceroy came to his aid. Few architects can have had clients so understanding. The Irwins' rapport with Lutyens contributed in rare measure to the abiding achievement at Raisina.[62]

# 7

# Quarrel at Raisina

The face of New Delhi might well have been different had harmony prevailed between the two principal architects. But early in their Indian partnership, incipient distrust was swiftly transformed to feelings of betrayal, and cooperation between Lutyens and Baker was tragically destroyed. Lutyens's crucial support for Baker's association with the capital city had of course not been an act of pure altruism. Lutyens saw that the proposed collaboration promised to enhance his own opportunities at New Delhi, and that given Hardinge's original four-year deadline, he could not possibly design everything himself. He had, moreover, pleasant memories of Baker's helpfulness on his visit to South Africa and of their youthful friendship, and the prospect of shared enthusiasms and a sympathetic exchange of ideas (notably lacking in his married life) excited him. "I do wish you were with us," he wrote to Baker while en route to India. "What fun it would be!" And a month later in Delhi he confided, "I often think of you & want you here."[1]

When Baker returned to England from Africa, Lutyens offered him use of his office and the hospitality of his home. In India their partnership began auspiciously: the two architects agreed "on all big points." The fellowship and conversation Lutyens so relished left him exhausted but happy. "It is such fun," he wrote delightedly. Baker was "so gentle & wise" that his presence was a great strength and joy. But their first difference, when Baker favored the northern site for the capital, elicited comments from Lutyens that augured ill. While his company was a "great comfort," Lutyens thought his colleague treated architecture less seriously than he did himself, making its practice "the handmaiden of sentiment."[2]

Rejection of a northern Ridge site and the choice of Raisina Hill provoked a decision in March 1913 destined to poison relations between the two architects for three decades. Baker, who had so often built effectively on an eminence in South Africa, suggested placing the Secretariats not at the foot of Raisina, but on the same elevated platform as Government House, conspicuously crowning the hill. The administrative and executive powers would then together form "one composition expressing unity in the instrument of Government." Despite additional costs and compounded difficulties in fitting buildings to the site, Lutyens promptly agreed to sign a joint letter outlining this proposal. Sent to Lord Hardinge on March 8, the document was replete with the historical imagery and political symbolism so characteristic of Baker.[3]

Hardinge had early envisioned the Viceregal residence in solitary majesty atop Raisina, seen from every part of the city. He nevertheless accepted the architects' scheme as possessing "inherent merit," but he was keenly aware that Government House would thereby sacrifice its exclusive dominance to "the intervening Secretariat buildings." No one implied, however, that Government House should be seen without interruption along any road. Three years later Hardinge was to write that it had been "perfectly obvious" that the crest of Raisina Hill would obscure Government House for part of the processional route. Certainly, a perspective sketch prepared by W. H. Nicholls after the architects' departure in March 1913 and exhibited to the pertinent authorities in India during the summer, made this fact abundantly clear even to the layman. But Hardinge had judged such a defect of "trivial importance" once he had surrendered his principle of universal visibility for Government House.[4]

The effects of this hasty, fateful decision are evident to this day. Approaching Government House on the King's Way, the visitor begins to lose sight of the monumental portico a half-mile from the brow of Raisina Hill, while at the Great Place he sees merely the palace dome above the rise. Finally even this is wholly obliterated until he reaches the crest of the inclined way leading to Government Court and its flanking Secretariat blocks. Similarly, from the Viceregal portico there is no view of the Great Place, at the foot of the hill, and the processional avenue cannot be discerned before its midpoint. [49, 50]

Lutyens perceived none of this. The capitol site selected, and its treatment agreed upon, he sought desperately to complete the final town planning report and to revise his plans for Government House before leaving Delhi on March 21. He had not only to reduce the rooms from an eight to seven ratio and the building from thirteen to eight and a half million cubic feet to meet Hardinge's budget, but also to design a higher dome and substructure to suit the Viceroy's wishes. The new palace site moreover was some 400 yards further west. For Keeling, Lutyens prepared eleven drawings necessary for preliminary estimates, and for Viceregal comments and criticism he roughed out five sketches of Government House. As if this intensive regime were not exhausting enough, he contracted a painful and highly fatiguing stomach ailment.[5]

Baker's chalk perspectives depicted his area of responsibility as officially defined on March 11. A rendering of the Secretariats, looking west, was among those the Viceroy viewed with general approval after lunch on March 17. In Baker's diary that day a thumbnail sketch showed the east facade of Government House as seen from the Great Place, looming between the Secretariats. Five days later the two architects were steaming toward Aden, working amicably together on the captain's bridge deck, in agreement on "the general disposition" of the central buildings. In London, their contract was drafted and considered at the India Office before Baker left for South Africa.[6]

Only one or two small clouds darkened the new Delhi's bright sunrise, hinting at the impending storm. In the summer of 1913, Lord Pentland, Governor of Madras, inspected the architects' chalk drawings with some dismay: clearly, he observed, Government House should have been built as first intended at Point A, now site of the Secretariats. Criticism in October from *Town Planning Review*, conspicuous as a proponent of the Grand Manner, was equally candid. The journal's perceptive editors—Patrick Abercrombie, C. H. Reilly, and S. D. Adshead—declared that the

49. Half a mile from Raisina Hill on King's Way, New Delhi, the portico of Government House disappears behind the brow of the inclined way between Herbert Baker's Secretariat blocks.

50. From the Great Place, only the dome of Lutyens's Government House is visible.

Delhi Town Planning Committee design did not bear careful scrutiny: the more closely its plan was studied, the more obvious its defects. Chief among these was the arrangement of the capitol. How reluctantly the Secretariat blocks separated to allow a view of Viceroy's House from the Central Vista! Above all, how pitifully the Viceregal palace, partially hidden from the approaching visitor by Raisina Hill, cried out to be acclaimed the climax of King's Way! Wholly absent, mourned the editors, was anything akin to that "majestic dominance" of the Capitol Building among Washington's public edifices. Rather than a single satisfying whole, a unified conception, the crowning feature at Delhi presented two perversely severed halves.[7]

Baker's return to London in late October left less than three weeks to complete the architects' joint agreement. The two colleagues had little time to correlate their designs for William Walcot, who had been selected to create his renowned colored perspectives at Apple Tree Yard. With consummate artistry, Walcot produced brilliant renderings from sketches Baker and two assistants had roughed out on the voyage from South Africa. Taken to India, they subsequently commanded a widespread audience in 1914 at the Royal Academy and in the Indian and British press.

Later, when storms of controversy raged over Raisina, one panoramic perspective [51] showing Government House seen between the Secretariats played a conspicuous role in the vehement discussions. A commemorative column stood at Point A on the processional approach to Government House, near the easternmost pavilions of the Secretariats, and at the crest of the steep gradient from the Great Court. Prepared from Baker's sketches in November, Walcot's rendering showed an impressive view of the palace's eastern facade, when in fact the inclined way actually masked all but the dome—as Nicholls's perspective demonstrated so clearly. The Imperial Delhi Committee itself, while dismissing Lutyens's proposals in 1916 to alter the gradient, did record that the drawing was "imaginary in its view of Government House." Lutyens remarked bitterly that the drawing exceeded even the bounds of artistic license. He felt certain that had Baker submitted a true perspective from the Great Place or Court, showing only the palace dome above the

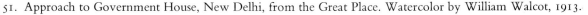

51. Approach to Government House, New Delhi, from the Great Place. Watercolor by William Walcot, 1913.

inclined way, the Royal Academy or public opinion would have rejected the drawing.[8]

Baker had harbored misgivings about collaborating with Lutyens on Delhi from the very first suggestion. An unhappy experience in early 1911 had raised serious doubts in his mind. In that year, with Baker's support, Lutyens had been appointed architect of both a municipal art gallery and a regimental monument in Johannesburg. He had then behaved, however, with such willfulness, with such "a ruthless want of consideration for the wishes and instructions of his friends and clients," that Baker had written he would find it difficult ever to collaborate. Hence Lutyens's initial soundings on Delhi had found Baker hesitant. The offer was too tempting, however: Baker thought it "providential fulfilment" of his dream since youth to join Lutyens on "some great Imperial work."[9]

When proposing collaboration in 1912, Lutyens had anticipated that disputes and disagreements "in a friendly way" were inevitable. On Baker's return to England in October 1913, difficulties over the two architects' private collaborative agreement quickly soured their friendship. The agreement specified that receipts be paid into a joint "pool account" from which office expenses and an allowance would be deducted. Baker's greater expenses in his South African practice, however, made him certain to draw more heavily on the "pool." As a result Lutyens evidently first refused, then reluctantly assented to a pooling of profits which aimed at "mutual all around equality," but set no specific limits on expenses.[10]

At 4:30 on the afternoon of November 12, Baker's solicitor wired him at Owletts, his home in Kent: Lutyens's lawyer insisted on an ironclad limit on Baker's expenses relative to those of Lutyens, with a maximum ratio of two to one in Baker's favor. Constantly anxious over his finances, Lutyens had had second thoughts about an arrangement based only on trust; together with his solicitor Francis Smith, he devised, in his words, "a lawyer's safeguard in the interests of my family." Baker's adverse reaction to the proposed restriction convinced him that he could not sign "for life & death any kind of clause without limit." He had vowed to endow his wife with all his worldly goods, and so believed he could not surrender any control over his earnings.[11]

Lutyens had changed his mind the day before the architects were to sail to India. Baker, angry and upset, had time only for a hurried conference with his lawyer the next morning. The proposed clause, he recorded, would have hit him unfairly, binding him financially "hand and foot" to Lutyens.[12]

At Victoria Station, reciprocal accusations marked the scene on the platform, much to the astonishment of George Swinton, who promptly sent Lord Hardinge warning of this "serious row" which had caused "a rift within the lute." For three days tension persisted. Baker, "awfully hurt and bruised," muttered that happy days were over. After Lutyens's behavior at Victoria, he thought it "the work of a Christian" to cooperate with him at all! Finally on the fourth day, aboard the *Egypt* in mid-Mediterranean, tempers cooled. In playfully exaggerated legal jargon ("whereas-to-before-as-hereafter-why-not'), Lutyens drafted an alternate financial formula that allowed for disproportionate expenses, yet protected profits. Half the gross earnings were to be equally divisible. If Baker's expenses rose above sixty per cent of the other half, the excess would not be pooled but paid instead by Baker. As

Swinton had predicted, the two old friends, away from their lawyers, resolved their differences, and on December 23 in Delhi they signed a revised agreement.[13]

The wounds festered, however, and the architects never recovered that memorably happy companionship they had known in February 1913. Lutyens's letters home grew increasingly critical. Baker's more flexible and businesslike methods, which simplified relations with officialdom, earned his disdain. "I don't think Baker really cares so long as he makes his pile & pleases the powers that be," he wrote. Indeed, Lutyens found his partner so ignorant of what was good and fine, and "so accustomed to cheap work," that he proved of no real help. Rather than confronting problems, he got over them "in a slovenly way," creating something muddy. This was, Lutyens remarked acidly, a very colonial attitude, reflecting a world view bounded "by the range of a pom-pom gun." Moreover he pinpointed a basic difference in philosophy when he deplored Baker's attempts to express human and national sentiments—essentially literary concepts—in architecture.[14]

Lutyens's hostile air of superiority and contempt was, in turn, of little help either to his partner or to the creation of Imperial Delhi. Baker confessed that he yearned for "a sympathetic companion," but instead increasingly worked at Raisina amid disparagement and veiled sneers. This atmosphere, so hard to create in, induced depression and the false belief that he had never achieved "any good anywhere." Returning from inaugural ceremonies in 1931, Baker recorded his sadness and regret at the harm to New Delhi caused by the architects' failure to collaborate. Appointed, as he realized, to "exercise a wholesome control over the wilful masterfulness of a genius," Baker's experiences convinced him that there could be no compromise course between maintaining an independent stance and becoming a puppet.[15]

While two such strong personalities with differing philosophies may have been fated to disagree, the gradient linking the Great Place to Government Court was undeniably catalytic in creating a bitter breach lasting more than twenty years. While agreement in March 1913 to resite the Secretariats atop Raisina Hill was crucial, decisions taken in early 1914 rendered confrontation virtually inevitable.

The two architects reached India on November 28, 1913. Bombay's High Victorian skyline was as familiar, and repugnant, as the profile of an old adversary; Baker thought it "a nightmare" as confused as Babel's tongues. Both men carried numerous small sketches of Delhi, in addition to Walcot's impressive perspectives, but plans for Government House and the Secretariats proved to exceed the sanctioned estimates. With help from his South African partner Francis Fleming, Baker rapidly revised his scheme virtually to its present form. The Government House excess was far larger, and hence the task more demanding. With great reluctance, Lutyens undertook the second major reduction in ten months, paring and consolidating. He had to reconcile contradictory demands for economy and monumental splendor without injuring either the palace's proportions or its relationship to the Secretariats. The new site west of point A required expensive foundation and retaining walls for Government House and its forecourt—an immense building mass for the actual floor area of the house. Baker marvelled as Lutyens worked "night and day" with "amazing skill and energy" to reduce the scale of his elaborate plans. Altering the palace in turn meant changing the

Secretariats' center lines. Finally, on the eve of the architects' departure in March 1914, the Imperial Delhi Committee exacted an important formal assurance, based on preliminary designs recently submitted. Anxious to begin excavating for foundations on Raisina Hill, the Committee insisted that further changes in Lutyens's plans, still less advanced than Baker's, must not affect the Secretariats. Consequently, on March 17, both architects signed an agreement which guaranteed the main buildings' dimensions and, in particular, their relative positions.[16]

From December to March, the architects and Committee members had repeatedly considered relationships between the capitol buildings. On December 18 the Committee discussed the threefold effect of Government House on the two Secretariat blocks: on their distance apart, on their height, and on their scaled height. In January 1914 the Committee and architects twice considered shifting both the Secretariats (to the north and south) to increase the distance between them. But the resultant proposal to enlarge Government Court, and hence the vista of the palace, foundered on its cost, estimated at four to five lakhs of rupees. Clearly concerned to ensure a unified conception, Committee members, with the architects at their elbows, adopted a maximum distance between the Government House dome and the Secretariat domes of 2,044 feet.[17]

At this point—January 1914—the Committee, with Lutyens and Baker present, established yet another upper limit of genuine consequence. After discussing the approaches to Government House, members formally resolved that no grade be steeper than one foot in twenty-five. Before the architects left Delhi on March 20, this ratio had been altered sufficiently to end the inclined approach from the Great Place near the easternmost pavilions of the Secretariats. During May, the Committee President, Malcolm Hailey, noted in the *Times of India* that the grade had been "limited to an ascent of 1 in $22\frac{1}{2}$," while in the *Times* he wrote simply that the incline had "a rise of about one in $22\frac{1}{2}$."[18]

En route home aboard the *Macedonia* and in England, the two architects' discussions were evidently intimate and amicable. Lutyens asked that the memorial column shown at point A (in Baker's sphere of work) be moved westward to the forecourt of Government House. Baker agreed that the suggested site was preferable, for, as his colleague argued, it permitted valuable vistas of the monument from north and south. Lutyens said nothing about any other effects of removing the column from atop the inclined approach.[19]

Did Lutyens fail to grasp the significance of the gradient agreed upon? Clearly he was ill, depressed, and above all preoccupied with recasting the intricate Government House plans. Illness had dogged him from soon after his arrival in India in late 1913; Baker had noted his colleague's poor health as early as December 18. During the critical month of March 1914, he was painfully afflicted with hemorrhoids and attendant ailments.[20]

Exhaustion and frustration bred depression. India's exotic novelty no longer held its initial charm. In Benares Lutyens was appalled by "the hideousness of everything": the stench, the squalor, and the "barbarism" of bull, cow, and monkey worship. Baker he found more and more unsympathetic and unhelpful. The task of revision—"cutting Govt. House into pieces and bits"—was sheer torture. The Viceroy's insistence on stringency constantly grated, and in London, Lady Emily proved of little or no help in assembling influential allies. Complaining bitterly about Hardinge, he wrote to his influential friends Lionel Earle and Edwin Montagu, then thought better of it and destroyed the letters. He did send Lady Hardinge a deeply pessimistic note about defects in Government House imposed by economy. This brought the Vicereine promptly to his doorstep in distress, miserable over his "black" letter and begging him not to voice criticisms that might be quoted. His dark mood persisted. "Everything is anxious-making here," he concluded. "It is like composing an opera & they leave out the fiddles & give you bows with one string & [leave out] all but one wind instrument—the Viceroy's. A drum, a triangle is what they leave you & a cornet perhaps, but they save one skin of the drum."[21]

On return to London, while a doomed generation enjoyed its last fling before the holocaust, Lutyens found himself even more harassed than in India. Instructed at Delhi to lower the dome and reduce the size of Government House, he had orders at the same time to enlarge the ballroom and dining room. Despite his herculean efforts at revision, the Imperial Delhi Committee had judged his preliminary designs as inadequate as a basis for estimates. Now he had to divide his labors between their complicated completion and an active practice which that summer included a church, a country house, a full-blown castle, a corporate guest house, a society's headquarters, and a host of redecorations, reconstructions, additions, and alterations. Small wonder perhaps if he showed little concern for a gradient at Delhi—an upper limit at that. After all, was Baker not responsible for that sphere of their scheme? Did not Walcot's vivid perspectives, on exhibit at Burlington House since May 1, depict the architects' grand design as jointly conceived, with the portico and dome of Government House crowning the ceremonial King's Way?[22]

In June 1914, Lutyens filed a design with the Imperial Delhi Committee that showed an inclined way or ramp from the Great Place terminating east of point A. The plan, C.E.-221-9, series II, would return to haunt him the rest of his life. The grade it affirmed, Committee members noted in 1916, was the basis for all subsequent work. His signature on that drawing, Lutyens confessed later, was "a great mistake," for it bound the Committee to a gradient whose effect was "ugly and clumsy." He argued his error was made "in good faith," on the understanding that Baker's Government Court would be designed to realize an unobstructed view of the Viceregal palace from the King's Way and Great Place.[23]

During the cold weather season of 1914–15 in Delhi, maximum gradients of lateral approaches and of the processional route to Viceroy's Court were the subject of renewed discussion. The topic became practical when the level of the Great Place was settled. The architects, Lord Hardinge, and the Committee all drove up short lengths of road (in effect full-sized experimental models) built with inclines of one in 20, $22\frac{1}{2}$, and 25. A grade of one in $22\frac{1}{2}$ was confirmed in February 1915 with Lutyens's acquiescence. A year later, however, he denied the finality of this ratio which he said he had regarded as simply a limit to ensure easy ascent—"useful data," but not dictating any design, as the Government had interpreted the figure. "Absorption in my profession," Lutyens protested to Hardinge's successor, "has prevented me realizing the rules that control bureaucratic methods."[24]

Relations between the architects during the 1914–15 visit, if not strained, were plainly less than ideal. On the outward voyage, Lutyens found Baker evasive.

Instead of settling pending problems, his colleague proclaimed a moratorium on work—which Lutyens promptly labelled a "tomorrowtorium." By mid-January he thought Baker "very troublesome," forever serving Mammon rather than fine building. Despite Baker's acknowledged "great good qualities," Lutyens deplored his practical politics; the sacrifice of good work to accommodate others he thought "very selfish." Lutyens wrote in despair to his wife that he had to fight his colleague and indeed the world to achieve at Delhi what he believed right. His words were to prove more prescient than he could ever have dreamed, for during the architects' next visit to India, in 1915–16, the battle over the gradient was royally joined.[25]

In January 1916, Lutyens suddenly perceived the inclined way's full effect. Because of an alleged misunderstanding, Baker had failed to provide a section drawing depicting his designated area of responsibility, despite continued requests from his colleague beginning in 1914. Lutyens consequently prepared his own. What he saw surprised and appalled him. Baker, he told Lady Emily, had "designed his levels so that you will never see Government House at all!! from the Great Place. You will just see the top of the dome!!" Walcot's perspective of the capitol, prepared at Baker's direction, had been published in the press, exhibited at the Royal Academy, and shown to visitors at the architects' Raisina office as a true representation. Lutyens now realized the drawing was "imaginary & wrong," and about as truthful as a seaside resort's poster advertising its amenities! He felt grossly misled. In a formal protest to Baker, he wrote angrily that from the Great Place the view of Government House "would be obliterated," the palace dome and Jaipur Column "awkwardly truncated," and Secretariat towers so high as to be almost outside one's field of vision. "This," he declared emphatically, "is not satisfactory collaboration."[26] [52, 53]

In reply, Baker penned extensive marginal notes on Lutyens's letter, reminding his colleague that plans for the Secretariats (including the disputed gradient) had been officially approved the previous year. Confident of the verdict on any proposed changes, Baker suggested his colleague lodge his grievance with the Imperial Delhi Committee.[27]

While insisting he hated such fights, Lutyens was a determined antagonist when aroused. Appeals to both the Committee and the Viceroy were only his first skirmishes in a six-year battle to alter the inclined way. His avowed purpose, expressed in his initial letter to the Committee on February 10, never wavered: to modify Baker's design so that Government House could be seen from the Great Place, thereby effecting "the original & advertised intention" shown in Walcot's perspectives. On February 11, Lutyens broached the subject of the gradient at an informal Committee breakfast. After some discussion, Hailey (as President) asked the two architects to make a joint written representation. A week later, the Committee considered in detail Lutyens's letter—dated St. Valentine's Day!—and Baker's dated the following day. Lutyens reiterated his argument that to realize the intended conception would require materially reducing the level of the processional way, carrying the slope almost to the railings of Viceroy's Court. Baker, on the other hand, considered the steep grade to be inherent in the nature of the raised platform. To take the slope further westward would drastically mutilate Government Court, shattering its special aura as a privileged sanctuary and

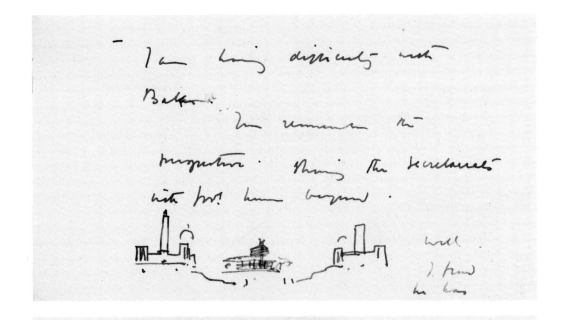

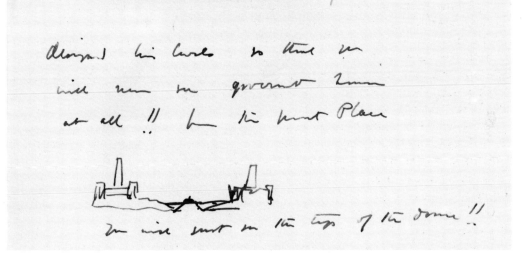

52 & 53. Approach to Government House, New Delhi, as depicted in William Walcot's perspective (above) and as designed (below). Sketches by E. L. Lutyens, January 27, 1916.

rendering access between the Secretariat blocks difficult. Treatment of the sides of the slope would require either extensive series of steps rising north and south to the Secretariats (in the manner of tiered stadium seats), or retaining walls pierced by long flights of steps. In both cases, the multiple stone surfaces, Baker argued, would augment the Court's heat and eliminate pleasant stretches of lawn.[28] [54, 55]

At a meeting on February 18, Committee members admitted that Walcot's panoramic perspective depicted an "imaginary" view of Government House. But the Committee cited the architects' earlier agreement to the steep gradient, confirmed in a plan filed by Lutyens in June 1914, showing the incline ending east of point A. Echoing Baker's words, members declared they could not accept a long

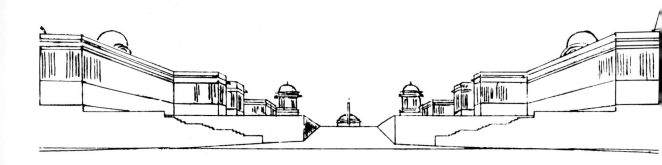

*Outline perspective view from centre of Great Court,*
*Grade ( as agreed.)*

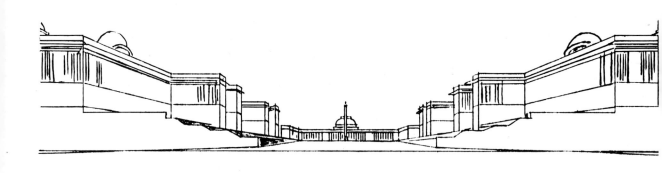

*Outline perspective view from centre of Great Court*
*Slope cut back to a point 160 feet from centre of Column*
*showing bases of pillars of Government House (as proposed)*

54 & 55.  Approach to Government House, New Delhi, as designed (above), and proposed by E. L. Lutyens (below).
Drawings by W. H. Nicholls, Architect Member of the Imperial Delhi Committee, March 28, 1916.

sloping grade for practical and financial reasons: Lutyens's proposal would impair access between the Secretariat blocks, virtually eliminate Government Court, open the privacy of Viceroy's Court to public view from the Great Place, and cost at least one and a half lakhs of rupees.[29]

Lutyens's other immediate resort was Lord Hardinge, who could overrule the Committee and indeed even his own Viceregal Council. "All finality," Lutyens told Lady Emily on February 1, "rests with the Viceroy." His perceptiveness had been an enormous boon during the arduous search for a capital site. But Lutyens, while acknowledging Hardinge's attainments, thought him "rather unknowing" about visual relationships and indeed "almost unapproachable on such matters." At this critical moment, Lutyens sorely missed his ally inside Government House, the Vicereine, who had died unexpectedly in July 1914 while visiting England. Hardinge's secretary, Du Boulay, while himself "horrified" by the effects of the gradient, reported the Viceroy opposed to any change in design. Lutyens waxed bitter. Baker's scheme was "an awful faux pas," and Hardinge's attitude "a cruel shame," governed by his first fanciful estimate. Du Boulay's report of the Viceregal position prompted an official letter from Lutyens. Should his own views not prevail, Lutyens felt history must know that Baker bore full responsibility for the result.[30]

Lutyens's letter (shown to Baker) substantially repeated his argument to the Committee, but with one alternative proposal. Instead of extra steps to the longer, lower slope, he suggested connecting the two Secretariat blocks with a tunnel, to preserve intact the flat lawns and gardens of Government Court. In a reply addressed to Hardinge, Baker attacked this covered way as undignified, despite its similarity to a "crypto-porticus" he himself had earlier proposed. The scheme already approved, he insisted, was "an inherently good one" in both aesthetic and practical respects.[31]

Lutyens returned on March 10 in a depressed mood after lunching at Government House. Hardinge would not consider "the merits of the case," insisting that the architects had previously agreed to a specific gradient. Baker emerged from a similar luncheon three days later scenting victory: the Viceroy had revealed he strongly supported the Imperial Delhi Committee's judgment. The same day, in a lengthy note to Hailey as President of the Committee, Hardinge rehearsed New Delhi's history and set down his own views in detail. The subject of Lutyen's complaint, an interrupted and obscured vista of Government House, had been "patent to everybody two years ago"; Hardinge had himself accepted such a result as inevitable once the Secretariats had been placed atop Raisina Hill. Lutyens's remedy he thought aesthetically and functionally objectionable. The long, deep ramp would resemble "a glorified railway cutting" and impair access between Secretariat buildings. An underground passage serviced by lifts Hardinge rejected in hyperbolic language: it would be "extremely inconvenient," would cause "great delays," and would be "very costly" to construct and maintain. In conclusion, he thought it "little short of a scandal" that Lutyens should now contest such a major but obvious feature of plans approved two years before. Since his own departure was imminent, however, he would leave the controversy to his successor for final decision.[32]

As early as February 4, 1916, Lutyens had grasped at the slender hope that Hardinge's successor, Lord Chelmsford, might "see more justly" and realize "the stupidity & ugliness of Baker's line." Meanwhile, the deepening controversy proved daily more worrisome and distracting. "Ought I to resign?" he asked Lady Emily in despair. Claude Hill, the Member of the Viceroy's Council in charge of Public Works, counted this possibility real enough to merit investigating. Did Baker think his colleague would quit? "I said *no*! emphatically," Baker wrote in his diary. But when Hill and Hailey both suggested that the Government of India appoint a professional arbitrator to settle the dispute, Baker (hitherto confident of winning) in turn hinted at resignation. To permit appeals beyond the Viceroy, and have the constant threat of arbitration, he told Hardinge, would be intolerable and make his own position impossible. "I can serve a master and be loyal to him," he wrote Hailey, "but I don't think that I could stand continual appeals beyond him."[33]

After conferring with Hailey, Hardinge appears to have squelched the idea of arbitration. Baker was "under a misapprehension." The wishes and intentions of the Viceroy and Government of India, and not of a given architect or (by implication) arbitrator, were paramount in all disputes or decisions. As for appeals to other authorities, Hardinge reasserted that Luytens and Baker must appreciate their status as servants to the Government of India.[34]

Heated confrontations marked the architects' return voyage aboard the *Caledonia*. The third Sunday in Lent was especially acrimonious. Baker begged Lutyens to try to see the better side of people and to understand their point of view. But instead, his colleague grew intemperate and "quite impossible to talk to," declaring he would resign and carry his complaints to the King himself. At this last threat, Baker recorded in his diary, "I asked him to try and have a sense of humour with regard to himself sometimes, but I got never a smile."[35] [56]

Much of the journey seems to have been consumed in drafting letters to principals in the gradient dispute, including the Viceroy-designate, Lord Chelmsford. Lutyens's missives to Chelmsford, while covering familiar territory, responded to recent statements by both Baker and Hardinge. The inclined way could hardly be called "a pleasant break"; rather it destroyed the processional avenue as a competent scheme. "It is bad design," Lutyens asserted, "to terminate an architectural vista and Avenue with a disappearing Target." To insist that the remedy, a lower incline, would resemble a railway cutting constituted "a libel on one's architectural skill." In his proposed revision, the King's Way would rise between pleasant tiers of terraces, "ever disclosing without mutilation Baker's charming facades," its terminus the raised and private platform of Viceroy's Court, screened by impressive iron grilles. He offered to have models of various alternatives made at his expense, and furthermore to accept arbitration by a third architect "of recognized and agreed eminence."[36]

Baker similarly addressed Chelmsford with familiar arguments. The panoramic perspective of 1914 (executed by Walcot) he admitted did show Government House nearer the Secretariats than actually designed; whether such artistic license was justified or not, Baker declared, Lutyens had not questioned its accuracy for two years. Anxious to preserve Government Court intact, he insisted that a steep slope (found at the Agra Fort and many Rajput citadels) was essential at Delhi to express the spirit of a raised and privileged sanctuary. At both Athens and the Capitol in Rome, the crowning building dominated its environs, then disappeared altogether as one mounted a steep approach; Baker envisaged his Secretariats as a worthy

*Tweedledum & Tweedledee*

56. "Tweedledum & Tweedledee": Lutyens versus Baker. Drawing by W. H. Nicholls, 1916.

propyleum to Lutyens's Parthenon. Arbitration of the dispute he denounced as a pernicious precedent which would spawn endless appeals.[37]

Lord Chelmsford's selection as Viceroy at age forty-seven had been an unexpected choice. While he was certainly handsome, dignified, and sociable, his highest preferment hitherto had been as Governor of an Australian state. When the Asquith Government offered him the Viceroyalty, he was a captain in the Fourth Dorset Territorials, guarding a wireless station near Simla. Protocol dictated his departure from India until the incumbent's term expired, but not before Hardinge had personally conducted him around the Raisina site. On assuming office, Chelmsford at once examined all papers pertinent to the gradient dispute; although deferring immediate action, he confessed agreement with Hardinge's experienced views and those of the Imperial Delhi Committee. Not surprisingly, after a further careful review with Hailey and Hill (the Council Member directly responsible), he upheld the decision to reject Lutyens's proposals. On May 13 a priority telegram ended Baker's suspense: "GOVERNMENT INDIA HAVE ISSUED OFFICIAL ORDERS DIRECTION COMMITTEE TO RETAIN INCLINED PLANE AT GRADIENT ONE IN TWENTY TWO ALREADY DECIDED ON."[38]

Letters from Hill to the two architects expressed the hope that Lutyens would "loyally accept" this decision, but not for six years, in fact, would Lutyens abandon his struggle. His appeals were laid before yet another Viceroy, two Secretaries of State, a prestigious India Office committee, and the King and Queen. Determined to win redress, he nevertheless fully realized the waste of time and energy expended on the dispute; the continual battling, he lamented, all detracted "from what should be ever our real endeavour, the best."[39]

His appeal to the new Secretary of State, Austen Chamberlain, gained Lutyens nothing but a clear conscience for his effort; Chamberlain adhered strictly to the Government of India's decision. Queen Mary's visit to Apple Tree Yard the same summer proved more supportive, for Her Majesty generally deplored all alterations and reductions of designs shown her at Balmoral in 1912. Then on November 4 at Buckingham Palace, Lutyens used plans, perspectives, and photographs to explain the gradient dispute in careful detail to both sovereign and consort. After this briefing, the King quite naturally objected to the inclined way's effect: to mask the palace was to impair its dignity and intended predominance. Lutyens realized, however, that royal advocacy in his dispute might be a futile achievement. Four years before, he had remarked how little real power King George possessed: he was scarcely more than "a speaking trumpet."[40]

Circulated in January 1917, Lutyens's report of his Palace interview created ripples of annoyance, followed by defensive activity. Chamberlain told Lord Stamfordham, King George's Private Secretary, that Lutyens was "an artist with no regard for money and little aptitude for business"; the expense to alter the contested gradient would be "very serious." He made it plain the Government's decision should be upheld. Concerned to protect the Viceroy and himself from Lutyens's "vagaries" and the meddling royal interest the architect had aroused, Chamberlain established a committee to advise the Secretary of State in Council on the New Delhi project, especially the furnishings and decorations of Government House.[41]

Hardinge, now Permanent Under-Secretary at the Foreign Office, angrily moved to counter Lutyens's influence. He arranged for Baker to see Queen Mary, and he made a point to discuss Delhi with the royal couple himself. "It is so like Lutyens to try in a spiteful way to stir up mud," he told Hailey bitterly, "but happily in this instance he has failed entirely." The Queen, he thought, put no trust in Lutyens, and Their Majesties displayed no apparent desire to upset the accepted scheme at Raisina, now sanctioned by the Cabinet. Lutyens boasted of having obtained an extra £100,000 for Government House after his interview with Queen Mary. This indiscretion may have been costly, prompting a letter from Lord Stamfordham which ruled out any changes at Raisina involving fresh expenditure. In May the Queen reproached Hardinge for having appointed Lutyens! Prospects for help from the Palace grew bleak.[42]

In his unrelenting quest to alter the gradient, Lutyens turned to the New Delhi Advisory Committee created by Chamberlain. As early as 1912, Lutyens had himself suggested such a body to ensure continuity at Delhi despite changes of Viceroys, Ministers, and other officials. Immediately after Lutyens's visit to Balmoral in September 1912, the King's Private Secretary had badgered Lord Crewe to consider creating a permanent trust like the Royal Commission of 1851 which would administer the project finances and act as an advisory committee. Crewe's response had been negative. Who would compose such a body? Its operations would be futile unless conducted in India, which effectively barred many likely candidates. Nor could the India Office and Government of India shed responsibility for expenditure on the Delhi scheme. Nine months later Stamfordham renewed his proposal with even greater insistence. Passage of time, he noted, had made King George "no less anxious" that there should be a competent, representative committee to advise the Secretary of State and Viceroy on the new city and especially on Government House. Both Crewe and his Permanent Under-Secretary remained adamant. Montagu foresaw only "friction, worry, and trouble"; the obstacles appeared "insuperable" to forming such a body in London. "We have abandoned the idea," he wrote firmly.[43]

Lutyens persisted. Finally, seventeen months later at the India Office, the Secretary of State took up his idea. On December 1, 1914, Crewe chaired an inaugural meeting of the "Home Advisory Committee on the Furnishing and Decoration of Government House, Delhi." Lutyens had suggested the names of all but two of its nine members. The group's function was to tender expert advice to the Secretary of State, and its conclusions on matters "of art, style, or taste" took precedence over any similar Viceregal body. The Committee promptly agreed that the general style of furniture and decoration at Government House should be Western (preferably English) and asked Lutyens to submit provisional schemes for furnishing the palace on his return from India.[44]

The Imperial Delhi Committee greeted word of this new creation with undisguised astonishment. How were they to reconcile their own cost estimates with the Home Committee's instructions to Lutyens? Hardinge was even more perturbed. Such a body, with its threat of continual intervention, he felt impinged on his ultimate authority. He did not mince words: "I do not wish to have anything to say or do with the self-constituted Committee in London for the furnishing of Govt. House, as I disapprove entirely of their meddlesome interference." Harcourt Butler's observation that Viceroys eventually "cease to want opinion or advice & only desire agreement or assent," proved very apposite. Hardinge's obdurate opposition, as well as the wartime stringency, effectively suspended the committee's work. There was no second meeting.[45]

Twenty months later, while emphasizing to the new Secretary of State her interest in Delhi, Queen Mary enquired about the committee's fate. Chamberlain, hitherto ignorant of its history, welcomed the concept; he thought it a much more satisfactory procedure than "allowing a series of Viceroys and Vicereines to work their wicked will." To avoid Viceregal fears of impaired prerogatives, the "rock of offence" which had wrecked the old committee, Chamberlain proposed a new body advisory solely to himself. Although Government House would be the committee's special concern, the Secretary of State might solicit members' advice on any aspect of Imperial Delhi. Chelmsford's response to this scheme was favorable, the Palace heartily approved, and Lord Crewe accepted the chairmanship. Other members included Lord Hardinge; Lord Carmichael, late Governor of Madras and Bengal and former Trustee of the National Galleries of Scotland and of the National Portrait Gallery; the Countess of Minto, Vicereine from 1905 to 1910 and Lady of the Bedchamber to Queen Mary; Sir Thomas Holderness, Permanent Under-Secretary at the India Office; Sir Cecil Harcourt Smith, Director of the Victoria and Albert Museum; and Commander Frederick Leverton Harris, a Privy Councillor and Unionist Member of Parliament.[46]

The committee first convened on May 18, 1917. Two months later, the Chairman read aloud Lutyens's account describing his royal audience in November, when His Majesty had censured the inclined way. What role could an advisory committee play in the gradient controversy? Members agreed to consult the Secretary of State. Hardinge privately expressed anger at the committee's meddlesome ambitions "to take too much upon themselves," and Holderness counselled Chamberlain's recent successor, Edwin Montagu, to reject efforts to revive the debate. But Montagu exhibited his customary openmindedness, authorizing the committee to reconsider the Government of India's decision. After three meetings and testimony from both Baker and Lutyens, members recommended against reopening the gradient question. While acknowledging that a majority felt the present scheme regrettable, they noted the heavy cost for any remedy. Their report, however, suggested the Secretary of State broach the topic on his forthcoming visit to India.[47]

After conferring at length with Keeling and Hailey upon his arrival at Delhi in November 1917, Montagu decided that work had progressed too far to permit any change. "I sympathize with Lutyens," he declared, "in that for some distance the view of Government House along the main avenue of prospect will be obscured, but it is too late to alter this." The Viceroy's Council rejoiced in their vindication, and at the India Office Holderness smugly concluded that the subject was closed.[48]

The Under-Secretary misjudged Lutyens. Despite the Advisory Committee's decision, Lutyens revived the gradient debate in 1919 with "hopes of getting the Baker mistakes put right." At Delhi, Sir Claude Hill arranged a meeting with the two architects to seek an amicable resolution of the controversy. Under such official pressure, Baker (to Lutyens's astonishment) modified his position; while preferring the existing scheme, he waived any architectural objection to reducing the inclined way. Not surprisingly, therefore, after Hill's subsequent appointment to the Home Advisory Committee in London, members met to discuss the Raisina gradient once more. Sir Claude, citing the architects' disagreement as a previous obstacle to any change, advanced Baker's new attitude as a basis for reopening the question. Both architects again testified. Under questioning, Baker made it clear he had no objection to Lutyens's proposals on abstract achitectural grounds. Rather his reasons were practical and political: cost, delay, danger from blasting, heat from the stone steps, inconvenient communication, and injury to the dignity and importance he sought to embody in the Secretariat buildings. Committee members' opinions, frankly expressed, were sent without revision to Montagu. They revealed sharp divisions: Hardinge and Holderness were firmly opposed to re-examining the issue; Crewe felt sure that despite their "unquestionable advantage," Lutyens's new designs were too costly to consider; and Hill, Harris, Carmichael, Smith, and Lady Minto—a majority—were all eager to implement the suggested alterations.[49]

Montagu forwarded the committee's views to the new Viceroy on March 16, 1921. Lord Reading carefully considered Lutyens's proposals and all opposing arguments, then on July 3 decided against reopening the case: the Government of India could not "afford the time or the money to carry out the cutting now advocated."[50]

Ignorant of this judgment, Lutyens remained undaunted. During his next cold weather visit he presented his case for the first time to Lord Reading as well as to the New Capital Committee, successor to the Imperial Delhi Committee. This body queried both architects and inspected the Raisina capitol in their company, but decided against reconsideration. The committee, however, left it to Lutyens's discretion to initiate further appeals to higher authorities.[51]

Keeling's estimate in March of twenty-five lakhs (about £166,650) to alter the processional way cast Lutyens into despair. This was a staggering sum—nearly half the cost of Government House. In 1916 the figure had been £8,000! Especially with Hailey as Finance Member, Reading doubtless would reject such a costly scheme. Lutyens's mood darkened; he feared above all his professional reputation would suffer from criticism of the gradient. "I have—if Reading is against me—to resign," he told his wife. "I cannot go on with Delhi." Instead he had to "chuck it." Resignation and a statement in the *Times* would clear him of responsibility for "Baker's mess." To relinquish his Indian post, he acknowledged, would make "a great difference" financially. In Madras, at Mrs. Annie Besant's Theosophist colony, Lady Emily took alarm: she promptly telegraphed her husband, urging perseverance and begging him not to resign. At Delhi, an anxious Keeling made made similar pleas. A harassed Viceroy, preoccupied with challenges from Mahatma Gandhi, delayed any decision on the revised scheme. Lutyens returned to England, and amid the urging of his friends and family, abandoned his dire threats.[52]

Lord Reading, sympathetic to Lutyens's aesthetic aims, but determined to restrict expenditure, ordered his Council to consider the gradient issue. In a detailed memorandum reiterating familiar arguments against Lutyens's proposals, the Public Works Department, with exasperation, advised Councillors to reject "any such alterations." Subsequently, in affirming this position, Council Members dealt Lutyens's hopes a fatal blow. The Secretary of State notified both architects on June 16. Vastly increased costs clearly made major changes unrealistic. The New Capital Enquiry in November, as well as the Inchcape recommendations and Hardinge's appointment as chairman of the Home Advisory Committee in 1923, precluded any attempt to reopen the controversy.[53]

Baker, victorious, offered Lutyens the olive branch. "We have got to get through together," he wrote, suggesting they meet, and recalling their once happy friendship. On the voyage from India, Lutyens had resolutely refused to speak to his colleague, and he now spurned this gentlemanly gesture. Although persuaded not to resign, he effectively abandoned collaboration with his official partner, forsaking any direct communication for five years. At their Raisina office the two lunched daily at the same long table, with Lutyens's men around Baker and Baker's around Lutyens. Even then, the principals exchanged words only through intermediaries; such extraordinary behavior of course proved embarrassing to visitors and assistants alike. Small wonder Baker called those years "the unhappiest in all my life's work." Only after 1926, during Lord Irwin's Viceroyalty, did the two men resume a more normal, albeit still distant, relationship. Mutual reliance and affection had graced their early lives and the outset of their imperial quest. But once distrust had sundered these bonds, neither could recapture, in Browning's words, "glad confident morning again."[54]

In 1931, when visiting the completed capital at Delhi, Lady Emily pronounced the inclined way a "crying iniquity" which spoiled her husband's grandest work. But was it? It is difficult to resist the Home Advisory Committee's majority opinion

57 (following pages). The approach to Viceroy's House from the Great Place.

that Government House would better have remained at Point A as first conceived. As the sole occupant of Raisina's highest point and the focus of eight axes, the Viceregal residence envisioned by Lutyens and Hardinge would have been the city's predominant feature, visible from all directions. The Secretariat blocks, set on the plain around an impressive plaza and silhouetted against the hill's slopes, would have formed a worthy propyleum to the acropolis. But one can appreciate Baker's perfectly human desire to have his buildings on the hilltop site, duplicating his many successes with South African kopjes. Hardinge and Lutyens only reluctantly accepted his argument that Viceroy and bureaucrat should share the same platform, expressing the instrument of Government "as a united whole." Hailey, on the other hand, after a stint as a departmental head, found Baker's image more persuasive. He did not yearn to see Government House in symbolic solitude but felt the executed design rightly recognized priorities: the Indian Civil Service had always been more important than the Viceroy. Their towers and domes looming high above the hill's crest and processional way, the Secretariat buildings seemed living proof, Keeling told Lord Reading, that the babu or native clerk ruled India![55]

Baker's unified scheme had several advantages. Chief among these was the creation of a capacious privileged place, removed from the traffic of the city streets. This raised court could accommodate ceremonies, furnish sightseers with panoramic views, and provide an imposing vista of Government House flanked by Secretariat porticoes. Endowed with broad lawns and water courses, the level space would give relief from the heat and glare of surrounding masonry. Communication between the two blocks would be easy.[56]

No one could deny, however, that the inclined approach to Government Court gradually obscured, then wholly masked Government House from the westbound traveller on King's Way. To a planner in the Grand Manner like Lutyens, this obstruction was a mortal sin: it was neither "right nor fine" that the central object should disappear and reappear. Vertical breaks could be placed down the length of an avenue (like the cultural edifices at Point B on King's Way). But an avenue necessarily stopped at the first horizontal break across its line of continuity. Baker's gradient, Lutyens felt, produced an ugly "tumor" in the intended vista, making Government House an ever-varying focus, rather than a constant terminus. The Star of India atop the Jaipur column would likewise sink inelegantly below a horizon of macadam, then suddenly reemerge.[57] [57]

Lutyens's chief remedies each comprised lowering the gradient of the inclined way to one in forty or more, so that the slope ended near the gates of Viceroy's Court rather than east of Point A in Government Court. The principal solution proposed widening the vista between the Secretariats by cutting steps and terraces north and south from the road, creating the effect of a tiered stadium. Lifts and a well-designed tunnel—or use of a telephone—could have obviated problems in communication between the two Secretariat blocks. But this terraced scheme, while potentially attractive in appearance, would have all but eliminated Government Court, preventing its ceremonial use and transforming it from a garden oasis to a heat trap.[58]

One alternative—sloping lawns—was quickly discarded: Baker stressed that grassy plots must be flat in dry countries for easy irrigation. Lutyens's other main scheme, designed to preserve the Secretariat lawns, proposed a long inclined grade sunk between retaining walls, an average of twelve feet below Government Court. While conserving green areas, this depressed roadway emphatically severed the courtyard and afforded only a slitlike vista of Viceroy's House. The ramp's depth would have largely obscured any view from it of the Secretariat facades. Baker and Hardinge justifiably condemned this "railway cutting" as aesthetically repugnant.[59]

Had Viceroy's House become an absurd jack-in-the-box? Baker and Hardinge felt not. On the contrary, Baker found a prospect pleasing which for part of a two-mile vista hid and then revealed itself again. Like the Capitol at Rome and acropolis at Athens, mystery and surprise he felt enhanced the interest and beauty of the central monument. As Robert Byron observed in 1931, even when Viceroy's House sank from sight, the enigma of an asphalt gradient leading to the sky still riveted one's eye to the axis of the design. Hardinge argued that a traveller coming from Indrapat would first enjoy a distant vista of towers and domes, then be "diverted in pleasant anticipation" of fountains and sculpture in the forecourt or plaza, next be absorbed in viewing the Secretariats while mounting the incline, and finally would relish the panorama of Secretariats and Government House from the hill's crest. Such serial vision, a Picturesque phenomenon rather than Baroque or Beaux-Arts, Gordon Cullen also found (in 1961) a most desirable feature of the King's Way. The drama of changing levels and different foci, the contrast of existing view and emerging view, Cullen felt rescued the long straight axis from monotony, heightening its emotional impact. Given the failure to erect Lutyens's four imposing buildings as vertical accents at Point B, the injection of a major horizontal break does enliven the processional route with variety. But any merit this effect may possess is more than counterbalanced: the truncated dome is undeniably disquieting, even repellent, as it hovers above the hill, its base hidden "like a great bloated bubble."[60]

At the root of the problem of course lay the agreement to place both architects' structures on top of Raisina Hill. Given this decision, should the Secretariats have been sited further apart to enlarge the view of Viceroy's House? Would an awkward sense of disjunction have marred Baker's buildings? Official proposals in January 1914 to expand Government Court had foundered over cost, not aesthetics. But even had the vista been successfully widened, the hill's crest would still have masked Viceroy's House on approach; a different solution was necessary. At the outset of the gradient controversy, Baker had perceived the key: to realize the view shown in Walcot's fallacious perspectives would have meant moving the palace eastward, toward the Secretariats. By then such a change was impossible. Ten years later as the buildings neared completion, Malcolm Hailey came to much the same conclusion: he regretted that New Delhi's early masters had not seen "a way of bringing the Government House somewhat closer to the Secretariats," thereby "presenting the buildings as a composite whole rather than as two units."[61]

In 1916 Baker argued that major alterations to a partly executed design would invite ridicule and scorn. His colleague felt on the contrary that the scheme, if not changed, would inspire widespread derision. Lutyens's belated remedies, as objectionable as the malady itself, were never attempted. After sixty years, "Mistake of Conception," the very label both architects hoped to spare New Delhi, is writ large across Raisina Hill.[62]

58 (following pages). The Jaipur Column and the east front of Viceroy's House.

# 8

# Edwin Lutyens

"So I go to India," Edwin Lutyens wrote to his wife, "full of courage & high endeavour in the likeness of that poor little knight that swore fealty to you some 16 years ago." Radiant with the romance of what fellow architect Herbert Baker called the Great Quest, Lutyens set out for Delhi in 1912. A dozen years afterward he could be seen striding determinedly among the rising walls of his fairytale city, puffing at perpetually unlit pipes and grunting out explanations of his great plan. By then he was laden with worldly honors. Knighted by his sovereign in 1918, he was a member of the Royal Academy, recipient of the Royal Gold Medal for Architecture and the Gold Medal of the American Institute of Architects, member of the Royal Fine Art Commission, and Vice President of the Royal Institute of British Architects. Married to the daughter of a Viceroy, and practitioner of an architectural style which was imperial in both scale and content, he had placed much distance between himself and his origins.[1]

The eleventh of fourteen children born to an Irish girl and an impecunious army captain turned artist, Lutyens was virtually self-educated. Picturesque gabled cottages, simply and "wittily portrayed" by Randolph Caldecott, a childhood mentor, sparked his imagination, and an inquisitive nature prompted frequent visits to the local carpenter and builder at Thursley and Godalming in Surrey. He spent two years at what is now the Royal College of Art, South Kensington, without finishing the course, and a year as an "improver" in the office of Ernest George and Peto, where he first met Herbert Baker, a senior assistant. Unlike Baker, who filled notebooks with comments and quick sketches during country rambles, Lutyens held up a framed pane of glass to any interesting view, then traced its lines with pieces of sharpened yellow soap. Later he only stood and looked. All essentials, including color, texture, and material, he committed to memory "with astonishing exactitude." Vestiges of what he saw often emerged decades later in a design. "I hear things, see things—unconsciously almost—& store them," he once explained, "& they turn up afterwards, from whence I know not."[2]

In Lutyens's early picturesque houses, details appear that betoken his eventual embrace of the classical tradition. Increasingly, classical discipline governed his imagination, although he always remained at heart a romantic in his love of pictorial effect. After the turn of the century, Lutyens realized that as British architecture assumed a new imperial stance, his future lay in the classical idiom. His stylistic evolution from the rural vernacular to the classical mode was more rapid than that of

59. Sir Edwin Landseer Lutyens. Drawing by Sir William Rothenstein, 1922.

60. Sir Edwin Lutyens, right, with Arthur Gordon Shoosmith, his resident representative at New Delhi (1920–31), on the site at Raisina.

his paragon Norman Shaw and occurred at the outset rather than the finale of his career. By 1903 Lutyens's convictions had crystallized:

> In architecture Palladio is the game!! It is so big few appreciate it now & it requires considerable training to value & realize it. . . .
> To the average man it is dry bones but under the mind of a Wren it glows & the stiff material becomes as plaster clay.[3]

Lutyens's conversion placed him squarely in the mainstream of British architecture.

Despite his adoption of Palladian classicism, Lutyens felt strongly that archaeology should not be the architect's lodestar. Lutyens urged his British colleagues to create their own patterns according to their needs, rather than hiring them to fit a slogan. This advice applied equally in India, where he discerned two ways to build: either to parade a building "in fancy dress" as at a costume ball, mixing dates and styles, or alternatively to "build as an Englishman dressed for the climate," conscious only that the tailor was Indian and not English. The latter method was clearly his preference: to work within the Western classical tradition, but "unconscious of all

61. The east front of Viceroy's House.

52. The east front of Viceroy's House. Watercolor by William Walcot, 1913.

but essentials." Early Hindu architecture might inspire admiration, but it was beyond European understanding; like Indians' music "it was worked out to their own weird rhythm." British architects in India should use their own ratios of proportion, adapting them to the climate.[4]

Lutyens swiftly rejected the proposal to use Indian draughtsmen for "orientaliz-ing" the New Delhi designs. Such a tactic, he argued, contradicted "the essence of fine architecture," in which plans, elevations, and sections composed a single, integral organism. Emblematic ornament was acceptable if discreetly subsumed within the controlling geometric system. Universal classical principles were quite capable of comprehending within their framework the exoticism of Indian ornament. But such decoration could not be allowed to seize command and actually determine the architectural outline and profile, as in the popular Indo-Saracenic style Lutyens had scorned in Bombay. Rather, in the manner of the Palladians, decoration had to be "within reason." Then its novelty and luxuriance, modestly displayed, might provide a foil for rational classical order.[5]

The only architectural language that could represent "the ideal of British Empire" and be adaptable to various climates, Lutyens asserted, was "of course classic"; it was "better, wiser, saner, & more gentlemanlike" than the sham sentiment of imitation Indian styles. Lutyens made no secret of his disdain for "Mogulese & Hindoo contraptions," and he resolutely defended the properties of the round arch against official insistence on the four-centered, tip-tilted Mughal arch. Like Wren he considered simple geometrical shapes the best, and the classical arch, based on the true circle, was fundamental to his conception of architecture in the Indian capital.[6]

Lutyens's august, supremely ordered Viceregal palace at New Delhi not only expressed "the ideal and fact of British rule in India," but achieved that fusion of traditions which both politics and climate dictated. Just as his early houses in Surrey joined paradoxical elements of the picturesque and the classical, so at Delhi the hues and shadows of Mughal facades were married to the sculptural massing and subtle proportions of European architecture. Majestic, imposing, even daunting, Viceroy's House was planned and realized on a scale reminiscent of Hadrian's Tivoli or Shah Jahan's Taj rather than Lutyens's familiar cottages and country houses in the Home Counties. Six hundred thirty feet wide and 530 feet from east to west, measuring nearly two-thirds of a mile around its foundations, the Viceregal edifice when completed comprised over 200,000 square feet, including internal courts—larger than the Palace of Versailles.[7] For generations, aspiring students at the Ecole des Beaux Arts had prepared for such a monumental opportunity; by a supreme irony, the chance came to a largely self-taught genius from an English village.

The Delhi Government House was the realization of Lutyens's long-held wish to design a grandiose palace, a romantic conception he committed to his sketch book as early as 1896. The delicate pencil and watercolor drawings for a "Château d'Ease, en Air, sur Fleuve des Rêves," [63, 64] embodied his deepest dreams—aspirations one day fulfilled on top of Raisina Hill in India. Viceroy's House is assuredly that fairytale palace, a castle in the air come true. Perhaps it may also be (as one critic has observed) the greatest folly in Britain's time-honored tradition of architectural

63. "Château d'Ease, en Air, sur Fleuve des Rêves: Port d'Amour." Watercolor with pencil, by E. L. Lutyens, between 1893 and 1896.

64. "Château d'Ease, en Air, sur Fleuve des Rêves: Cour d'Honneur." Watercolor with pencil, by E. L. Lutyens, between 1893 and 1896.

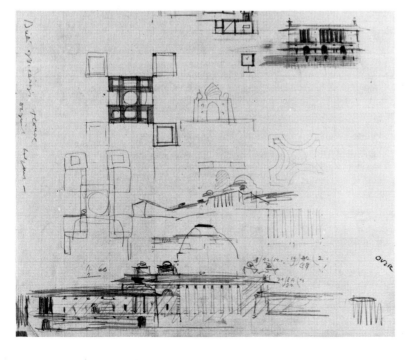

65. Experiments with plans and elevations for Viceroy's House, New Delhi. Pencil sketches by E. L. Lutyens, 1912.

66. The southwest wing of Viceroy's House.

67. The east portico of Viceroy's House.

68. Viceroy's House, east front from the southeast, showing the continuous line of giant dentils above the chujja.

69. Ink sketches of Viceroy's House by E. L. Lutyens, including a detail of a chattri, and inscribed, "Chattris are stupid useless things." September 16, 1913.

follies. Certainly it expressed the British imperial ideal as perfectly as Lutyens's country houses expressed the domestic ideal.[8]

Straddling a rocky saddle between the summit of Raisina Hill and the lowering slopes of the Delhi Ridge, Viceroy's House exhibits a scale to defy man and nature, a challenge not only to neighboring mausolea but also to the vast landscape they dot. To the visitor, Lutyens's creation seems to be at once a giant Indian bungalow, embattled Rajput fortress, and Mughal tomb. Majestically sited astride a granite outcrop, the palace boasts two basement stories, the lower at street level and the upper continuous with the Viceregal forecourt and elaborate gardens. Above this imposing plinth, colonnades and dark voids punctuate clifflike walls, and a titanic dome crowns the whole. Envisioned from the outset as a nearly square form, the Viceroy's residence presents a unified conception, grand and harmonious, as impersonal and abstract as the Escorial, which Lutyens much admired in 1915. From every direction the palace is as insistently horizontal as almost any house by Frank Lloyd Wright, a striking contrast to the verticality characteristic of High Victorian edifices and British-built Indo-Saracenic architecture. Yet, aside from its horizontal emphasis, Viceroy's House has the hard, clipped edges, flat, broad walls, recessed ornament, and sculptural solidity which suggest High Victorian affinities. [58, 61]

The very colors of the building contribute to the impression of low length. Buff and rhubarb-red sandstones not only echo the hues of nearby Shahjahanabad but, laid only in horizontal bands, stress lateral dimension as well. A broad ribbon of red stone defines a high plinth typical of neighboring Muslim monuments. Its assertive color enhances the solidity of this massive base and helps bind in continuous union the palace's diverse parts. [71]

Still another characteristic Indian architectural element acts as a crucial unifying feature of Lutyens's palace: the chujja, a beetling, downswept stone cornice common in Mughal buildings and found in Indo-Aryan temples as early as the eleventh century. Boldly girdling Viceroy's House beneath its blind parapet, the principal chujja juts eight feet from the wall face. The brightly sunlit upper surface of this immense blade as well as its deep shadow lengthen and link the palace fronts, an expression of Lutyens's dictum that light is an architect's "most important instrument" for composition. Directly above, giant dentils introduce a persistent but gentle dissonance: repeated at unvarying intervals of forty and a half inches, they are rarely centered over either columns or intervening spaces. On the tall north and south facades, a second chujja projects some five feet at the upper basement level, its lateral emphasis offsetting the walls' greater height. The dramatic slash of shadow at both levels is not merely aesthetic contrivance but a device to reduce the heat that is readily absorbed by Dholpur sandstone. The overhanging stone also serves as an eave or drip, throwing water clear of the buildings and permitting doors and windows to remain open during the humid monsoons. Effective as heat and water shields, the chujjas help as well to protect palace interiors from what Lutyens called the "tremendous violence" of Indian light; they plainly give substance to his belief that climate must govern all construction in India.[9] [68]

In his earliest sketches during the summer of 1912, Lutyens reinforced the dominant horizontality of Viceroy's House with a repetitive march of colonnades

70. Ink sketch of Viceroy's House by E. L. Lutyens, showing saucer fountain and inscribed, "I want ½ domes overflowing with water." September 5, 1913.

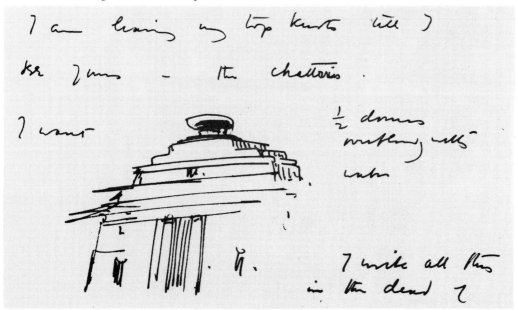

2. The north entrance to Viceroy's House. Watercolor by William Walcot.

. The south front of Viceroy's House. The towers were not executed. Watercolor by William Walcot.

. The south front of Viceroy's House, looking east to the Secretariats.

that recalls Neoclassical projects by J. N. L. Durand or even E. L. Boullée. Such lateral emphasis gives the building a visual stability appropriate to the supreme monument of the Raj, and indeed, as it stretches across Raisina Hill, its giant pavilions firmly grasping the brow, the palace does seem to embody all the self-assurance of the Britannic lion itself. [58, 69]

If solid and stable, Viceroy's House is by no means static or dull but, quite the contrary, full of invention. Vertical surfaces are battered and profiles progressively set back so that masses taper to pyramidal forms. At the same time, the dome generates interpenetrating lines of force, a circular motion which pervades and unites vaulted corridors and rooms, classical arches and tiny chattris or cupolas. Capping the four pyramidal wings like inverted and fragmentary domes, ingenious fountains in their turn inflect one's sight toward the imperial centerpiece. [70] Coordinated elements in a coherent and symmetrical whole, giant pairs of stone saucers crown each facade. Their duality emphasizes the supreme position and importance of the dome; their skyward gesture prefigures forms at Le Corbusier's Chandigarh. The sparkling overflow that once rivalled the glitter of the copper hemisphere has vanished, however, having been judged unsuitable for a drought-racked republic. But lively courtyard fountains are objects of perpetual delight.

Yet if the splash of rooftop fountains is silenced, the palatial facades are still alive with the ever-changing light and shadow of enormous colonnades that punctuate the otherwise solid grandeur of the building. Loggias, by masking in shadow many varied openings, help to endow the building with a remarkably austere appearance. The colonnades conceal the complexity of internal arrangements, everywhere maintaining the big external public scale even when private-scale patterns prevail within the wings. Skillfully manipulated, the palace facades achieve that paradoxical duality found in Lutyens's best work. Voids become positive elements in the design. Massive load-bearing walls are contrasted with dark loggias; thickly layered for enclosure, the walls are punctured for ample ventilation. The building has the openness of a summer house, despite its construction as a fortress against the Indian climate. Though it is a behemoth of some 340 rooms, the palace is still kin to the humble bungalow. [77, 78]

Lutyens's gigantic colonnades very nearly become continuous on the east front. The columns of the dodecastyle portico are especially huge—and are unequally spaced. Intervals opposite the three entrance doors measure ten and a half feet rather than nine feet between centers. While virtually indistinguishable from 500 feet, this compositional irregularity generates a subtle variation that helps avert monotony in the columnar rhythm. The impressive pillars, distinctive in scale and spacing, focus interest on the most exclusive entrance of the building and give the edifice an air of standing at attention, eyes front, heels together. [81]

The portico columns boast a remarkably original kind of capital; compared by one critic to "the headpiece of a caryatid, swollen round the middle by a corrugated band," and supporting a flat mortarboard with dependent bells, it derives ultimately from an orthodox acanthus leaf version.[10] Lutyens has distilled and abstracted his prototype to pure geometrical essence, conceiving the novel Delhi Order. Even the angle bells, which suggest the drop ornaments common in Mughal architecture,

74. Cobra fountain, designed by E. L. Lutyens, South Court, Viceroy's House.

5. Chattris crowning the east front of Viceroy's House.

5. The cobra fountain in the South Court of Viceroy's House.

77. South front, Viceroy's House, showing the Indian character of the kitchen entrance colonnade.

78. Massive kitchen entrance columns, Viceroy's House.

invert the normal downward taper of their model to create an eye-catching pendant form. [84]

In India, furthermore, the bell is replete with allusive meaning. As a symbol of vibration, the cosmic creative force, the bell played a part in early Buddhist ceremonial and has an integral role in Hindu worship today. The bell-shaped fruit of the sacred lotus represented for Hindus the womb of the universe. Could there be a more appropriate emblem to adorn the Viceregal residence than the lotus, seat and footstool of the gods? Moreover, given the ancient Indian belief that bells would sound the demise of a dynasty, what could be more reassuring to Britons than Lutyens's clapperless stone inventions?[11]

Austere, yet richly complex in conception, the dome is the quintessential expression of the palace itself. It rears proudly 166 feet above the forecourt, precisely at the center of the rectangle bounded by the outer angles of the four wings and athwart the plan's principal diagonals. Hence it appropriately lies nearer the state entrance than to the garden, while at the same time it presents a symmetrical appearance from every side. More than three times the hemisphere's height, its imposing base of circular drums and ponderous square plinth creates an undeniable impression of strength and permanence recalling funerary and reliquary monuments of Pharaonic Egypt and the Asokan Empire. [85, 88]

79. East front, Viceroy's House, experiment with loggias and dome. Pencil drawing by E. L. Lutyens, *c.* September 1913.

80. The East Loggia of Viceroy's House. Marble statue of Queen Mary.

81. The east portico of Viceroy's House.

Wren at St. Paul's and Lutyens at Raisina each sought the same effect in his dome: an elegant silhouette, impressively high to dominate the cityscape, and a ceiling low enough to avoid the awkward appearance of a cylindrical shaft from inside. Lutyens's initial ideas for a Government House, conceived in 1912 before his appointment as architect, embodied a rather different dome, both lower and wider. This design, especially when coupled to a pedimented portico boasting a giant order, recalled the Pantheon as well as sundry projects by Palladian adherents in Britain and America and by the French Neoclassicists, all of whom shared a common inspiration in Roman Imperial architecture. [91]

As ultimately built, the Viceregal dome did not wholly satisfy its creator. On its completion, Lutyens confessed he would have liked to soften the pronounced step between upper drum and hemisphere by reducing the diameter of the stone railing. He felt, too, that the dome's plinth and drum rose too precipitously from the long parapet. Undoubtedly, the imperfections he lamented sprang from his early and frequent recasting of the dome, the result of vacillation about its size by the Viceroy, Lord Hardinge.[12] [79, 82]

Lutyens's dome expresses the very essence of art for empire's sake. It broods over the city, astoundingly animate, like the topeed head of a British soldier, district officer, missionary, or Viceroy, while great arms below grasp to subdue in their embrace an alien land and culture. The hard, blank surfaces and tough, compacted solidity of the dome challenge time and the elements. Lutyens's creation dominates city and plain, an intended testimony to British power and its efficacy. [83]

With our hindsight, however, the magnified scale of the Viceregal dome, meant to impress, may signify not so much boundless self-assurance as insecurity. Britons in

82. North elevation, Viceroy's House, showing low dome. Detail of ink drawing, office of E. L. Lutyens, June 1914.

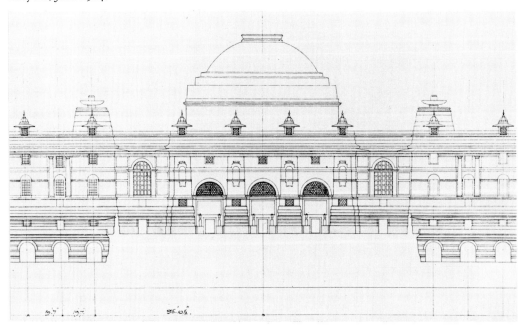

3. East front, Viceroy's House.

India had been looking over their shoulders since the Mutiny of 1857, and the spectacle of British weakness in the Boer War had been unnerving. Similarly, in American architecture, it seemed as though only the exaggerated bulk of Richardsonian Romanesque, with its implication of permanence, could sufficiently compensate for the profound uncertainty of the post–Civil War era. Later, German Nazis, haunted by the specter of their fatherland's humiliation in 1918 and by their own lack of established roots, would design on an even greater scale, in an effort to triumph over history itself.

As the silhouette of Lutyens's monumental hemisphere climbed above Viceroy's House in 1929, it became the visual focus both of palace and city, dominating and unifying them, the epitome of their character and of British rule. The dome stood at the heart of the Indian Empire as a palpable reminder of British suzerainty. In general form as well as details, it married past and present, linking the legacy of the Roman, Asokan, and Mughal empires with Britain's physical and spiritual heritage. As the Orient spurred Lutyens to new levels of experiment and assimilation, so the dome became an ecumenical metaphor in stone, a transcendent symbol for that supreme synthesis of cultures, the British Empire.

Imagined visitors to Delhi in 1930, bound for a Viceregal reception in the newly built Raisina palace, face a delightful prospect. They first see the full panorama of the Raisina acropolis from Lutyens's War Memorial Arch—a breathtaking vision of

84 (following page). In the east portico of Viceroy's House.

86. Durbar Hall, Viceroy's House.

authority made manifest. Tree-lined water channels and greensward, proclaiming order in the desert, direct progress undeviatingly along the gentle rise of King's Way.

Ordinary reception guests alight in the saucer-domed and barrel-vaulted Upper Basement Entrance Hall and enter the contrasting brilliance of the North or South Main Staircase Hall. Grandeur is the keynote on the cascading half-turn stairs. Lutyens, after a visit to Genoa in 1909, had confessed that "the lavish space given away in staircases" made him "sick with envy"; he thought the stairways as well as the detailing of the sixteenth- and seventeenth-century palaces and the planning of their courtyards were "splendid." [13] [89]

At the head of the Main Staircases of Viceroy's House, guests customarily proceed through domically vaulted corridors to the north–south axis of the Durbar Hall, whence the imperial thrones are seen obliquely. The thirteen-foot portico doors, however, admit princes and other privileged persons; the monumental scale and the gilt guilloche and bronze ornament celebrate not only the distinction of such persons but the importance of entry as a symbolic act.

As visitors move like moths almost involuntarily toward the brightness, the space before them is compressed between massive piers, then suddenly swells to new and startling dimensions beyond. The guests step down and look up: the Durbar Hall!

85 (preceding page). The north front of Viceroy's House.

They have reached their goal in a carefully calculated succession of constrictions and exhilarating releases, repeatedly experiencing a sense of overcoming difficulties and attaining splendidly ordered open spaces. Human control over the world stage—British imperial control—is insistently, inescapably dramatized. [86]

Seventy-two feet in diameter and seventy-nine feet high, the Durbar Hall appears much bigger, even comparable in scale to the Pantheon in Rome (145 feet by 147 feet) or the inner dome of St. Paul's Cathedral (100 feet by nearly 215 feet). The unadorned plaster ceiling doubtless helps create this impression of size.

In a supreme paradox, India's blazing sunshine, which Lutyens thought so "violent," floods the very heart of this fortified palace, the void at the core of its cubic mass. Rays pour from the outer oculus through the inner eye and also penetrate the Durbar Hall from staircase windows on the north and south. A dozen jaalis set in the attic admit additional sunlight, diffused through stylized vegetal designs as classical in inspiration as they are Indian. At night, concealed artificial lighting bathes the dome, its effect supplemented by marble lamp stands in each apse and by a retractable crystal chandelier suspended from above the inner oculus. Reflected light from the marble pavements endows the room at all times with that remarkable opalescent quality characteristic of so many Indian monumental edifices. [92]

Lutyens designed new Viceregal thrones for the Durbar Hall in 1920 to replace those from Government House in Calcutta. The flamboyant new creations in gold and crimson, each capped by two lions and a crown, were impressively scaled. They fairly enveloped their occupants and provided a theatrical backdrop even when the Viceroy and Vicereine stood. The text of their inscription, chosen by Lord Irwin from a list Mrs. Marjorie Shoosmith gave Sir Edwin, came from Proverbs 14:33, "Wisdom resteth in the heart of him that hath understanding."[14]

Lutyens acknowledged in a classic understatement that the decoration of

87. Durbar Hall, Viceroy's House.
Watercolor by William Walcot.

89. The South Main Staircase in Viceroy's House.

88. Details of the dome of Viceroy's House.

Viceroy's House was a question of "considerable difficulty," and was as well, he declared, a matter of genuine importance to India's artistic reputation. For the palace's plethora of vaults, domes, and ceilings, whose unadorned surfaces are so satisfying to today's eye, Lutyens proposed elaborate schemes of ornamentation.[15]

Instead of coffering for the great domed ceiling of the Durbar Hall, Lutyens contemplated a continuous painted ribbon telling India's story, adapted from indigenous works of art. As conceived, Lutyens's friezes were factual, documentary art as in Roman narrative sculpture and painting, in which action flowed with assurance from one episode to the next. This convention of the "continuous style," whose masterpiece is Trajan's 100-foot column, can be traced from Pergamon and Persia to the Buddhist art of India, where it occurred as early as the second century B.C. Lutyens's proposed narratives, glorifying an imperial past, reflected the literary nature of much British art, in which works were a medium for preaching. [87]

But the dome and pendentives of Durbar Hall have stayed blissfully unadorned; Lutyens's scheme for their decoration has remained a pipe dream. So, too, has the school for artists and craftsmen which he and Baker early envisioned. Destined to be the victim of financial economy, the school was meant to meet the decorative needs of Viceroy's House and to "spread its influence & its labors over the whole peninsula." Without the benefit of such a school, or meticulous tutoring and supervision, Lutyens lamented, no Indian painter was sufficiently imaginative and adaptable to create a coherent design for Durbar Hall. No wonder, therefore, that

90. Viceroy's Council Room, Viceroy's House. Percy Brown and Indian artists at work on mural maps.

91. Interior of the Pantheon, Rome. Oil painting by Giovanni Paolo Panini, *c.* 1750, National Gallery of Art, Washington, D.C.

Robert Byron suggested in 1931 that Indian frescoes on the inner dome were "a justifiable field for economy."[16]

Lutyens and Lord Irwin approved mural decoration for only one of the palace's 340 rooms—and to a design proposed by an Englishman. Percy Brown conceived pictorial maps to resemble sixteenth- and seventeenth-century European cartography for the four walls of the Viceroy's Council Room. Under Brown's direction, Munshi Ghulam Husain and a staff of Indians executed the oil paintings, which illustrated India and its neighbors as well as the air route from Delhi to London. An ample complement of people, buildings, animals, ships, and sea monsters helped create a playful effect.[17] [90]

Today's visitors to the Durbar Hall find their delight in nonpictorial features. The chief ornament of the room consists in its proportions and the colorful events it still houses. The perfect geometry of circles and squares—articulated in cylindrical and hemispheric volumes, diametrical axes, giant exedrae, and emphatic paving patterns—implies an empire of ordered unity and permanence, of effective laws, and of universality transcending the local and sectarian. As sunshine streams through the outer and inner oculus, it suffuses the domed hall with its extraordinary brilliance. Heaven's rays, arrogated to human purpose, bathe the raised thrones with a dramatic intensity never enjoyed even by the Sun King at Versailles. The tangible and ethereal, the manmade and natural, are here inextricably linked in a setting for human action. Surely the Durbar Hall is no less than the image of a man-centered cosmos: to use Palladio's description of the Pantheon, it bears in its plan and dome "the figure of the world."[18]

Although roughly twice the size of the Viceroy's throne room, Hadrian's Pantheon is the most obvious source of inspiration for Lutyens; it was familiar to him from visits and standard texts such as Palladio. [91] In Delhi drawings dated December 1914 (later superseded), the analogy is even more precise: like the Pantheon, and in accordance with Vitruvian canons, the radius of the Durbar Hall floor, and the height of the vertical cylinder and of the coffered dome, are all identical. In both Rome and New Delhi today's traveller can thrill to the same electric pleasure, the visual and emotional impact of a giant soaring space, lit dramatically from high above, and radiant with color and glittering marble. If he stands beneath the great oculus on Raisina Hill and ponders the purposes of those who built there, he may recall John Davidson's lines, written scarcely a decade before the initial designs for Imperial Delhi:

> It is with nations as with men:
> One must be first. We are the mightiest,
> The heirs of Rome.[19]

British imperialists routinely compared themselves with their most illustrious predecessors. The Romans had achieved dominion not simply by the sword, but by codified laws, a universal language, and the enticements of citizenship in a civilized community. Under the Pax Romana new highways and canals and safe shipping lanes linked disparate, distant lands to their general benefit. Order and imperium had been synonomous. Was not their own empire even greater, Britons asked—a vastly

92. The Durbar Hall in Viceroy's House.

93. Bust of Sir Edwin Lutyens by Sir William Reid Dick. In the Staircase Court of Viceroy's House.

94. Stone coving framing the sky in the Staircase Court in Viceroy's House.

larger domain bestowed with physical and spiritual order, to the profit of all?

The architects of New Delhi sought to express in permanent and unmistakable form the order and unity that were central to the meaning of the Indian Empire. Viceroy's House, the principal and pivotal monument in the capital from the very first, best captures the intended effect of ordered unity, not only in its facades but in its plan. Much as the coro expresses the essence of a Spanish cathedral, so too the Durbar Hall is the heart of its great house. Visitors to the monumental throne room and its mantle of adjacent passages and stairs experience intricate patterns of color and materials and complex changes in volume, light, and axial direction that animate the entire building. They encounter as well a pervasive geometry, symmetry, and hierarchy. Just as the giant copper dome dominates the palace exterior which serves as its base, so too the singular significance of the Durbar Hall is felt throughout the centralized plan. Every detail of the plan is coordinated with the others in a coherent system, a consummate expression of the classical mind. All parts are related to a single point, in the way that the Viceroy was supreme governor and linchpin of the sprawling Indian Empire. That hierarchy of order so beloved by Kipling, and conveyed to the furthest outposts of imperial authority, here assumes tangible form.

While the principal entrances other than the east front permit the visitor to circumvent the Durbar Hall, the importance of the room nonetheless asserts itself in the plan. Sited athwart the main axes of Viceroy's House, the giant void which confronts the guest from the vestibule inspires circumambulation simply by its awesome and clearly ceremonial character. Moreover, the room lies an inhibiting three steps below the contiguous corridors, and, most important, its emphatic east–west axis stops abruptly at the imperial thrones. The consequence is axial ambiguity and circuitous movement in a plan that is fundamentally symmetrical and axially conceived.[20] [95]

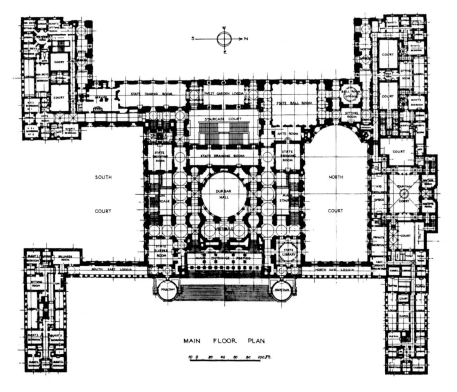

95. Plan of Main Floor, Viceroy's House.

96 (facing page). Council Chamber, Viceroy's House. Plan of Main Floor (left); section on north–south axis, looking west (right); and elevation of interior, south side (top). Ink sketch by E. L. Lutyens, September 5, 1913.

To achieve the desired "sense of pervading equanimity" in a house, Lutyens declared, required painstaking care and trouble. After the first intuitive ideas, it was a time-consuming job "to make the outside fit in effect with the inside of a house." Much of Lutyens's success surely came from his sheer enjoyment of his task, the delight he found in the exacting challenge to his imagination. "It is fun," he remarked with obvious gusto, "designing a building to fit within a defined cube" and weighing the almost limitless variations possible.[21]

Lutyens's commission at Raisina did not lack for such challenge. The scale of Viceroy's House was urban, rather than simply domestic. Meant to dominate an entire cityscape, it had to be equally impressive from all angles. A long garden wall like the château at Versailles or a pinwheel of patulous extensions would not have suited the intended scenic and symbolic purposes. Lutyens preferred instead a sculpted cube, its massive look of British solidity made more imposing by pyramidal propensities recalling Hindu and Muslim monuments.

The basic plan of Viceroy's House, which had crystallized when Lutyens first visited India, is typical of his earlier buildings: a symmetrical arrangement of rooms within a square or an H-plan, a void (more often a solid mass) which deflects movement around the intersection of the main axes, circumambulatory circulation, and symmetrical massing.[22] The palace as eventually executed, its portico framed by outstretched L-shaped wings, remained remarkably faithful to a pair of hasty sketches Lutyens sent Herbert Baker from Simla on June 14, 1912. From the outset the circular Durbar Hall, inscribed within a square, formed the centerpiece. Other areas designated in mid-1912 for the use of the Viceroy, King, ADCs, Council Members, and Comptroller, and as the State Rooms and Council Chamber, stayed unchanged except for postwar removal of legislative functions to a separate building. Even the rectangles labelled "State Garden" and "Privy Garden" reflected the eventual pattern of ceremonial and domestic activity in the Mughal Garden. [18]

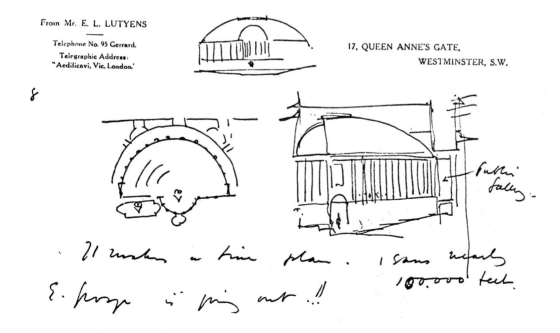

98. The West Garden Loggia, Main Floor.
Watercolor by William Walcot.

99. The Ball Room in Viceroy's House. Watercolor by William Walcot.

100. The State Dining Room in Viceroy's House.

97. The Ball Room in Viceroy's House.

Sketches for Raisina dating from 1912 and 1913 uniformly display a Council Chamber between the north wings. [96] The important Morley-Minto constitutional reforms of 1909 expanded the Imperial Legislative Council from twenty-five to sixty members, instituting direct election for nearly half and broadening the scope of debate. The decision to house this Council at Delhi under the Viceroy's roof, however, aroused prompt opposition, highlighting the important symbolic role of New Delhi and its architecture. As early as August 1912, one Member of Parliament protested that both practical and political expediency suggested a separate council building "worthy of the dignity of the new city," as a "visible sign of the new era of political development." In reply, the Government's spokesman, Edwin Montagu, offered assurances that the Councillors would have a separate entrance to Government House. Given that the Imperial Council was simply "an addition" of other Members to the Viceroy's Executive Council, he declared, the Government believed a site immediately adjacent to the Viceregal residence was altogether proper. Not until after the next step from consultative toward responsible government—enactment in 1919 of Montagu's own reforms—did the Government of India commission an independent Council House.[23]

Because Lutyens planned Viceroy's House essentially as processional architecture, its forms a catalyst for movement, he expended much care and space on transition areas, especially the vertical linkages. The pivotal Durbar Hall is everywhere surrounded by stairs, eminently practical for large-scale entertaining and for evoking a useful impression of awesome imperial might. On the east, the mountainous portico steps join Viceroy's Court and the city's ceremonial axis to the Viceregal throne. To the north and south, the Main Staircases provide appropriately grand entrance from the carriageways and North and South Court. [89] Twin stairs beneath the great hall descend to the Lower Basement and the voluminous cloakrooms necessary for receptions of a thousand persons, and four newel staircases ascend to the gallery of the palace dome, with vistas across the Delhi plain under the over-arching heavens. Near the portico, modest half-turn stairs with landings offer swift, direct access from the Lower Basement kitchens for official functions on the Main Floor. On the west, monumental sandstone steps virtually fill an entire courtyard, connecting the carriageways with all the State rooms, and rivalling in their generous scale not only the Genoese examples that Lutyens admired but even Piranesi's fantasies. [94]

Southwest of the Durbar Hall rises the most imaginatively and complexly wrought staircase of all, intended solely for the Viceroy's family and connecting on three floors the semi-State rooms, State apartments, and private Viceregal quarters. Built between walls and gracefully tall in its proportions (as though under compression), it recalls much of the mysterious drama of Lutyens's Castle Drogo in Devon. Delicately recessed vertical surfaces interweave with a meticulous combination of both slightly and boldly projecting horizontal members, all bound in an integral whole by massively deep round arches. To cap this tour de force, Lutyens has linked his composition with that special heritage of Mughal palaces, the music and sight of running water. In a design at once lively and restrained, the glistening liquid—so precious in India—spills into six shallow basins from the marble jaws of eight Britannic lions. [101]

101. Viceroy's Staircase, Viceroy's House.

104. Long State Drawing Room, Viceroy's House, looking south.

105. West Garden Loggia, Viceroy's House, looking south. Vaulting decorations at the behest of Lady Willingdon, Vicereine from 1931 to 1936.

Nearby, the view of the red and buff sandstone Staircase Court from the State Drawing Room's five western windows may at first seem severely architectural until the visitor looks up. A deeply overhanging stone cove captures a dazzling panorama of azure heaven; at night its gently lit soffit frames a thousand glittering diamonds in the black velvet sky. [94, 104]

The adjoining North Corridor ends as a vestibule of the State Ball Room, one of a suite of State apartments overlooking the gardens. Three—the State Dining Room, West Garden Loggia, and Ball Room Loggia or anteroom—are the same width, but their different lengths and heights endow the visitor's procession with variety. The Ball Room, moreover, is nearly twice the others' width. The dancing area, thirty-four feet in height and panelled with mirrors, leads at each end through three arches to vaulted vestibules twenty-four feet high, where those not dancing can witness the swirling kaleidoscopic spectacle without crowding or collision. Lutyens has used the same Order and gleaming floorboards to effect visual unity of the lobbies and central area. But by omitting in the vestibules the three-quarter attached columns, he has correctly given the principal room primacy in splendor. [97, 98, 99, 106]

The forceful east–west axis which divides in half the Viceregal palace and the capital city, bisects as well the West Garden Loggia. [105] That lofty prelude to the Ball Room and State Dining Room is the noblest of the loggias that are important aesthetic and functional features of Viceroy's House. Double pairs of columns, repeated six times on the long walls, frame gorgeous vistas across luxuriant gardens to the Ridge and, alternatively, over the pageant of guests and towering Viceroy's Body Guards on the steps of Staircase Court. Between the columns, gurgling fountains in the sills cool the breezes from the Delhi plain. In either end wall, square-pillared Venetian doorways bound views across the respective vestibules toward

102 (preceding page, left). The State Library in Viceroy's House.
103 (preceding page, right). The semi-state rooms of Viceroy's House open on the garden.

106. State Ball Room, Viceroy's House.

107. State Dining Room, Viceroy's House.

108. The West Garden Loggia, Upper Basement Floor, in Viceroy's House.

109. Wardrobe by E. L. Lutyens in the southwest wing of Viceroy's House.

110. Door handle by E. L. Lutyens in Viceroy's House.

111 (facing page). A Viceregal bathroom, with shower.

112. State Library, Viceroy's
House.

113. Private Dining Room,
Viceroy's House.

114. Card Room, Viceroy's
House.

round-headed niches and glazed entrances to the adjacent State rooms and emphasize the insistent north–south axis of the suite by the recession in depth.

Fine materials enliven the grand State Dining Room, once the setting for Viceregal banquets. An impressive gallery of portraits were hung on teak panels, part of a display Lutyens dreamed might eventually rival the Vandyke Room at Wilton.[24] Depicted were Governors-General and Viceroys, lofty rulers over a subcontinent but also intensely individual beings: not idealized Greeks, but very human Romans. They were flanked by Delhi Order pilasters, which in turn supported a rich teak entablature with a boldly bracketed frieze. Above, the ceiling cove sprang from a thin teak cornice. At the south end, Viceregal gold plate glittered against dark red velvet in a niche that rose to the parapet of a Minstrels' Gallery. Crystal chandeliers illuminated the shining table (seating 104), and light leather chairs, pale damask curtains, elaborate Kashmiri carpet, and gray-and-white stars in the marble floor. Below the dado rail, handsome side tables by Lutyens echoed in inverted form the pierced entablature brackets, while ingenious lyre-shaped clocks graced the overmantel of the two marble fireplaces. Behind the distinguished guests, 112 native khitmatgars waited attentively, their uniforms a blaze of scarlet and gold, underscoring by their race and numbers the imperial flavor of the scene. [100, 107]

Beneath the dramatic succession of State rooms at New Delhi lay another suite, the semi-State or Private State rooms used for all but the most elaborate official functions. Opening on the garden between the original Viceroy's apartments and the northwest or Guest Wing, they corresponded to the principal rooms of a peer's country house and were emphatically British. Lutyens's Viceregal edifice, like Wren's work for William and Mary at Hampton Court, paradoxically combined public grandeur and private domesticity, functioning admirably as both ceremonial stage set and comfortable residence. If the Main Floor State rooms at Raisina were reminiscent of Hampton Court, the more intimate semi-State apartments recalled John Evelyn's estimate of Wren's and Hawksmoor's work at Kensington Palace: "very noble tho not greate."[25]

A procession of seven rooms composed the semi-State suite. All possessed a common width, but different lengths and heights varied the visitors' successive volumetric sensations. Uniquely patterned ceilings, wall panelling, marble floors, and carpets from Kashmir and Amritsar gave each room a distinctive personality. No mantelpiece design, here or elsewhere in the palace, was repeated—"& Lady Irwin likes them all," Lutyens told his wife exultantly in 1929. Furniture was built of Indian woods in Delhi workshops; the local climate proved lethal to the soft woods of antiques which the New Delhi Advisory Committee sent from England. Chinese craftsmen, soon joined by increasingly expert Sikhs, faithfully executed Lutyens's designs.[26] [112, 113, 114]

Areas intended for the reception of visitors on State business display in their plan typical Lutyens complexity. Three identical entrances grace the apsidal west end of the North Court. The central archway issues at right angles into a cross-vaulted corridor that serves also as a lobby, while the entrance axis continues to the blank wall of an elliptical vestibule, behind which lies the Viceroy's lavatory. Entry to the waiting room or to the Viceroy's Private Office is at ninety degrees on the north–south axis.

116. The Nursery anteroom,
Viceroy's House.

117. Day Nursery electroliers,
Viceroy's House. Ink sketch by
E. L. Lutyens, January 24, 1929.

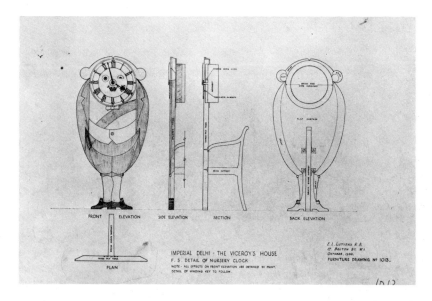

118. Nursery clock, Viceroy's
House. Ink drawing, office of E. L.
Lutyens, October 1930.

115 (facing page). The Nursery
Cloister, Viceroy's House.

During five Viceroyalties, the floor below the semi-State rooms teemed with a staff not found even in the greatest British country house. There were rooms for a steward, a housekeeper, valets, and a barber, and workshops for three tailors, tinsmiths, a mason and stone-cutter, a blacksmith, a painter, a carpenter, and electricians. Multiple godowns provided storage for tents and camp equipment, coal and wood, furniture, boxes, stationery, linen, china and glass, and carpets. Scattered throughout this Lower Basement were a still room, a bakery, a pastry room, a pot scullery, kitchens and kitchen stores and larders, wine and beer cellars, refrigerating and ice-making rooms, a boiler-house, a European servants' hall, a cinema theater, and the Viceroy's Press, where sixty men produced a never-ending torrent of invitations, menus, seating plans, and minutely detailed programs of Viceregal tours and events.[27]

The four wings of the palace accommodated bedroom suites and offices, and in each wing, stairways and interior courts dictated nonaxial circulation. Supplemented by light from loggias, they ensured that corridors avoided the appearance of long, dark tunnels. The Viceregal quarters, originally located in the southwest wing, markedly resembled an eighteenth-century English house, from servants' hall and housekeeper's office in the basement to nursery beneath the roof. If the State rooms of the main block served, like a traditional royal palace, to accent the ruler's exalted role, the southwest wing was a self-contained cocoon of well-protected domesticity and privacy, urbane but comfortable, secluded but with sweeping vistas of the Ridge and Delhi plain. Its furnishings designed by Lutyens, its art selected and hung by the Irwins, its staff ample and punctilious, the Viceroy's wing recalled Henry James's judgment that the "well-appointed, well-administered, well-filled

119. Plan of Upper Basement floor, Viceroy's House.

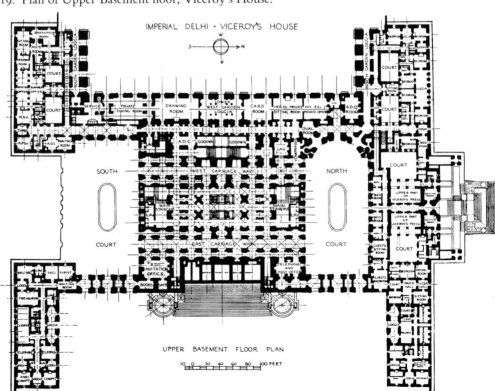

120. Vicereine's Bedroom, Viceroy's House.

country house" was a compendium of English social genius and manners, the most perfect and characteristic national invention.[28] [109, 110, 111, 120]

The top floor of this house-within-a-house was devoted to children and guests. Lutyens took special pleasure in the painted wood electroliers of the nursery, conceived in "a very lightsome mood": four praying angels for the Night Nursery, four galloping horses in the anteroom, and in the Day Nursery, four hens and their chicks with broken eggs spilling their yolks as the light bulbs![29] After the imperial grandeur of the State rooms, replete with thrones and boldly patterned marble floors, Lutyens obviously enjoyed the paradox of creating children's chairs or a giant red and white chessboard in the floor. He fenced the nursery light court for safety, but introduced a playful parrot's cage in each side of the wooden screen. It was a perfect example of his exuberant wit: an imprisoning barrier transformed into an attractive object of great charm. [115, 116, 117, 118]

At first, even the Irwins, accustomed to big houses, found the palace all quite confusing. "We still feel rather as if we were moving in a labyrinth of Crete," the Viceroy wrote after three days in residence, "and if we leave our regular runs are apt to get lost." Yet, as he predicted, with greater familiarity grew admiration and affection. Years later he recollected that "in spite of its size, it was essentially a liveable-in house"; he and Lady Irwin came to love it more every day.[30]

The garden was one of the chief pleasures of the palace. The Viceregal garden scheme which Lutyens submitted to the Government of India in 1918 was explicitly intended to be "of the Moghal type"; the sources for this model were actually much

121. The west front of Viceroy's House, from the gardens. The towers were not built.

122. The west front of Viceroy's House from the Mughal Garden.

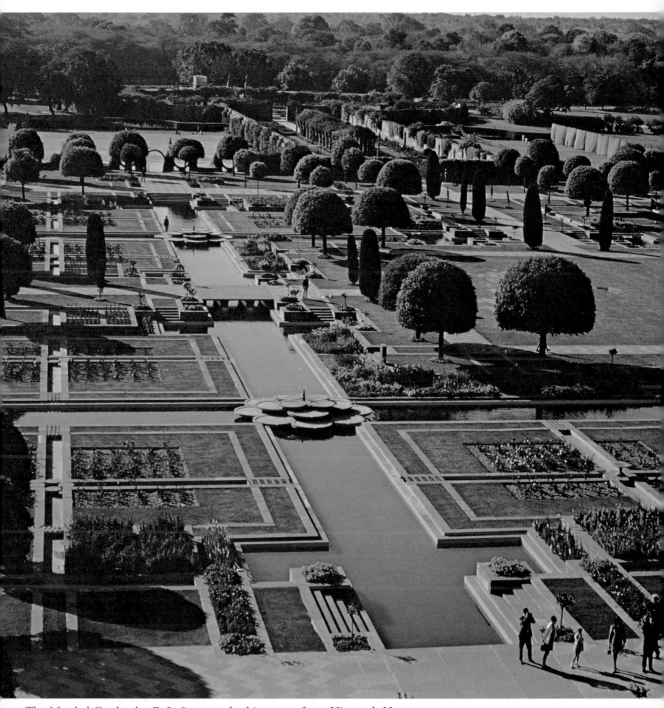

23. The Mughal Garden by E. L. Lutyens, looking west from Viceroy's House.

older. Constance Villiers-Stuart, whose pioneer research on Indian water gardens Lord Hardinge knew and admired, emphasized that quadripartite plans figured in Muslim conceptions of paradise, Hebrew visions of Eden, and the Hindu mythological geography of the world. Lutyens had ample opportunity to observe such fourfold designs on his visits to the Red Forts at Agra and Delhi, the Taj, the Shalimar Gardens both at Lahore and in Kashmir, and even the Escorial. Decorative use of water was the single aspect of Indian architecture which most captivated Lutyens. After all, in contemporary judgment it was he who had "more than any other man" promoted a renaissance in British water gardening. Not surprisingly, the Viceroy's garden mirrored this renewed popularity in Britain for formal water gardens, raised paved walks, color groupings, and pergolas.[31]

Certainly Lutyens's Viceregal garden may be regarded as an extension of the house; the massive, nobly severe walls which enclose the garden literally grow out of the Lower Basement, resembling an imposing fortress by Marshal Vauban, while the interlocking rectangles of the house plan pervade the parterres. Walls and terraces cascade across the landscape in three waves down to the level of the plain, where the tranquillity of a circular pool climaxes the main urban axis and faintly echoes the War Memorial rotary, more than two miles distant. [121, 124, 125]

Water gives a theatrical unity to the whole. Two glistening channels run westward from beneath the Garden Loggia and intersect with a pair of north–south canals. Circular fountains of sixteen-tiered lotus leaves, carved from sandstone, scatter liquid pearls in perfect rainbows from their twelve-foot jets. Beside the

124. Aerial view of Viceroy's House and Mughal Garden.
125 (facing page). Plan of the gardens of Viceroy's House.

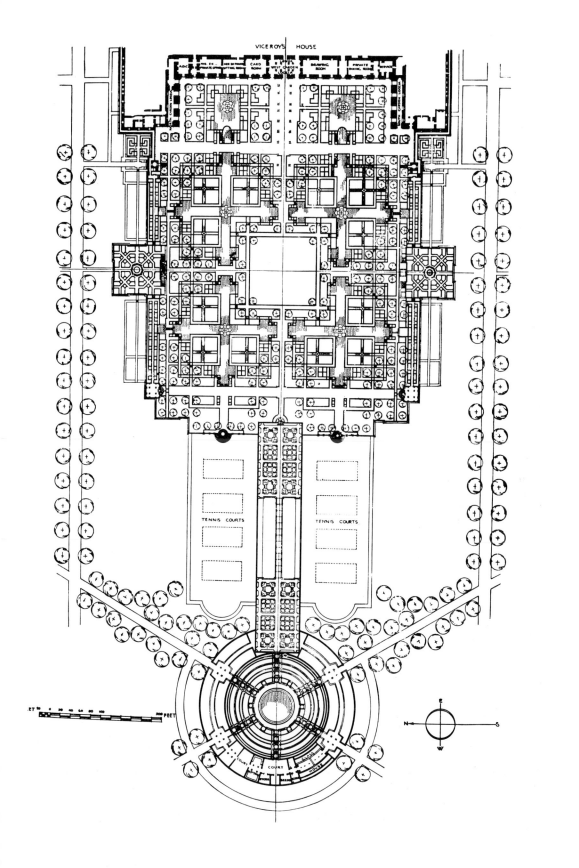

VICEROY'S HOUSE

TENNIS COURTS          TENNIS COURTS

126. The stone screen marking the boundary of the Mughal Garden and the tennis courts.

127. The stone pergola between the Mughal Garden and the Round Pool Garden at Viceroy's House.

28. The Round Pool Garden steps.

129. West front of Viceroy's House from the Mughal Garden.

130. Tiered fountain in the Mughal garden, looking northeast.

131. A diminutive Gurkha guarding a Viceregal gazebo.

132. North Fort grotto, Viceroy's House.

palace, two larger fountains of eighteen leaves grace rectangular pools, where reflections repeat with double charm the blossoms and building. At the heart of the watercourses, a 200-foot-square island provides a pleasant greensward for a garden-party marquee and outdoor receptions. Intricate variations in level, as well as scores of topiary trees and two tall sandstone gazebos, endow Lutyens's composition with a sculptural quality. [122, 123, 129, 130, 131]

Amid this splendid panorama, the aptly named North and South Forts, each ninety-four feet square, are set like bastions along the garden boundary. Their sharply battered walls rise solidly from plain to parapet, where formal terraces of English flowers are spread beneath the sun. In the southern enclosure a fountain jet stabs the sky from an octagonal pool; on the north terrace, a perforated pipe girdles a round void. Water cascades twenty feet in a showery circle to a grotto tank where a slender jet splashes. Troughs of placid water frame the frothy square basin, as if to assert the triumph of order over tumult in British India. [132]

The visitor's odyssey nears its end. A western wall of relentless stone hoops screens and also announces by its circular geometry the tennis courts below. Beyond, a narrow but 430-foot-long garden, dividing grass tennis courts from clay, directs the visitor toward the Ridge between walls enlivened with niches like those Lutyens had admired at the Escorial. A rhubarb sandstone pergola, twelve feet wide, is bridged in part by cantilever beams, counterweighted by remarkable pendants that

34. The Round Pool Garden at Viceroy's House.

33. The Round Pool Garden, at its best in February.

resemble elephant trunks. The procession culminates in a butterfly garden, its brilliant colors arranged in tiers about a round pool, with a high orchard wall ensuring privacy and peace. Here the Viceroy would retreat with his wife from a world increasingly alien and uncertain to take afternoon tea and savor the last hour of sun and its magic afterglow. Then a gray haze would steal over the gardens, and on the Ridge, jackals would cry at the moon. The fragrance of roses and mignonettes perfumed the air, and, to Lutyens's delight, the fountains formed lunar rainbows. Small wonder that Indians called the garden "God's own heaven," and one Viceroy pronounced it "a paradise".[32] [126, 127, 128, 133, 134, 135, 136]

The lushness of the Viceregal garden accentuated the inhospitable nature of the surrounding landscape. The patterns of water, color, and symmetry from Lutyens's hand were in marked contrast to the arid, drab wilderness outside the estate. The formal palace edifice and its geometric garden, juxtaposed against the untamed Delhi Ridge, was meant to be a telling affirmation of power and of the passionate British resolve to bring order to India—tangible proof, to use poet John Davidson's words, of the "ruthless obligation . . . to be despotic for the world's behoof."[33]

The fifteen acres of bright hues and bold patterns fashioned west of the palace by Lutyens and W. R. Mustoe, Director of Horticulture, were but a small fraction of the extraordinary 250-acre grounds. A handful of British estates might possess a comparably impressive landscaped park of specimen plantings, but how many had as well a swimming pool, squash court, cricket ground, nine-hole golf course, and eight tennis courts? None could boast a garden staff of 418, of whom fifty devoted themselves largely to scaring depredatory birds and another twenty entirely to flower arrangements. Within the Viceregal compound a "utility garden" alone comprised sixteen acres, providing abundant cut flowers for the palace, seasonal

135. Gardeners planting the Mughal Garden, next to the Viceregal tennis courts.

136. Sandstone pergola framing construction of Viceroy's House and gardens.

vegetables and citrus fruit for its kitchens, and rose bushes sufficient to replace three thousand each year.

In all respects the Viceregal establishment was appropriately imperial in scale. At the close of British rule in 1947, over two thousand persons served Lord Mountbatten at Viceroy's House in New Delhi: aides and clerks, soldiers and police, and a veritable army of servants and staff throughout the palace and its grounds, stables, garage, post office, and dispensary. Including families and other dependents, altogether more than six thousand persons had permanent housing in the Viceregal compound at Raisina, and over a thousand more lived at Simla and Calcutta.[34] [137, 139]

The Viceregal staff quarters at Delhi became known in official parlance simply as "Schedule B," nomenclature coined in 1913, when the Imperial Delhi Committee determined the scale of accommodation required at Raisina and the limits of permissible expenditure. The document listing the requisites for the palace or Government House, and allowable expenses, was entitled "Schedule A."

The challenge for Lutyens was to concoct a staff village close to the palace, complementary in appearance and clearly subsidiary to this principal focus—a formal and symbolic microcosm of the garden city then in conception. Lutyens's first scheme proved abortive. Stables and menials' quarters, screened by an elaborate wall, would have flanked the northern approach to Government House and to the intended Imperial Council Chamber. The consequence of such a design, the Imperial Delhi Committee objected, would have been costly decorative treatment of Schedule B to ensure a dignified entrance avenue. Instead the Committee advocated "a different but equally convenient" placement of the staff buildings, in the northwest corner of the Viceregal compound, where they would impinge less

137. Lord and Lady Mountbatten and their daughters Patricia and Pamela at Viceroy's House in 1947 with liveried servants.

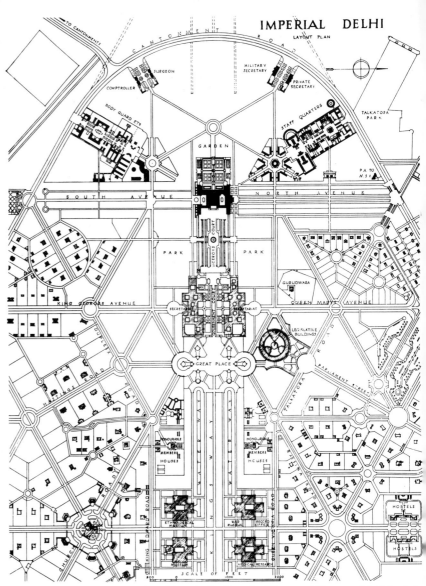

139. Faiz Mohd, the Head Butler
at Viceroy's House during the
Viceroyalty of Lord Mountbatten.

140. Detail of the layout of Raisina, including the Viceregal Estate with Schedule
B or staff quarters, Body Guard Lines, and senior Viceregal staff bungalows, all by
E. L. Lutyens.

directly on the view from the palace and on the Council House approach. Suitably
proximate and decorous quarters for the Governor-General's Body Guard remained
problematical. In 1918 the New Delhi Advisory Committee in London threw its
influence behind Lutyens's proposal for a site in the Viceregal estate southwest of
Government House, symmetrical in plan and skyline with staff housing in Schedule
B. This scheme was ultimately realized in the present Body Guard or Escort Lines, a
cantonment completed in 1927 for two companies of British and Indian infantry and
twice that number of Body Guards.[35]

Schedule B and nearby military lines reflected many of the same concerns for
ordered, hierarchical unity and uniformity that had inspired Imperial Delhi as a
whole. These two villages echoed both the form and intent of the garden city capital
in the precise geometry of their interwoven radial and grid plans, whose principal

138 (preceding pages). Stone pergola leading to the Round Pool Garden.

axial vistas focused on the aloof monument of executive power astride an adjoining eminence. Quarters were designed and assigned as befitted rank: from single rooms for palace "menials" and pairs of rooms for "married syces" or grooms to commodious bungalows, replete with spacious garden and servants' compound, for principals in the Viceroy's Secretariat. The potential monotony inherent in a range of white-plastered bungalows and barracks was skillfully averted in both plan and elevation. Among the predominant quadrangular groupings Lutyens interspersed other basic geometric forms—circuses, crescents, and wedge-shaped designs—at varying distances from common axes. Emphatic axiality, clear-cut symmetry, and focal terminal features gave vigorous expression to imperial preoccupations with order, conformity, and stability. Above a uniform cornice line and consistently flat roofs Lutyens set obelisks, urns, and lantern-capped towers on a dozen and a half buildings to create a picturesque skyline. He employed details such as coining and rustication with accustomed dexterity in the stable blocks to produce lively shadow patterns and surface textures despite the corrosive glare of the sun. While the attenuated dome and drum of the Band House remotely recalled the Horse Guards in Whitehall, an unimpeachably English source, Lutyens achieved a subtle blending of East and West in the stable towers whose domical vaulting and lanterns suggested inspiration from Hindu temple sikharas, expressed in the language of Wren. [141, 143, 144, 145, 146, 147]

Lutyens tackled the planning process with artistry, endowing buildings meant for diverse functions with a harmonious unity: the stables and Band House had a domestic note, while careful detailing and massing of small bungalows and of syces' quarters gave them a surprising monumentality. Ranges of menials' cells or modest cottages were dexterously manipulated to look like single large residences, so that, as at Hampstead Garden Suburb, all the houses in a group enjoyed an enhanced grandeur and appeared equally agreeable to inhabit. [148]

Consistent symmetry, proportion, vocabulary, and materials (white plastered brick, although Lutyens and the King had preferred stone) invested the Viceregal compound with a homogeneity that was a metaphor of British paternalistic goals in India as framed a century earlier by Governor-General Lord William Bentinck and his Councillor, Thomas Babington Macaulay. Lutyens orchestrated the architectural components at Delhi much as the government marshalled resources to integrate an entire subcontinent. But within the comprehensive codes that governed classical architecture—and within those that governed dominions—there was room for remarkable variety and novelty. Even within the chafing budgetary constraints and physical confines of Schedule B, Lutyens exhibited his ingenuity. He could, for example, endow entries to a circle of servants' quarters with all the imposing dignity of a city portal or triumphal arch; or he could transform normally sturdy, even stolid, gate piers into arresting skeletal sentinels by deeply scalloping adjacent faces with huge niches. A measure of Lutyens's genius was his ability to do the unexpected—and to succeed.[36]

Lutyens's wit and penchant for surprise had to contend with the realities of Indian climate. From the very outset of the new capital, the Government of India's seasoned bureaucracy frankly deprecated "any radical departure" from traditional principles of residential design at Delhi. The essential elements were lofty central rooms to

141. Schedule B. The Band House, stables, and staff quarters from Viceroy's House.

42. Bungalow of the Private Secretary to the Viceroy in the Viceregal Estate.

43. Schedule B.

145. Schedule B, Viceregal Estate, from the northwest. Perspective by Cyril A. Farey, 1922.

144 (left). Stables at Viceroy's House. Perspective by Cyril A. Farey, 1922.

146. Schedule B, looking southeast to Viceroy's House.

147. The Band House, Schedule B, Viceregal Estate.

148. A unified design for multiple staff quarters, Schedule B.

149. The south approach to Viceroy's Court and the Jaipur Column. Elephants by C. S. Jagger.

150. From the dome of Viceroy's House. The Jaipur Column and All–India War Memorial Arch, framed by the Secretariat blocks.

151. Entrance front, bungalow of the Surgeon to the Viceroy.

152. Garden front, bungalow of the Private Secretary to the Viceroy.

153. Garden front, bungalow of the Surgeon to the Viceroy.

store cool air during the hot hours, smaller rooms around these main rooms for protection from hot wind and sun, devices such as clerestory hopper windows for changing the air rapidly on opening up a house at night, and verandahs to protect windows and doors from the direct sun. Plastered brick columns were spaced more widely than in European classical colonnades to permit better ventilation. The typical flat roof in a classical bungalow—a sandwich of packed mud on five inches of concrete laid over bricks resting on reinforced concrete joists—acted as an insulator and incidentally served as a cool nighttime refuge for sleeping.[37]

Lutyens's faithful adherence to these principles in early schemes for Raisina bungalows, however, swiftly provoked the charge that he had designed hot-weather rather than cold-weather residences. The Viceroy's Private Secretary singled out the internal atria and loggias and "very large external loggia" to illustrate this complaint in his own projected bungalow. The subsequent discarding of these features reflected the fact that ranking government officers and their retainers spent only the six coolest months in the Indian plains before retreating to their Himalayan aerie. But by the mid-1920s the Calcutta and Simla press smugly reported critical brickbats for the new bungalows from those Raisina residents who were not part of the annual migration. Houses designed merely for cold weather and built with thin walls and no verandahs were "like ovens" by April. Even Herbert Baker privately expressed unhappiness over the "shadeless" and "shadowless" buildings which had sprouted across Delhi to Government designs.[38]

Lutyens sited the four principal Viceregal staff bungalows symmetrically at the termini of major axes which united with geometric precision the palace, gardens, Schedule B and Body Guard Lines. The plan of the compound was linked in turn to the whole intricate urban web of sixty- and ninety-degree angles that it echoed: estate became epitome of city in the quest for a unified hierarchical order. As elsewhere in Delhi, the size and appointments of each house faithfully reflected the occupant's specific official rank: the Viceroy's Private Secretary had seven bedrooms, the Military Secretary had five, and the Surgeon and Comptroller had appropriately smaller quarters with three bedrooms each.[39]

In the four Viceregal staff bungalows the long, low lines, underscored by shadows from prominent string courses and cornices, had their counterpoint in the thrust of bold chimneys and in the elegant verticality of portico, garden loggia, and tall round-headed recesses. Designing primarily for cold weather (and for appearance),

54. Entrance front, bungalow, Surgeon to the Viceroy. Ink drawing, office of E. L. Lutyens, January 1918.

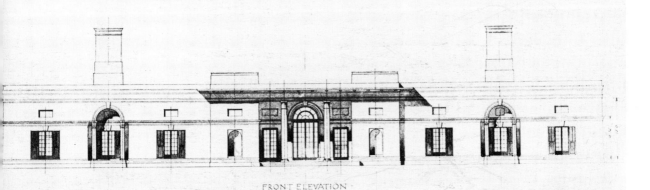

FRONT ELEVATION

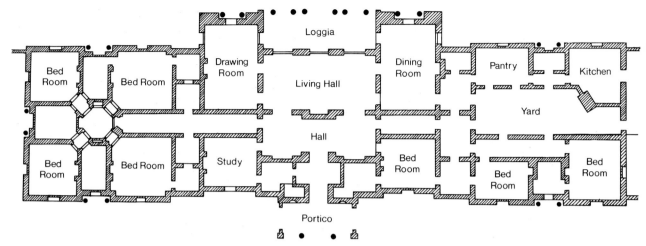

155. Plan of the bungalow of the Private Secretary to the Viceroy.

156. Living Hall, bungalow of the Private Secretary to the Viceroy.

Lutyens omitted peripheral verandahs and made little provision for cross ventilation. But his concessions to hot weather in March included thick walls, high-ceilinged rooms, clerestory openings, deep-set shuttered windows, and a loggia and portico shielding the entrances, supplemented in daytime with "chicks" or tatti screens of split bamboo or plaited cuscus grass. Visitors to the Private Secretary's residence, after a typically Lutyensesque circumambulation from the portico, reached the main rooms—a drawing room, living hall, and dining room—which were clustered on the garden front and bracketed by the bedrooms and by the kitchen and service rooms. Indian servants and their families were housed separately, as usual, a discreet distance away. [151, 152, 153, 154, 155, 156]

Conceived as early as 1913, designs and budgets for buildings and gardens in the Viceroy's estate were periodically altered for more than a decade. The house destined for the Private Secretary was habitable by the cold weather of 1920–21, when Lutyens promptly moved in, using it annually for nine years until the Viceregal Court came to Raisina from Old Delhi. By 1922 the bungalow had plumbing but still no water, which even the architect's unconventional wife pronounced "primitive." Its wood fire, Lady Emily and her daughters recalled, did

157. Sir Edwin admires a parrot in his bungalow garden at New Delhi, 1928.

158. Lutyensesque levity in the garden. Left to right, A. G. Shoosmith, W. R. Mustoe, and Lutyens.

159. Viceroy's Court, Jaipur Column, and east front of Viceroy's House.

little to combat the icy wind that seemed to make even the white roses blue with cold. Moreover the chimney "smoked in the best Lutyens tradition." (Sir Edwin himself expressed astonishment that fireplaces in Viceroy's House did not "go badly amiss.") A round blackboard covered the dining room tabletop, and chalk was laid beside the knives at each place. Enchanting drawings and games of noughts and crosses helped enliven mealtimes, which were normally crowded with guests. Lutyens abhorred nothing more than the solemnity and "Church-all-day feeling" that accompanied a visit in 1925 from Theosophist Annie Besant.[40] [142, 157, 158]

The forms that Lutyens created in Schedule B, Body Guard Lines, and the main staff bungalows exerted a potent influence over residential design everywhere in the new city. Herbert Baker's Delhi representative later testified unequivocally to their powerful example. [41] The principal evidence existed of course in scores of houses at Raisina, work by Lutyens's disciples both in private practice and in the office of Robert Tor Russell, Chief Architect to the Government of India, where most official quarters at Imperial Delhi were designed. Although modest in extent, Lutyens's contribution to housing at Raisina helped to define a style and set a standard. An harmonious and unified appearance embodying the image and ideals of British rule, coupled with location in the capital city and the renown of the architect, helped ensure that this handful of buildings inspired residential architecture in the Indian Empire for a generation.

To the east, Viceroy's Court formed a physical and symbolic extension of Lutyens's palace. The red sandstone retaining walls that enclosed the 1,150-foot-long forecourt emerged directly from the north and south facades at the Lower Basement level, binding British edifice and native hillock in a powerful embrace.

Western technology had even altered and subdued the landscape to serve imperial purpose: blasting levelled twenty feet from the crest of Raisina Hill, and a constant flow of precious water brought fountains and lush greenery to the arid eminence. Along the lateral entrances to the expansive quadrangle, sentinel ranks of lions in rhubarb stone as well as sandstone elephants modelled by sculptor Charles Sargeant Jagger, their caparisoned flanks emblazoned with royal monograms, boldly proclaimed British guardianship over India. [149, 160]

Focus of the forecourt was the Jaipur Column. Gift of Sir Sawai Madho Singh, Maharaja of Jaipur, to commemorate creation of the new capital, the monument was the centerpiece of Viceroy's Court both as a unifying spatial marker and an imperial and ecumenical symbol. It towered more than 145 feet against the sky, a slender pillar and its pedestal, supported on a red sandstone base and crowned remarkably by a glass star sprouting from a bronze lotus blossom. The buff sandstone drums of the shaft, an average of six and a half feet in diameter, had a spinal tube of drawn steel, anchoring the five-ton lotus and star finial to a reinforced concrete core in the base, a precaution prompted by memories of a 1905 earthquake. Observations using a theodolite—to refute early charges that the column had been built out of plumb—disclosed a welcome elasticity when the tip of the star oscillated in a stiff wind five or six inches to a beat of three seconds.[42] [150, 161]

Straddling the main axes of Viceroy's Court, the Jaipur Column helped orient the visitor, acting as a visual terminus of the north and south avenues and a directional

160. Elephant, minus the imperial cypher, guarding the lateral approach to Viceroy's Court. Designed by C. S. Jagger.

point in the processional path to Viceroy's House. Paradoxically it obstructed the visitor's most direct route to his goal, forcing him to choose movement to the left or right, as in so many of Lutyens's entrance vestibules. Symmetrically placed between the eastern wings, its slender shaft and brilliant glass star in emphatic contrast to the massive palatine edifice, the column inflected attention toward center stage, underscoring and enhancing the importance of the State Entrance. Was it not, one admirer asked, the lightning which anticipated the thunder of the mighty dome beyond?[43]

The Jaipur Column assumed primary significance, however, in its symbolic role. Above all, it was a metaphor of dominion and victory, the primordial staff or stake thrust in the soil, the flag driven into a windswept hilltop or tropical shore, the cavalry lance impaling a foe. Free-standing commemorative pillars were of course hardly new to India: among the most notable were the some thirty stone lats erected at the behest of the Buddhist Emperor Asoka in the third century B.C. Ten have survived, two in Delhi. Later equivalents which Lutyens saw in the capital territory were the renowned Iron Pillar—a standard of the Lord Vishnu to the memory of a Gupta king—and the thirteenth-century Qutb Minar, whose inscriptions and very

161 (facing page). Jaipur Column, Viceroy's Court, by E. L. Lutyens.
162. Plan of New Delhi on the Jaipur Column.    163. Detail of the Jaipur Column.

name proclaim it as a pole or pivot of just rule and divine faith, and exultant emblem of Islam's eastward spread. On the greensward of Calcutta's Maidan, a 152-foot monument honored Sir David Ochterlony, the general who conquered Nepal in 1816. Preeminent among modern pillars in the West were those raised in both London and Dublin to Nelson's triumphs and in the Place Vendôme to Napoleon's campaigns; their most celebrated precedent was the marble pillar to Emperor Trajan in a forum often acclaimed as the premier monument of Imperial Rome. A germinal sketch for Delhi by Lutyens in June 1912 had depicted a spacious forum with two pillars, each labelled "Trajan Column," [18] and a sketch in September had shown a single shaft with distinctive spiral markings and crowned by a human figure. In June 1915 William Walcot executed a pair of alternative perspectives of the pillar, one capped with the figure of King George, the other with a lotus finial. Later that month, Lutyens urged the second design upon Lord Hardinge; marble statues of the King and Queen, commissioned in 1913, eventually adorned the State Entrance of Viceroy's House.[44]

The allusion to Trajan could be read as a compliment to King George: the Roman emperor had been a masterly administrator at the climax of Rome's military power, a ruler who set a premium on the welfare of his imperial subjects. Had not the King-Emperor shared such aims when he proclaimed at his Durbar his "earnest desire" that the transfer of the capital to Delhi might lead "to the better administration of India" as well as "the greater prosperity and happiness" of its people? Appropriately those very words were incorporated in the dedicatory inscription on the west panel of the Jaipur Column pedestal.

Indian and imperial details were joined in an ecumenical union. The north and south pedestal panels represented the obverse and reverse sides of the Great Seal. The King appeared in bas relief on the north as a mounted Sovereign in State above images of British naval and air might and beneath a baldachin held aloft by turbaned Indians. Royal approval for this allegorical scene of omnipotence proved necessary to squelch the wishes both of Viceroy and donor for depictions of actual events from the Durbar visit. (Lutyens dismissed their plan as too journalistic, making the King's person appear insignificant.) The south relief displayed the heraldic arms of Britain, while the east face bore the plan of Imperial Delhi, carved at Lutyens's direction in the style of "the diagram on the obelisk in the Place de la Concorde." [162] At the base of the pedestal stood a white marble statue by Jagger of Lord Hardinge, founding father of the new city and its first Viceroy, his face set resolutely toward the east, along the straight spine of King's Way to Purana Qila and the Jumna and to the great Gangeatic Plain beyond—monarch, it seemed, of all he surveyed. Perched on the topmost corners of the pedestal, four imperial eagles straight from Roman legionary standards recalled prophetic words by a Druid sage in William Cowper's ode to Queen Boadicea:

> Regions Caesar never knew
> Thy posterity shall sway,
> Where his eagles never flew,
> None invincible as they.

Above the shaft of the column, which was wholly carved in a pattern of British oak leaves, rested a giant buff sandstone egg. From this apposite representation of genesis flowered a sacred lotus, secured by a bronze coronal decorated with two ancient symbols: the bell-shaped lotus fruit, seed of future worlds to Hindus, and lions, both a Britannic royal device and most honored beast in the oldest Hindu scriptures, the Rig-Veda. That supreme touch of Lutyensesque wit and bravado, a glass star which burst from a pillar as if from a rocket, was the star of India, emblem of her chivalric orders and ever-present testimony at Raisina to national ideals transcending the routine machinery of governance. For many Britons who spent their lives as imperial servants in the subcontinent, such idealism was a credo that sustained endeavor; its tenets informed the draft inscription which Lutyens composed for the Jaipur Column:

> Endow your thought with faith
> Your deed with courage
> Your life with sacrifice
> So all men may know
> The greatness of India.[45]

Early during Lord Irwin's term in India, with his explicit encouragement, Lutyens completed an ambitious scheme for an iron grille across the east end of Viceroy's Court. Arrayed in martial ranks, the fourteen-foot railing uprights stood as sentinels, their closely-spaced sequence broken at staccato intervals by sturdy

64. Iron grille at the east entrance to Viceroy's Court.

165. The iron grille at the east entrance to Viceroy's Court.

166. The Secretariats framing the approach to Viceroy's House. Reduced towers were built. Watercolor by William Walcot.

167. Secretariat blocks framing an obelisk fountain at the Great Place.

upswept red stone piers. These in turn supported buff-colored stone elephants carrying lamps and urns which climaxed in imperial crowns. Inspired by the gates at Chiswick, whose craftsmanship and detail he counted "amongst the best" Englishmen had produced, Lutyens created portals that had an intricacy recalling antique lace; the very complexity of design proclaimed their ceremonial importance. The outward bulge of the central fifty-five feet not only gave the grille an appearance of strength at its most delicately wrought point, but its expansive quality suggested the fluid line of territorial conquest and aggrandizement: offense as the best defense. Mounted cannon and turbaned cavalry sentries, their lances anticipating the forms both of the grille and the Jaipur Column, were clear expressions of Viceregal and imperial power.[46] [164, 165]

The Great Place, or present Vijay Chauk, forecourt to the entire palatine acropolis at Raisina, was equally unambiguous as a statement of imperium. Within its geometric bounds Lutyens tamed the limitless plain, uniting indigenous and alien forms in a symmetrical plaza where the martial might of British India could parade in awesome splendor. Red stone Sanchi railings screened either end, recalling the plait that girdled the dome at Viceroy's House, while six rhubarb-red obelisk fountains evoked at once memories of piazzas in Renaissance and Baroque Italy. Indeed critic Robert Byron unhesitatingly compared Lutyens's forum to St. Peter's Square "for spaciousness and economy of design." Like that celebrated plaza, the Great Place served a ceremonial purpose, and its austerity provided an effective foil to brilliant pomp on ritual state occasions. Even sated Delhiwallahs or residents, readily confessed to their unashamed delight at the annual Beating of the Retreat—a twilight spectacle of Indian infantry in Scottish kilts, bagpipes skirling, with the camel corps silhouetted on the Raisina ramparts against the dying sun.[47] [171, 172]

If order and unity were numbered among the supreme goals of British rule, water

168. Body Guard at the east entrance to Viceroy's Court.

169 (facing page). King's Way, New Delhi. Secretariats frame Viceroy's House; Record Office, right; and circular Council House, top right.

and roads were most surely among its instruments, not least in New Delhi. The half-dozen reflecting pools of the Great Palace were literally filled to the brim, so that the basins captured on their surface and within their geometry a likeness of the overarching heavens. From the plaza, broad canals carried the eye down the vista of King's Way, "a silver chain of water mirrors" linking the acropolis to Indrapat, the newest Delhi to its oldest site. These monumental waterways asserted not simply a local but an imperial scale, just as irrigation canals drawn across India's parched face had helped transform and unify a subcontinent. [169, 175] The mile-and-a-half King's Way, too, embodied an image of disciplined action and achievement, recalling those straight trunk roads that betokened authority over India. [176] Good roads were among the most persistent and valiant endeavors of British rule. Kipling, as so often, caught the spirit of the imperial credo in his "Song of the English":

> Keep ye the Law—be swift in all obedience—
> Clear the land of evil, drive the road and bridge the ford.[48]

The Central Vista was enthusiastically used as a park from the outset. Its riding paths afforded a lengthy canter, and the alternate quick-growing temporary and slow-growing permanent trees created intimate shady spaces within the attractive sweep of greensward. On his last trip to Delhi in 1938, Lutyens happily recorded that King's Way had become "very popular" for evening walks by the Indians, and twenty years later architect Henry Medd used the same words. Use steadily increased, and by 1968 a resident town planner reported a "very large number" of persons congregated along the avenue every evening, and on Sundays and holidays he noted that it was very common to see the Central Vista "packed with people" from one end to the other. In fact concern existed about overuse of the space. A

170. The approach to Government Court and Viceroy's House at the Great Place. Watercolor by William Walcot.

171. The departure of dignitaries after the Beating of the Retreat at the Great Place, New Delhi.

172 (facing page). Camel Corps on the ramparts of Government Court at the Beating of the Retreat.

children's playground and boating on the waterways were welcome additions, but certain activities and groups threatened the amenity: ubiquitous student drivers created a nuisance, a nearby regiment used the park as a parade ground at all hours, local colleges and high schools made the lawns their daily playing fields, and events at the National Stadium brought temporary car parks and hawkers' booths. For two months before and after the Republic Day parade in January, materials for spectators' stands littered the length of the vista. But the noble green expanses of the capital managed to transcend such abuse. Indeed the parks of New Delhi and other imperial cities have remained one of the most enduring legacies of British genius, the work of men confident in their authority, shaping nature for the common weal.[49]

The masters of this Empire displayed not only an ardent interest in the exercise of power, but also on occasion a keen attention to matters of beauty and science. Nowhere was this more tangibly embodied than in the heart of New Delhi. A singularly explicit expression of this concern was meant to stand at the main cross axis of King's Way and indeed of the city, at Point B on the planners' charts. Here in a symmetrical cluster of four edifices, whose very size implied permanence, was to be a cultural focus of the capital: an Oriental institute, a national library and record office, an ethnological museum, and after 1918, a war museum and a medical research institute. East and West were inextricably intertwined in a repository of Indian art and an archive of British rule, museums to explore comparative racial history and to celebrate British and Indian military victories in France, and, not least, an institute of Western technology and philanthropy for the conquest of Eastern disease. In this "centre of intellectual interest," paternal autocrats in the Government of India intended variously to educate, flatter, entertain, and serve the King-Emperor's Indian subjects: in sum, to seek their welfare and court their good will.[50]

A fragment of one building in Lutyens's ambitious scheme—the Record Office—is all that ever rose to his design. Initially the report of the Delhi Town Planning Committee illustrated four square edifices forming an impressive plaza on King's Way near its midpoint, rivalling the nearby acropolis in dramatic scale. But by 1914 official opinion deemed "a clear view" along the parkway to Indrapat and Raisina Hill as paramount, and all four buildings withdrew to the margins of the cross axis. Defeating Baker's official request for responsibility over the buildings at Point B, Lutyens forged ahead with drawings for the Ethnological Museum, soliciting helpful advice from Sir John Marshall. The eminent head of the Archaeological Survey volunteered that the plan for a record office was the best he had ever seen.[51] [173]

Watercolor perspectives depicting Lutyens's monumental grouping of cruciform structures, as exhibited at the Royal Academy in 1922, displayed a pervasive classical vocabulary, skillfully adapted to Indian tradition and weather. The wide expanse of basement walls, their battered red stone punctured at intervals by shadowy entrances and recessed windows and semidomes, conveyed a calculated impression of timeless solidity and strength. The continuous sweep of cornices and string courses and the rhythmic beat of paired columns reinforced a dominant horizontality appropriate to a uniformly flat riverain. The airy central courtyard of each structure, its deep loggias, thick walls, and splashing rooftop fountains acknowledged the preponderantly hot and arid Delhi climate. Failure to execute the projected plaza to Lutyens's original design has remained one of the tragedies of New Delhi. [174]

173. Record Office or National Archives, New Delhi, by E. L. Lutyens.

174. Proposed cultural center of New Delhi at the intersection of King's Way and Queen's Way. Watercolor, 1922.

WAR MUSEUM        RECORD OFFICE        ETHNOLOGICAL MUSEUM

IMPERIAL DELHI     BUILDINGS FACING ROAD LEADING TO GOVERNMENT HOUSE

175. Morning bather on the canals of the Central Vista, New Delhi.

176. Seen from the All-India War Memorial Arch, Viceroy's House and the Secretariats crown King's Way.

From the very conception of King's Way, Lutyens intended a decorative feature at the east end of the avenue: the layout map in the town planners' final report of 1913 showed a "commemorative column." Anticipating an early conclusion of hostilities in Europe, Lutyens voiced hopes to Lord Hardinge in 1915 for "a bountiful crop of lakhs" to make possible a truly great monument. By 1917, with his commission for a war memorial almost a certainty, Lutyens's ideas began to crystallize into sketches for a big stone arch set in a symmetrical colonnade. Three years later the New Capital Committee approved his designs for a huge commemorative arch, and the King's uncle, the Duke of Connaught, laid its foundation stone in February 1921.[52]

The 139-foot All-India War Memorial Arch, eventually completed in 1931, exhibited a scale appropriate not only to a subcontinent but also to recent battlefield contributions and sacrifices. India had been a critically important reservoir for the manpower which made final victory possible in 1918. The Delhi monument honored 60,000 Indian soldiers who died overseas and recorded on its walls the names of 13,516 British and Indian officers and men of no known grave who fell fighting on the North-West Frontier and in the third Afghan War of 1919.[53] [177]

Proportional relationships were fundamental to the success of the Delhi memorial, as was an array of visual devices. Here as elsewhere, Lutyens created (in Baker's words) a "geometrical web" by the "magic of mathematics," forming "rhythmic crystals" from the "dull mass of material." The main opening of the arch was thirty feet wide and its impressive height two and a half times that width. Multiples or fractions of thirty appeared throughout, and in the attic story reciprocals of seventeen and a half feet figured prominently. Seven small setbacks between the base and the frieze increased the height optically, while lateral arches and concave attic recesses relieved the massiveness of the north and south facades, and prominent cornices and rayed suns carved on the metopes both enlivened and united the many buff sandstone surfaces. Giant pine cones stood in urns beneath the smaller arches, evoking apposite Oriental, Roman, and Christian associations of pine-cone fonts with purification and rebirth. At the summit, the curve of a dome and the lip of its open oculus distantly echoed Viceroy's House, while on the facades flanking the main archway, designs in low relief recalled the Whitehall Cenotaph, set here forever beneath stylized wreaths. The memorial provided not only a majestic sculptural terminus to King's Way, but acted as well as its portal, earning the local sobriquet "India Gate."[54] [178]

Lutyens's war memorial spanned the processional route in New Delhi much as the Arch of Titus bridged the Via Sacra to the Forum. The Romans, who adopted the arch from the Etruscans, had transformed it into an isolated monument, and under Augustus it had become a conventional symbol of empire. The Islamic rulers of India later appropriated the form, and their British successors erected at Bombay the best-known arch in the subcontinent, the "Gateway of India," to mark the Durbar visit of the King-Emperor. London itself boasted the Wellington Monument and Marble Arch; Paris had the Arc du Carousel and, most conspicuously, the Napoleonic Arc de Triomphe de l'Etoile, dedicated "à la gloire des armées impériales" and sharing with the Indian war memorial a heavy attic, sparse relief, and an absence of columns. As with Lutyens's masterpiece at Thiepval, the design at

Delhi was partly determined by the number of dead to be recorded, but the imposing scale could hardly compare with Albert Speer's projected 400-foot-high arch for Berlin, which would have listed a prodigious 1,800,000 names.[55]

However much the Delhi monument may have been a disciplined geometric abstraction, it was at the same time profoundly symbolic in form and intent. Domed portals had a venerable lineage of imperial, celestial, and cosmic significance dating in the West from the Late Roman and Byzantine Empires, and in Islamic India from before the Mughals. The Roman triumph or victory procession ultimately became a species of emperor worship, and passage through the arch was celebrated as the apotheosis of a divine ruler. The Delhi memorial, the Duke of Connaught proclaimed in 1921, was "a monument of great and overwhelming victory" and an edifying reminder of India's response to her King-Emperor's call. At the official dedication ten years later, Lord Irwin emphasized the "unquestioning" loyalty to the King-Emperor that Indian manhood had shown, fighting beside Britons in the cause of justice. Lutyens had hoped from the very first that the monument might have an important symbolic function, helping to bind the subcontinent in "a common service & purpose." From the summit of the arch he proposed to have a pillar of flame glow by night and a column of smoke rise by day, as he had originally planned at the Whitehall Cenotaph. By these ancient symbols he could express the eternal nature of the sacrifice commemorated.[56]

Duty, discipline, unity, fraternity, loyalty, service, and sacrifice: these were the meanings which the All-India arch was meant to convey to a country witnessing renewed political agitation and turbulence. Small wonder that the King's uncle, mindful of a world "dark with trouble," called upon Indian soldiers to be worthy heirs of those who had faithfully served the Raj. Like a huge noticeboard, the arch honored by name cherished comrades, as well as extolling exemplary fidelity to common values, encouraging continued partnership in the established order, and celebrating the "ideal and fact of British rule over India."[57]

By 1921, however, the Delhi monument was more truly an epitaph to long-held beliefs in a permanent British autocracy on the subcontinent. In the years after Lutyens's first tentative sketches for a memorial, Indian political changes had been astonishingly rapid. The Lloyd George government altered the very foundations of imperial rule in August 1917 with an express commitment to prepare India for responsible government within the Empire. But in the aftermath of General Dyer's massacre of an Amritsar crowd, the Indian National Congress adopted a policy of noncooperation with a government that Gandhi called "satanic." Riots and a boycott greeted the Prince of Wales the following year, only a decade after his father's triumphant Durbar visit. As the editor of the *Times of India* observed, the age of consent had passed.[58]

In 1936, a quarter of a century after the conception of Imperial Delhi in which he took such a conspicuous part, King George V was dead. Lutyens designed a dignified seventy-three-foot monument to the late monarch some 500 feet east of the All-India War Memorial, at the terminus of a dozen converging vistas. A white marble figure of the King-Emperor faced westward from beneath a graceful sandstone baldachin set in a raised circular basin at the center of a rectangular pool. A deep concavity reduced each side of the twenty-foot-square canopy base to the

177. Laying the last stone of the All-India
War Memorial Arch, Princes' Place.

178. All-India War Memorial Arch by
E. L. Lutyens. Watercolor perspective by
William Walcot.

179 (facing page). The All-India War Memorial
Arch by E. L. Lutyens

dimensions of a slender white marble pedestal, from which the monarch surveyed his capital city. Round scalloped basins projected from the four recesses, creating an harmonious rhythm of curve and countercurve. [180]

Ornamental use of water in the royal memorial, complementing a tissue of symbolic meanings and associations, tempered and enlivened the severity of the abstract geometric patterns. The plan of the baldachin and its site in a circular basin forcefully recalled the complex medley of convex and concave curves in Hadrian's island villa or Maritime Theater at Tivoli as well as the elaborately curvilinear fountain at the center of the private wing in Domitian's imperial residence on the Palatine. A sketch plan by Lutyens, early in the conception of Viceroy's House, exhibited striking similarities. Both alien and native heritage were fused in explicit symbols which emphasized the majesty of the King-Emperor's person and of his proconsuls and servants. Emblems of kingship abounded: the British imperial crown, orb, and robes, the chivalric star of India, the baldachin, and even the water itself evoking ancient Oriental traditions of a divine monarch as mystic giver of the waters of life. Sculpted nautilus shells implied British dominion of the seas and conjured memories of the sovereign's oceanic pilgrimage for his Coronation Durbar. The baldachin was not only an image of kingship but also of the heavens, of that abode of the divinities and cosmic canopy which compassed the whole British Empire. With unintentional irony the monument—the very embodiment of an order now mortally challenged—faced directly into the setting sun.[59]

Framed by the War Memorial Arch, the Sovereign's monument not only served as a stately conclusion to King's Way, but also helped screen the visually disruptive Irwin Amphitheater. Begun in 1931 at the easternmost end of the main urban axis, the stadium marred the important vista of Indrapat's fortress walls which had been a principal feature of the Town Planning Committee layout. The planners' report, at Herbert Baker's suggestion, provided for a Durbar amphitheater excavated from the Ridge just west of Government House. Much expensive machinery was purchased to quarry the hard Delhi quartzite for roadfill and concrete and to create the projected amphitheater. Levelling the summit of Raisina Hill, however, yielded more than abundant building material. Moreover, the Imperial Delhi Committee deemed such an expensive item to be nonessential, and for future Durbars members suggested the 1911 site. In 1929, the eastern end of King's Way was mooted. The town planners had designated the site for an 120-acre irrigation reservoir formed by a barrage on the Jumna—an ornamental lake reflecting and enhancing Indrapat and visible from almost the entire Central Vista. The Imperial Delhi Committee promptly reduced this "elaborate treatment" of the river frontage, recommending a smaller but nonetheless decorative lake. Water effects were later abandoned in favor of a sunken garden, completed to a Lutyens design. In 1931 keen interest by the new Viceroy and Vicereine, the Earl and Countess of Willingdon, and a generous gift by the Maharaja of Bhavnagar, prompted construction of an Olympic stadium on the site to designs by Robert Tor Russell, Chief Architect of the Government of India. A plea by Lutyens to blue-pencil the drawings came to nothing, and even Russell's reluctance to dot chattris along the stadium skyline could not prevail against an insistent Vicereine. The vista Lord Hardinge had cherished and championed slipped unceremoniously behind a brick wall.[60]

180. King George V Memorial, Princes' Place, by E. L. Lutyens.

By this time the first half-dozen pleasure domes projected for the other sides of Princes' Park and for neighboring avenues had appeared on ample sites. These majestic town houses for India's native rulers had a splendid swagger befitting their status. There were over 560 rulers whose principalities together encompassed one-fifth of the population of India and two-fifths of its area. Most states were petty chieftainships, some merely a few acres in size, while others were larger than England. Hyderabad was as big as England and Scotland combined and had a population of fourteen million. Relative precedence among the leading 149 states was distinguished by the number of guns in the salute a ruler received on ceremonial occasions. The pride of palaces at the east end of King's Way, each guarded by sentries in brilliant uniforms and set in some eight leafy acres, was meant to be as worthy a terminus of the great avenue as the Viceregal estate. But the prominent elevation of the Raisina acropolis and the focal position of the King-Emperor's statue among the princely residences seemed to underline the fact of ultimate British paramountcy even in the native states.[61]

Lord Minto, Hardinge's predecessor as Viceroy, had infused traditional British support for the ruling chiefs with a new sensitivity and vigor, in part to balance the increasing influence of nationalist politicians and Legislative Councils. George V, himself an admirer of the personal and paternal rule exercised in the princely states, had much sympathy for the idea of "a Council of all the Chiefs" to act as a unified conservative force in politics. Hardinge took the initiative in March 1913 by calling a conference of rulers, the first step toward a formal body for collective consultation. Eight years later at the Red Fort in Delhi, the Duke of Connaught inaugurated a permanent Chamber of Princes on a wintry February afternoon, surrounded by the fateful vestiges of the vanished Mughal Court. The Maharaja of Bikaner, probably the most distinguished prince both in appearance and achievements, was first Chancellor of this body. He was more than a match for any Briton: Lady Reading had "positively radiated happiness" as Vicereine, he told her successor, "but it was perhaps a pity that she had eaten cheese on her knife."[62]

The transfer of the capital had been justified in part by arguments of its superior convenience over Calcutta for visits from most chiefs, especially the loyal Rajput rulers. Hardinge took advantage of this new proximity to make Viceregal relations closer and more cordial, explicitly emphasizing British dependence on the princes in the task of Indian governance. The Viceroy expressed delight that by 1913 the new Delhi had attracted numerous applications from ruling chiefs for housing lots. He was glad to give them good sites, he explained, so they would have "a permanent stake in the Imperial capital." Sir George Birdwood acclaimed this news as a "master-inspiration": an announcement that ten prominent rulers had taken plots would "electrify Hindu and Muslim India," striking men's imagination and incalculably strengthening the Raj. Sir George, who had a keen sense of propriety, however, urged Hardinge to "keep the 'jumped up' low castes, the *setha* of Calcutta, Bombay and Madras and Karachi from entering as landlords the sacred precincts reserved for the Rajputs and *Rajas* generally—and our British officials—white, black, and brown."[63]

Official opinion at first favored excluding rajas' villas from the capital boundaries altogether, relegating them to the city environs. Geoffrey de Montmorency cited

81. Main entrance, Hyderabad House, Princes' Place, New Delhi, for Nizam of Hyderabad, by E. L. Lutyens in association with Abdulla Peermahomed.

problems liable to arise concerning sanitation, noise and dust, traffic control, and "discipline of unruly retainers." The Secretary to the Public Works Department thought native residences would spoil the ornamental lake planned between Indrapat and Kingsway, declaring darkly that however attractive the buildings initially, anyone could foresee the eventual nature of their surroundings. Such judgments, however, wholly ignored the likely reaction of the princes, who were always acutely sensitive in matters affecting their prestige. Any blow to their izzat, Lord Chelmsford recognized, would arouse widespread resentment. The rajas, for example, emphatically preferred making lump sum payments for land and utilities in Delhi rather than accepting annual leases or levies that might imply the inferior relationship of a tenant to a zemindar or landlord. Britain could scarcely risk offense to such useful allies. By 1916 a layout of prime sites for the chiefs, centrally located, was complete. Eventually the Government of India allocated three dozen lots on perpetual lease, seven for senior rulers around Point C at the east end of Kingsway. The plan of each site and design of its buildings required approval by the Government of India.[64]

Not surprisingly the rajas' houses resembled the Viceroy's House in their hybrid union of classical orders with indigenous motifs in everything from loggias to jaalis. Two palaces (and drawings for three others) were by Lutyens, while the rest were by architects who admired him and had observed his work close at hand. Moreover Lutyens and Baker enjoyed supervisory or censorial powers over new construction as "architectural advisers" to the capital, much as the Viceroy himself exercised a parternal and paramount authority over the native states. As pioneer art historian Ernest Havell repeatedly emphasized, the example set by the Imperial Government in public edifices necessarily had "a potent influence" not only with Indian craftsmen but also with Indian patrons—princes and aristocrats—who looked to official architecture "for correct models of taste and fashion."[65]

Lutyens built the biggest and costliest (£200,000) of the princes' palaces for the Muslim ruler of Hyderabad, the seventh Nizam, reputed to be the richest man in the world. His main residence in his own state—one of four palaces—was riddled with caches of gold ingots and astonishing gems as well as millions of paper rupees. His psyche was a bundle of contradictions: miserly, averse to personal ostentation, increasingly frugal in the extreme, he nevertheless engaged in periodic bouts of spectacular spending, had a thousand servants, and a harem of some two hundred concubines. His mistresses accompanied him on a special train during his brief visits to New Delhi.[66]

Building restrictions and allotted sites (normally about eight acres) did not permit any Delhi palaces which would eclipse Viceroy's House. But Lutyens, in association with Abdulla Peermahomed, conceived an edifice for the Nizam which befitted his role as premier prince of India. At the wrought-iron gates guards stood at attention in blue tunics touched with gold and in headdresses boldly marked with the yellow ocher of Hyderabad, while above the palace floated the Nizam's standard. Mughal chahar bagh gardens flanked the forecourt like Oriental carpets, ablaze with roses set with bold geometry amidst stone paths and water channels rippled by cascading lotus-leaf fountains. On the two-story palace facade the dark shadows of arcaded verandahs and prominent cornices, the laciness of jaalis, and the small-paned glazing of generous loggias punctuated the smooth texture of broad surfaces. Obelisks and urns adorned stepped tiers of stone and stucco, climaxing in the dramatic gesture of a dome against the sky. The result was an impression of strength and splendor, of extravagance indifferent to mere utility, an effect wholly appropriate to the Nizam's exalted worldly status. [181, 182, 183]

Lutyens's butterfly-shaped plan for the palace was a variant of a design popular in Britain for more than three decades. Lutyens had already devised a three-quarters butterfly in 1902 at aptly-named Papillon Hall, following the example elsewhere of Norman Shaw, E. S. Prior, and Detmar Blow.[67] At Delhi he halved the butterfly to two wings and with characteristic wit turned custom on its head to achieve an original orientation. Beneath the dome he set a pivotal entrance hall from which symmetrical wings radiated at an angle of some fifty-five degrees. These symmetrical blocks, however, did not reach forward like welcoming arms to contain the forecourt but were swept back, as if to shield the zenana from public view. Only the concavity of the arcaded porte-cochère echoed the circular Princes' Park beyond the gates. [184]

As at Viceroy's House, Lutyens made staircases an especially featured attraction. Opposite the main portal, convex steps spilled into the low-domed circular reception hall, their ceremonial grandeur enhanced by a runner carpet of deepest red. Monumental statuary at their foot diverted the visitor's direct approach in a characteristic Lutyensian fashion. At their summit the zenana lay beyond a dark

182. Mughal Garden, Hyderabad House.

183. Arcaded verandah, Hyderabad House.

184 (below left). Sketch plan of Hyderabad
House by E. L. Lutyens.
185 (below right). Loggia, piano nobile,
Hyderabad House.

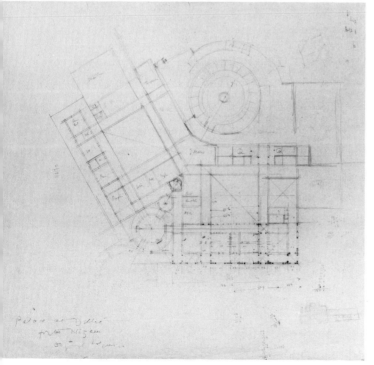

velvet curtain, enticingly drawn back. But the Nizam's dinner guests turned right or left up stairs which rose easily within concentric walls to the state rooms. In the piano nobile, motifs everywhere evoked Viceroy's House, yet never competed in size. Loggias trapped gentle breezes as well as the cooling music of a Mughal fountain. Crystal chandeliers tinkled from a coved ceiling, light reflected from mirrored walls and glittered on marble fireplaces and boldly patterned floors that could have fittingly adorned an English ducal seat. [185]

Indeed the European character of the Nizam's palace earned complaints from his two legitimate sons, who considered it "unsuitable for an Oriental house." In 1931 when Lord Hardinge visited New Delhi for official inaugural ceremonies, he thought the residence a fine one, but Lutyens's design of purdah quarters for favorite concubines lent credence to the complaints. The zenana, Hardinge noted, comprised

> a circular court with about 12 or 15 rooms round it, each the size of an ordinary horsebox & with only one window close to the roof. A rough bed was the only furniture. There were six tiled bathrooms, but no baths, only taps of hot & cold water under which each lady has to sit! There seemed to be no means of mixing the hot & cold water, as it pours on to the ladies![68]

The Gaekwar of Baroda harbored no complaints about the palace Lutyens designed for him at Delhi. [186] The British had placed the maharaja on a vacant throne in 1875 at the age of twelve after deposing his predecessor and excluding the descendants from succession. Surrounded by Englishmen, he was educated to be a model of Victorian rectitude and progressive politics. After his first wife died, he wed a Maratha noblewoman whose "Brindian" sophistication equalled his own, and they enjoyed fifty years of happy married life. Unlike other native rulers, he kept no mistress and hence Lutyens made no provision for a concubines' zenana. The house at Princes' Place exuded an atmosphere of British affluence: its furnishings were "comfortably Anglo-Saxon" and its plumbing American, as in the sprawling palace at Baroda. The cook and bandmaster were French, the stablemaster Irish, and the valet and maids English. Table linen was woven to order in Belfast, and the dinner service was fashioned in Bond Street. Scarlet-liveried servants offered guests whiskey or hock with seltzer at breakfast, champagne and port in the evening. The maharaja hired Britons to run his army and police force, his hospitals and colleges; it was only fitting that he employed the Viceroy's architect, an Englishman celebrated for his country house designs.[69]

The Gaekwar's new palace at Delhi shared not only a boundary with the Nizam's residence but much else besides. Its butterfly plan had wings set at an angle of fifty-seven degrees, a concave central porte-cochère, and a pivotal circular salon. [187] In both buildings the plan ensured that most rooms had several windows but at an extravagant cost in walling and roofing. The two houses each boasted arcaded verandahs, loggias, and courtyards, its share of deep-set jaalis and ornamental parapet urns, and a prominent dome. Interest at Baroda House, however, centered not so much on rather repetitive facades but on the difficult triangular spaces inevitably generated by a butterfly plan, which Lutyens resolved in a graceful succession of circular and long round-ended vestibules and cunningly contrived lavatories around the lofty salon. Staircases were again a focal feature: a visitor to the

186. Main entrance,
Baroda House, Princes'
Place, New Delhi, for
the Gaekwar of
Baroda, by E. L.
Lutyens.

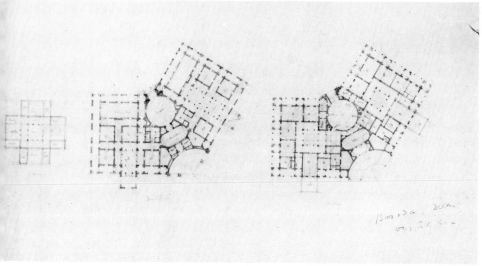

187. Sketch plan of
Baroda House by E. L.
Lutyens.

188. Brick dome under
construction, New
Delhi.

second floor climbed one of a magnificent matched pair, worthy of Renaissance Genoa, to arrive at a gallery-cum-corridor that offered bewitching views over the meticulously detailed salon. Opposite this vista he entered an elongated sitting room lit by four internal windows in its round ends and from three glazed doors. A shady verandah of similar shape led to a curved terrace where jaalis pierced a parapet to afford the benefits of both privacy and cool evening breezes.

The plastered brick saucer domes that embellished these palatial corridors, as well as Viceroy's House, were constructed without temporary support or centering by a method ancient in Asia and known to the Byzantines. The Indian contractors' foremen would in each case organize a tight ring of laborers at the lip of the circular void they planned to close. Fresh mortar was already laid along the rim. At a given signal—often the beat of a drum which punctuated accompanying music!—every man placed a brick from each hand simultaneously, creating an instant circle. When the mortar dried, the workers repeated the procedure. So they raised a dome, course by course until it stood entire, its last bricks held in place by callused fingers till the mortar set.[70] Barefoot, scantily clad, covered with dust, braving scorching sun and chilling winds, India's peasants built a princely city. [188]

As a rule, palaces in the capital were occupied for scarcely two or three weeks each year. In February, rulers and retinues left their states for meetings of the Chamber of Princes and events of Delhi Week, highpoint of the social season. Nearer twenty than seven days in length, the gala program boasted the Annual Imperial Horse Show and the Annual All-India Polo Tournaments as its central fixtures and numerous other engagements, including the Delhi Hunt Ball, the Freemasons' Ball, a Viceregal ball and garden party, and a State Investiture. Hundreds of officers and wives accompanied regimental polo teams; governors, residents, ministers of state, and Indian gentry deserted their provinces and posts. Princes without Delhi palaces took whole floors at Maiden's or the Cecil Hotel, and lobbies were crowded at cocktail hour with slim equerries in tight-fitting tunics, civilians and their ladies in white silk suits and light summer dresses. At Princes' Place, the sound of saxophones wailing the tune of "I'm Forever Blowing Bubbles" wafted from open loggia windows beneath a floodlit dome. Pennons in state colors snapped above the hoods of sleek limousines, and imperious honking from deep-throated klaxons announced the arrival of rajas at a fellow ruler's festive tamasha.

The King-Emperor's representative himself inaugurated Delhi's grand Week, arriving in his state carriage at the new stadium for opening ceremonies, resplendent in a gray morning coat beneath a regal umbrella, surrounded by bodyguard lancers. Custom dictated that on reaching His Excellency's box, gentlemen of the Viceregal party exchanged their white topis for felt hats delivered on trays by scarlet-clad orderlies. Conspicuous among the princes and vividly-attired princesses in nearby boxes was the donor of the stadium, the handsome young Maharaja of Bhavnagar, his swarthy face and English clothes a foil to the immaculate white of his Prime Minister's beard and traditional Rajput costume.[71]

The sheltered world of the maharajas vanished like a dream with unimaginable speed. During the First World War, the Indian States committed men and money to the common cause with startling liberality. At its close they had earned the esteem of the whole British Empire and stood at the zenith of their powers. But the maharajas, patently autocrats and unable ever to act in concert, were doomed: the end came quickly. In 1940, seven were still building palaces for themselves in New Delhi, as though their order would endure for eternity. But in 1947 the paramount power hastily withdrew the protection of the Crown and abandoned the states to the mercies of independent Pakistan and India. The princes, as one Member of Parliament remarked, were obliged to sign away their birthright for the promise of a pension. Some 550 acceded to India. The Gaekwar of Baroda, after he signed the Instrument of Accession, openly wept like a child; the Nizam, who resisted the surrender of his powers, saw Hyderabad forcibly integrated into the new Dominion. Eventually the Government of India stripped the former rulers of their titles and allowances and occupied their Delhi palaces. Baroda House became railway offices. Memories of generous hospitality and festive pomp lingered on. But something rooted in the traditional life of the East, colored in hues of the Orient, had disappeared from the political landscape of India forever.[72]

If the princely order could claim to be indigenous to India, Gothic and classical churches raised on the subcontinent had a decidedly exotic appearance. Often this was explicitly intended, not the least at New Delhi, where spiritual and secular leaders from the outset planned an Anglican cathedral worthy of the British Raj. Sir George Birdwood, a veteran of many years' Indian service, acknowledged the intimate connection between church and state when advising Lord Hardinge in 1913. A Delhi cathedral, he wrote, must have a commanding site and spire, for it would forever symbolize the piety that helped Britons triumph during the Mutiny. Indians, moreover, held religious Englishmen in "highest esteem," while labelling officials neglectful of public worship as "devils." The Viceroy himself envisioned the proposed edifice not only as reflecting the Church's response to new opportunities, but as commemorating "the benign results and influences" of the King-Emperor's Durbar visit.[73]

The Delhi Town Planning Committee assigned the cathedral a suitably prominent location, south of Kingsway at the junction of Queensway with Akbar and York Roads. The generous lot on a traffic island was initially called "the Close," then later York Place, and finally Motilal Nehru Place. On their first expedition to India, the Committee lunched with the Bishop of Lahore, whose diocese included Delhi, and the architect member at once pressed the merits of a big edifice. Lutyens even threatened to advise "a back-seat site" unless the bishop promised a quick start on an appropriately large church. When the Chaplain at Raisina began conjuring up visions of an English medieval cathedral, Lutyens promptly denounced any plans for "a true Christian Gothic Farce." If such talk persisted, he warned, he would banish the church to an outer ring on the city plan, with "the rank of a 3rd-rate building." Despite its beauty, Westminster Abbey with its acres of glass was only fit in India "for frying bacon."[74]

Five years later at Delhi Lutyens himself embarked upon preliminary sketches for a cathedral, one of his earliest and most explicit ambitions. As a young man, pacing up and down excitedly before his mentor Gertrude Jekyll, he had confessed a burning desire "to build palaces and cathedrals." Now in 1917, already engaged upon Viceroy's House, he found the prospect of a great church exhilarating and could be heard singing Te Deums throughout the day.[75] But his splendid vision of a cathedral at Delhi, as at Liverpool, was destined for disappointment. Nearly two decades later an elegant church to designs by one of Lutyens's disciples rose on a site near Viceroy's House.

Blissfully ignorant of future events, Lutyens stood at his drafting board, feet firmly planted apart, as he sketched a striking central plan for his oft-imagined cathedral. Its radial design of three equal arms or wings created a triangular core bounding a circle inscribed by the lofty dome—a singularly suitable trinitarian design for a circular site in a triangulated city. The liturgical problem of a centrally planned church engaged Lutyens no less than it did those Renaissance architects who had pondered its functional complexities. In one wing he fitted the choir stalls and choir room, chapter house, and lady chapel; in another the baptistry and library; and in a third, chapels for the chivalric orders of the Star of India and Indian Empire, underlining the relation between church and imperial state. The aisles of each wing were sufficiently long for ceremonial processions; however, the site of principal ritual activity, the central domed space on which a triad of naves focused, posed the greatest challenge to Lutyens's ingenuity. In the angles of the triangular crossing he placed the Viceroy's tribune (in front of the great organ), a lectern, and, on axis with the main nave, the pulpit. Directly opposite the Viceroy's elevated seat, Lutyens placed the high altar, as if to emphasize the complementary efforts of priest and proconsul amidst an alien culture. In 1917 tradition as well as acoustics militated against setting the altar beneath the central dome. The result was very Protestant: the axial pulpit and the interpretation of the gospel assumed a visual prominence rivaling Holy Communion at the altar. The central void in its entirety became a setting charged for action. Lutyens joined ideal and real with customary skill. The geometry of a circle within an equilateral triangle was as perfect as any Italian architect might have desired some five centuries before and expertly embraced the disparate functions of modern Anglican liturgy. The Archbishop of Canterbury himself sanctioned the design.[76] [189]

Lutyens's most detailed elevation sketch of the proposed cathedral exhibited the usual converging vertical lines that his freehand perspectives often displayed. The observer's point of view lay below ground level, so the edifice had a vertical vanishing point. This "very strange and personal distortion," in his son's words, he frequently achieved in his buildings by use of batter or setback or recession of superstructures, creating a sensation of sturdiness and permanence aloof from "the tumult of frantic progress." In Lutyens's depiction of Delhi cathedral, his technique underscored the monumentality conveyed by giant pilasters and arches, the grand sweep of Palladian porticoes, and the powerful thrust of a massive dome. The enormous wings with their overhanging chujjas appeared outstretched as if to embrace the furthest reaches of India in a gesture appropriate to an evangelizing church. A towering cross on the lantern affirmed Christian presence and missionary aspirations as forcefully as the Union Jack above Viceroy's House proclaimed British dominion.[77] [190]

Lutyens's confident, authoritarian control over his commissions, reflecting a virtually intuitive mastery of geometrical form, can be discerned even in his tiny germinal sketches for a Delhi cathedral. This passionate discipline over every detail was at the heart of his credo: "the whole point and essence of fine architecture," he

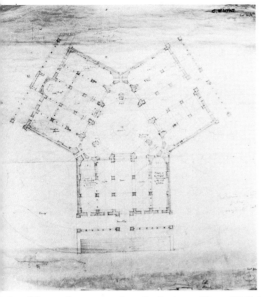

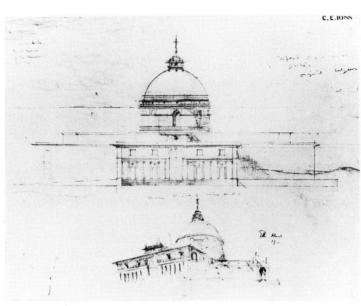

189. Plan of proposed cathedral at New Delhi. 190. Elevation of proposed cathedral at New Delhi. Pencil drawing
Pencil drawing by E. L. Lutyens, March 1917. by E. L. Lutyens, March 1917.

told Lord Hardinge, was the careful coordination of plans, elevations, and sections to "make one complete organism, perfect and inseparable." In this quest for cohesive, integral design, Lutyens emphasized the role of tradition, which he defined as the "inherited sense of structural fitness, the evolution of rhythmic form by a synthesis of needs and materials, the avoidance of arbitrary faults by exercise of common sense coupled with sensibility." No architect, he hoped, would compromise with the merely "good enough," but would always seek to fashion a graceful statement, with distinction and humor, akin to the conversation of a civilized man. Basil Spence, as an enthusiastic twenty-two-year-old employed on the Delhi drawings in 1929, observed at close hand the master's insistence on excellence. Lutyens's work exhibited a generosity in conception that precluded "anything mean" and bespoke the high value he placed on traditional qualities of scale and proportion as well as on fine materials and workmanship.[78]

At New Delhi Lutyens rose superbly to the challenge, transcending his earlier Tudor vernacular and neo-Georgian designs to rival Greenwich, Blenheim, and Hadrian's Pantheon. At Viceroy's House he created a paradoxical edifice at once ceremonial and intimate, replete with domestic as well as scenic and dramatic elements—a palace that, despite its scale and sumptuousness, was in many ways lovable. Much of its success was due to Lutyens's wit, his ability to combine familiar forms in unexpected ways to create lively new shapes. As one critic has remarked, he knew how "one minute touch of strangeness can color a whole design and make magic out of the trite." He often startled colleagues by the swiftness of his perceptions. His genius at discerning unexpected connections helped Lutyens to express the essential qualities of Indian architecture "in pure English idiom," uniting Eastern and Western ideas to produce buildings full of vigor and intelligence at every turn. In Herbert Baker's words, Lutyens recoined old gold, recreating Renaissance architecture "to new forms of use and beauty. His art had a Shakespearean quality with its wit, fun, vitality, and rare beauty."[79]

At Raisina Lutyens wrote an enduring epitaph for himself and his generation. The city Lutyens and his colleagues created provided posterity with a window on the life and values of Edwardian and Georgian society. Raisina commemorated the vitality and creative enterprise of a tiny island kingdom at the dawn of the twentieth century. It stood as a notable example of human power to organize disparate experience and aspiration into unified action and achievement. It enshrined the belief in the governance of a world and its art by rules and ordered discipline. By its very scale and majesty it reflected the magnitude and audacity of rule over a subcontinent of 320 million persons by a scattered community of fewer than 200,000 resident Britons. Imperial Delhi was the last and supreme monument of the British overseas empire before powerful winds of change swept away colonial rule forever. Even as its walls rose, India's new capital became a summary of the imperial legacy, a distillation into architectural form of doomed ideals and paternal purposes at the threshold of a new era.

Indeed New Delhi's sheer size and its style of architecture sounded a haunting and persistent note of insecurity. The splendor of the monuments seemed an attempt to bolster beliefs already seriously undermined and an effort to sustain the outward appearance of power. In their hybrid elements, these Indo-British edifices represented an explicit recognition of the increased partnership of Indians in governing the subcontinent. Viceroy's House, Lutyens acknowledged, was assuredly a British gentleman's residence, but also unmistakably Indian: its originality derived from its being "built in India for India."[80]

By Lutyens's own admission, the buildings of New Delhi displayed India's age-old capacity for assimilation and synthesis. It was her way, Jawaharlal Nehru declared, "to welcome and absorb other cultures," and to survive repeated invasions with her spirit unbowed. Fresh contacts, he felt, had always renewed and transformed the dynamic core of Indian civilization, while never sundering the intimate relationship with the past. The Imperial Delhi of Lutyens and Baker embodied India's response to yet another alien challenge and testified to the astonishing power that has helped her hold fast, in Nehru's words, to what is "true and beautiful and good" in her own heritage.[81]

# 9

## *Herbert Baker*

A shrill fanfare of trumpets pierced the crisp air of a cloudless January day in 1927 as Lord and Lady Irwin arrived at opening ceremonies for India's new Council House. Earlier, hundreds of automobiles had headed toward Raisina, Daimlers and Rolls-Royces weaving among bullock carts and idling at railway crossings for scores of freight cars laden with building materials. Now throngs of spectators along King's Way jostled behind impassive soldiers for a view of the Viceregal carriage and six, with magnificent postilions and outriders and the golden umbrella of royalty borne above Their Excellencies by a liveried attendant. Pennons fluttered above two squadrons of cavalry escort and bright sunshine flashed from lances of the impressive Body Guard, clad in scarlet and mounted on silken-black steeds. Hoofbeats resounded on the pavement to the accompaniment of jingling accoutrements. While the pattern of pageantry was familiar to the delighted crowds, its setting was novel: it was the first ceremonial use of the Central Vista and Great Place, a long-held dream at last come true.

Within the Council House precincts, a banked amphitheater seating 2,000 guests encircled a crimson pavilion and English and Punjabi regiments which served as guard of honor. Jewels blazed on the Durbar dress of Indian princes, and colorful military uniforms vied in splendor with parasols and gold-edged saris. The cerise turban of the Maharaja of Patiala towered conspicuously above a sea of topis and gray top hats. As the Second Battalion of the Royal Warwickshire Regiment crashed out the bars of "God Save the King," the brilliant company rose at the Viceroy's approach, all under the scrutiny of innumerable coolies precariously perched nearby on builders' refuse heaps. Only the day before these peasants from the Punjab and Rajputana had held undisputed sway over the site, men and women alike swarming by the hundreds in feverish last-minute efforts to clear rubble, lay turf and gravel, and set out feathery potted palms. Now, while prince and peasant watched, the Union Jack broke for the first time above the Council House and loudspeakers—an innovation—broadcast brave words by Sir Bhupendra Nath Mitra and Lord Irwin as well as a hopeful message from the King-Emperor himself. Then, at the private entrance for the President of the Legislative Assembly, came the ceremonial climax: Sir Herbert Baker presented a golden key to the Viceroy, who threw wide the door and declared the building duly open.[1]

For Baker, that brief moment on a sunny Delhi morning marked a major milestone in an imperial career that spanned thirty-five years in Africa and Asia. No architect of any era had done so much important work throughout the British

191. Herbert Baker. Pencil drawing by Sir
William Rothenstein, 1925.

Empire. Baker was supremely happy in his generation, to use Wren's much earlier
phrase: his personality, ideas, and art coincided to an uncommon degree with the
needs and aspirations of his clients. Quintessentially English, from a land-owning
family long established in Kent, he enjoyed from his youth an affinity with country
life that inspired his devotion to traditional materials and workmanship. This
fidelity fortified the prevailing precepts of Ruskin and Morris, and of the Arts and
Crafts movement, which he absorbed from evening classes at the Royal Academy
School, from Gertrude Jekyll's generous friendship, and from colleagues in the
office of Ernest George and Harold Peto. On walking tours, armed with a bulging
coat pocket of colored chalk stubs, he filled tiny notebooks with jottings and
thumbnail sketches.[2]

Baker received his boyhood education at Tonbridge, where in addition to cricket
and the classics, the public school regimen sought to inculcate those qualities of
leadership and piety deemed appropriate to a class privileged to rule an empire.
Baker's own faith in that empire, and in its potential as a force for good in the
governance of the world, was lifelong. In addition to his imperial convictions, the
other articles in Baker's creed, both personal and more generally British, which
found expression in his architecture, were his rugged yet dignified simplicity; his
spirit of adventure and openness to the influences of foreign ideas and methods,
counterbalanced by a passion for orderliness; his literary and narrative rather than
abstract turn of mind, allied to his delight in symbolic associations; and his fervent
belief in the marriage of all the arts, with an emphasis not so much on novelty as
quality of craftsmanship. All of these help to explain his distinctive significance
today, as well as the sympathetic chord he touched in his own era, especially with
Cecil Rhodes, who proved to be a congenial Maecenas.

The "Colossus" and his architect shared not only a lofty code of imperial duty, but had in common as well a love of learning and a deep fondness for vigorous outdoor life. An inveterate horseman, Baker rode daily before breakfast in all weather at Raisina and when past fifty he habitually ran the three miles to Delhi Gate at Shahjahanabad and back after a long day at his drafting board. At Owletts, his ancestral seat, he was devoted to the garden, particularly a fernery which he tended himself. He loved poetry, and he adorned his letters and memoirs with apposite quotation and his own graceful translations from the French. Without being priggish, he enjoyed cultured company and made many friendships, although his protégé Charles Wheeler deemed him not an especially good "mixer." To intimates he revealed an appealing boyishness behind the earnest and respectable mien: Wheeler recounted how at age eighty Baker and the courtly Montague Rendall, former Headmaster of Winchester, linked arms to do a two-step on the sculptor's studio floor while chanting, "We are the octogents."[3]

In the last decade of his life, writing of Rhodes, Baker recalled John Buchan's description of Augustus Caesar: "Combined in him were the realism of a man of action, the sensitiveness of the artist, and the imagination of the creative dreamer."[4] These were the qualities that Baker's contemporaries in Africa, India, and imperial London looked for and admired in themselves and him. Pericles's tribute to the Athenians, often quoted by Baker, could well have served as his motto and that of his colleagues: "We are lovers of the beautiful, yet simple in our tastes; and we cultivate the arts without loss of manliness."

As with Rhodes, Baker was fortunate in his association with an entire handful of splendid Periclean figures, the celebrated "Kindergarten" of bright young Oxford graduates whom Lord Milner gathered about him to administer South Africa. Baker shared their company and their beliefs, not the least their vision (like Rhodes) of "a better ordering of the world through the civilizing genius of the English-speaking races."[5] As each of these colleagues rapidly achieved distinction and success, one commission led to another for the youthful architect. On Robert Brand's recommendation, he was appointed to design the Pretoria railway station, which led in turn to the Union Buildings and thence directly to his appointment in New Delhi.

In 1912, before he had been selected to collaborate with Edwin Lutyens, Baker alluded to the main elements of his artistic credo in an article in the *Times*. He declared that in the architecture of New Delhi

> there must be no conscious straining after invention or originality. . . . There must be good building and a frank acceptance of modern methods and materials. The controlling mind must heat and weld into his orderly conception all that India has to give him of subtlety and industry in craftsmanship. And lastly, he must so fire the imagination of the painters, sculptors, and craftsmen of the Empire, that they may, interfusing their arts with his, together raise a permanent record of the "history, learning, and romance" of India.[6]

Baker made it clear that he conceived the role of architects and artists as that of creating "historical records" which would embody the English character, much in the same way that Inigo Jones and Christopher Wren had in the earliest days of the

Empire "stamped sanity and sobriety" on English architecture. In a passage that suggests his own values, Baker wrote, "The best buildings of that period have eminently the attributes of law, order, and government, to the extent, some might say, of dullness, the defect of these qualities."

Unlike Lutyens, whom he thought concentrated his intellectual talents on abstract and geometrical qualities to the neglect of human and national sentiment, Baker felt that content in art was of the first importance. In building New Delhi, therefore, English classical architecture in the manner of Inigo Jones and Wren should be adopted in order fearlessly to "put the stamp of British sovereignty" on the subcontinent of India.

Drawing an analogy with the Roman Empire, Baker quoted his friend William Marris: "Only Rome in her greatest days did what England has been doing, as a matter of course, for one hundred years!" Baker felt that architects, with their allied artists and craftsmen, had an opportunity "to immortalize through their arts" the law and order which British administration had "produced out of chaos." Like Alexander the Great or the Romans, the British might put "their own impress on the arts which they had at first absorbed."

In a paper entitled "Architecture of Empire," prepared for the *Round Table*, Baker underlined the value he attached to the principles of classical architecture, the "dearly bought experience of over 2,000 years," culminating in the language or style of Jones and Wren and their followers of the eighteenth century. He saw parallels between architecture and British colonial rule itself.

> Our rule confers order, progress and freedom within the law to develop national civilizations on the lines of their own tradition and sentiment: so in architecture there is infinite scope within the limits of order, true science, and progress for the widest self-expression in every field of art; but without the orderly control of the great principles, there might result a chaos in the arts such as in governments which History records our rule was ordained to supersede.[7]

Thus, while there might be as many types or dialects as there were races, laws, and provisional governmental systems within the Empire, there was "one supreme law and the same common ideal of which the Crown stands as the symbol." Similarly the underlying rules and ideals of classical architecture were "fixed stars to guide the Architect through the difficult sea of his art." The mission of the architect—and the poet—was, Baker felt, to give outward expression to Britain's national ideals and then to adapt them to diverse colonial situations, "to turn them to shape and give them a local habitation and a name" throughout the Empire.

At Pretoria, Baker envisioned an administrative capital for South Africa which would express the idea of the new union of the four colonies and of the English and Afrikaner peoples, in buildings and a site which would "give dignity and beauty to the instrument of Government and the symbol of the Union." Baker rejected a location in the centre of the city as "unworthy of the capital buildings of a united South Africa." He chose instead Meintjes Kop, overlooking the valley, a site which he felt had the nobility of a city set upon a hill, with all the historical associations of the Acropolis at Athens or Corinth. Reginald Blomfield's description of the temples and great curved colonnades on the hill-terraces of the Hellenic city of Pergamos had deeply impressed and inspired him. From the Mediterranean travels on which Cecil Rhodes had sent him, he also recalled the temples and theater of Segesta and the hillside temples of Agrigentum. From all these influences, Baker later wrote, a vision came to him of two great buildings connected by a semicircular colonnade overlooking an open theater or place of democratic assembly.[8]

The sketches and drawings which Baker produced for the approval of the country's leaders showed two dome-capped towers, which recalled Wren's at the Royal Naval College at Greenwich and which, linked by an impressive colonnade, symbolized the newly united English and Afrikaner peoples. Above and behind the towers of the kopje ridge, Baker envisioned a Hall of Fame, either a classical temple or a large low dome, "a greater symbol of final union." Another unrealized project was a via sacra, a broad sculpture-lined pathway, along the ridge of the kopje, with a small circular Temple of Peace to the two peoples, such recent enemies. [200]

Baker's symbolic conceptions, typical of the essentially literary or narrative nature of much British art, appealed at once to the imagination of the Afrikaners Smuts and Botha. Like Cecil Rhodes, Baker records, the two generals perceived the power and usefulness of symbolic and associational architecture, a perception which Wren had put into words some two centuries before: "Architecture has its political Use: publick Buildings being the Ornament of a Country; it establishes a Nation, draws People and Commerce; makes people love their native Country, which Passion is the original of all great Actions in the Commonwealth."

At New Delhi, Baker similarly endued his work with symbolic meaning and import. His two vast Secretariat buildings, each three stories high and nearly a quarter of a mile long, housed every administrative department of the Government of India. Their dominating hilltop position—a "sahib site" removed from ordinary traffic—was meant to impress Indians and indeed to inspire a sense of reverence in all who approached. Such a piazza sacra, Baker felt, reflected the spirit of Indian tradition as found at "all the palaces & big tombs & mosques," which were raised upon a natural plateau or manmade plinth. Ample precedents existed elsewhere in the East, notably at Persepolis, Babylon, and the ruined mound sites of Mesopotamia.[9] [201, 202]

The Secretariats' location served practical needs by convenient proximity to Viceroy's House. But equally the site expressed an ideal, the unity and "common dignity" of the Government of India as a whole, as implied in the Viceroy's constitutional title, Governor-General in Council. Baker thought that for Government House to have been sole splendid occupant of Raisina's crest would have given too pointed an emphasis to the Viceroy as supreme authority. Baker believed, too, that Members of the Council and departmental Secretaries, when installed in grand new buildings, would rise to the distinction thus given their office. Creation and encouragement of such influences was one of the loftiest missions of an architect and was certainly his own earnest intent. He had faith that future generations would not charge him, in Wordsworth's phrases, "with vain expense" or "ill-matched aims" for his efforts at Delhi.[10]

The government officers who peopled the Secretariat buildings were leading actors in the symbolic drama of Imperial Delhi, a chosen few perched by day on a rocky mount in an enclave as artificial as any Himalayan hill station. The Raisina acropolis was a majestic stage set for the spectacle of the Indian Civil Service, the tiny corps who were governors over a quarter of the human race. Normally of long tenure, members of this exalted cadre were known in common parlance as the "heaven-born" and enjoyed a reputation for matchless integrity and scrupulous fairness. By comparison, Parliamentary control seemed remote and insubstantial, Indian legislators' rhetoric biased and ineffectual, and Viceregal policies transient and erratic. As one leading newspaper editor recalled, "The Government of India was the Indian Civil Service and woe betide the iconoclast who dared to lay sacrilegious hands upon it." Malcolm Hailey, when Governor of the Punjab, remarked privately that the Government of India had always been more important than its head. How appropriate, then, was the site accorded Baker's two Secretariat blocks, its aloofness an acknowledgment of Olympian detachment, its preeminence an explicit recognition of real authority. The lawns and fountains that united the twin buildings in dignity and ordered beauty Baker envisioned as a temenos or sacred precinct, where dwelt the genius loci of the Government of India.[11] [206]

His guiding principle at Raisina, Baker recorded, was "to weave into the fabric of the more elemental and universal forms of architecture the threads of such Indian traditional shapes and features as were compatible with the nature and use of the building." He thought his duty not simply to draw upon the collective knowledge of great masters of European architecture, but also to accept the best of Indian sentiment and achievement in art. In a word, like Wren, he sought to fuse classical grace with native energy. Such a course, he felt, would express the spirit of British administration, itself based on accumulated experience and increasingly on a union of East and West. "As we look forward to some happy marriage between the two ideals in politics," he remarked, "so must we also in the matter of architecture."[12]

As at Viceroy's House, indigenous architectural forms in the Secretariats were a response to practical climatic needs as well as to the requirements of political symbolism. Baker employed the characteristic Indian features of the open canopied chattri, an ancient royal emblem; the widely overhanging stone chujja, which protected walls and windows from driving rain and midday sun; and the intricately carved stone and marble jaali, which admitted air but not noontime sun. Unlike Lutyens, he also used the nashiman or recessed porch, a re-entrant vaulted portal that distinguishes many Mughal buildings. In Baker's adaptation a rectangular architrave enclosed a round-headed arch of two or more stories. Designed originally as cold-season offices, the Secretariats were constructed without the continuous verandahs which normally served in India as sun shields. Instead, windows were kept small in proportion to wall area, and their glass was deep-set in thick walls away from high rays of the sun. Teak jalousie shutters screened the low sun of morning and evening. Lighting of rooms could be better adjusted as a result, and offices were not as gloomy in winter as with verandahs. [192, 193, 207, 210, 211]

Baker rejected the "prettinesses" of much Indian ornament, however, preferring "a simplicity which subordinates details of design to a big conception." Indian ingenuity was too often spent on "superficial fantasies" and elaboration: Hindu architecture merely aped wooden construction in stone, with "grotesque, meaningless" carving, while Mughal building, though of a higher order, consisted of "masses of brick & concrete covered with decoration." Jaalis he acknowledged as

92. South front of the North Block, Secretariats, New Delhi, by Herbert Baker.

93. Dome of the North Block, Secretariats, from a chattri in the South Block.

"perfectly beautiful" and suitable for Raisina, but he emphatically enjoined his subordinates C. P. Walgate and William Harvey to avoid "dreadful Hindo stuff" on brackets and other Delhi detailing. Those qualities of indigenous architecture most attuned to the character of British rule were the thickness of arches and vaults, massiveness of walls and domes, plain repetition in plans, depth of open halls and courts, and solidity of foundation plinths. Together these suggested the orderly coherence, austere power, and permanence of British governance.[14]

The Secretariats represented the Grand Manner as Baker defined it: a careful avoidance of pilasters and engaged columns, with wall surfaces kept simple, shadows deep, and lines fluid. Remarkable pavilions crowned every wing, their huge colonnades and dark voids enhancing the impression of sculpted strength. Situated on the second floor or piano nobile, fifty-two feet above the plain, these temples echoed features at Baker's Union Buildings in Pretoria and, their architect noted, at palaces in Isfahan. Each pavilion marked the office of a Chief Secretary or Member of the Viceroy's Council, commonly called simply an "Honorable Member." The deliberate emphasis in design recognized their ultimate rank in the divine hierarchy of official India, a society of civil servants deemed more exclusive than royalty, scorning even Calcutta's richest Scottish merchants as pedlar box-wallahs or "counter-jumpers." But in fashioning his lofty pavilions, Baker recalled Cecil Rhodes's way of taking narrow-minded men outside to look up at the mountains. At Delhi Rhodes's disciple hoped the Honorable Members might find similar inspiration in a breathtaking prospect embracing ruined Hindu and Muslim cities ranged beside the capital of an India united under British dominion.[15] [212, 213]

Like platoons at rigid attention, the colonnades lined the processional route, their ramrod verticality punctuating the horizontal sweep of the two blocks. The grouping of columns followed no known law of combination. But it was this unorthodox and loose-limbed quality that prompted contemporary comparison of Baker's work with Wren's experiments. Ready to dash in where others feared to tread, Baker often forewent the rules and avoided the purely logical solution, with great effect. This same adventurousness, which had led him to Africa and success, mirrored the imperial spirit incarnate in giants like Rhodes. Baker quoted with approbation Robert Browning's dictum:

> It were better youth
> Should strive through acts uncouth
> Towards making, than repose on things found made.[16]

At the Great Place, the Secretariat walls which ultimately rose from the plain resembled an embattled stronghold, as though Indian nationalism and the debilitating breadth of the landscape rendered all building defensive by necessity. The term "qila," traditionally used in Delhi parlance for Shah Jahan's palace, soon came to mean not Viceroy's House but the Secretariats; one wag remarked that the sword had been beaten into the pen. Thirty-foot-wide flights of red stone stairs set at right angles to King's Way evoked visions of imperial Persepolis and the approaches to its sanctum. [217, 218] A pair of towers framed the processional axis to the acropolis like sentinel guardians, half as high as first designed but still embodying the intended attribute of majesty. These are bracketed in turn by two triumphant domes,

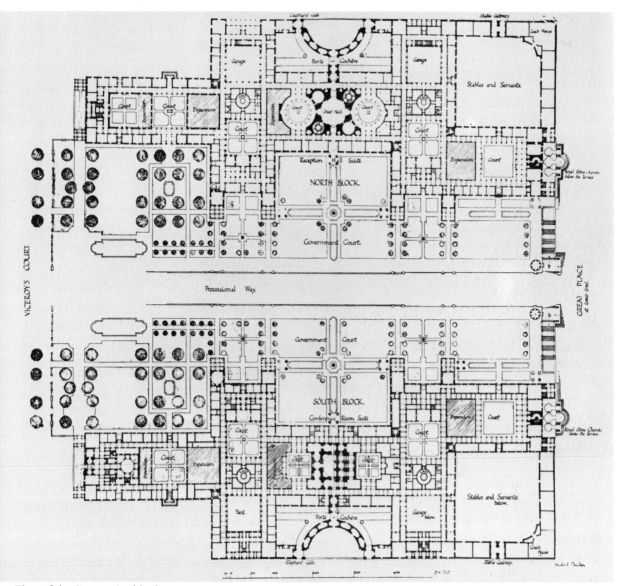

94. Plan of the Secretariat blocks.

specimens much indebted to St. Paul's and as splendid and audacious as those by Wren at Greenwich Hospital, which Baker much admired. [195, 221] But they are alive with Indian detail, embraced by chattris and adorned with jaalis, carved lotuses, and sculpted elephants. Baker's handling of these motifs predictably earned disapproval from Lutyens and author Robert Byron, but even the latter critic confessed admiration of the general effect of the domes. Certainly more important to Baker was Lord Hardinge's warm endorsement of his designs, elephants included.[17] [196]

The two blocks, each about the size of the British Houses of Parliament, reminded newspaper tycoon Alfred Northcliffe of an Atlantic City hotel, "bigger than the Savoy, Cecil, Carlton, and Ritz combined." Curiously, they often look smaller than they are, perhaps because, as one Chief Commissioner explained, they are "low compared to their vast spread" and are normally seen only from distant avenues. In each behemoth, the basement contains garages, godowns, and archives; the first two

195. London from Greenwich. This foxed engraving of the painting by J. M. W. Turner hung in the office of Herbert Baker.

196. One of the elephants adorning the Secretariat domes.

floors comprise officers' rooms; and the top floor houses clerks. Bureaucrats bustle along six and a half miles of passages, where official notices specifically prohibit bicycling. The multitude of high-ceilinged rooms are ranged around a series of open, arcaded courtyards which Baker called the "most important feature" of the Secretariats' design. These courts forcefully conjure visions of elegantly harmonious Renaissance palazzi. But Mughal balustrades and the arches of the middle tier, broader than those below, inject a gentle dissonance of culture and proportion. The deep, vaulted arcades of Tuscan columns and piers preclude the normal darkness of long corridors. Adjacent offices as a result enjoy a welcome airiness, and plastered domes in nearby hallways glow with reflected light. The straightforward plan is an evident heir of palatial sixteenth- and seventeenth-century schemes, giant symmetrical piles interwoven with inner courtyards, such as the Escorial and the Tuileries or, in particular, Inigo Jones's projected Whitehall, which Baker illustrated in an article in 1908.[18] [194, 197]

Baker's imagination demanded more than just a series of stable-box rooms where civil servants worked "amidst a mad hurricane of flailing fans flapping weighted-down papers." He had scarcely been appointed architect before asking Lord Hardinge for freedom to design public rooms and reception areas to enhance the impression of his buildings. He hoped that future generations would exclaim, with Wordsworth, "They dreamt not of a perishable home who thus could build."[19]

Baker eventually created on the short north-south axis beneath the Secretariat domes that dramatic succession of spaces he craved. Clearly he revelled, as always, in the challenge which a steep natural site posed. Because the hilltop Government Court was meant primarily for ceremonial use, vehicular arrivals usually took place below at the level of the plain, through domical porte-cochères highlighted with vigilant sandstone elephants. Centerpiece of the north block interior was a high-domed octagonal hall, its soaring marble faces reflecting light from a galaxy of jaalis and inlaid with Indian heraldic devices. The climb from the main south block

197. Arcaded courtyard in the Secretariats.

entrance was equally theatrical, a labyrinthine stage set of ingenious, vaulted staircases opening to courts and fountains on either side. The shadowy arches and massive masonry piers intersecting at varying levels all powerfully evoked Piranesi's emotive prison etchings. From the ground floor, double flights led to an imposing domed conference room surrounded by libraries and reception rooms for official government hospitality. Elsewhere the arcaded staircases which spiralled to the topmost floor were an eye-filling sight, but civil servants shivered when December winds gusted through the unglazed jaalis. [198, 199, 225, 226]

At Baker's instance, decorative experiments brightened the bare walls and ceilings of seven Secretariat rooms. From the outset at New Delhi, he had promoted schemes to encourage indigenous artists and craftsmen, believing fervently that they and the architects should collectively "raise a permanent record of the 'history, learning, and romance' of India." Artists chosen for the Secretariat project readily found suitable subjects in the rich traditions and mythology of the subcontinent. Methods of applying mural paintings proved thornier. Ultimately two techniques were employed: tempera and marouflage. The well-known artist S. Fyzee Rahamin used tempera, with stone colors and a vegetable black, and linseed, gum, and sugar as an adhesive vehicle. These colors he applied directly to the dry plaster, as in the Ajanta and Bagh Cave paintings, depending on line rather than light and shade for modelling and perspective. While keeping the typical flatness of Rajput art, the

artist exercised his own inventiveness in the arrangement of his selected subject-matter, Hindu and Islamic allegory, on two domes in the north block.[20]

In the Princes' Waiting Room in the south block, G. H. Nagarkar of Bombay executed a chronicle of Hindu Aryan life in marouflage, painting the design on canvas and affixing it to the dome and spandrels by adhesives. Except for the low tone of coloring, Nagarkar's compositions won praise from Percy Brown, the distinguished curator of the Victoria Memorial Hall in Calcutta and a principal figure in support of native artists. Brown applauded the standard of drawing, pleasing flat spaces of color, and graceful placement of figures in relation to the architecture, as well as the effective treatment of symbolic content.

Not all murals in the Secretariats won uniform plaudits, however. Even Brown's well-disposed sympathies did not extend to poor arrangement of compositions in their architectural frames. Failure to compensate for curved surfaces and overhead placement inevitably caused distorted perspectives and proportions. Another knowledgeable critic found cause to deplore faulty draftsmanship and lack of vigor and breadth, condemning maudlin romanticism which merely reproduced mannerisms from traditional work.[21]

Baker felt that an artist's work should be endowed with meaning and even moral content. Public monuments ought to be more than objects of beauty, art for art's sake; they should express principles and beliefs. Although the Secretariat murals had

198 (facing page). Porte-cochère at the Secretariats. Watercolor by William Walcot.

199. A principal staircase in the Secretariats.

200. The Union Buildings, Pretoria, 1910–12, by Herbert Baker. Watercolor by William Walcot.

201. The north front of the North Block of the Secretariats.

202. The east front of the Secretariat blocks, New Delhi, by Herbert Baker, from a fountain in the Great Place.

203. Aerial view, Council House and Secretariats under construction.

proved to be more decorative than inspirational, the inscriptions selected in 1925 and later to adorn those temples of imperial governances were undeniably explicit. One announced baldly, "Liberty will not descend to a people; a people must raise themselves to liberty; it is a blessing which must be earned before it can be enjoyed." Lord Irwin, beset by clamorous demands for prompt Indian independence, told Baker the aphorism was "rather pointed." Another inscription, from Queen Victoria's proclamation of 1858, seemed to affirm permanent British presence with remarkably unruffled serenity: "In their prosperity will be our strength, in their contentment our security, and in their gratitude our best reward." After seventy years of direct Crown rule, however, important numbers of Indians were neither content nor grateful.[22]

In 1926–27 government departments completed their transfer from temporary prewar quarters in Civil Lines. Fifteen years had elapsed since the King-Emperor and his consort had laid the foundation stones of the new city at the Durbar camp, and a dozen years since those two cumbrous blocks had been trundled across the plain to Raisina. Awkwardly, as it turned out, King George had proclaimed the stones as the site of Imperial Delhi. To avoid arousing further censure from critics in Calcutta, Lord Hardinge decided simply, in his words, "to let sleeping dogs lie." Not until 1915 did he direct Baker to proceed with designs to house the newly renamed "commemorative stones" in the Secretariats' eastern platform wall. Decorated with the King or Queen's insignia in bronze and the legend "15th December 1911," each stone was set on a pedestal and recessed in a niche within its own vaulted chamber. The respective royal coat of arms was cut into the red stone wall, an explanatory inscription of inlaid white marble encircled the chamber, and protective iron gates displayed the royal monogram. In a gesture of the most explicit symbolism, a fountain sprang from each chamber to feed the large fountains and water channels of King's Way, before joining the Jumna on an imperial journey to a Britannic sea.[23]

Baker's resident representative, Henry Medd, laid the top stone of the Secretariats' north block on September 30, 1927, perched with contractor Baisakha Singh on a perilous wooden platform at the lantern to the dome; [208] seven months later the Chief Engineer, Sir Alexander Rouse, performed the same ceremony with Sobha Singh at the south block. By then, Baker's persistent efforts had set in motion plans to complete his composition on Raisina Hill with an addition to Government Court: four graceful columns, gifts of the Dominions of Canada, Australia, South Africa, and New Zealand as a gesture of imperial friendship. Baker had shown the columns in his earliest designs, including William Walcot's perspectives at the Royal Academy in 1914, and had suggested them as Dominion gifts in a letter to Lord Chelmsford in March 1916. The project had won the Viceroy's favor, but had been

204. The Great Hall, North Block, Secretariats, under construction.

205. Vaulted chamber in the Secretariats containing one of a pair of commemorative Durbar stones.

208. The "topping-off" ceremony at the North Block, Secretariat, on September 30, 1927. Henry Medd, in helmet, appears at the right, hand on hip.

dropped owing to especially strained relations between South Africa and India. Lutyens meanwhile coolly refused his backing unless Baker consented to reconsider his design for an inclined way from the Great Place. In 1920 and 1921 Baker revived his proposal, but not until Lord Irwin's Viceroyalty did it win unanimous support from the four Dominion governments. Irwin, however, sympathized with Lutyens's desire to locate the columns in the Great Place, that architect's area of responsibility, but Baker prevailed with his argument that sculpted legends and details would be better appreciated in the tranquil greensward of Government Court than amid sizzling heat and traffic in the big plaza.[24] [228]

Columns which the Emperor Asoka had set up throughout his united Indian empire suggested the form of the Raisina pillars. Baker had particularly admired examples at Sarnath and in Firoz Shah's ruined city at Delhi. The name and floral emblem of the donor Dominion adorned the pedestal of each column. [227] Longer inscriptions, reminiscent of Asoka's carved edicts, were abandoned when Canadian Prime Minister Mackenzie King objected to use of the term King-Emperor. Surmounting a globe atop each stone monolith was a full-rigged bronze ship, symbol of the ocean link of Britain's empire. By 1931 and the formal unveiling, Irwin had proclaimed Dominion status as the official goal of British policy for the subcontinent, and the four Dominion columns not only represented common loyalty to one monarch, but also betokened India's inevitable equality.[25]

Baker's Council House at New Delhi likewise reflected the march of constitutional progress. Already in December 1917 the Secretary of State had approved proposals to omit the Imperial Legislative Council Chamber from plans for Government House and instead to use space in the new Secretariats. If, as

206 (preceding pages, left). The east front of the North Block of the Secretariats.
207 (preceding pages, right). Indian details woven into Baker's work at New Delhi.

anticipated, need for a larger chamber arose, the India Office agreed that a separate building could be erected.[26]

The Montagu-Chelmsford reforms of 1919, which created a large Legislative Assembly, an upper house of notables, and a Chamber of Princes, furnished the catalyst for construction. The location selected for the Council House had two major advantages. Directly northeast of the Secretariats, the site was especially convenient for Honorable Members and Secretaries who sat in the legislature. It had the virtue, moreover, of providing a dignified terminus to the major axis from Shajahanabad. Originally meant to focus on a solitary Viceregal residence on Raisina Hill, the vista now ended awkwardly on the north flank of the Secretariats, a fact the editors of the *Town Planning Review* had been quick to decry as early as 1913. The projected legislative building, which promised to screen this unfortunate junction, did destroy the symmetry of the urban layout, however, and looked plainly like the afterthought it was. Even before completion of the Council House, Lutyens publicly underlined the need for a comparable structure, perhaps a court building, to restore balance to the central city plan. He was not alone: in 1931, for example, both Lord Hardinge and the *Daily Telegraph* correspondent in Delhi echoed his proposal.[27] [229]

The chosen site formed an equilateral triangle of more than a thousand feet each side. Baker first designed a monumental edifice of three wings, each containing a council chamber and linked to a high central dome representing unity of the three estates under the Raj. [209, 214] Lutyens protested that the scheme was "all wrong" for the location, not properly related to vistas and inadequate in masking the offensive junction of Secretariats and avenue. He assailed Baker's preliminary elevations as too fussy and elaborate, declaring that neither Michelangelo nor God could make anything of them. He proposed instead the simplicity of basic geometry—a circular colosseum design.[28]

Baker staunchly resisted, suggesting alternative plans and even a different site, but after a crucial meeting of the New Capital Committee on January 10, 1920, Lutyens could exult, "I have got the building where I want it & the shape I want it." Lord Chelmsford and his Council confirmed the committee's decision, and Baker

209. Elevation of original proposal for a Council House or Legislative Building, New Delhi, by Herbert Baker.

210. A nashiman or recessed porch at the Secretariats, New Delhi.

211. An arcaded inner courtyard in the Secretariats.

212. The South Block of the Secretariats. Detail of a watercolor by William Walcot.

213. The dome and a pavilion of the South Block of the Secretariats.

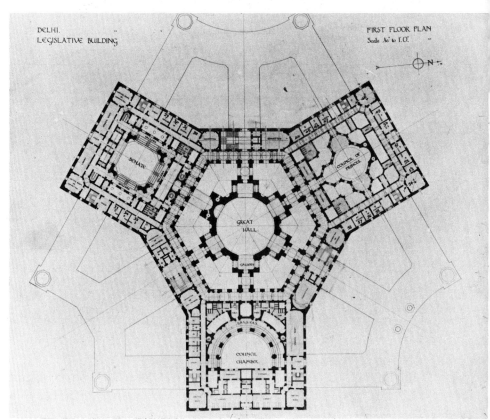

214. First floor plan of original proposal for a Council House by Herbert Baker.

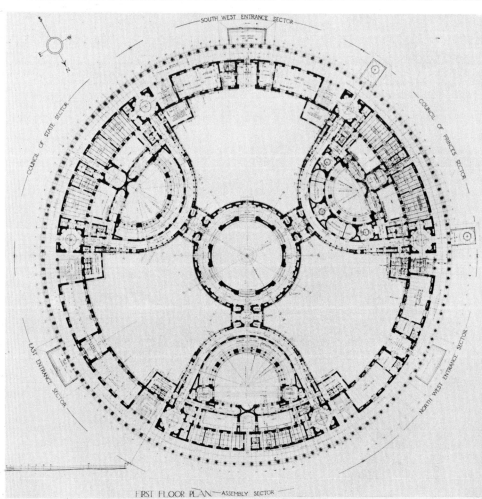

215. Plan of the circular Council House, New Delhi, as completed, by Herbert Baker. Scale 1 : 1500.

216. Main entrance, Council House.

withdrew further objection, acknowledging that he had been given "out," as in cricket. He quickly devised what he called "a fairly good" plan whose three chambers placed at equal angles around a low-domed circular hall precluded disputes over cameral precedence, but he dubbed it the "merrie-go-round" and expressed doubts privately that it would be "the best for the purpose." He had to abandon his vision of a high dome seen rising from its base, for the outer perimeter wall would have cut in two any close views of it. The unifying symbolism of a prominent dome was lost. It was yet another case, he lamented, of geometry overruling sentiment and expression.[29] [215, 230]

Baker's good friend Sir William Marris, now Home Secretary in the Government of India, shared these reservations. The unusual arrangement of three semicircular chambers at 120-degree intervals, Marris mused, would "always seem a little fantastic & undignified—like elephants dancing." He half-expected to see the periphery and three giant spokes "go slowly turning round." Despite the intrinsic strength and beauty of its basic shape, moreover, he felt a circular colosseum did not represent any expression of the parliamentary principles.[30]

217 (following pages, left). View of the South Block of the Secretariats at the Great Place.
218 (following pages, right). Thirty-foot-wide stairs at the North Block of the Secretariats.

As the Council House rapidly rose on its site, critics variously compared it to a gasometer or bull-ring, and once to a "dreary-go-round." The length of its passages, a half mile, prompted one facetious legislator to suggest installing a tramway! More serious was censure in 1922 by the New Capital Enquiry Committee, which condemned the circular design for adding to the cost and problems of construction. Three Members emphasized the extravagant proportion of corridor space and actually urged creating a new plan on a different site. Other Members, with one exception, believed a better scheme might have been originally possible. Only the practical need to house the councils expeditiously prevented abandonment of the work already done.[31]

Baker, saddled with a design not of his choosing, himself complained that the circular plan made the building even more expensive and difficult to build than expected. Moreover, its rapid execution in addition to the Secretariats required his hiring a larger staff, amounting at one time to twenty-seven draftsmen in London and two representatives in Delhi. Baker's public defense of the Council House shape understandably lacked conviction. He focussed on its generous accommodation of offices and committee rooms and noted that the circumferential corridors offered more convenient and sheltered communication than did an open tripartite plan.[32]

The visitor looking toward Old Delhi from a balcony in the Secretariats' north block is treated to an eye-filling panorama of the Council House. As befits its importance, its size is impressive: 570 feet in diameter and over five acres in area. The circular perimeter is divided into three levels: a rhubarb-red foundation, a middle story girt around by 144 buff-colored pillars, and a small attic story in plaster above the cornices. From Raisina Hill, the visitor can see the low central dome and its cupola, once unmistakably capped with the crown imperial. At intervals, bracketed arches with sculpted bells support a red sandstone carriage porch, enriched with a chujja and sometimes a chattri. [234] The porches deliberately inject a decorative Indian flourish, meant to meet demands for indigenous motifs as well as to give human scale to the $27\frac{1}{2}$-foot columns. There is, indeed, a coldly impersonal quality to the peripteral colonnade, with something of the grandiose monumentality of schemes by French Neoclassical architects E. L. Boullée and J. N. L. Durand, as well as public buildings designed in the 1930s not only at Rome, Berlin, and Moscow, but Paris and Washington. The porches are meant as well to steady the uninterrupted sweep of the circle. Should in fact Baker's pillars be fewer, grouped to vary the repetitive rhythm? Some contemporary critics thought so, and at least one thought the colonnade would have been best omitted altogether, to give an impression of massive solidity to a building so low in proportion to its area. The attic story, moreover, has an insubstantial air. Added to the completed edifice in 1929 to expand clerical space, it was unfortunately executed in plaster as an economy measure. As the visitor approaches the building at ground level, its dome is wholly screened and its cupola hovers above the attic, then disappears. Disclaiming this combined result of a circular plan and an extra story, Baker admits bitterly in his memoirs that the effect resembles a Jack-in-the-box.[33]

From inside the giant verandah or gallery, the visitor notes at once that its continuous curve is intentionally arrested at intervals by doorless entrances, two columns supporting a lintel and semicircular jaali, while masonry screens join several

219. Courtyard verandah, Council House.

221. The Secretariats seen from Viceroy's Court.

220. Government Court, between the Secretariats.

pillars of the colonnade to signify porte-cochères below. [222] The verandah may shield the visitor from monsoon rains, but the very height of the pillars prevents protection from burning rays. Sunshine streams through the columns to the inner wall and to the rooms and passages beyond. On those days when "the bare red bones of the Delhi landscape shimmer as if they were boiling in some enormous cosmic stewpot," there is no denying that this is a cold-weather building.[34] The restful splash of fountains sounds across garden courtyards but the sun blazes powerfully through the succession of groined lunettes. The present air-conditioning is a luxury unknown to early legislators, cooled only by electric fans. [219, 223]

The interior appointments of each chamber intentionally differed according to the degree of dignity of the occupants: the Legislative Assembly [224] was housed the most simply, as befitted its popular nature, while the Chamber of Princes boasted the most opulent furnishings. In every case, however, Baker selected a semicircular design on the Continental model, recalling Jules de Joly's well-known Neoclassical Salle des Séances for the Palais Bourbon. The obvious alternative, a rectangular House, was deemed certain to encourage two-party government, fostering dangerous divisions along strictly religious lines between Hindus and Muslims. Baker designed an Assembly chamber able to accommodate 400 members, but initially the provision of interior brickwork and supplemental galleries compressed its size to ensure that the 144 original Members would not appear lost in its space.[35]

222. Giant verandah, Council House.                223. Garden courtyard, Council House.

224. Legislative Assembly chamber, Council House.

Acoustics presented difficulties because of the semicircular shape as well as the height needed for dignity and coolness and to permit clerestory lighting, as skylights were impracticable under the Indian sun. A Member, moreover, spoke from his seat in the House, according to the British custom, so that often he had a number of listeners behind him. Various devices were used to reinforce voices, but others were required to reduce confusing reverberations. Baker gave the teak panelling convex facets and tilted them forward, in order to distribute reflected sounds evenly and downwards. He lowered the room height eleven feet below his first designs and was obliged to convert the ceiling into an enormous jaali, lined with felt matting. Buff-colored acoustic tiles of American origin were affixed over 6,500 square feet of wall and ceiling area. Sound was judged to be good in the legislators' seats and fair in the galleries, but the Governor of one Province, in a wry disparagement of all Indian legislatures, told Baker he did not think much of the Council House at Delhi; his own was much better, where he could not hear a word said![36]

226. Interior of the Great Hall in the North Block of the Secretariats. Watercolor by William Walcot.

227. The emblems of a Dominion adorn each Asokan column in Government Court. Above, the arms of Austra

228. Four Dominion columns grace Goverment Court.

Debate was greatly enlivened on March 16, 1927 when one poorly cemented six-inch-square acoustic tile landed resoundingly on a Member's desk, and deliberations were resumed only after erection of a temporary awning of wire mesh. Events on April 8, 1929, however, were far more serious and dramatic. As the Assembly President rose to speak, two bombs exploded in the hall with shattering force, and cries mingled with dust and falling plaster. Amid the ensuing chaos, pistol shots rang out from the galleries as terrorists fired on the Government benches. Miraculously, there were no serious casualties, but the occasion highlighted the mounting challenge to British rule.[37]

The two other Houses had more ornate, if less turbulent, quarters in the new legislative building. The chamber of the Council of State, arranged to seat sixty elder statesmen but able to accommodate 200 in comfort, was elegantly panelled in Bombay blackwood. Marble pillars decorated galleries to either side of the chair, and a circular Mughal jaali, backed by black acoustical felt, embellished the ceiling. [235] The even more elegant Chamber of Princes sufficed for 120 rulers, most of whom enjoyed permanent dynastic salutes of eleven or more guns. A dozen Members were elected as representatives by 127 lesser princes. Carved blackwood walls and benches as well as panels and pillars of glistening black and white and colored marble adorned this jewelbox chamber. From galleries screened with pink marble jaalis, purdah ladies watched while the Maharaja of Bikaner addressed the House in ringing tones or Alwar underlined a point with emphatic gestures, his black silk gloves a marked contrast to the snow-white majesty of Patiala's costume.[38] [236]

The princes' heraldic escutcheons, meant to compose a colorful frieze around their chamber, raised unexpected problems in precedence, for several rulers claimed the privileged position to the right of the King-Emperor's arms. The Maharaja of Alwar, self-styled reincarnation of the god Rama, provided the solution: a lottery, which dictated a random order.[39] The chamber is now altered to form a library, but the shields, tinctured in enamel with golden mantlings and set against dark panelling, recall the splendors of a vanished world.

Baker placed the original legislative library and reading room in the galleried circular hall at the heart of the Council House. Three hundred tons of structural steel supported an impressive ninety-foot-wide dome, and at night cornice lighting enhanced the lofty coffered interior. Baker intended that on state occasions the Viceroy might address there a joint session of two or three of the Houses or perhaps a high Durbar summoned from throughout India. The hall, and in fact the entire building, was meant to symbolize the integral unity of the Indian Empire. Under one roof and within one circle would gather representatives of the three estates from the British provinces and presidencies and the native principalities, working to common ends in allegiance to a single King-Emperor.[40] [237]

Coats of arms representing the twelve provinces of the Indian Empire girdled the legislative library. In order to "infuse interest and meaning" into the decoration of Delhi, Baker had formed committees in London and India with Lord Hardinge's blessing to devise arms for each province. The aim was to express within the limits of two or three symbols the chief historical and geographical facts of the province. A tiger and an English East India Company ship shared the shield of Bengal, for example, and Bombay's escutcheon displayed a river, a hill fort, and ships, emblems for the mighty Indus in Sind, martial Maharattas in the Deccan, and early sea powers—Arab, Portuguese, and British—in the Indian Ocean. Baker's committees exercised great care to avoid offending any religious sensibilities and combed both art and archives for ideas appealing to Indian imagination.[41]

In the Assembly chamber (now the Lok Sabha or House of the People), the teakwood panelling sparkled with thirty-five enamelled and gilded coats of arms, representing not simply the Indian provinces but the four Dominions and a clutch of British colonial territories. In 1928, as the Viceroy spoke from the Assembly dais, one legislator discerned a portent in the display of India's arms beside the shields of Canada, Australia, South Africa, and New Zealand. For perceptive persons, the Member observed, "there was a whole world of promise in those plaques which caught the hard, glaring sunlight of a brilliant February morning in Delhi and transmuted it into soft colours, sending blue and crimson and purple bars across the motes dancing in the shafts of sunlight." Beneath the bold escutcheons Lord Irwin explained the road India must take to become "an acceptable and accepted" Dominion, raised to equality in the Commonwealth of Nations, just as her heraldic device glittered among theirs on the chamber walls.[42]

The Assembly which Lord Irwin addressed in 1928 was a striking measure of the distance India had travelled since prewar days. The House now elected a presiding officer from among its number. To the right of the incumbent President, Vithalbhai Javerbhai Patel of Bombay, were Government officials and nominated Members, to be sure, but in front of him a mere handful of Europeans mingled with Muslim Members, among whom Sir Abdul Qaiyum Khan, "as rugged as his own frontier hills," and the tall Sir Zulfiqar Ali Khan stood out in particular. To the left sat the distinguished Motilal Nehru, whose Congress supporters, in rough white homespun, rose behind their leader in tier upon tier. Only a decade and a half earlier, Lutyens recalled, Lord Hardinge had opposed any separate edifice for the Legislative Council, declaring emphatically that representatives would meet under the Viceregal roof. Reactionary officials who yearned for that autocratic era might irreverently nickname the new chambers "the Monkey House." But this monument embodied as none other could the fact of India's progress toward constitutional maturity. The building's massive grandeur proclaimed the dignity and importance of the Houses it embraced. The Council House expressed, in Lord Irwin's dedicatory words, "the set purpose and sincere desire of the British people" to establish responsible government in India. Twenty years afterward, from a gallery in the great central hall of that very building, a bugler clad in simple cotton khadi would sound a sonorous note on a seashell, a haunting knell for empire and a summons to self-government. Later in that same room, now sanctified by history, Indians would draft the constitution of a republic.[43]

The bold geometry of the Council House climaxed the axis from Shahjahanabad. Athwart this imperial vista, another giant circle marked the map of New Delhi: Connaught Place, which had borne the name of the King-Emperor's uncle since his farewell visit to India in 1921. In their final report, the Delhi Town Planning Committee had envisioned a monumental plaza at this focal site, ringed by shops, hotels, and businesses and dominated by a terminal railway station, that expressive

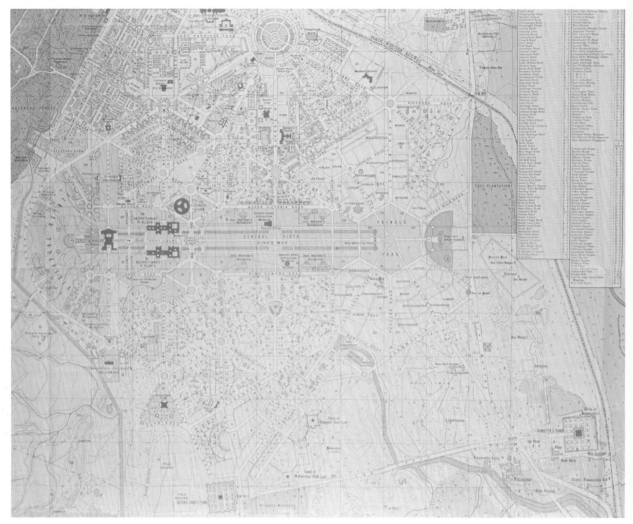

229.  Detail of an official Survey of India map of New Delhi in 1931.

230.  The Council House (now Parliament House), New Delhi, by Herbert Baker.

231. The Council House, New Delhi.

emblem of British progress and centralizing power in India. The Imperial Delhi Committee, who considered the plaza next in importance to the Raisina acropolis, strongly seconded this ambitious scheme. Members suggested municipal and local administrative offices as well as a post office on the projected circus but acknowledged that private enterprise must provide most of the buildings. W .H. Nicholls, the Committee's architect from 1913 to 1917, emphasized the need for uniformity to ensure a dignified and harmonious architectural effect. To enclose the circus, 1,100 feet in diameter, Nicholls proposed seven colonnaded facades, each 177 feet in length and at least three stories or sixty feet in height, symmetrically treated, with their main horizontal lines at one level. Since the average 110-foot width of the seven roads piercing the ring impaired its visual integrity, Nicholls recommended spanning three avenues by great archways and a continuous upper cornice. Financial realities, he recognized, would permit nothing approaching the munificent spirit evident at Akbar's Fatehpur Sikri, but he hoped that the projected structures, while simple and straightforward, might display good workmanship and durable materials.[44]

Railway authorities, however, decided that a terminal station at Connaught Place was impracticable and abandoned the idea in favour of a large interchanging station at Paharganj, nearer Shahjahanabad. Without the catalyst of government building, private enterprise proved reluctant to invest. Not until 1928 were all lots on the inner circus sold and construction begun on the first two blocks of shops. The ring was only completed three years after New Delhi's inauguration ceremonies in 1931.[45]

R. T. Russell, Chief Architect to the Government of India, and his office prepared the detailed designs for Connaught Place along lines which Nicholls had advocated before leaving Delhi in 1917. Airy stuccoed colonnades, punctuated by Palladian archways, afforded protection to shoppers from sun and rain alike, and the elegant, understated classicism prompted admiring comparisons with terraces at Bath and Cheltenham. Built only two stories tall, however, the blocks failed to achieve the intended effect of urban enclosure, even before trees in the central park grew to obscure views across the circus. Furthermore, as Nicholls had feared, the sheer width of avenue entrances interrupted the desired circular continuity and rendered the boundaries of the plaza ambiguous. But these visual defects did not hamper the magnetic popularity of the stylish shops, which eventually eclipsed fashionable Chandni Chauk in Old Delhi. Indeed forty years after its first bricks were laid, one Indian planner recorded that Connaught Place, full of hustle and glamor, had become the Delhiwallah's abiding image of his city far more than even that widely recognized symbol, the historic Qutb Minar.[46]

Many persons have mistakenly believed that New Delhi was solely the work of Lutyens and Baker. Russell and his staff designed not only Connaught Place but all the government housing, upwards of 4,000 flat-roofed residences of stuccoed brick, from quarters for menials and clerks to bungalows for junior and senior gazetted officers, as well as hospitals, post offices, police stations, and in fact every official building required for the capital city. Government of India residences wholly by Lutyens were confined to the Viceregal estate, and, by Baker, to six houses on King George's Avenue and one rather hot bungalow on Akbar Road, known as "Baker's

232. Connaught Place, New Delhi.

233. A. G. Shoosmith in the garden of his bungalow at 13 Asoka Road, New Delhi, 1928.

234. Princes' Porch, at the entrance to the Chamber of Princes in the Council House, with the Secretariats to the south. Watercolor by P. D. Hepworth, 1924.

235. The Legislative Assembly Chamber in the Council House.

236 (below, left). The Chamber of Princes in the Council House.

237 (below right). The Library and Reading Room in the Council House.

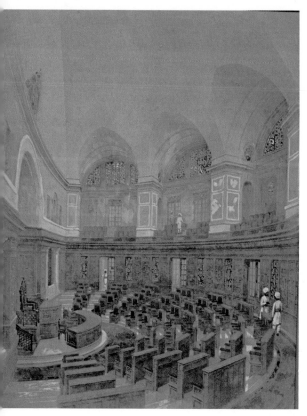

oven" to the Lutyens apostolate. Besides New Delhi, Russell's responsibilities for twenty years until his retirement in 1939 embraced designs for all Government of India buildings on the subcontinent, among them the Indian national military academy at Dehra Dun, Government House for the province of Sind at Karachi, offices in Bombay, and civil airports at Delhi and Karachi. At one time his staff comprised three British Assistant Architects and some twenty Indian draftsmen. Russell first accepted appointment to Indian government service in 1914, and Nicholls's handling of climatic problems and Lutyens's mastery of the classical orders both influenced him from the outset. Nicholls, who readily admitted a debt to Lutyens, pronounced Russell "a first-class man" whose work not only paralleled but improved upon his own.[47] [233, 239, 240, 241]

Russell's two principal works at New Delhi other than Connaught Place were a pair of stuccoed hostels for legislators that flanked Queen's Way and a princely residence for the Commander-in-Chief, Flagstaff House. [238] The scale of the three-story twin blocks, known as Eastern and Western Court, reflected the importance accorded representative bodies under the reformed constitution. Russell treated the two floors above the massive, arcaded basement plinth as a single continuous verandah. Giant Tuscan columns rose through both upper floors toward the knifelike shadow of a bold cornice, but the pillars proved as ineffective as those of the Council House in shielding rooms from heat and glare. Moreover, the top-floor balustrade intersected the columns, effectively breaking the depth of shadow between them. When Russell exhibited at the Royal Academy in 1922, his hostel designs inspired unfavorable comparison with Lutyens's technique and complaint about the lack of collaboration with the new capital's architectural advisers.[48] [158]

Perhaps partly in response to such criticism as well as to the proximity of Viceroy's House, Russell's stone and stucco mansion for the Commander-in-Chief appeared to exude the very spirit of Lutyens at his most imperial. Its long symmetrical mass, completed in 1930, echoes motifs recalling not only the Viceregal palace, Schedule B, and Hyderabad House, but in particular the cluster of cultural edifices Lutyens designed for the heart of King's Way. Conspicuous string courses, a black ribbon of shadow beneath the cornice, and the rhythm of paired columns in garden loggias all underscored the predominant horizontality. Recessed windows and deep arcades implied a massive solidity that would defy the assaults of men and elements. The restrained classicism of the palatial interior, exemplified in the serene and even severe cornice and fireplace details of the barrel-vaulted reception room, admirably befitted a soldier's residence. Later this austere dignity suited equally well the Anglicized tastes of Jawaharlal Nehru when Prime Minister, and appropriately the house became a museum and library devoted to the man sometimes known as "the last of the Viceroys." [245, 246]

Handsome axial vistas of Government House from the north windows of the Commander-in-Chief's residence emphasized the direct and intimate connection between Viceregal and military power. High fences and stout iron gates barred easy access to this veritable stronghold, set deep in ample grounds, aloof on a rising site. The Commander-in-Chief's exalted rank in the table of precedence, second only to the Viceroy's, dictated the palatial scale of his residence. By 1930, however, the size of the house seemed to accent the insecurity of British India and the heightened

238. Eastern Court, Queen's Way, New Delhi. R. T. Russell, architect.

importance of those armed forces which its occupant commanded.

Russell's successor as Chief Architect, Henry Medd, had worked for Lutyens at Apple Tree Yard from 1915 to 1917 before he came to Raisina in 1919 as Herbert Baker's assistant representative. Walter Sykes George already had been Baker's resident architect at Delhi since 1915, and C. P. Walgate had accompanied Baker on five visits to India between 1913 and 1918. When George resigned from Baker's service for private practice in 1924, Medd became responsible for interpreting and if necessary adapting the voluminous drawings sent from the London office. By his admission, he actually designed "very few features" of the Secretariats and Council House which the Public Works Department engineers executed. But top honors in competitions for the design of New Delhi's original Anglican and Roman Catholic churches, now both cathedrals, won for him an enduring place on the city skyline.[49]

By 1923, funds collected for an Anglican cathedral were clearly inadequate for anything resembling Lutyens's projected monument at the Close, and it appeared unlikely that Delhi would be created a separate see. The new Chaplain of Raisina, moreover, convinced the Bishop of Lahore that the proposed edifice south of King's Way would be too distant from the quarters of the clerks who formed the bulk of the congregation. The architectural competition held in 1925, therefore, stipulated a site which a parish committee recommended as convenient, north of King's Way on Asoka Road and east of the Gurudwara Bangla Sahib. As sole assessor, Sir Edwin Lutyens chose Medd's entry, a design in his own "Wrenaissance" mode and devoid of Indian motifs.[50]

40. A Government bungalow for a senior gazetted officer in the Indian Civil Service.

41. Government housing designed for Members of the Legislative Assembly.

39. Government housing for clerks in New Delhi, designed by W. H. Nicholls.

Building funds still proved insufficient, however, until the arrival in 1926 of Lord Irwin, an Anglo-Catholic of singular and exemplary piety. His ardent interest furnished the catalyst for substantial subscriptions from Britain. The competition site, which Medd considered to be "of no particular distinction," was abandoned in favor of the present location just north of Viceroy's Court. But when foundation ceremonies were held on February 23, 1927, the building appeal was in progress and the size of the church still unknown, so Irwin laid the stone at the crossing, the only certain point in the plan.[51]

Late the next year construction began to a design whose plan recalled aspects of Lutyens's churches at Hampstead Garden Suburb and, by Medd's admission, Palladio's Il Redentore in Venice. With its altar at the east end, the church was properly oriented to the rising sun, traditional symbol of the resurrected Christ, but the main view was from the south, where the building terminated an axial vista from the Jaipur Column and the palace forecourt. The powerful massing was symmetrical on both axes, rising by logical stages, and a long chancel balanced the nave, enduing the altar with a remoteness attractive to Irwin's High Church tastes. Medd designed a high central tower, possibly too tall, instead of the modest dome of his competition drawing, which had strongly echoed Lutyens's Free Church of 1910 at Hampstead Garden Suburb. Immense foundations for this lofty feature were laid deep on stable soil, but no tower was completed until 1935, when a third design by

242. Competition drawing by H. A. N. Medd for an Anglican church, New Delhi, 1925. Side elevation.

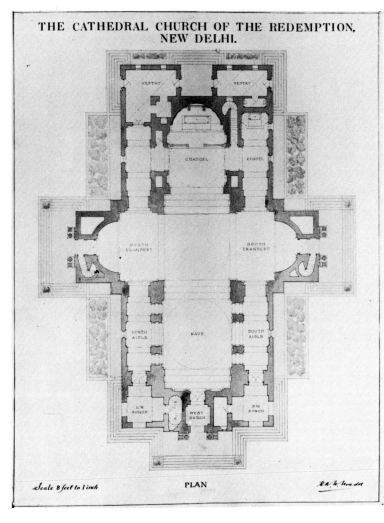

THE CATHEDRAL CHURCH OF THE REDEMPTION,
NEW DELHI.

Scale 8 feet to 1 inch          PLAN          H. A. N. Medd del.

243. Plan of the
Cathedral Church of
the Redemption, New
Delhi.

244. Revised design by
H. A. N. Medd for an
Anglican church, New
Delhi, after 1926. View
from the southwest.

245. The north front of the Commander-in-Chief's residence, New Delhi, designed by R. T. Russell.

246. The south front of Flagstaff House, the Commander-in-Chief's residence.

Medd, one of intermediate height, was built during his absence from India. All cornices and decorative features, including columned openings at the cardinal points of the tower, were executed in plastered brick rather than the intended buff-colored ashlar Dholpur sandstone used elsewhere in New Delhi. The dismayed architect later remarked that the guiding spirits in this enterprise, Lady Willingdon and F. T. Jones, then Chief Engineer, made a dangerous combination: their taste failed to match their energy.[52] [242, 243, 244, 247, 249]

Although Medd would have preferred the entire external facing to be in finely hewn ashlar stone, funds permitted its use only for the porches and molded courses. In contrast to these smooth-cut details, the buff Dholpur sandstone of the main walling was composed of roughly hewn rubble masonry, but the whole internal surface was ashlar. The floor was laid in patterns of red and buff stone, except for the sanctuary, which boasted Indian marble. The sanctuary apse was panelled in teak. In addition to his earlier subscription of £100, the King-Emperor gave the silver cross, a token of his personal interest in the new city and its buildings. Lord Irwin, a Yorkshireman, prompted the gift of the altar and altar rails, the figures above the reredos, and the pulpit by York Minster, as part of its celebration of thirteen centuries of Christianity from the baptism of King Edwin of Northumbria in 627.

The coursed rubble masonry and split red sandstone roofing may have hinted at Medd's Cotswold origins, but the severe facades, relieved only by tiny windows and concentrated classical ornament, were eminently appropriate to Delhi and its violent sunshine. The spacious chancel and transepts, and the height of the shadowy vaulted interior and its giant Corinthian Order, created an impression of monumental dignity and expansive scale that belied the actual size. The rich chancel furnishings

and the graceful Venetian or Palladian arch motif in the aisles and chapels, incorporating a subsidiary Order, helped avoid any feeling of austere coldness.

Lord Irwin's devoted concern never flagged, and often in the evenings he could be seen at the site on Church Road, inspecting the progress and discussing details with Medd. The Viceroy was genuinely delighted with the result, and he recorded his enthusiastic approval of its consummate unity, especially the way the interior scheme carried the eye forward naturally to the high altar. Acoustics, however, distinguished by a pervasive echo, caused disappointment to architect and client alike, but the application of "Limpet-Asbestos" plaster to the vaults and upper walls, on the expert advice of Hope Bagenal, brought marked improvement after 1931. Irwin's well-known interest in the building, and its final location close to the palace, led to a popular misnomer, "Viceroy's Church," which has persisted for half a century.[53]

The actual name of the church (created a cathedral in 1947) was in fact the subject of prolonged debate. Lutyens and Irwin favored dedication to God the Father. But the Metropolitan, the Bishop of Calcutta, expressed doubt about a title for which there was little or no precedent in the Western Church. The example of Palladio's Il Redentore suggested the Redeemer, or Holy Redeemer, to Medd, but eventually the building was consecrated as the Church of the Redemption, which the architect and others considered exotic for an Anglican edifice.[54]

Medd was successful, too, in the competition of 1927 to design the Roman Catholic Church of the Sacred Heart, now a cathedral. Competition assessors included both Lutyens and R. T. Russell. Construction, not begun until 1930, lasted until 1934.[55] Choice of a site at Alexandra Place, a major circus terminating a vista

247 (facing page). Cathedral Church of the Redemption, New Delhi, completed 1935, from the southwest.

248. Chancel of the Cathedral Church of the Redemption, New Delhi. Watercolor by Walter Sykes George.

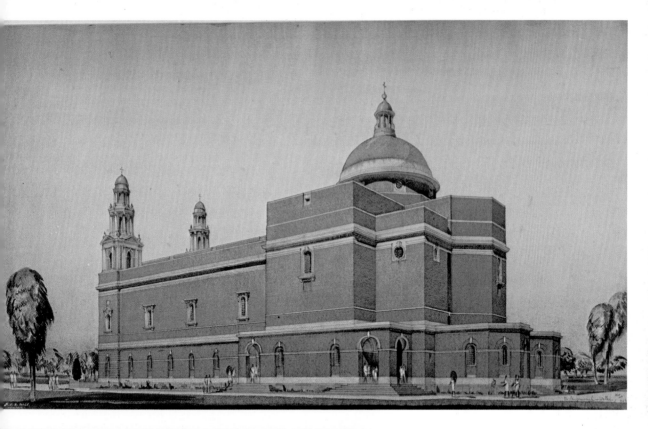

250. The Roman Catholic Cathedral of the Sacred Heart, New Delhi, designed by H. A. N. Medd. Watercolor by R. Myerscough-Walker.

251. The nave and chancel of the Roman Catholic Church of the Sacred Heart. Watercolor by R. Myerscough-Walker.

249 (facing page). The Cathedral Church of the Redemption, New Delhi, designed by H. A. N. Medd.

from the north block of the Secretariats, required the longer church axis to run north and south. The dexterous design, even more powerful than Medd's earlier Anglican scheme, expressed the might and confidence of a worldwide Church, nearly 2,000 years old, facing new challenge with courage and conviction.

At the north end of the cathedral, great spare rectangular masses stood shoulder to shoulder above the fluid rhythms of the huge plinth. Twin projecting vestries again recalled Lutyens at Hampstead Garden Suburb, as did dome and cupola. The original south or main entrance front was equally robust. The rectangular and pyramidal geometry of the single, open tower was a perfect foil to the solid hemispheric dome, and the simplicity and vigorous verticality of both tower and colonnaded loggia created a strong focus and climax to the intended vista and to the long plain surfaces of the side elevations. The bold lines of cornices and string courses not only underscored the horizontal sweep of the church, but their taut ribbons of buff stone on the contrasting red brick appeared to bind the whole composition indissolubly together. The darkness of the deep entrances emphasized the massive quality of the building, and as at Church Road, tiny openings in the huge blank walls testified to the architect's acquaintance with the bitter winds of winter and the summer's heat at Delhi. [250, 252]

Unfortunately the entire south front had to be reworked to include an oval mosaic cartouche of St. Francis, ordered from Florence without Medd's knowledge. The clients, moreover, pressed their architect to replace his integrally conceived

252. Competition drawing by H. A. N. Medd for a Roman Catholic church, New Delhi, 1927.

253. South front, the Cathedral Church of the Sacred Heart, New Delhi, completed 1934.

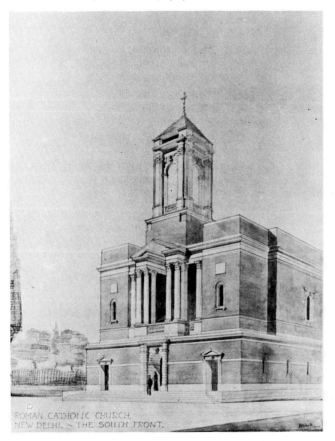

254. St. Thomas's Church, New Delhi, completed 1932. W. S. George, architect.

tower with a twin pair. The result was duly Italianate but delicate and complexly wrought compared to the rest of the stalwart design. Medd later admitted with characteristic candor that the towers were "rather banal," adding ruefully, "I could have done better than that."[56] [253]

Medd's plan derives from Giacomo Barozzi da Vignola's influential sixteenth-century church in Rome, the Gésu. Inside the Sacred Heart Cathedral, the cohesive proportional system echoed Lutyens's war memorial at Thiepval, where arches grew progressively larger as each sprang in hierarchic succession from the level of the previous keystone. The bright flood of sunshine from the transepts and domed crossing frame the chancel and highlighted the distinction between the laity seated in the barrel-vaulted nave and the sanctity of priests gathered at the focal altar. [251]

Much the same impression of scale is evident in Walter George's small Anglican church for Indian sweepers, St. Thomas's, built in 1931–32 on the northern margin of the city near Paharganj. Meager funds permitted only the simplest possible brick structure. Every brick, in the architect's words, did its duty; there was neither steel nor reinforced concrete in the fabric. The plinth was made of Delhi quartzite for practical reasons: every monsoon brought up soil salts that destroyed brickwork but could not damage the hard local stone. Only the sturdy tower, which the congregation required, was not purely functional. Large blank surfaces of simple brickwork arranged in stepped setbacks, pierced with little windows and a deeply receding round-arched portal with splayed jambs, captured all the rugged muscularity and sober nobility characteristic of Romanesque architecture.[57] [254]

THE GARRISON CHURCH, DELHI CANTONMENT.

A.G.SHOOSMITH. OBE. ARIBA
ARCHITECT

255. St. Martin's Church, the cantonment or garrison church at New Delhi, designed by A. G. Shoosmith. Watercolor by the architect.

THE LADY HARDINGE SERAI, DELHI.
A. G. Shoosmith. O.B.E. ARIBA Archt.

56. The Lady Hardinge Serai in New Delhi, designed by A. G. Shoosmith. Watercolor by the architect.

The bare brick-walled interior of St. Thomas's proved to have acoustics good enough to prompt boasts from the architect. The altar and its baldachino, the altar rail, pulpit, and fonts, completed to George's designs in 1943, were in buff Dholpur stone, rigorously plain: there was no ornament except inscriptions with touches of paint and gilding. The benches of Burma teak, meant to seat 296, had wheelwright's joints rather than joiners', to ensure strength and permanence. George took care that no source of light was visible when looking up the nave. But although the windows were small, when the doors of the nave and crossing were open (as always during services), a worshipper in any seat could read the fine print of a hymnal. Light and form were handled so adeptly that the effect of solemn dignity inspired at once a devotional attitude.

Three years earlier in designs for the Garrison Church of St. Martin, Arthur Shoosmith had expressed even more powerfully the same qualities of breadth and simplicity with a virility and discipline appropriate to a military outpost. Educated at Haileybury and the Royal Academy Schools, Shoosmith had worked in the offices of H. S. Goodhart-Rendel and Sir John Burnet before winning the prestigious Soane Medallion in 1920. The same year, on the recommendation of the Royal Institute of British Architects, he was appointed to succeed John Greaves as Lutyens's representative at New Delhi. During his tenure of this post, Viceroy's House was completed, and Henry Medd has recorded that "its success was in no small measure due to his meticulous insistence on the highest standards of workmanship in his interpretation of the drawings sent out from London."[58]

Shoosmith's standards of excellence were equally rigorous at St. Martin's. The flat, stony site lay west of the Delhi Ridge, about three miles from Raisina Hill. Beyond the bungalows and barracks of the new cantonment, designed by John Begg and the Military Works Department, the dusty plain stretched hot and almost treeless, burnt tawny by the sun.[59] On this unpromising site Shoosmith raised perhaps the most remarkable church in India, a timeless monument of brick, transcending all entanglements of detail, majestic in its bold modelling, directness, simplicity, and severity. [255, 257]

Lutyens, who had suggested his lieutenant for the job after he had placed second in the competition for both Raisina churches, offered him some pithy advice. "A building of one material," he wrote, "is for some strange reason much more noble than one of many. It may be the accent it gives of sincerity, the persistence of texture, and definite unity." He strongly cautioned against fussy design. "Don't use—whatever you do—bricks on edge and any fancy stuff; it only destroys scale and promotes triviality." His prescription was to "get rid of all mimicky Mary-Anne notions of brick work and go for the Roman wall." Britons, he felt, should be able to use bricks as magnificently as the Romans had.[60]

Shoosmith heeded his mentor's advice in waging friendly but frequent battles with the superintendent engineers to acquire three and a half million first-class, two-inch red bricks and to obtain the requisite standard of brickwork, whose minutely recessed joints enlivened the church facades with their shadow lines. Powerful battered walls rising with successive setbacks from a stone plinth, sparing use of windows, and subtle proportions combined to produce an edifice which defied labels of modern or traditional, Eastern or Western. If its sublime abstractness

257. A brick pit in New Delhi.

258. A brickyard and kilns in New Delhi.

259. A few of the 3½ million bricks for St. Martin's Church at the New Delhi cantonment.

260. St. Martin's Church under construction.

261. A lattice of scaffolding surrounding St. Martin's Church.

suggested the work of Willem Marinus Dudok and the Dutch and German Expressionists, and Lutyens at his most elemental, the parapet of the 128-foot tower, modelling of the side elevations, and recessive entrance jambs hinted at the battlements, buttresses, and portals of medieval Europe. The massiveness and monumentality of St. Martin's not only recalled the legacy of ancient Persian brickwork, but betrayed, too, Shoosmith's lifelong admiration for those very qualities as seen in English barns and the warehouses of Bristol dockyards.[61] [262, 263]

A tile-and-concrete barrel vault arched fifty-six feet above the wood-block floor of the wide nave, intersected by smaller barrel vaults, three to each aisle. Above the square chancel a brick dome appeared to hover weightlessly. Both in its general form and in its structural principle of balanced compression the nave resembled the Basilica of Constantine. Because the church was of necessity nondenominational, the architect deliberately eliminated imagery and iconic ornament.[62] The stripped classicism of the church interior seemed to underscore the severity of cantonment barracks and the rigors of military life as well as to embody the imperial code of ascetic duty and that stern doctrine of Curzonian efficiency which discarded nonessentials. [264]

One critic not only praised Shoosmith's responsiveness to the Delhi climate, but thought he had created a church which looked admirably like "a fortress against the

262. The remarkable west and south elevations of St. Martin's Church.

263. St. Martin's Church interior, facing the chancel.

264. The brickwork seen to advantage at the south door, St. Martin's Church.

powers of evil." To diehard imperialists steadfastly opposed to the forces of Indian nationalism, the metaphor was all too apt. Certainly the thick walls and tiny windows of St. Martin's earned approval from local soldiers, who deemed the church "a good place to hold in an emergency." Those were not the only plaudits. Robert Byron thought St. Martin's "superb." One article in *Country Life* called it "impressive," and another complained that had the church been the work of a French or German architect, Europe would have been "flabbergasted" by its splendidly simple and straightforward design.[63]

Prominently ranged beside Viceroy's House or standing tall amid the clerks' or sweepers' or soldiers' quarters, New Delhi's churches appeared almost to suggest British rule as a divine mission and to ask, as had more than one eminent Victorian, "Can we suppose otherwise than that it is our office to carry civilization and humanity, peace and good government, and, above all, the knowledge of the true God, to the uttermost ends of the earth?" By their very presence, the churches offered assurance to Britons in Raisina of the rightness of their island kingdom's self-destined supremacy. But for those who foresaw the swift approach of empire's end, the churches had an altogether different symbolism, that of security deferred and hope transferred to another realm.[64]

The design of New Delhi's churches captured much of that austerity, nobility, and quiet strength which British imperial ideology proclaimed as personal virtues in its many scattered agents who bore the "White Man's burden." They were virtues, too, in Herbert Baker's credo, attributes displayed in his work and personality. Baker was, one contemporary remarked, like his buildings: "strong, even rugged, but simple." There was "no nonsense, no sham about him," but in fact much of the force and character of St. Francis, which made the man lovable and his creations understandable. A later critic saw in him the traits of an adventurous pioneer, including flexibility and idealism. This meant his architecture, while often devoid of subtlety, was fresh, direct, and vital, but with an orderly quality that derived from the sound principle of freedom within discipline. The loose-limbed nature of his work also sprang from his belief that what forms said was as important as the composition. Buildings should state a creed, and they were of little worth unless they conveyed social or national identity or even some moral message. Indeed the significance of Baker's life and buildings lay not so much in stylistic innovation but in eloquent expression of contemporary convictions. His very freedom of method helped him successfully interpret concepts or sentiments, and as Lord Hardinge emphasized, no people were governed by sentiment more than in India.[65]

Baker espoused the view that buildings could embody ideas as an influence for good. Men and governments, he remarked in 1927, tended "to live up to the dignity of their habitation," and "this high service" justified the art of architecture. Winston Churchill expressed this notion in 1943 when he observed that "we shape our buildings, and afterwards our buildings shape us." For Baker, the monuments of Britain's empire prompted individuals to seek the common goals of imperial society. Small wonder, then, at his pleasure over the Viceroy's compliment in the new Legislative Assembly chamber: Lord Irwin expressed a wish that the conduct of business might reflect the harmony of Baker's conception.[66]

Baker and Lutyens and their colleagues at Raisina raised a city that bespoke the disciplined imagination and indomitable tenacity that had built a worldwide empire. This tiny band mirrored one imperial servant's description of himself and his peers as "acolytes of a cult"—Pax Britannica—for which they worked happily and, if necessary, died gladly; all "loved and laughed much" and fearlessly acknowledged their inevitable common end, secure in the knowledge that their work would live after them and that by their fruits they would be judged in the days to come. New Delhi was an ample memorial and reward for its authors: as Vitruvius had written of Augustan Rome, its eminent dignity proclaimed the majesty of the Empire.[67]

# 10

# *Twilight and Dawn, 1931*

Ominous black clouds hung heavily over New Delhi, and unseasonable cold and rain greeted guests who arrived for the official inauguration ceremonies. Gloomy skies mirrored the mood of those who discerned at Raisina the sepulcher of an empire. The city that Lord Hardinge envisioned in 1912 was meant to testify to "the ideal and fact of British rule in India." The Viceroy had intended the new capital to express peaceful British authority over a composite European and Asian civilization. The undeviating geometry of the city plan had appeared symbolic of Britain's efforts to impose order and unity on the subcontinent, while the monumental scale of the avenues and principal buildings had implied a permanence that challenged time itself. As the domes and towers fashioned by Lutyens and Baker rose on Raisina Hill, bright against the sky above city and plain, they had seemed to proclaim the success of British discipline and power. By February 1931, however, many persons acknowledged that New Delhi's inaugural celebrations were but a requiem for that dream of abiding dominion. Curzon's prewar prophecies continued to haunt his Viceregal successors with an accuracy at once astonishing and infuriating; not only had the capital cost more than £10,000,000, but it was already destined to become the predicted "gilded phantom," as the power of initiative ebbed to nationalist forces.[1]

If even in 1921 British suzerainty seemed to the Prince of Wales to be "solid, secure, and timeless," by 1931 a new imperial ideal of partnership had replaced the old proprietary concept of empire. Already, the *Observer* declared, the old Empire had become the British Commonwealth of Nations at the Crown's initiative. The inscription which Lutyens envisaged for Government House in 1914—"Govern them and lift them up forever"—now only seventeen years later seemed impossibly jarring in its explicit paternalism.[2]

Not surprisingly, little was heard in 1931 of New Delhi as embodiment of imperium, but instead much was made of its perceived role as emblem of a new era. The very week of its inaugural ceremonies, delegates returned to India from the first Round Table Conference, which had been convened in London to chart the course toward Indian self-rule. Leading British newspapers agreed that the coincidence was "almost miraculous," for it was now possible to regard Raisina as representing the government's "altered spirit." History would associate New Delhi with the beginning of real self-government; its buildings would not be seen as "vainglorious gestures" of dominion and the trappings of imperial power, but rather as the offices and council chambers where India would plan and direct her own future. Those who sought to rewrite the Indian constitution could regard New Delhi as a parable in stone, a hopeful symbol of cooperation and successful creation in the face of enormous obstacles.[3]

One astute observer discerned in the long procession of majestic Delhis the unique character of the newest city. Its predecessors defied the world behind massive walls and bristling gateways, admitting strangers only grudgingly to its central fortress, "where military despotism was enthroned." By contrast New Delhi was open to the plains and welcomed the visitor along tree-lined avenues to its very heart, where constitutional government was administered and India's representatives met together in council. New Delhi, the critic thought, was "well named"; it truly stood for a new epoch.[4]

Amid these paeans and colorful festivities, however, bitter memories lent sharpness to continued controversy over the form and timing of the imperial denouement. Opening of the Lady Hardinge Serai on February 4, first of the inaugural ceremonies, evoked recollections of that fateful State Entry into Delhi eighteen years before, indelibly marked by the explosion of an assassin's bomb. In thanksgiving for the Viceregal couple's escape, the women of India had subscribed a lakh of rupees in small contributions for Lady Hardinge to use as she thought best. She began the New Delhi Cathedral Fund with a donation of Rs. 25,000, and before her death she proposed use of the rest to construct a serai or hostel for indigent travellers opposite the new railway station. Because the station site long remained unsettled, the serai was not begun until 1930, to skillful designs by Arthur Shoosmith, inspired by early Mughal architecture. [256]

Lutyens's capitoline palace, although itself already occupied for fourteen months, nevertheless captured the spotlight during much of New Delhi's inauguration. Awestruck guests thought the beauty of its marble halls and Mughal garden beggared description. Abandoning customary restraint, Lord Hardinge wrote "glorious" repeatedly in his diary. Lutyens's devoted friend Edward Hudson, proprietor of *Country Life*, was moved to exclaim, "Poor old Christopher Wren could never have done this!" Lady Emily thought her husband had created a miracle which was both a palace of immense dignity and "an ideally comfortable country house." She remarked, too, on the "immense luck" in having Lord and Lady Irwin, so charming and appreciative, as first occupants of the house.[6]

During the fortnight's festivities, the Viceregal couple presided with equal ease over a banquet for 100, formal reception, garden party, and investiture ceremony, as well as light-hearted luncheon parties and lively after-dinner games for house guests, including charades, at which the Viceroy excelled. Despite the simple and delightfully unsophisticated side of his character, Lord Irwin nonetheless kept due state as the King-Emperor's representative. He might walk to church unattended and in mufti, but he appreciated the effect of splendor on appropriate occasions, especially in the Orient. His investitures were deemed to rival even Curzon's in magnificence. On February 12, carefully orchestrated pomp in the Durbar Hall caused the Viceroy's good friend and guest, the redoubtable Bishop Gore, to say, "When I get home I shall suggest that Edward Irwin be impeached for exceeding the King in grandeur!" After the same occasion Lord Hardinge commented that Viceroys behaved far more like royalty than in his term, a fact he attributed to Lord

Reading, who had first visited India as cabin boy on a Glasgow cargo boat.[7] [265]

The Irwins in fact had relaxed Court etiquette at Delhi. The requisite curtseys at dinner, as many as seven in an evening under the Reading regime, were reduced to three. Guests were still shepherded into a drawing room by a platoon of aides-de-camp and ranged in two solemn lines, men opposite women, to bow and curtsey as Their Excellencies swept past. But then various dogs who tumbled all over the house would scamper in behind the Irwins, giving a reassuring impression that the Viceroy was, after all, essentially a country squire.[8]

Welcome sunshine broke through the prevailing wintry gloom on February 10 to grace a brilliant spectacle of imperial pageantry, the unveiling of Herbert Baker's Asokan columns, gifts of the four Dominions. Massed bands, trumpet fanfares, and a thunderous thirty-one-gun salute heralded arrival of the Viceroy's carriage and scarlet-clad bodyguard. Nearly five thousand guests, including Dominion representatives, the Commander-in-Chief, and Lord Hardinge had assembled in Government Court, while hundreds of Indian clerks and chaprassis jockeyed for position on the Secretariat rooftops. In a brief address, inaudible after loudspeakers failed, Lord Irwin described the pillars as emblems of common loyalty to the sovereign of an empire which eschewed uniformity of custom and instead preserved diversity within unity—the very adjustment which Baker envisioned for classical architecture in the differing corners and climes of Britain's overseas territories. Successive Dominion envoys reiterated the theme of comradeship, declaring the columns to be permanent tokens of their affection and concern and symbols of that Commonwealth in which India must soon stand an equal. Speeches concluded, the four representatives simultaneously pressed electric buttons, draperies fell from the pillars, a fanfare sounded, and bands struck up "God Save the King," all an earnest, it seemed, of India's welcome to the family circle as the fifth Dominion.[9] [268, 269]

The People's Fête, which the Raisina contractors organized the next day in Old Delhi, was full of all the spirited swagger and flourish and contrast of a peculiarly Indian occasion. Inside the Fort, which harbored memories of the Peacock Throne, General Lake and Emperor Shah Alam, and blood-red Mutiny horrors, selections from "The Student Prince" and "Madame Butterfly" enlivened the halls and gardens, and pipers entertained 3,000 honored guests with "Maids of the Black Glen" and the "Inverness Reel." Below the battlements on the Jumna mud flats, horsemen and Highlanders delighted a crowd of 50,000 with tent pegging, musical rides, and broadsword dances. From his vantage adjoining the octagonal darshan tower, where Mughal Emperors had daily shown themselves to their people, the Viceroy witnessed a remarkable pageant of Indian travel and transport. Elephants in war paint led a procession that included rickshaws, wooden-wheeled bullock carts, buffaloes laden with firewood, tongas burdened with whole families, hillmen from beyond Simla carrying curtained litters, and gaily caparisoned camels drawing a landau and the Punjab state carriage. This panorama of life on the Grand Trunk Road comprised as well wandering musicians, jugglers, clowns decorated with fearful designs, and dancing bears mincing past with comical steps. In the vanguard of a long file of motorcars was a battered and rusty veteran said to be the first ever imported. Overhead, Bristol fighters of the Royal Air Force swooped in maneuvers as skyrockets exploded and guns boomed on the Ridge. By an extraordinary

265. The first Baron Irwin (later first Earl of Halifax), Viceroy of India, 1926–31, gracing the frontispiece of *Country Life*.

# COUNTRY LIFE

Vol. LXIX.—No. 1794.     SATURDAY, JUNE 6th, 1931.     Price Two Shillings. [ Postages: Inland (Parcel Post) 9d. Canada 3½d., Abroad 1s. 1d.

Matzene, Simla.

LORD IRWIN.

*The first Viceroy of India to sit on the Vice-regal throne at New Delhi.*

266. The Republic Day parade, held annually on January 26. The Central Vista continues to serve as a setting for ceremonial.

267. The President of India in the former Viceregal carriage at Republic Day festivities.

268. Inaugural ceremonies for New Delhi. Unveiling of the Dominion Columns designed by Herbert Baker, February 10 1931.

269. Indian spectators on the rooftop of the North Block, Secretariats, to enjoy Viceregal pomp, February 10, 1931.

coincidence, when Lord Irwin stepped to the parapet to acknowledge the salute, a brilliant rainbow appeared in the heavens, a happy augury.[10]

Nineteen years before, on the spot where the Viceroy sat at sunset, King George and Queen Mary—enthroned, robed, and crowned—had received the Durbar homage of 100,000 Indians. These loyal subjects had approached in wide, successive waves with shouts of "King-Emperor" and cries of joy. Now, in 1931, rumors abounded of hostile agitation. Pickets tried to prevent attendance at the fête, and political demonstrators attempted disruption. An army of police, many of them hidden, encircled the Fort and guarded its gates with elaborate precautions. Security officers promptly vetoed Lord Irwin's expressed wish to join Indian spectators on the plain outside the walls.

Imperial duty and Dominion fraternity were solemn keynotes of the commemoration ceremony held on February 12 at Lutyens's Indian War Memorial. As the pale winter sun dropped behind the domes of Raisina, the Viceroy stood bareheaded, wreath in hand, before the monumental arch that not only paid tribute to common imperial sacrifice but also formed a symbolic gateway to the new Delhi. A special guard of honor of much-bemedalled soldiers, men who had ridden the cobbled streets of France and filled its sodden trenches or fought on Himalayan frontiers, framed the scene to perfection, while red and white pennons of the Central India Horse proudly brightened King's Way. A "fire of remembrance" blazed on the summit of the arch, and a single bugler sounded the Last Post, whose sad refrain seemed as much a final salute to the Indian Empire as to her recent war casualties. As scarlet-clad horsemen and infantry in khaki passed under the arch and Royal Air Force planes roared overhead in formation, regimental bands crashed into familiar martial tunes, with "A Long Way to Tipperary" a poignant echo from the tragic inferno of conflict. The lofty sacred fire that had begun in a dark pillar of cloud assumed a ruddy glow as the angry twilight sky burned crimson and gold. There was, recalled one official, "something terrible" about the scene, as if Indian soldiers were marching to rejoin the dead in a fiery imperial Valhalla.[11]

Consecration of the Church of the Redemption on February 15 brought to a climactic conclusion New Delhi's inaugural events. Everything, the Viceroy recorded, looked "most august," with three bishops in full regalia, including copes and miters, and the building crowded with people. After assembly of the congregation, the Bishop of Lahore went outside the west door to meet a body of residents who presented a petition praying him to consecrate the church. Assenting, the Bishop knocked three times on the closed door, saying, "Lift up your heads, O ye gates, and be ye lifted up, ye everlasting doors, and the King of Glory shall come in." From within, the people replied, "Who is the King of Glory?" Upon the Bishop answering, "The Lord strong and mighty, even the Lord mighty in battle," the door was thrown open, and as the procession entered, the choir sang Psalm 122, "I was glad when they said unto me, Let us go into the house of the Lord." After the Bishop pronounced the formal consecration, the stone edifice resounded with the triumphant verses of the apt and well-known hymn, "City of God." Lord Hardinge thought the church interior "very fine and simple," and Lord Irwin concluded that visitors were greatly impressed with the church, which had turned out "wonderfully well." The splendid service left the Viceroy with a great feeling of

270.  Viceroy's House, the dome of the Cathedral Church of the Redemption, and the Jaipur Column, seen from the former New Delhi residence of the Commander-in-Chief in India.

271. A Britannic lion guarding the forecourt of Viceroy's House.

happiness: "It was," he told his father, "a wonderful climax to the hopes and efforts of the last four years."[12]

Commemorative ceremonies for the new capital could not hope to rival the Delhi Durbar of 1911. While the inauguration in 1931 was, in Lord Irwin's words, "a landmark in the history of India," economic depression and consequent financial stringency made impossible the lavish expenditure of nineteen years before. Even the sum of £22,000, the cost of bringing a representative Indian army to Delhi and supplying the essentials of a simplified pageant, raised protests from the European community. Their heightened concern about the future of British interests following the Round Table Conference undercut any festive sentiments. One English journalist reported glum descriptions of inaugural events as "the funeral of our Indian Empire."[13]

Physical dangers posed by political extremists, moreover, had ruled out an anticipated visit from the popular Duke and Duchess of York, destined in a half-dozen years to become King-Emperor and Queen-Empress. Acts of terrorism, although strongly condemned by Gandhi and other leading adherents of nonviolence, continued unabated. On December 23 Sir Geoffrey de Montmorency, who years earlier had served the Imperial Delhi Committee and was now Governor of the Punjab, had barely escaped assassination. Precisely a year before, Lord Irwin had survived an attempt to derail the Viceregal train with a bomb; with customary sang-froid, he had not let events interrupt his study of an eighteenth-century theologian. "I heard the noise," he recorded, "and said to myself 'that must be a bomb,' and fully expected to hear something further happen. I then smelt all the smoke which came down the train, and concluded that it was a bomb; but, as nothing happened, I went on reading Challoner till someone came along and told me it had been a bomb and I went to see the damage."[14]

Not everyone shared Lord Irwin's indifference to danger. Lady Emily thought many persons would be greatly relieved when the inauguration was safely over. "You never know," she wrote home, "what mad man may throw a bomb." Viceroy's House and grounds were "chock-a-block with policemen & sentries," and the *Times* correspondent on February 10 reported that all approaches to New Delhi were "plastered" with police to discourage demonstrations. A visiting Member of Parliament described the capital as "an armed camp."[15]

Understandably, fewer than fifteen Indian princes attended the inauguration ceremonies. The *Daily Mail* in its role as Cassandra interpreted this absence as a vote of no confidence in continued British authority. Other journals detected a "general lack of enthusiasm" for New Delhi among most Indians, an attitude the *Daily Mail* had discerned six years earlier when reporting the native belief that Raisina would eventually go the way of its ruined predecessors. In 1926 Malcolm Hailey had attributed this apathy to the recent focus of Indian political energies on the provinces, emphasizing local rather than general concerns. This development, Baker agreed, reduced interest in the attempt to embody the spirit and sentiment of India in a national capital.[16]

Congress politicians, in any case, were in no mood for festivity in 1931 as they gathered in Allahabad to mourn the death of their leader Motilal Nehru and to ponder the consequences of the Round Table Conference. Indeed Nehru's son

Jawaharlal later heaped bitter scorn on the imperial ritual of Britons in India, "their court ceremonies, their durbars and investitures, their parades, their dinners and evening dress, their pompous utterances." All this awesome display in fact had impressed Indians, a people admittedly "given to ceremonial observances." But the persistence of what Nehru called "this elaborate show," despite revolutionary changes in values, began to inspire ridicule and jest. Nehru depicted Viceroy's House as the "chief temple where the High Priest officiated," and he assailed the new Delhi as the "visible symbol of British power, with all its pomp and circumstance and vulgar ostentation and wasteful extravagance."[17]

Mahatma Gandhi was equally critical, as befitted his fervent advocacy of the cause of the poor and his belief in India's villages as the source of her social and economic strength and identity. He deplored "the waste of money on architectural piles" and felt strongly that India could not afford Viceregal residences at Raisina, Simla, and Calcutta. The new capital was an artificial imposition on the country, with no relation to rural life. Its buildings were "in conflict with the best interest of the nation"; they did not represent India's millions, especially those with neither place to sleep nor bread to eat. New Delhi was, in his estimate, a "white elephant."[18]

Fate decreed that only two days after New Delhi's inaugural celebrations, Gandhi found himself at the gates of the city's grandest palace for an interview with the King-Emperor's Viceroy. Important constitutional proposals that had been mooted at the recent Round Table Conference now required the assent of Congress nationalists. Consequently it was in a bold effort to break a political impasse that Lord Irwin had given Gandhi and his colleagues an unconditional release from their year-long internment and then had agreed to meet the Mahatma as "man to man."[19]

Punctually at 2:20 on the afternoon of February 17, therefore, Gandhi made his way past the stone gauntlet of Britannic lions guarding Viceroy's Court and was ushered into Lord Irwin's study. [272] His arrival was in vivid contrast to official processions the previous week. A torn woolen shawl, loin cloth, and bamboo stave had replaced the scarlet uniforms and flashing lances of an imperial Body Guard. A prisoner only days before, Gandhi nonetheless came as no humble supplicant, but much more like the plenipotentiary of a sovereign power, "on equal terms with the Viceroy." While he had never led an army or a government, this frail priest-king "commanded the allegiance of his countrymen while the King-Emperor commanded only the Government of India." He was the first in a succession of colonial leaders over the decades who would languish in British jails, then grace British conference chambers.[20]

In England, Winston Churchill, who had seen Victorian India first-hand as a young cavalry officer, perceived the pattern of the future with remarkable clairvoyance. He realized that the end of British rule in India spelled the demise of an entire empire. For Britain to lose India, he had declared in January, "could not fail to be part of a process which would reduce us to the scale of a minor Power." In his most forcible language he deplored the "spectacle" now taking place at Raisina: "It is alarming and also nauseating to see Mr. Gandhi, a seditious Middle Temple lawyer, now posing as a fakir of a type well-known in the East, striding half-naked up the steps of the Viceregal palace, while he is still organizing and conducting a defiant campaign of civil disobedience, to parley on equal terms with the representative of the King-Emperor."[21]

Churchill was not the only Briton distressed by the meeting of the "two uncrucified Christs," as a mutual friend dubbed the Viceroy and Gandhi. The King-Emperor disclosed to Irwin that he was "troubled at the comical situation of the religious fanatic with his very restricted covering being admitted to your beautiful new house" for "interminable and irksome conversations." Had Churchill and King George been present in the Viceregal study, they would have been even more astonished, for it was a remarkable scene: a distinguished-looking, six-foot-five-inch English aristocrat, an expert horseman, born in a castle and schooled at Eton and Christ Church, Oxford, and seated opposite him, a tiny Hindu guru clad in dhoti and shawl, with thick glasses, big ears, a bald pate, and a grin that showed few teeth except when he inserted a set to eat a diet of dates and goat's milk.[22]

Lord Irwin set down his impressions of Gandhi for the King:

> I think most people meeting him would be conscious, as I was conscious, of a very powerful personality, and this, independent of physical endowment, which indeed is unfavorable. Small, wizened, rather emaciated, no front teeth, it is a personality very poorly adorned with this world's trimmings. And yet you cannot help feeling the force of character behind the sharp little eyes and immensely active and acutely working mind.

Indeed Irwin thought Gandhi had "a very good mind: logical, forceful, courageous, with an odd streak of subtlety." Moreover, as one British memsahib recorded with

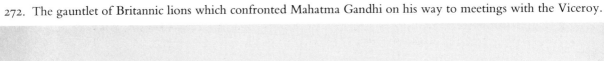

272. The gauntlet of Britannic lions which confronted Mahatma Gandhi on his way to meetings with the Viceroy.

273. Gandhi in the Viceroy's garden, 1947. During the Viceroyalty of Lord Mountbatten, India became an independent member of the Commonwealth of Nations, finally fulfilling Gandhi's wish that his motherland should "become a partner with Great Britain."

delight at the time, he had a real sense of fun, with twinkling eyes and "a most disarming smile." Other observers were less impressed. An official who was present at one of the eight meetings recalled: "I remember Gandhi squatting on the floor and after a while a girl coming in with some filthy yellow stuff which he started eating without so much as by your leave." When the Viceroy's dogs bounded in, they sniffed all around him as if they had never seen the like in the whole of their lives. But when Lord Irwin was asked if Gandhi had been tiresome, he replied, "Some people found Our Lord very tiresome."[23]

An affectionate bond grew between the pair as they huddled in the great palace at Raisina, hour after hour, for talks which were conducted, Gandhi said, "in the friendliest possible manner and with much sweetness." Irwin was set in the Antique mold, an exemplar of qualities which Rome had highly prized: gravitas, pietas, integritas, and virtus. These stood him in good stead. His "faith in a higher Power and sincere allegiance to moral principles," one Congress chieftain later declared, were what won Gandhi's esteem. "I succumbed," Gandhi confessed, "not to Lord Irwin but to the honesty in him." The two men did not kneel together in prayer, as was reported, but they did laugh over Churchill's lurid description of the "half-naked fakir." Initially "consecrated knights in opposing camps," they became friends in a common cause.[24]

At noon on March 5, at Viceroy's House, archrebel and King-Emperor's representative signed a truce that became known as the Delhi Pact. Essentially both sides pledged their best efforts to bring about peace. The Indian Government offered to release political prisoners and withdraw repressive ordinances, while Gandhi agreed to suspend the civil disobedience movement and to attend the second Round Table Conference as sole Congress representative.

If the pact was a victory, Gandhi said, it belonged to both sides. He had negotiated with the Viceroy as an equal, as no Indian had done before. Irwin had allayed the Mahatma's suspicions and convinced him of Britain's honest intentions; the promise of self-government was manifestly sincere. Future controversy would center not on this common goal but on the rate of progress toward it. Gandhi and Irwin helped ensure that contact between India and the West would be not only close but sympathetic. Their conversations in the wintry sunlight of the Viceroy's study averted the indefinite separation of Briton and Indian by "an uncomfortable gulf of mutual hatred and miscomprehension" just when that catastrophe seemed inevitable. The foundations that the "two Mahatmas" laid for the peaceful transfer of power survived the vicissitudes of the next sixteen years, and India chose to remain within the Commonwealth after her independence in 1947. Then Gandhi's desire, expressed in 1931, that India should "become a partner with Great Britain," was fulfilled.[25] [273]

Almost at once, Lord Irwin's term drew to an end. On April 7 he gave a final gala ball at Viceroy's House. It was a warm evening, and the illuminated gardens were more popular than the mirrored ball room. Lutyens's fountains, the bright uniforms and flowing dresses, and the music of the band evoked visions of Versailles for one guest. But it was, he thought, "the kind of atmosphere that must have pervaded the closing years of the Second Empire."[26] The sense of both an impending finale and a dawning order gave every experience double piquancy.

Eleven days later at Bombay, "looking unutterably sad," Lord Irwin stood holding his hat and acknowledging cheers as the Viceregal launch carried him to a waiting ship. As the forlorn figure faded from view in the tropic haze, one British journalist recorded that the climax of the Viceroy's farewell address lingered on in memory: the classic inscription on the Jaipur Column, distilled from Lutyens's suggestions. Carved at the heart of the subcontinent, it was a noble epitaph for British rule and fitting counsel for the future masters of India:

> In Thought Faith
> In Word Wisdom
> In Deed Courage
> In Life Service
> So may India be great.[27]

But the words of another statesman and visitor are printed perhaps most memorably on a landscape littered with the remnants of earlier capitals. They are lines resurrected annually in June, when the hot south winds from Rajasthan raise great clouds of red dust and the air of New Delhi grows heavy and dark. Those who venture into this tempest along the broad avenues leading to Raisina see nothing of the imperial acropolis and the proud house built for a British Viceroy. It is as though Lutyens's fairytale palace and its mammoth neighbors by Baker have disappeared into the turbulent air. Then parts of the splendid edifices materialize, hauntingly incomplete. In those unreal moments, one is apt to recall Georges Clemenceau's words, when he first gazed upon the half-built city in 1920: "This will be the finest ruin of them all."[28]

# NOTES

## Abbreviations

*Persons*

| | |
|---|---|
| AC | Sir Austen Chamberlain |
| AS | Arthur Gordon Shoosmith |
| CH | Charles Hardinge, first Baron Hardinge of Penshurst |
| DB | Sir David Barr |
| EB | Sir Edward Baker |
| EL | Sir Edwin Landseer Lutyens |
| FR | Frederick Sleigh Roberts, first Earl Roberts |
| GB | Sir George Christopher Molesworth Birdwood |
| GC | George Nathaniel Curzon, first Marquess Curzon of Kedleston |
| GD | Sir Geoffrey de Montmorency |
| GL | General Gerard Lake, first Viscount Lake |
| GS | George Sitwell Campbell Swinton |
| GW | Sir Guy Fleetwood Wilson |
| HB | Sir Herbert Baker |
| HL | Henry Vaughan Lanchester |
| HM | Henry Alexander Nesbitt Medd |
| JB | John Begg |
| JD | Sir James Houssemayne Du Boulay |
| JH | Sir John Prescott Hewett |
| JI | John Poynder Dickson-Poynder, first Baron Islington |
| JJ | Sir John Lewis Jenkins |
| JM | John Morley, first Viscount Morley |
| JT | Frederic John Napier Thesiger, third Baron Chelmsford |
| LI | Edward Frederick Lindley Wood, first Baron Irwin |
| LL | Lady Emily Lutyens |
| LS | Leonard Stokes |
| MS | Arthur Bigge, first Baron Stamfordham |
| RB | Reginald Barratt |
| RC | Robert Offley Ashburton Crewe-Milnes, first Marquess of Crewe |
| RO | Sir Robert Warrand Carlyle |
| RR | Sir Richmond Thackery Ritchie |
| RW | Richard Colley Wellesley, first Marquess Wellesley |
| TD | Thomas Denman, third Baron Denman |
| TH | Sir Thomas William Holderness, first Baronet |
| TS | Thomas Henry Sanderson, first Baron Sanderson |
| VC | Sir Valentine Chirol |
| VS | Mrs. Constance M. Villiers-Stuart |
| WH | William Malcolm Hailey, first Baron Hailey |
| WL | Sir Walter Roper Lawrence, first Baronet |
| WM | Sir William Stevenson Meyer |
| WS | William Stantiall |

*Other Abbreviations*

| | |
|---|---|
| *AAJ* | *Architectural Association Journal* |
| ASA | Arthur Gordon Shoosmith and Marjorie Cartwright Reid Shoosmith, papers, property of Mrs. Marjorie Cartwright Reid Shoosmith, Slindon, Arundel, West Sussex |
| ASD | Arthur Gordon Shoosmith, drawings, Royal Institute of British Architects, Portman Square, London |
| ASP | Arthur Gordon Shoosmith, papers, Royal Institute of British Architects, Portland Place, London |
| *B* | *Builder* |
| BFL | Sir Banister Fletcher Library, Royal Institute of British Architects, Portland Place, London |
| BLM | Louis Mountbatten, first Earl Mountbatten of Burma, papers, Mountbatten Archives, Broadlands, Romsey, Hampshire |
| CEL | Library of the Chief Engineer, Government of India, Central Public Works Department, New Delhi |
| CHC | Charles Hardinge, first Baron Hardinge of Penshurst, papers, Cambridge University Library, Cambridge |
| CHK | Charles Hardinge, first Baron Hardinge of Penshurst, papers, Kent County Archives Office, Maidstone, Kent |
| CHP | Charles Hardinge, first Baron Hardinge of Penshurst, papers, property of the Dowager Lady Hardinge, South Park, Penshurst, Kent |
| CHPD | Charles Hardinge, first Baron Hardinge of Penshurst, diary, property of the Dowager Lady Hardinge, South Park, Penshurst, Kent |
| CHPS | Charles Hardinge, first Baron Hardinge of Penshurst, Sanderson correspondence, property of the Dowager Lady Hardinge, South Park, Penshurst, Kent |
| *CL* | *Country Life* |
| CMP | Robert Offley Ashburton Crewe-Milnes, first Marquess of Crewe, papers, Cambridge, Uni- |

versity Library, Cambridge

DNB     *Dictionary of National Biography*

ELP     Sir Edwin Lutyens, papers, Sir Banister Fletcher Library, Royal Institute of British Architects, Portland Place, London

GGIC     Governor-General in Council

GOI     Government of India

HBD     Sir Herbert Baker, diary, property of Henry Edmeades Baker, Owletts, Cobham, Kent

HBK     Sir Herbert Baker, papers and drawings, property of Henry Edmeades Baker, Owletts, Cobham, Kent

HDD     Home Department: Delhi, Proceedings, National Archives of India, New Delhi

HDP     Home Department: Political, Proceedings, National Archives of India, New Delhi

HDU     Home Department: Public, Proceedings, National Archives of India, New Delhi

HMD     Henry Alexander Nesbitt Medd, drawings, Royal Institute of British Architects, Portman Square, London

HML     Henry Alexander Nesbitt Medd, papers, property of Mrs. Marjorie Lloyd Medd, London

HMP     Henry Alexander Nesbitt Medd, papers, Centre of South Asian Studies, University of Cambridge, Cambridge

HSAS     Sir Harry Haig and Lady Haig, papers, Centre of South Asian Studies, University of Cambridge, Cambridge

IOR     India Office Records, London

ISRM     *Indian State Railways Magazine*

JRSA     *Journal of the Royal Society of Arts*

JSP     John Lewis Sale, papers, Centre of South Asian Studies, University of Cambridge, Cambridge

LEL     Lady Emily Lutyens, papers, property of Miss Jane Ridley, London

NDD     Office drawings for New Delhi, drawings archives, Government of India, Central Public Works Department, New Delhi

OCC     Office of the Chief Commissioner, Delhi, papers, Delhi Public Administration Record Office, Delhi

PCSI     Council of State of India, *Proceedings*

PDC     *Parliamentary Debates* (Commons), 5th series

PDL     *Parliamentary Debates* (Lords), 5th series

PLAI     Legislative Assembly of India, *Proceedings*

PLCI     Legislative Council of India, *Proceedings*

PP     Great Britain, *Parliamentary Papers*

PWD     Central Public Works Department, Government of India, Proceedings, National Archives of India, New Delhi

RIBAJ     *Journal of the Royal Institute of British Architects*

SIDC     Secretary, Imperial Delhi Committee

SPWD     Secretary, Government of India, Public Works Department

TPR     *Town Planning Review*

WNP     William Henry Nicholls, papers, Royal Institute of British Architects, Sir Banister Fletcher Library, Portland Place, London

WSG     Walter Sykes George, papers, British Council Library, New Delhi

## Notes to Chapter 1

1. Fort William, GGIC to the Secret Committee, April 12, 1804, IOR, Home–Misc., 492: 203–4.

2. Headquarters Camp, Delhi, GL to RW, September 21, 1803, ibid.: 349–50.

3. Spear, "Cities of Delhi," p. 404; Thompson, "Delhi as Capital," p. 109; and Ferrell, "Delhi, 1911–22," pp. 1–2.

4. Heber, *Narrative of a Journey*, 1: 306–7; Spear, "Cities of Delhi," p. 412.

5. OCC, file 196, cited in Spear, *Twilight of the Mughuls*, p. 221.

6. Ferrell, "Delhi, 1911–22," pp. 3, 6–10, 14–15, 38–9.

7. *Capital* (Calcutta), August 4, 1916; *Statesman* (Calcutta), May 5, 1916; and "General report dated 15th April 1913, by Lieutenant A. H. L. Mount," annexure no. 1 to enclosure to despatch no. 59, Railway, of 1913, IOR, L/PWD/6, vol. 908, file 3671.

8. CHPD, November 26 and December 16, 1910.

9. Memorandum titled "Their Majesties' Visit to Delhi, January 1912," December 21, 1910, CHK, U927/Va 16, p. 36e; Hardinge, *Old Diplomacy*, Ch. 7–13; and memorandum by DB, December 21, 1910, CHK, U927/Va 16, p. 36a.

10. Calcutta, CH to TS, December 22, 1910, CHPS. Hardinge had succeeded Sanderson in 1906 as Permanent Under-Secretary at the Foreign Office. Calcutta, GW to JD, December 13, 1910, CHK, U927/Va 16, no. 15, pp. 31–2; and Calcutta, JD to GW, December 14, 1910, ibid., p. 33. Hardinge's Council is properly referred to as the Council of the Governor-General of India, but the shorter term, Viceroy's Council, in common usage, will be employed hereinafter. Calcutta, CH to TS, March 2, 1911, CHPS.

11. Memorandum by DB, December 21, 1910, CHK, U927/Va 16, pp. 36a–36b.

12. Viceroy's Camp, CH to TS, November 30, 1911. CHPS.

13. London, King George V to JM, September 8, 1910, Royal Archives, Windsor Castle, N/293, quoted in Nicolson, *King George the Fifth*, pp. 167, 168; CHPD, November 2, 1910.

14. Simla, CH to TS, September 14, 1911, CHPS. A Council of State, comprising the Archbishop of Canterbury, the Lord Chancellor, the Lord President of the Privy Council, and the Duke of Connaught, was established on November 10, 1911 to act in the King's name.

15. CHPD, June 23, 1911 and July 5, 1911; and Montagu, *PDC*, 36 (March 28, 1912): 598.

16. Camp Delhi, CH to JH, November 27, 1911, CHK, U927/Va 16, pp. 1045–6, and Delhi, JH to CH, November 27, 1911, ibid., pp. 1048–9.

17. "Their Majesties at Bombay," *Pioneer* (Allahabad), December 5, 1911.

18. "The Royal Pageant at Delhi," *Pioneer* (Allahabad), December 14, 1911; and Sharp, *Good-Bye India*, p. 181.

19. *PP*, "Announcements by and on Behalf of His Majesty

the King-Emperor," no. 3, p. 6.

20. Simla, GW to CH, July 10, 1911, IOR, MSS Eur. E. 224/17; Hardinge, *My Indian Years*, pp. 40, , 49; "New Delhi: This Month Marks a New Era," *Daily Gazette* (Karachi), October 25, 1926; and London, RC to CH, July 28, 1911, CHC, 113, pp. 93–4. The twelve persons in India whom Hardinge says in his memoirs knew the secret were presumably the Viceroy and his private secretary, the Vicereine, the Council, Diamond Hardinge's nurse, and one of the Secretaries to the Government of India. The latter is said to have copied out repeatedly in his own hand (in schoolboy fashion!) the despatch of August 25, 1911 in which the Governor-General in Council officially proposed the scheme. London, RC to CH, August 11, 1911, ibid., p. 96.

21. Fortescue, *Narrative of the Visit to India*, pp. 165–6; Government of India, *The Historical Record of the Imperial Visit to India, 1911*, pp. 174–6; and Hardinge, *My Indian Years*, p. 54.

22. "Coronation Durbar: The New Capital, Foundation-Stones Laid," *Pioneer* (Allahabad), December 16, 1911.

23. Hardinge, *Speeches*, 1: 177, 179; and Government of India, *The Historical Record of the Imperial Visit to India, 1911*, pp. 208–11.

24. "Delhi 'Kambukht'," *Indian Daily News* (Calcutta), undated clipping, *c.* April 1919. Lord Ronaldshay was an aide-de-camp to the Viceroy, 1900; M.P. for Hornsey, Middlesex, 1907–16; Governor of Bengal, 1917–22; and Secretary of State for India, 1935–40.

25. "The Wreck of the Delhi," *Pioneer* (Allahabad), December 15, 1911; and A. Al-Ma'mun Sahrawardj to GC, February 28, 1912, IOR, MSS. Eur. F. 111/434 A.

26. Hardinge, *My Indian Years*, p. 56.

27. Viceroy's Camp, India, CH to TS, December 17, 1911, CHPS; and CH to JH, December 19, 1911, copy, IOR, MSS. Eur. E. 220/1 A, p. 35. Interestingly, the dress rehearsal, witnessed by the Viceroy, was "a complete fiasco." Hardinge, *My Indian Years*, p. 44.

28. Alwar, Maharaja Sawai Sir Jey Singh Bahadur of Alwar, to GC, December 22, 1911, IOR, MSS. Eur. F. 111/434 A, pp. 72–3. One member of the Viceroy's Council was later to deplore "the dreadful experiences of the Durbar in respect of traffic." Minute by Butler, September 14, 1912, on note by GD, "Estimate of the area required," August 24, 1912, HDD Deposit, October 1922, no. 10. Reay, *PDL*, 11 (February 22, 1912): 198. Lord Reay was Governor of Bombay, 1885–90, and Under-Secretary of State for India, 1894–5. CHPD, January 10, 1911.

29. Nicolson, *King George the Fifth*, p. 173; and CHPD, January 10, 1911.

30. Richard Barry, "Trip of George V, First English Ruler to Set Foot on His Empire in the Far East, Is of Great Political Significance," *New York Times*, December 3, 1911, Part 5. To create the appropriate impression, some £660,000 was expended on the Durbar and royal visit. Hardinge, *My Indian Years*, p. 43. Richard Barry spoke of British rule as "fast drawing to a close." Eighteen months later, the senior member of the Viceroy's Council wrote that "the days of patriarchal government are past and a benevolent despotism is no longer suitable nor acceptable to India." Minute by GW, May 8, 1913, IOR, MSS. Eur. E. 224/16.

## Notes to Chapter 2

1. "Minute of the Honble. the Governor-General for removing the seat of Government from Calcutta to Colgong, dated June 4, 1782," cited in Davies, "Calcutta as Capital," pp. 139–44. Hastings's minute, addressed to his Board of Control, was never actually submitted. Smith, *The Oxford History of India*, p. 777; and Record of a conversation in Stanhope, *Notes of Conversations with the Duke of Wellington*, p. 306.

2. Ascot, Berkshire, FR to GC, December 25, 1911, IOR, MSS. Eur. F. 111/434 A, p. 75; and *DNB*, s.v. "Lawrence, John Laird Mair, first Lord Lawrence."

3. *PP*, "Announcements by and on Behalf of His Majesty the King-Emperor at the Coronation Durbar," no. 4, p. 12.

4. "A Strategic Blunder: Delhi from the Military Point of View," *Englishman* (Calcutta), January 25, 1912.

5. London, WL to CH, April 19, 1912, CHC, 110, pp. 134–5. Hardinge recorded that Sir Valentine Chirol, correspondent and member of the Board of the *Times* as well as author of three important books on India, told him that Curzon considered the removal of the capital to Agra, but did not press it. Hardinge, *My Indian Years*, p. 38. In 1901 while explaining the selection of Calcutta as the site of an Indian national memorial to Queen Victoria, Curzon had declared, "It is now too late—I sometimes wish it were not—to turn Delhi again into an imperial capital." Curzon, *Speeches*, 2: 199–200. Curzon admitted in Parliament that the question of the capital at Delhi had been often on his mind during his Viceroyalty. Curzon, *PDL*, 11 (February 21, 1912): 157. He later said that if one granted the transfer was necessary, Agra would have been preferable to Delhi. GC, "The New Capital at Delhi," June 13, 1916, IOR, MSS. Eur. F. 111/436; and Smith, *Oxford History of India*, 3rd ed., p. 777. Minto, *PDL*, 11 (February 22, 1912): 191.

6. Simla, GW to CH, June 22, 1911, CHC, 113, p. 36.

7. Balmoral, King George V to CH, September 14, 1911, CHC, 113, p. 109. For the Rajput princes, who came from the west of India, Delhi of course represented a much less strenuous journey than Calcutta.

8. King George V diary, January 11, 1912, cited in Gore, *King George V*, p. 267; and King George V to JM, September 18, 1910, cited in Nicolson, *King George the Fifth*, p. 167.

9. London, RC to CH, August 11, 1911, CHC, 113, pp. 96–7; and London, RC to CH, January 27, 1911, ibid., p. 2.

10. London, EL to LL, September 20, 1912, ELP.

11. "The Viceroyalty: Lord Hardinge's Work," clippings from unidentified newspaper, April 1, 1916, CHK, U927/Zpl/1; Calcutta, CH to TS, December 1, 1910, CHPS; *DNB, 1941–1950*, s.v. "Hardinge, Charles, Baron Hardinge of Penshurst"; Viceroy's Camp, CH to RR, November 28, 1911, CHC, 113, p. 122; Calcutta, CH to TS, December 1, 1910, CHPS; and minute by GW, June 18, 1913, IOR, MSS. Eur. E. 224/16.

12. Delhi, JH to GC, December 20, 1911, IOR, MSS. Eur. F. 111/434 A, and Simla, GL to LL, June 18, 1912, ELP.

13. One critic, after Hardinge had been eighteen months in India, remarked that the Viceroy seemed "very unknowing about things & how to do them," and was "in the hands of his Council here, more or less." Delhi, LL to HB, May 2, 1912, HBK.

14. Simla, GW to CH, May 4, 1913, IOR, MSS. Eur. E. 224/6–7; Debate on the Budget for 1913–14, *PLCI*, 51 (March 24, 1913): 629, 633, 644, 650, 653, 655, 656, 659, 660, 664, 666, 667, 671, 674, 677, 682; and Simla, CH to TS, June 19, 1912, CHPS.

15. CHPD, December 16, 1910.

16. Calcutta, CH to RC, January 25, 1911, CHC, 113, p. 1; Calcutta, CH to RC, February 16, 1911, ibid., p. 4; and Simla, CH to RC, July 6, 1911, ibid., p. 58.

17. Lieutenant-Governor's Camp, Sir Lancelot Hare to JD, February 20, 1911, CHC, 113, p. 15; Calcutta, EB to CH, February 14, 1911, ibid., pp. 8, 13; note by JJ in Calcutta, JJ to CH, February 14, 1911, ibid., p. 6; Calcutta, CH to RC, January 25, 1911, ibid., p. 1; Calcutta, CH to RC, February 16, 1911, ibid., p. 4; and Calcutta, CH to RC, February 22, 1911, ibid., p. 24.

18. CHPD, June 18 and 19, 1911; and Hardinge, *My Indian Years*, p. 36.

19. Simla, JJ to CH, June 17, 1911, CHC, 113, p. 29.

20. Hardinge, *My Indian Years*, pp. 36–7; and CHPD, May 23, 1911.

21. Note by JJ in Calcutta, JJ to CH, February 14, 1911, CHC, 113, pp. 7–8; and Simla, JJ to CH, June 17, 1911, ibid., p. 29.

22. Simla, note by CH, June 20, 1911, CHC, 113, pp. 30–4. In 1909, when the Minto–Morley reforms were under discussion, Lord MacDonnell put down a motion in the Lords suggesting the union of Bengal under one Governor, the amalgamation of Bihar, Orissa, and Chota Nagpur into one Governorship, and the relegation of Assam to a Chief Commissionership. MacDonnell, *PDL*, 10 (December 12, 1911): 804.

23. Hardinge, *My Indian Years*, p. 37.

24. Simla, GW to CH, June 6, 1911, IOR, MSS. Eur. E. 224/17; and Simla, CH to GW, June 21, 1911, ibid.

25. GW, "India: Transfer of the Capital to Delhi," January 1, 1912, IOR, MSS. Eur. E. 224/17. Two days earlier, Sir Guy had requested that the notes written by Members of Council on the original proposals be printed and treated as official confidential records. Calcutta, GW to JD, December 29, 1911, CHC, 110, p. 41.

26. Significantly, when Sir Guy left India, the Viceroy gave him a bound copy of the correspondence relating to the transfer of the capital, "as a souvenir of our cooperation in that great measure." Simla, CH to GW, April 29, 1913, IOR, MSS. Eur. E. 224/6–7. Five days after the Durbar, Hardinge solicited Lord Sanderson's opinion of the King's announcement. "It is my scheme," he asserted, "for which I accept entire responsibility." Viceroy's Camp, CH to TS, December 17, 1911, CHPS.

27. Note by GW in Simla, GW to CH, June 22, 1911, IOR, MSS. Eur. E. 224/17.

28. Simla, CH to RC, July 6, 1911, CHC, 113, pp. 58–9; Simla, GW to CH, July 10, 1911, ibid., p. 59; Simla, CH to GW, July 10, 1911, IOR, MSS. Eur. E. 224/17; and Simla,

CH to RC, July 13, 1911, CHC, 113, pp. 59–63.

29. CHPD, July 26, 1911; London, RC to CH, August 7, 1911, CHC, 113, p. 63; Simla, CH to RC, August 3, 1911, ibid., p. 94; and CHPD, August 8, 1911.

30. Mashobra, CH to GW, August 4, 1911, IOR, MSS. Eur. E. 224/17; GW to CH, August 5, 1911, ibid.; and Simla, CH to RC, August 10, 1911, CHC, 113, p. 98.

31. "New Delhi: This Month Marks a New Era," *Daily Gazette* (Karachi), October 25, 1926; Simla, note by JJ to CH, June 24, 1911, CHC, 113, p. 39; Hardinge, *My Indian Years*, p. 39; CHPD, August 11, 1911; and Simla, GW to CH, August 14, 1911, CHC, 113, p. 98.

32. London, RC to CH, August 11, 1911, ibid., p. 96; Simla, CH to JJ, August 13, 1911, ibid., p. 98; Simla, CH to RC, August 17, 1911, ibid., p. 99; London, RC to CH, August 15, 1911, ibid., pp. 98–9; Simla, CH to RC, August 17, 1911, ibid., pp. 99–100; and London, RC to CH, September 15, 1911, ibid., pp. 109–10.

33. CHPD, August 25, 1911; and *PP*, "Announcements by and on Behalf of His Majesty the King-Emperor at the Coronation Durbar," no. 3, p. 6.

34. Simla, notes by JJ and GW on note by CH, June 20, 1911, CHC, 113, pp. 35, 49.

35. Jenkins indicated that because of Calcutta's pervasive influence, "many people," including the Indian Congress leader, Gopal Krishna Gokhale, urged holding the central Legislative Council elsewhere, "such as Delhi or Agra." Calcutta, note by JJ in Calcutta, JJ to CH, February 14, 1911, CHC, 113, p. 6; and Simla, note by JJ on note by CH, June 20, 1911, ibid., p. 39.

36. Simla, GGIC to RC, August 25, 1911, ibid., p. 129. Hardinge had come to the same conclusion at the time of Crewe's initial proposals: "I think that, if ever a Governorship of Bengal is created, the Government of India had better clear out and go elsewhere." Calcutta, CH to EB, February 13, 1911, ibid., p. 5.

37. MacDonnell, *PDL*, 12 (June 17, 1912): 104. Lord MacDonnell had over thirty years' experience as an administrator throughout India, including Bengal. Simla, GGIC to RC, August 25, 1911, section 6, CHC, 113, p. 125. The wording of this portion of the despatch almost exactly repeats parts of a note by Jenkins on June 24 in which he predicted the transfer would be seen as "assertion of an unfaltering resolve to maintain British Rule in India." Simla, note by JJ on Simla, memorandum by CH, June 20, 1911, ibid., p. 38, and London, RC to GGIC, November 1, 1911, ibid., p. 134.

38. London, Abrahams to RC, no date, CMP, I/2 (4); Simla, note by O'Moore Creagh, on Simla, memorandum by CH, June 20, 1911, CHC, 113, p. 37; Simla, note by GW on memorandum by Hardinge, June 20, 1911, IOR, MSS. Eur. E. 224/17; "General report dated 15th April 1913," ibid., L/PWD/6/908, file 3671; and Simla, GGIC to RC, August 25, 1911, section 5, CHC, 113, p. 124. While Delhi's proximity to Simla earned mention, there is no evidence that the proponents assigned this argument any preeminence.

39. Curzon, *PDL*, 11 (February 21, 1912): 154; Calcutta, CH to TS, March 16, 1911, CHPS; Simla, CH to King George V, August 23, 1911, CHC, 113, p. 101; Calcutta,

CH to TS, March 14, 1912, CHPS; Simla, CH to RC, August 17, 1911, CHC, 113, p. 99; Kohat, CH to TS, April 10, 1912, CHPS; and Calcutta, CH to TS, March 14, 1911, ibid.

40. Simla, GW to CH, June 22, 1911, IOR, MSS. Eur. E. 224/17, and Simla, CH to Clark, July 2, 1911, CHC, 113, p. 55.

41. Memorandum by GW, "India: The Transfer of the Capital to Delhi," January 1, 1912, IOR, MSS. Eur. E. 224/17; Crewe, *PDL*, 11 (February 21, 1912): 174; Simla, note by CH, June 20, 1911, CHC, 113, p. 31; and Simla, JJ to CH, June 17, 1911, ibid., p. 29.

42. Viceroy's Camp, CH to TS, December 17, 1911, CHPS; VC to GC, December 12, 1911, IOR, MSS. Eur. F. 111/434 A; memorandum by GW, "Transfer of the Capital of India from Calcutta to Delhi," January 1, 1912, ibid., MSS. Eur. E. 224/17; Simla, minute by GW in Simla, GW to CH, June 22, 1911, ibid., and Simla, CH to RC, July 13, 1911, CHC, 113, p. 60.

43. Simla, GGIC to RC, August 25, 1911, CHC, 113, pp. 124–5, 133; and London, RC to GGIC, November 1, 1911, CMP, I/2 (4).

44. Simla, CH to RC, July 13, 1911, CHC, 113, p. 62; Hardinge, *Speeches*, 1: 48–50; and note by Butler on Simla, memorandum by CH, June 20, 1911, CHC, 113, p. 45.

45. Delhi, JJ to CH, December 15, 1911, ibid., pp. 4d–5; Delhi, JJ to CH, December 15, 1911, ibid., pp. 5–6; Calcutta, C. J. Stevenson-Moore to JD, December 16, 1911, ibid., p. 7; CH to Butler, December 20, 1911, ibid., p. 13; Simla, CH to GW, July 15, 1912, IOR, MSS. Eur. E. 224/5; and Hardinge, *My Indian Years*, p. 53.

46. Delhi, JH to GC, December 20, 1911, IOR, MSS. Eur. F. 111/434 A; Basu, quoted by Lord Ronaldshay, *PDC*, 39 (June 10, 1912): 549; and Basu, *PLCJ*, 50 (March 25, 1912): 696. Basu was later President of the Indian National Congress (1914) and a Member of the Council of the Secretary of State for India (1917–23). Raja Pramada Nath Ray of Dighapatia, ibid., 691.

47. *Amrita Bazar Patrika*, December 14, 1911, IOR, Bengal Native Newspaper Reports, L/R/5/38, no. 1540, p. 577; *Hindoo Patriot*, December 15, 1911, ibid., no. 1557, p. 582; *Dainik Chandrika* (Calcutta), December 16, 1911, ibid., no. 47, p. 1533; *Hitavadi* (Calcutta), December 22, 1911, ibid., no. 47, p. 1565; *Muhammadi* (Calcutta), December 29, 1911, L/R/5/39, no. 35, p. 15; and *Pallivarta* (Bongong), December 26, 1911, ibid., no. 27, p. 42.

48. Calcutta, H. M. Haywood to CH, February 2, 1912, HDD A, February 1912, no. 162; Calcutta, W. D. Madge to Secretary to the GOI, Home Dept., February 2, 1912, ibid., no. 163; Simla, note by RO on Simla, memorandum by CH, June 20, 1911, CHC, 113, p. 41; Simla, JJ to CH, September 28, 1911, ibid., pp. 11–12; Simla, CH to RC, September 28, 1911, ibid., p. 114; and Calcutta, A. Al-Ma'mun Sahrawardj to GC, February 28, 1912, IOR, MSS. Eur. F. 111/434 A.

49. Simla, note by RO on Simla, memorandum by CH, June 20, 1911, CHC, 113, p. 42; Extract from "Administrative Changes: Press Opinion," undated clipping from unidentified newspaper, CHK, U927/Va 21; Lieutenant-Governor's Camp, JH to GC, December 20, 1911, IOR,

MSS. Eur. F. 111/434 A; and Hardinge, *Speeches*, 1: 446.

50. London, GW to CH, September 1, 1912, IOR, MSS. Eur. E. 224/5; Calcutta, extract, in Calcutta, Pugh to GC, January 11, 1912, ibid., MSS. Eur. F. 111/434 A; Naraingunge, George Morgan to the Editor, *Statesman*, December 22, 1911, in Naraingunge, Morgan to GC, January 17, 1912, ibid.; and Rees, *PDC*, 39 (June 10, 1912): 543–4.

51. "A Strategic Blunder," *Englishman* (Calcutta), January 25, 1912.

52. Unidentified abstract, enclosed in Calcutta, Pugh to GC, January 11, 1912, IOR, MSS. Eur. F. 111/434 A; "Delhi's Place in History," *Pioneer* (Allahabad), December 8, 1911; *Nayak* (Calcutta), December 15, 1911, IOR, Bengal Native Newspaper Reports, L/R/5/38, No. 39, p. 1530; *Nayak* (Calcutta), December 19, 1911, ibid., no. 46, p. 1533; *Nayak* (Calcutta), December 25, 1911, ibid., no. 49, p. 1567; and *Phoenix*, December 16, 1911, Bombay Native Newspaper Reports, L/R/5/166, no. 4, p. 14.

53. Curzon, *PDL*, 11 (February 21, 1912): 162; and London, EL to HB, September 5, 1913, HBK.

54. Simla, CH to RC, August 31, 1911, CHC, 113, p. 103; Viceroy's Camp, CH to TS, December 17, 1911, CHPS; London, Barnes to GC, December 12, 1911, IOR, MSS. Eur. F. 111/434 A; and Delhi, JH to GC, December 20, 1911, ibid., MSS. Eur. F. 111/434 A.

55. Curzon, *PDL*, 11 (February 21, 1912): 161–2; Lansdowne, ibid. (February 22, 1912): 239; and Rees, *PDC*, 39 (June 10, 1912): 547.

56. Curzon, *PDL*, 11 (February 21, 1912): 138–41; Lansdowne, ibid., (February 22, 1912): 235; Minto, ibid.: 195; Law, *PDC*, 37 (April 22, 1912): 783–4; and Bourdillon to GC, January 31, 1912, IOR, MSS. Eur. F. 111/434 A.

57. London, minute of dissent by Barnes, December 11, 1911, IOR, MSS. Eur. F. 111/434 A; Curzon, *PDL*, 11 (February 21, 1912): 162–3 and 12 (June 17, 1912): 92, 94.

58. Curzon, *PDL*, 11 (February 21, 1912): 160; Rees, *PDC*, 39 (June 10, 1912): 537; Colonel Charles Edward Yate, former Resident at Jodhpur and Udaipur and Agent for Rajputana and Baluchistan, ibid., 37 (April 22, 1912): 794; and London, minute of dissent by Barnes, December 11, 1911, IOR, MSS. Eur. F. 111/434 A.

59. Curzon, *PDL*, 11 (February 21, 1912): 159; Lansdowne, ibid., (February 22, 1912): 238–9; François Bernier, *Travels in the Mogul Empire*, pp. 354–5; and Viceroy's Camp, Reading to LI, November 18, 1925, IOR, L/PO/441.

60. Curzon, *PDL*, 11 (February 21, 1912): 138, 144; and ibid., 12 (June 17, 1912): 87.

61. Barnes, minute of dissent, December 11, 1911, IOR, MSS. Eur. F. 111/434 A.

62. Curzon, *PDL*, 11 (February 21, 1912): 165.

63. Lansdowne, *PDL*, 11 (February 22, 1912): 237; Minto, ibid., pp. 193–4; and London, Bourdillon to GC, January 31, 1912, IOR, MSS. Eur. F. 111/434 A.

64. Calcutta, CH to TS, January 1 and 24, 1912, CHPS.

65. Calcutta, CH to TS, January 1, 1912, CHPS; London, Sir Charles Stuart Bayley to GC, January 25, 1912, IOR, MSS. Eur. F. 111/434 A; and Crewe, *PDL*, 11 (February

21, 1912): 172–3.

66. Simla, CH to TS, July 10, March 14, and July 25, 1812, CHPS.

67. Calcutta, CH to TS, February 12, 1912, CHPS; and Crewe, *PDL*, 11 (February 21, 1912): 180.

68. Calcutta, CH to TS, February 12, 1912, CHPS; Crewe, *PDL*, 11 (February 21, 1912): 181–2; Hardinge, *PLCI*, 50 (March 25, 1912): 703; Delhi, note by GD, October 8, 1912, enclosing "Preliminary Report and Estimate," October 1, 1912, New Delhi, CEL.

69. Calcutta, CH to TS, February 12, 1912, CHPS; London, GB to CH, August 1, 1913, in CH to WH, August 22, 1913, IOR, MSS. Eur. E. 220/1 A; and George Robert Canning Harris, fourth Baron Harris, former Under Secretary for India and Governor of Bombay, *PDL*, 11 (February 22, 1912): 201. Sir George Birdwood, author, sometime Registrar and Fellow of Bombay University, Secretary of the Asiatic Society in Bombay, and Sheriff of Bombay (1864), served as a special adviser to the Statistics and Commerce Department, India Office, from 1871 to 1902.

70. Ascot, FR to GC, December 25, 1911, IOR, MSS. Eur. F. 111/434 A.

71. Hardinge, *PLCI*, 50 (March 25, 1912): 704.

72. London, Buckle to GC, December 11, 1911, IOR, MSS. Eur. F. 111/434 A; Alwar, Alwar to GC, December 22, 1911, ibid.; Raja Partab Bahadur Singh of Partabgarth, *PLCI*, 50 (March 25, 1912): 680; Rama Rayaningar, ibid., 52 (March 24, 1914): 1017; and *Rast Goftar*, December 17, 1911, IOR, Bombay Native Newspaper Reports, L/R/5/166, no. 22, p. 24.

73. *Cochin Argus*, December 16, 1911, Madras Native Newspaper Reports, IOR, L/R/5/116, no. 5, p. 1782; *Oriental Review*, December 20, 1911, Bombay Native Newspaper Reports, IOR, L/R/5/166, no. 11, p. 18; *Indian Social Reformer*, December 17, 1911, ibid., no. 1, p. 11; *Indu Prakash*, December 19, 1911, ibid., no. 8, p. 16; H. H. Maharajadhiraja Sir Bijay Chand Mahtab Bahadur of Burdwan, *PLCI*, 50 (March 25, 1912): 677; Gopal Krishna Gokhale, ibid., p. 667; and Pandit Madan Mohan Malaviya, ibid., 50 (March 7, 1912): 418.

74. Rama Rayaningar, ibid., 52 (March 24, 1914): 1017–18; Madhusudan Das, ibid., p. 1019; and Rao Bahadur Vasuedo Ramkrishna Pandit, ibid. 54 (March 24, 1914): 1042.

75. Rai Sri Ram Bahadur, ibid. 52 (March 24, 1914): 1024; Khan Bahadur Mir Asad Ali Khan, ibid, 54 (March 24, 1916): 528; Nyapati Subba Rao Pantulu, ibid. 50 (March 25, 1912): 679; *Nayak* (Calcutta), December 16, 1911, IOR, Bengal Native Newspaper Reports, L/R/5/38, no. 29, p. 1523; and *Bengalee*, December 17, 1911, ibid., no. 1549, p. 579.

76. *Nayak* (Calcutta), December 17, 1911, ibid., no. 45, p. 1532; *Hitavadi* (Calcutta), December 22, 1911, ibid., no. 31, p. 1557; *Bangavasi* (Calcutta), December 23, 1911, ibid., no. 33, p. 1558; *Murshidabad Hitaishi*, December 27, 1911, ibid., L/R/5/39, no. 64, p. 20; *Dnyan Prakash*, December 14, 1911, IOR, Bombay Native Newspaper Reports, L/R/5/166, no. 20, p. 23; *Indian Mirror*, December 14, 1911, IOR, Bengal Native Newspaper Reports,

L/R/5/38, no. 1551, p. 580; *Hindoo Patriot*, December 15, 1911, ibid., no. 1557, p. 582; and *Hitavarta* (Calcutta), December 28, 1911, ibid., L/R/5/39, no. 28, p. 42.

77. *Hindoo Patriot*, December 18, 1911, ibid., L/R/5/38, no. 1593, p. 593; *Hitavadi* (Calcutta), December 29, 1911, ibid., L/R/5/39, no. 61, p. 19; *Samay* (Calcutta), ibid., no. 62, p. 19; *Hitavadi* (Calcutta), December 22, 1911, ibid., L/R/5/38, no. 47, p. 1565, *Hitavadi* (Calcutta), December 22, 1911, ibid., no. 51, p. 1568; *Sanj Vartaman*, December 14, 1911, IOR, Bombay Native Newspaper Reports, L/R/5/166, no. 14, p. 19; *Gujarati*, December 24, 1911, ibid., no. 12, p. 19; *Kesari*, December 19, 1911, ibid., no. 3, p. 12; *Comrade*, December 16, 1911, IOR, Bengal Native Newspaper Reports, L/R/5/38, no. 1576, p. 587; and *Madras Standard*, December 16, 1911, IOR, Madras Native Newspaper Reports, L/R/5/116, no. 6, p. 1782.

78. Hardinge, *My Indian Years*, p. 79.

## Notes to Chapter 3

1. Note by JJ, December 19, 1912, CHC, 110, pp. 28–30; and note by CH, December 23, 1912, ibid., p. 30.

2. Calcutta, GW to CH, December 27, 1911, IOR, MSS. Eur. E. 224/4 B; note by GW, December 30, 1911, HDD A, April 1912, nos. 103–39; note by Butler, January 1, 1912, CHC, 110, p. 34; and note by RO, January 3, 1912, CHC, 113, p. 38. Carlyle had suggested a Committee consisting of a former Chief Secretary to the Eastern Bengal and Assam Government; the Secretary to the United Provinces, Public Works Department; the Assistant Quartermaster-General, who had been responsible for sanitary engineering at the Durbar; and a British architect resident in Jaipur. He also advocated hiring an architect with town planning experience from Britain. Note by Syed Ali Imam, January 1, 1912, CHC, 110, pp. 34–5.

3. London, RC to CH, February 1, 1912, ibid., p. 66.

4. Note by TH in London, RR to CH, February 2, 1912, in Calcutta, memorandum by JD to Members of the Viceroy's Council, February 23, 1912, ibid., pp. 94–6; memorandum by TH, February 16, 1912, ibid., p. 88b; note by TH, February 2, 1912, ibid., p. 96; CH to HL, February 23, 1912, ibid., p. 94; and RC to CH, February 28, 1912, ibid., p. 102. Sir Thomas Holderness was Secretary of the Revenue, Statistics, and Commerce Dept., India Office, 1901–12, and Permanent Under-Secretary, India Office, 1912–19, succeeding Sir Richmond Ritchie.

5. Bombay, Reed to WH, January 13, 1912, IOR, MSS. Eur. E. 220/1 A; London, RB to VC, February 4, 1912, VC to CH, February 9, 1912, CHC, 110, pp. 81–2; memorandum by TH in RC to CH, February 16, 1912, ibid., p. 88b; CH to RR, December 30, 1911, ibid., p. 42; and RC to CH, January 25, 1912, ibid., p. 61.

6. RC to CH, January 25, 1912, ibid., p. 61, and memorandum by TH (n.d.) in RC to CH, February 16, 1912, ibid., p. 88b.

7. London, RB to VC, February 4, 1912, in VC to CH, February 9, 1912, ibid., p. 81; extract from CH to VC, February 28, 1912, ibid., p. 105; Liverpool, Derby to RC (n.d.), CMP, 1/9 (4). On April 25, 1910, Lord Crewe helped in laying the cornerstones of the Hampstead Garden

Suburb Anglican church, St. Jude-on-the-Hill, designed by Lutyens.

8. RC to CH, February 28, 1912, CHC, 110, p. 102.

9. London, Hamilton to Lansdowne, February 3, 1912, in London, Lansdowne to RC, February 7, 1912, ibid., pp. 88g–88h; Lord Montagu to RC, February 16, 1912, CMP, 1/9 (4); London, Jackson to RC, February 5, 1912, CHC, 110, pp. 88b–88c; memorandum by TH in RC to CH, February 16, 1912, ibid., p. 88b; Lucas, note on interview with GS in RC to CH, February 16, 1912, ibid., p. 88a; London, GS to TH, February 15, 1912, p. 88e; CH to RC, March 3, 1912, ibid., p. 107; note by TH in Calcutta, JD to Members of the Viceroy's Council, February 23, 1912, ibid., pp. 94–6; and London, Bigge, to Lucas, March 12, 1912, CMP, 1/9 (4).

10. RC to CH, March 12, 1912, CHC, 110, p. 112. To the original draft of the press notice announcing the Committee's membership had been added the sentence, "Mr. H. V. Lanchester, F.R.I.B.A., who is at present engaged in work in India, will join the Committee." Lanchester's position was therefore clearly a subordinate one, but for him to have withdrawn after the public announcement would have meant a loss of face. RC to CH, March 18, 1912, ibid., pp. 123–4; CH to RC, March 19, 1912, ibid., p. 124; and RC to CH, March 21, 1912, ibid., p. 126.

11. London, EL to HB, March 15, 1912, HBK; and London, EL to HB, March 24, 1912, ELP.

12. London, TH to RO, March 15, 1912, in RO to GD, April 4, 1912, HDD Deposit, April 1912, no. 28; and en route, EL to LL, April 1–12, 1912, ELP.

13. HB, Speech, London, June 23, 1921, HBK; Byron, "New Delhi," p. 708; Bombay, GD to JD, April 12, 1912, CHC, 110, pp. 132–3; en route, EL to HB, April 6, 1912, HBK; and "Sir E. Lutyens's Plans for the New Delhi," *Indian Daily News* (Calcutta), December 5, 1920.

14. Bombay, EL to LL, April 12, 1912, ELP; and en route, EL to LL, April 14, 1912, ibid.

15. London, EL to HB, March 24, 1912, HBK; en route, EL to LL, April 1, 1912, ELP; en route, EL to HB, April 6, 1912, HBK; CHPD, April 30, 1912; and Delhi, EL to LL, April 29, 1912, ELP.

16. Delhi, GS to CH, May 23, 1912, CHC, 110, pp. 152–4.

17. Delhi, EL to LL, April 17, 1912, ELP; Delhi, EL to HB, April 25, 1912, HBK; and Delhi, EL to LL, April 25, 1912, ELP.

18. Delhi, EL to LL, April 20, 1912, ibid.

19. Simla, EL to HB, June 14, 1912, HBK; Delhi, EL to LL, May 5, 12, 20, 1912, ELP; and Delhi, GD to JD, May 13, 1912, CHC, 110, p. 146.

20. Simla, EL to HB, June 14, 1912, HBK; and Simla, EL to LL, May 22, 26, 1912 and March 20, 1920, ELP.

21. Delhi, EL to HB, May 2, 1912, HBK; Simla, EL to LL, June 9, 1912, ELP; and *PP*, "First Report of the Delhi Town Planning Committee," p. 8.

22. Delhi, EL to HB, May 8, 1912, HBK; and Simla, EL to HB, June 14, 1912, ibid.

23. Delhi, EL to HB, May 8, 1912, HBK; CH to RC, June 2, 1912, CHC, 110, p. 161; Delhi, EL to HB, May 2, 1912, HBK; London, EL to HB, March 19, 24, 1912, ibid.;

London, EL to LL, March 19, 24, 1912, ELP; en route, EL to HB, April 6, 1912, HBK; Delhi, EL to HB, May 8, 1912, ibid.; Delhi, EL to LL, undated (*c.* May 15, 1912) and May 20, 1912, ELP; and London, EL to HB, March 24, 1912, HBK.

24. Simla, EL to LL, June 9, 1912, ELP; and EL to HB, July 20, 1912, HBK.

25. Dehra Dun, CH to GS, August 1, 1912, CHC, 111, pp. 3–4; and London, EL to LL, August 28, 1912, ELP.

26. Scott, *PDC*, 35 (March 19, 1912): 1695; Simla, JB to SPWD, April 12, 1912, PWD, Establishments-B, June 1912, nos. 22–3, letter no. 194; notes by LeMaistre, Gordon, and RO, dated April 20, May 7, and May 13, 1912, respectively, on id.; Simla, Deputy Secretary to the GOI, PWD, to Consulting Architect to the GOI, May 18, 1912, ibid., letter no. 475-E; London, RC to CH, April 9, 1913, CMP, 1/10 (2); and CH to RC, April 11, 1913, ibid.

27. King, *PDC*, 45 (December 20, 1912): 1946–50.

28. A number of good reports of the events of December 23 exist. For this account, the following have been used: Hardinge, *My Indian Years*, pp. 79–82; account by Colonel Frank Maxwell, December 23–26, 1912, CHP; *PP*, "Correspondence Relating to the Attempt upon the Life of His Excellency the Viceroy and Governor General," Cd. 6642, 1912–13; Sir Percy Lancelot Orde, Kt., C.I.E., former Inspector-General of Police, Punjab, eyewitness account, interview with the author, September 26, 1970; Sharp, *Good-Bye India*, pp. 178–81; and Delhi, EL to LL, December 26, 1912, ELP. The latter two descriptions are based on interviews with the Viceroy's wife. Two years before the State Entry, to the day, a Hindu Zadkiel, in telling Lord Hardinge's fortune, had prophesied that he would not complete his full five years as Viceroy. CHPD, December 23, 1910.

29. Hardinge, *My Indian Years*, p. 80.

30. Account by Colonel Frank Maxwell, CHP; and Delhi, EL to LL, December 29, 1912, ELP.

31. Leslie, "Delhi, the Metropolis of India," pp. 133–46.

32. Viceroy's Camp, CH to TH, February 6, 1913, CHC, 111, pp. 189–90; Delhi, GS to JD, January 16, 1913, ibid., pp. 164–5; Delhi, EL to LL, January 20, 1913, ELP; Delhi, GW to JD, January 20, 1913, CHC, 111, p. 173; Delhi, JD to FR, January 29, 1913, ibid., pp. 181–3; and Delhi, JD to GS, January 20, 1913, ibid., p. 172b.

33. Delhi, EL to LL, January 20, February 8 and 13, 1913, ELP; extract from CH to GW, February 12, 1913, CHC, 111, p. 204; and *PP*, vol. 20, "First Report of the Delhi Town Planning Committee," Cd. 6885, 1913; *PP*, "Second Report of the Delhi Town Planning Committee," Cd. 6888, 1913; and *PP*, "Final Report of the Delhi Town Planning Committee," Cd. 6889, 1913.

34. Hardinge, *Speeches*, 1: 178; and Delhi, JD to FR, January 29, 1913, CHC, 111, p. 182.

35. *PP*, "Second Report of the Delhi Town Planning Committee," Cd. 6888, p. 6.

36. *PP*, "First Report of the Delhi Town Planning Committee," Cd. 6885, p. 6; and *PP*, "Second Report of the Delhi Town Planning Committee," Cd. 6888, pp. 7–9.

37. "Note on Sir Bradford Leslie's scheme, March 11, 1913, Appendix to *PP*, "Second Report of the Delhi Town

Planning Committee," Cd. 6888, p. 1; *PP*, "Report of the Committee," March 4, 1913, accompaniment to "Second Report of the Delhi Town Planning Committee," Cd. 6888, p. 3; "Proceedings of a Committee," CHC, 111, p. 300; and memorandum by CH, March 4, 1913, CMP, I/10 (3).

38. CHPD, March 10 and May 25, 1912; *PP*, "First Report of the Delhi Town Planning Committee," Cd. 6885, p. 8; and *PP*, "Second Report of the Delhi Town Planning Committee," Cd. 6888, p. 9.

39. Ibid., p. 5, and *PP*, "Final Report of the Delhi Town Planning Committee," Cd. 6889, p. 2.

40. Memorandum by CH, March 4, 1913, CMP, I/10 (3).

## NOTES TO CHAPTER 4

1. Simla, CH to RC, May 31, 1912, CHC, 110, p. 159; Delhi, EL to LL, May 5, 1912, ELP; and Simla, EL to LL, May 26, 1912, ibid.

2. *PP*, "First Report of the Delhi Town Planning Committee," Cd. 6885, 1913, pp. 6–7.

3. Simla, EL to HB, June 14, 1912, HBK.

4. "New Imperial Capital, Delhi: Construction of Main Avenue," GS, EL, and Williams (for Brodie) to GD, note, June 1912, HDD, December 1912, no. 18, p. 11. The tentative layout of the Delhi Town Planning Committee which accompanied Hardinge's note of July 16, 1912 is missing and does not form part of the Crewe papers. The layout is, however, to some extent described in the July 16 note and another Viceregal note of July 31. "Note by His Excellency," July 16, 1912, CMP, I/10 (1); and "Note by His Excellency," July 31, 1912, ibid.

5. "Note by His Excellency," July 31, 1912, ibid.

6. "Note by His Excellency," July 16, 1912, ibid.

7. Delhi, GD to JD, June 28, 1912; and Bombay, GS to CH, June 29, 1912, CHC, 110, pp. 176–7, and "Note by His Excellency," July 16, 1912, CMP, I/10 (1).

8. "Delhi: First Report of H. V. Lanchester," CHC, 110, pp. 180–5.

9. "Note by His Excellency," July 16, 1912, CMP, I/10 (1).

10. "City of Lashkar: Preliminary Report on Improvements," in HL to JD, February 22, 1912, CHC, 110, pp. 91–3.

11. "Delhi: Second Report of H. V. Lanchester: The Extension of the Indian City," CMP, I/10 (1).

12. "Note by His Excellency," July 16, 1912, ibid.; and "Memo" by CH, July 22, 1912, ibid.

13. "The Arrangement of the Secretariats: Fourth Report of H. V. Lanchester," HDD Deposit, August 1912, no. 12. The sketch plan is missing from the report.

14. Dehra Dun, CH to HL, July 31, 1912, CHC, 110, p. 234. A lakh (or lac) is a unit of 100,000. In 1912, twenty-seven lakhs of rupees was the equivalent of about £180,000.

15. Dehra Dun, CH to GS, August 1, 1912, CHC, 111, pp. 3–4; CH to RC, August 11, 1912, ibid., p. 8; and note by CH, July 31, 1912, CHC, 110, pp. 229–33.

16. London, Lucas to RC, August 12, 1912, CMP, I/10 (1).

17. North Berwick, GS to RR, August 22, 1912, ibid.; minute by TH to RR, August 21, 1912, ibid.; and London, EL to RR, August 23, 1912, ibid.

18. Simla, CH to RR, July 11, 1912, CHC, 110, p. 189; and "Obituary: H. V. Lanchester," *B*, 184 (January 23, 1953): 154. According to Lodge, on more than one occasion Lanchester put a completed project away in a drawer for several weeks lest the client should think the work was done too easily and did not merit the fee. "Dr. H. V. Lanchester," an appreciation by T. A. Lodge, in the private collection of James Burchell, London. Simla, CH to GW, August 27, 1912, IOR, MSS. Eur. E. 224/5.

19. "Delhi: Fifth Report of Mr. H. V. Lanchester," CHC, 111, pp. 13–15, and "Note by His Excellency," August 14, 1912, ibid., pp. 9–11. The Committee's main avenue was 480 feet wide; Lanchester's three avenues were 250 feet wide. The plan of this third scheme is missing. Forty years later Lanchester was to claim that the concept of a main avenue from Government House eastward to Indrapat was his only real contribution to the final city plan. "The New Delhi," memorandum dictated by Lanchester to James Burchell, 1952, property of James Burchell, London. Although Hardinge had preferred such an arrangement for the main axis on first viewing the southern site in March 1912, he did not advocate this scheme until July 31, 1912, after Lanchester had prepared his "second revised layout," incorporating an avenue pointed on Indrapat. Note by CH, July 31, 1912, CHC, 110, pp. 229–33.

20. "Note by His Excellency," August 14, 1912, CHC, 111, pp. 9–11.

21. "Delhi: Fifth Report of Mr. H. V. Lanchester," ibid., p. 15, and joint note by M. Nethersole and C. E. V. Goument, August 14, 1912, ibid., pp. 11–12. Goument was Secretary to the Government of the United Provinces, Public Works Department, Buildings, Roads, and Railway Branches. Simla, CH to GS, August 15, 1912, ibid., pp. 16–17.

22. Simla, CH to GS, August 22, 1912, ibid., pp. 32–3, and "Note by P. H. Clutterbuck," August 18, 1912, ibid., pp. 22–5.

23. "Notes by Mr. T. R. J. Ward," August 17, 1912, ibid., pp. 27–9; and note by GD, August 20, 1912, ibid., pp. 29–31.

24. Simla, CH to GS, August 22, 1912, ibid., pp. 32–3; August 24, 1912, ibid., p. 35; Simla, CH to EL, August 27, 1912, ibid., pp. 36–36a; and Simla, CH to GS, August 28, 1912, ibid., p. 36b.

25. London, EL to HB, September 27, 1912, HBK; London, EL to CH, September 13, 1912, CHC, 111, pp. 74–6; London, EL to CH, September 20, 1912, ibid., pp. 81–3; minute by Craddock, August 28, 1912, on note by GD, August 20, 1912, on "Notes by Mr. T. R. J. Ward," August 17, 1912, HDD Deposit, August 1912, no. 20; London, GS to CH, September 20 and 24, 1912, CHC, 111, pp. 87, 90b–90c; and London, EL to CH, September 20, 1912, ibid., p. 83.

26. Simla, CH to GS, September 8, 1912, ibid., p. 46. In subsequent letters to both Lutyens and Swinton, Hardinge emphasized that wherever Government House was ultimately placed, he believed the building must face Indrapat with a view of the Jama Masjid on the left and of Safdar Jang's tomb on the right. Simla, CH to EL, September 17, 1912, ibid., p. 77; and Simla, CH to GS, September 17,

1912, ibid., p. 78.

27. London, GS to CH, October 3, 1912, ibid., pp. 95–6, and London, EL to CH, October 11, 1912, ibid., p. 107.

28. Kashmir, CH to GS, October 22, 1912, ibid., p. 112; and CHPD, November 4, 1912. Gordon held the important position of Secretary to the Government of India, Public Works Department. Delhi, CH to EL, November 6, 1912, CHC, III, 120–1. On November 5, the day following his visit to the site, Hardinge telegraphed Swinton, "Please ask Lutyens to prepare a lay-out for Raisina." CH to GS, November 5, 1912, ibid., p. 119.

29. Delhi, GW to JD, November 25, 1912, ibid., p. 129; and CHPD, December 8, 1912. For further information, see Appendix to Chap. 4, p. 367.

30. Only eleven days before, Lutyens's designs for the southern site had won the Viceroy's compliments: "Lord H. liked my layout today," Lutyens had reported to his wife. Delhi, EL to LL, January 7, 1913, ELP; memorandum by CH, March 5, 1913, CMP, I/10 (3); and Delhi, EL to LL, January 20, 1913, ELP. The last operation to remove bomb particles from Hardinge's shoulder did not take place until January 31, 1913. Viceroy's Camp, CH to TH, February 6, 1913, CHC, III, p. 190.

31. London, RC to CH, January 17, 1913, and London, TH to CH, January 17, 1913, ibid., pp. 166–7. Holderness was now Permanent Under-Secretary of State for India, succeeding Sir Richmond Ritchie. Delhi, GW to JD, January 20, 1913, ibid., pp. 172–3.

32. En route, EL to LL, February 6, 1913, ELP; HB, "Resume, 1913–20," HBK; Baker, *Architecture and Personalities*, p. 65; Delhi, EL to LL, February 14, 1913, ELP; and HBD, February 12, 1913, HBK. Baker describes Antique acropoli—Athens, Agrigentum, Halicarnassus, Pergamos—in Baker, "The Architectural Needs of South Africa." In "Architecture and Education," HBK, Baker declared that for public buildings, "wherever there may be a choice, the selection of a hill site is preferable." London, EL to HB, July 4, 1922, HBK; HBD, February 1913; and Simla, SPWD to Under-Secretary of State for India, PWD, India Office, April 23, 1913, PWD, Establishment-A, June 1913, no. 102.

33. Delhi, GS to CH, February 22, 1913, CHC, III, p. 298.

34. Copies of the layouts are at CMP, I/10 (5).

35. Delhi, GS to CH, February 22, 1913, CHC, III, p. 299; Delhi, JD to GS, February 27, 1912, ibid., p. 227; Delhi, GS to CH, January 14, 1913, ibid., p. 156; and Delhi, CH to EL, November 6, 1912, ibid., pp. 120–1.

36. HB, "Resume, 1913–20," HBK; Baker, *Architecture and Personalities*, pp. 65, 67; and London, EL to HB, July 4, 1922, HBK. Baker's account confirms that Lutyens agreed "without any controversy" to the idea of a shared platform. HB, "Resume, 1913–20," ibid.

37. Delhi, CH to WH, March 13, 1916, IOR, MSS. Eur. E. 220/1 C; and HBD, February 26, 1913.

38. Baker later claimed the location of this feature as his contribution to the city plan, in addition to the extended capitol platform. HB, "Resume, 1913–20," ibid. In a meeting with the architects on March 11, 1913, Hardinge predicted the King would oppose moving the amphitheater site from that used for his Durbar in December

1911. HBD, March 11, 1913, ibid. The amphitheater was never completed at this site.

39. Delhi, EL and HB to CH, March 8, 1913, ibid.

40. HBD, March 10, 11, 1913, ibid.

41. HBD, March 17, 1913, ibid.

42. "Proceedings of a Committee," CHC, III, pp. 299–301, and "Report of the Committee," March 4, 1913, ibid., pp. 293–6. This document confirmed information that the Director-General of the Indian Medical Service had reported as early as January 1912 in describing swampy and malarial conditions north of Shahjahanabad. Note by Sir Charles Lukis, January 20, 1912, CHC, 110, pp. 58–60d.

43. *PP*, "Second Report of the Delhi Town Planning Committee," Cd. 6888, pp. 2–3, and Delhi, EL to LL, February 5, 1913, ELP.

44. London, Keeling to HB, February 6, 1945, HBK; Viceroy to Secretary of State, March 8, 1913, CHC, III, p. 309; London, RC to CH, sent March 11, 1913, CMP, I/9 (3); and London, RC to CH, March 11, 1913, CHC, III, p. 320.

45. Delhi, JD to Lucas, March 20, 1913, ibid., p. 335; and near Bombay, GS to CH, March 22, 1913, ibid., pp. 340–1.

46. *PP*, "Final Report of the Delhi Town Planning Committee," Cd. 6889.

47. *PP*, "Second Report of the Delhi Town Planning Committee," Cd. 6888, pp. 1, 7; note by GS in Delhi, GS to CH, December 19, 1912, CHC, III, p. 138d; and Balmoral Castle, Scotland, MS to RC, September 12, 1912, CMP, I/10 (2).

48. The editors of the *Town Planning Review* (Patrick Abercrombie, C. H. Reilly, and S. G. Adshead) rejoiced in the decision "to project the grand axis on the river instead of on the old town" of Shahjahanabad as "a natural and noble idea." "The New Capital City at Delhi."

49. The ceremonial route was linked to a wide riverside and lakeside drive that Sir Bradford Leslie had suggested in his address to the Royal Society of Arts in December 1912. Sir Bradford's scheme to dam the Jumna, citing the proposed lakes at Canberra as "the finest feature" of the capital, may have served to inspire the Town Planning Committee's lake at Indrapat. Leslie, "Delhi, the Metropolis of India."

50. Accompanying the Delhi experts' final report, in addition to maps, were diagrammatic cross sections of the 440-foot-wide parkway, of avenues 300 and 150 feet wide, and of a road sixty feet wide showing trees, grass strips, irrigation ditches, riding paths, service roads, and carriageways. Raymond Unwin, in the most widely read of his treatises on civic design, had recommended that in designing roads "very great variation in widths should be provided for, and roads of different types and characters arranged," and he had illustrated his text in 1911 with cross sections remarkably like those of the Delhi experts in 1913. Unwin, *Town Planning in Practice*, illus. 176a, 177.

51. "Estimate of the area required," August 24, 1912, HDD Deposit, October 1922, no. 10.

52. "A Visit to the Delhi of Drab Design," *Statesman* (Calcutta), August 5, 1923.

53. London, EL to CH, September 13, 1912, CHC, III, p. 76; and "The New Capital City at Delhi."

54. Simla, CH to GW, August 27, 1912, IOR, MSS. Eur.

E. 224/5; and note by GS in Delhi, GS to CH, December 19, 1912, CHC, III, p. 138d.

55. Minutes by RO and Clark, September 15, 1912, on note by GD, August 24, 1912, HDD Deposit, October 1912, no. 10; minute by Butler, September 14, 1912, ibid.; minute by Craddock, October 1, 1912, ibid.; and minute by Craddock, January 30, 1913, on note by GS in Delhi, GS to CH, December 19, 1912, HDD Deposit, March 1913, no. 1.

56. "Notes regarding the Building of New Delhi and Viceroy's House," typescript, February 1933, ELP.

57. Spear, "Mughal Delhi and Agra," in Toynbee, ed., *Cities of Destiny*, p. 240.

58. Lanchester, *The Art of Town Planning*, pp. 204–5; Simla, EL to HB, June 14, 1913, HBK; Delhi, EL to Robert Lutyens, December 22, 1913, ELP; and Delhi, SIDC to SPWD, December 29, 1913, enclosure no. 1 to Simla, GGIC to RC, April 9, 1914, despatch no. 8-P.W., IOR, L/PWD/6/1182, file 3576.

59. Agra, Gordon Sanderson to Marshall, November 4, 1913, OCC, Proceedings 1–8, Part B, file/1914–Education.

60. Delhi, EL to LL, undated, between November 23 and 29, 1913, ELP. Lutyens deprecated Hardinge's concession to agitation at Cawnpore, where the partial removal of a Muslim edifice for a road widening scheme had prompted serious rioting in August 1913, and attracted nationwide attention. The Viceroy's compromise, Lutyens complained, would make demolitions at Delhi (where such buildings abounded) "impossible." Ibid.; and "Summary of the Administration of Lord Hardinge," CHC, 131, pp. 18–19.

61. "Plan for London," p. 41. Another critic attacked the manner in which Lutyens's ingenuity forced "London's divers and subtler rhythms" into "the strait-jacket of academic symmetry." Brett, "The New Haussmann," *Architectural Review*, pp. 24–5. President of the Royal Academy from 1938 until 1944, Lutyens was Chairman and presiding genius of its Planning Committee, a creation of his own devising.

62. Rome, EL to LL, January 10 and 16, 1912, ELP; and Delhi, EL and HB to CH, March 8, 1913, HBK.

63. Patte, *Monumens*; idem, *Mémoires*; Zucker, *Town and Square*, pp. 179–80; and Rosenau, *The Ideal City*, pp. 88, 89, 93, 108. At L'Enfant's request, Jefferson loaned him plans of Paris and eleven other European cities, including Karlsruhe's radial design. Philadelphia, Jefferson to L'Enfant, April 10, 1791, in Padover, ed., *Thomas Jefferson and the National Capital*, p. 58.

64. Baker, "The Architectural Needs of South Africa," p. 520; Hardinge, *Old Diplomacy*, p. 32; "Notes regarding the building of New Delhi and Viceroy's House," ELP; and en route, EL to LL, April 28, 1925, ELP.

65. Baker, "Architectural Design," p. xviii.

66. The drawings of the recent Washington and Chicago plans that Burnham sent to the conference were acclaimed as "the most striking exhibits" and the chief attraction of the items displayed at the Royal Academy. Adshead, "The Town Planning Conference," p. 181; "The Town Planning Conference," p. 787; and Moore, *Daniel H. Burnham*, 2:138, 141. Burnham's Chicago report gave an account of

the recent attempt to revive L'Enfant's ideas and specifically cited Baron Georges Haussmann's improvements in Paris of an existing urban fabric as an accomplishment deserving emulation. Burnham and Bennett, *Plan of Chicago*, pp. 18, 25. Baker, "The Architectural Needs of South Africa," featured an illustration of the Senate Park Commission plan.

67. Unwin, quoted in Creese, *Search for Environment*, p. 232; and Unwin, *Town Planning in Practice*, pp. xvii, 92, and illustrations 10, 56.

68. Unwin, quoted in Creese, *Search for Environment*, p. 231.

69. Even the name Canberra has a topographical significance, being an aborigine word referring to the area's resemblance to a woman's breasts.

70. "American Designs Splendid New Capital for Australia," *New York Times*, June 2, 1912, Part 5.

71. Commonwealth of Australia, *Parliamentary Papers*, vol. 2, 1914–17, nos. 153, 346; ibid., vol. 4, 1914–17, nos. 353, 354; Birrell, *Walter Burley Griffin*, p. 86; and Griffin, *The Federal Capital*, p. 13.

72. CH to TD, August 3, 1912, CHC, III, p. 4a; Melbourne, TD to CH, December 18 and January 20, 1912, ibid., pp. 134v, 172a; and Delhi, CH to TD, March 11, 1913, ibid., p. 322. The Viceroy had already seen a reproduction of Griffin's plan at least by the previous August, when he wrote the King's Private Secretary that the designs for Canberra were "very fine." Simla, CH to MS, August 4, 1912, CHC, III, p. 4b. At the end of the month, de Montmorency forwarded the July 4 issue of *Engineering News*, containing an account and an illustration of the scheme. Note by GD, August 31, 1912, CHC, III, pp. 41–2. Wigmore, *The Long View*, pp. 63–4. The editors of the *Town Planning Review* judged that, "as an essay in architectural grouping," the New Delhi design was "not equal to several of the designs submitted in competition for Canberra." "The New Capital City at Delhi," p. 187.

73. Balmoral Castle, MS to RC, September 12, 1912, CMP, I/10 (2); note by GS in GS to CH, December 19, 1912, CHC, III, p. 138d; and "Note by the Lieutenant-Governor of the Punjab," January 11, 1912, in Earle to JD, February 2, 1912, ibid., pp. 68–71.

74. "The Secretariats . . . range down the main avenue some 2 miles long." London, EL to HB, July 20, 1912, HBK.

75. Dehra Dun, CH to GS, August 1, 1912, CHC, III, pp. 3–4; and minute by Craddock, October 1, 1912, on note by GD, August 24, 1912, HDD Deposit, October 1912, no. 10.

76. Delhi, EL to LL, January 20, 1913, ELP.

77. Sharp, *Town and Countryside*, p. 163.

78. "Extract from a letter," CHC, III, pp. 4–4a.

79. "Wonders of New Delhi," *Daily Telegraph* (London), February 9, 1931. One less enchanted observer, in an obvious reference to Joseph Rowntree's New Earswick, George Cadbury's Bournville, and William Lever's Port Sunlight, criticized the hierarchical arrangement of dwellings, which he said resembled the monotonous model garden cities of British soap and chocolate manufacturers, except that an Imperial Secretariat had replaced the central

factory building. "A Visit to the Delhi of Drab Design," *Statesman* (Calcutta), August 5, 1923.

80. "New Delhi: The Problem of Style," *Times* (London), October 3, 1912; "Obituary: Sir Edwin Lutyens, O.M., P.R.A.," *Times* (London), January 3, 1944; and Curzon, *Speeches*, 4: 166.

81. "Extract from a letter," CHC, 112, p. 188.

82. Curzon, *Speeches*, 3: 437; Hussey, *The Life of Sir Edwin Lutyens*, p. 267; and Moore, *Daniel H. Burnham*, 2: 147.

83. Baker, "Architectural Design," p. xviii; idem, prepared comments, following Thompson, "Delhi as Capital," February 7, 1933, HBK; and HBD, February 24, 1913, ibid. Herbert Albert Laurens Fisher was Warden of New College, Oxford, 1925–40, and James Ramsay MacDonald, Leader of the Labour Party in 1913, was Prime Minister, 1924 and 1929–35. Both were in Delhi as Members of the Royal Commission on the Public Services of India.

## APPENDIX TO CHAPTER 4

Lord Hardinge's selection of a site for the Viceregal residence appears conclusively to date from December 8, 1912, when the Viceroy galloped with Hailey to Raisina Hill and confirmed his earlier inclination to build there. Hardinge's later accounts confuse and telescope his three visits to the southern Delhi sites, at the end of July, on November 4 and 5, and on December 8, as recorded in his diary. Hardinge's remarks before the Royal Society of Arts in 1926 are especially confused in his recollection of the chronology and participants. (Discussion of "The New Delhi," a speech by Sir Herbert Baker, *Journal of the Royal Society of Arts* 84, July 2, 1926: 788–89.) Hardinge's recollection in 1916, quoted by Christopher Hussey, puts the ride with Hailey to Raisina's top in October, when the Viceroy did not visit Delhi. (Delhi, CH to WH, March 13, 1916, HBK.) As for the July visit, Hailey was on leave overseas that month; and in both his diary entry for November 4 and his letter of November 6 to Lutyens, Hardinge mentions being accompanied by Ward, Gordon, and Goument. (CHPD, November 4, 1912, and Delhi, CH to EL, November 6, 1912, CHC, 111, p. 120–21.) There is no reference to a visit on the site with Hailey. Hardinge's diary records an interview with Hailey and de Montmorency on September 7, but no ride; indeed the day is noted as a wet one. More important, however, Hailey is described as "in favour of Raisina as the site of Government House," and the Viceroy comments that "it must be looked into." (CHPD, September 7, 1912.) Mention of a site visit only comes in the diary on December 8, the day Malcha, by then the leading alternative to Raisina, was emphatically ruled out by the Viceroy in his diary. Twenty-five years after the event, in 1937, in a conversation with Baker, Hardinge placed his selection of Raisina in the summer of 1912. According to this account, upon viewing the site the Committee had selected, "he decided at once that this would not do and rode straight away to Raisina Hill and said that would be the centre of the site." There is no mention of Hailey accompanying him. (Memorandum by HB, May 22, 1937, HBK.) In another rather misleading account, written in his journal at the time of the inaugura-

tion of New Delhi, Hardinge belittles the Committee's abilities relative to his own actions: "Swinton was one of the three experts sent from England to select a site for New Delhi and, after spending six months riding round Delhi on an elephant, they selected a site which, after 3 hours examination I rejected and myself in another selected the actual site of New Delhi." (CHPD, February 7, 1931.)

## NOTES TO CHAPTER 5

1. Notes by JJ, December 19, 1911, and January 1, 1912, CHC, 110, pp. 29, 36.

2. Simla, CH to RR, June 7, 1912, CMP, I/9 (4); London, RR to LS, June 11, 1912, ibid.; London, LS to RR, in London, RR to CH, June 21, 1912, CHC, 110, pp. 172–172a; "Notes of an interview," in London, RR to CH, June 21, 1912, ibid., p. 172a; and London, LS to RR, in London, RR to CH, June 28, 1912, ibid., pp. 174–5.

3. London, RR to RC, June 27, 1912, CMP, I/9 (4).

4. "Secretariat Competitions: 3rd Report of Mr. H. V. Lanchester," in Simla, GD to JD, July 23, 1912, CHC, 110, pp. 207–13; Delhi, GD to JD, August 6, 1912, CHC, 111, p. 4c–4d; and "Conditions of Proposed Competition," PWD, Notes on Civil Works-Buildings-A, May 1913, nos. 18–30.

5. Note by Hawkins, August 23, 1912, PWD, C.W.-Buildings-A, ibid.; and note by Nethersole, August 27, 1912, ibid.

6. Notes by JB, August 26 and September 3, 1912, ibid.; and minute by Nethersole, September 3, 1912, on note by JB, September 3, 1912, ibid.

7. Notes by CH on the proposed competition, August 28, 1912 and September 9, 1912, ibid.; and Simla, CH to GS, September 12, 1912, CHC, 111, p. 71.

8. Simla, GGIC to RC, despatch no. 27, September 19, 1912, PWD, C.W.-Buildings-A, May 1913, nos. 18–30, and "Conditions of Competition," enclosure no. 4 to despatch no. 27-P.W. of 1912, in ibid.

9. Note by Butler, September 12, 1912, ibid.; and Soames, *PDC*, 45 (December 20, 1912): 1950.

10. Falkner, "The Late Sir Edwin Lutyens," p. 31; and "A.A. Ordinary General Meeting," p. 57.

11. Simla, EL to LL, June 3, 9, 18, 1912, ELP; and Simla, EL to HB, June 14, 1912, ibid.

12. London, Earle to RC, June 11, 1912, CMP, I/9 (4d); and London, Montagu to RC, June 25, 1912, ibid.

13. Simla, CH to EL, July 18, 1912, CHC, 110, p. 203.

14. Extract from CH to RC, July 16, 1912, in Simla, CH to EL, July 18, 1912, ibid., pp. 204–204a.

15. Simla, CH to GS, September 23, 1912, CHC, 111, p. 90, and London, EL to CH, August 1, 1912, ibid., pp. 1, 2.

16. London, EL to HB, September 27, 1912, HBK. Robinson, who was only thirty-seven, had been ten years in South Africa as a civil servant and editor. In 1917 Robinson assumed by royal license the name and arms of Dawson, by which he is better known as the editor of the *Times*, especially during his second tenure of the office, 1923–41.

17. London, EL to HB, February 29 and March 19, 24, 1912, ibid.; en route, EL to HB, April 6, 1912, ibid.; Delhi,

EL to HB, April 25 and May 2, 8, 1912, ibid.; and Simla, EL to HB, June 14, 1912, ibid.

18. London, EL to HB, July 20, 1912, ibid.

19. Note by GW, December 30, 1911, HDD A, April 1912, nos. 103–39. Sir Hugh Keeling, Chief Engineer for the new Delhi, recorded that his information in 1912 and 1913 ascribed the architect's selection to Webster Boyle Gordon and not to Meston, as Baker supposed. London, Keeling to HB, February 6, 1945, HBK; memorandum by HB, May 22, 1937, ibid.; and Cobham, HB to Hussey, January 17, 1944, ibid. When Marris was appointed to the Home Department, Lutyens—ever vigilant—wrote, "So we shall have a friend there, wh. will be good." Delhi, EL to LL, February 18, 1913, ELP.

20. London, RB to CH, November 10, 1912, CHC, 111, p. 122; and RB to HB, April 23, 1913, HBK.

21. Baker, "The New Delhi: Eastern and Western Architecture," *Times* (London), October 3, 1912.

22. London, GS to CH, October 3, 1912, CHC, 111, p. 96; and London, GS to CH, October 10, 1912, ibid., pp. 106–7.

23. London, RC to Gladstone, October 18, 1912, CMP, I/9 (4c); London, Lucas to JD, October 18, 1912, CHC, 111, p. 111; and London, Lucas to RC, October 21, 1912, CMP, I/9 (4c).

24. London, EL to LL, October 26, 1912, ELP; London, EL to TH, October 30, 1912, ibid.; and en route, EL to HB, November 1, 1912. HBK.

25. Ibid.; London, TH to RC, November 22, 1912; London, RC to CH, November 22, 1912, CMP, I/9 (4); and en route, EL to HB, November 30, 1912, HBK.

26. En route, EL to HB, November 1, 30, 1912, ibid.

27. Delhi, EL to HB, undated, ibid.

28. CH to RC, January 5, 1913, CHC, 111, p. 150; London, TH to HB, January 8, 1913, CMP, I/9 (4f); and RC to CH, January 10, 1913, CHC, 111, p. 151.

29. Rome, HB to TH, January 12, 1913, ibid., pp. 168–9; London, TH to CH, January 17, 1913, ibid., p. 166; memorandum by HB, February–March, 1913. HBK; and Baker, *Architecture and Personalities*, p. 64.

30. Gladstone to RC, January 25, 1913, CMP, I/9 (4c); RC to CH, January 22, 1913, CHC, 111, p. 176; and HBD, January 24, 1913.

31. Memorandum by CH, January 13, 1913, CHC, 111, p. 155; Delhi, EL to LL, April 20, 1912; and Dhar, EL to LL, December 16, 1912, ELP. Richard Burdon Haldane was appointed Lord Chancellor on June 10, 1912. Delhi, EL to HB, December 29, 1912. HBK.

32. London, TH to Jacob, January 20, 1913, and Biarritz, Jacob to TH, January 22, 1913, PWD, Establishment-A, June 1913, nos. 86/1 and 86/2; and London, Jacob to CH, April 11, 1913, CHC, 111, p. 368a.

33. Simla, CH to GS, September 23, 1912, CHC, 111, p. 90; London, GS to CH, October 18, 1912, ibid., p. 110; and RC to CH, October 22, 1912, and CH to RC, October 24, 1912, ibid., pp. 112–13.

34. En route, EL to HB, November 1, 1912, HBK; London, Earle to RC, June 11, 1912, CMP, I/9 (4d); and en route, EL to HB, November 30, 1912, HBK. Earle was Private Secretary to the Secretary of State for the Colonies, 1908–12, and Permanent Secretary to H.M. Office of

Works, 1912–33. Lady Emily Lutyens was a first cousin. In 1925 he recommended that the Government appoint Lutyens to design the new British Embassy at Washington. Earle, *Turn Over the Page*, p. 192.

35. Dublin, Gordon to CH, December 18, 1912, and Delhi, Thomas to JD, January 11, 1913, CHC, 111, pp. 134u–134v and 152–3.

36. Delhi, EL to JD, March 1, 1913, CHC, 111, p. 234; en route, EL to HB, November 30, 1912, HBK; and Peshawar, Blomfield to CH, December 23, 1912, PWD, Establishment-A, June 1913, nos. 80–109.

37. Blomfield, *Memoirs*, pp. 148–9; Cobham, HB to Hussey, January 17, 1944 and April 19, 1945, HBK.

38. Simla, JB to Gordon, April 12, 1912, PWD, Establishment-B, June 1912, nos. 22–3; Simla, Le Maistre to JB, May 18, 1912, ibid.; and Simla, GGIC to RC, September 19, 1912, GOI despatch no. 27-P.W. of 1913, PWD, C.W.-Buildings-A, May 1913, nos. 18–30.

39. RC to GGIC, February 4, 1913, register no. 271-B.D., PWD Notes, C.W.-Buildings-A, May 1913, no. 20; Simla, GGIC to RC, May 8, 1913, GOI despatch no. 24-P.W., PWD, C.W.-Buildings-A, May 1913, nos. 18–30; and annexure no. 1 to GOI despatch no. 24-P.W., ibid.

40. London, RC to CH, March 9, 1913, CMP, I/10 (2); King, *PDC*, 47 (January 30, 1913): 1658–9; and Baker, ibid.: 1662–6.

41. Simla, CH to Gordon, June 18, 1912, CHC, 110, p. 170; Simla, Nethersole to JD, August 8, 1912, CHC, 111, p. 4d–5; Viceroy's Camp, CH to Gordon, February 15, 1913, ibid., p. 207; and Delhi, Gordon to CH, February 28, 1913, ibid., p. 230a.

42. WS to TH, July 7, 1914, IOR, L/PWD/6/1183, file 3577; and Simla, GGIC to RC, October 1, 1914, GOI despatch no. 28-P.W., C.W.-Buildings, IOR, L/PWD/946, file 3963.

43. Simla, EL to LL, June 3, 1912, ELP.

44. Delhi, EL to LL, April 20, 1912, ibid.; and Delhi, EL to HB, May 8, 1912, HBK.

45. Simla, EL to LL, June 3, 1912, ELP; Delhi, EL to LL, February 16, 1913, ibid.; and Colombo, Ceylon, EL to LL, April 23, 1920, ibid.

46. Simla, CH to EL, August 19, 1912, CHC, 111, p. 26; Viceroy's Camp, CH to GC, October 22, 1912, IOR, MSS. Eur. E. 111/434 B; Dehra Dun, CH to EL, March 28, 1913, CHC, 111, p. 350; Simla, CH to HB, August 30, 1913, HBK; and Dhar, Malwa, EL to LL, December 16, 1912, ELP.

47. Hardinge, *PLCI*, 50 (March 25, 1912): 703; Delhi, EL to LL, January 2, 1913, ELP; Simla, CH to EL, August 4, 1913, CHC, 112, p. 68b; and CHPD, November 15, 1911, January 11, 1912, and February 18, 1912.

48. Simla, CH to RR, July 11, 1912, CHC, 110, p. 189; and Simla, CH to EL, August 27, 1912, CHC, 111, p. 36. The Mughal style suffered from the "taint of Hindu architecture." Viceroy's Camp, CH to GC, October 22, 1912, IOR, MSS. Eur. F. 111/434 B.

49. Simla, CH to RR, July 11, 1912, CHC, 110, p. 189; Simla, CH to LL, August 27, 1912, CHC, 111, p. 36; Viceroy's Camp, CH to GC, October 22 and 30, 1912, IOR, MSS. Eur. F. 111/434 B; and Simla, CH to EL,

August 4, 1913, CHC, 112, p. 68b.

50. "Indian Architecture," pp. 19, 20; Adshead, "The Architecture of Delhi," pp. 617–18; "The New Delhi," p. 429; and "The Building of the New Capital," *Pioneer* (Allahabad), May 3, 1912.

51. Soames, *PDC*, 45 (December 20, 1912): 1950; RB to HB, March 23, 1913, HBK; and "Extract from a letter," CHC, 112, p. 117.

52. London, EL to HB, March 24, 1912, HBK; Dublin, EL to LL, no date, ELP; Dhar, EL to LL, December 16, 1912, ibid.; and Chitnavis, PLCI, 51 (March 5, 1913): 291.

53. "Delhi: Second Report of H. V. Lanchester," CHC, 110, p. 197. "City of Lashkar," in HL to JD, February 22, 1912, ibid., p. 93; and Lanchester, "Architecture and Architects in India," p. 294.

54. Havell, "Imperial Delhi and Indian Art," *Times* (London), December 22, 1911. Ernest Binfield Havell, Principal of the School of Art and Keeper of the Government Art Gallery in Calcutta from 1896 to 1906, had reorganized art education on Indian lines and initiated the movement for the renewal of hand-loom weaving throughout India. Idem, *The Building of the New Delhi*, CMP, I/9 (4c); "The Future Delhi," *Times* (London), October 22, 1912; Havell, "The Message of Hope for India,"; and idem, *Indian Architecture*, Ch. 15, pp. 250–7.

55. London, Voysey to Havell, October 27, 1912, IOR, MSS. Eur. D. 736/1; "The Future Delhi," *Times* (London), October 22, 1912; Leslie, "Delhi, Metropolis of India," p. 141; Chisholm, contribution to discussion, *RIBAJ* 61 (December 27, 1912): 146; Oertel, "Indian Architecture and Its Suitability for Modern Requirements," IOR, MSS. Eur. F. 11/435; Teddington, Oertel to GC, June 15, 1913, IOR, MSS. Eur. E. 111/434 B; CHPD, August 28, 1912; and note by JB, December 2, 1913, "Manner In Which Building Operations at New Delhi Are To Be Conducted," Appendix to Notes, PWD, C.W.-Buildings-A, September 1913, nos. 48–50.

56. King, *PDC*, 45 (December 20, 1912): 1949.

57. Baker, "The New Delhi: Eastern and Western Architecture: A Problem of Style," *Times* (London), October 3, 1912; HBD, March 12, 1913; and Johannesburg, HB to CH, July 25, 1913, CHC, 112, p. 60.

58. "Delhi," *Town Planning Review*, pp. 167–8. The editors were Patrick Abercrombie (later to work with Lutyens on a city plan for Hull), C. H. Reilly, and S. D. Adshead.

59. Viceroy's Camp, CH to GC, October 30, 1912, IOR, MSS. Eur. F. 111/434 B, and "Extract from a letter," CHC, 112, p. 130a.

60. Simla, CH to EL, August 27, 1912, CHC, 111, p. 36; London, RC to MS, September 28, 1912, CMP, I/10 (2); London, Brassey to RC, April 10, 1913, ibid.; and London, RC to Brassey, April 14, 1913, ibid.

61. Barua, *PLCI*, 51 (March 24, 1913): 682; Delhi, WH to CH, August 16, 1913, CHC, 112, p. 77; Madras, Besant to EL, February 14, 1913, ELP; and Keith, "The Projected European Renaissance Architecture for the New Capital at Delhi," *Pioneer* (Allahabad), February 7, 1913.

62. London, Rolleston to Under-Secretary of State for India, November 20, 1910, appendix to Sanderson, *Report on Modern Indian Architecture*.

63. Petition to RC, February 6, 1913, enclosure no. 1 to Simla, GGIC to RC, April 24, 1913, despatch no. 15-P.W., PWD, C.W.-Miscellaneous-A, May 1913, nos. 1–2. The petition is also printed in Havell, *Indian Architecture*, pp. 271–4.

64. Simla, GGIC to RC, April 24, 1913, despatch no. 15-P.W., PWD, C.W.-Miscellaneous-A, May 1913, nos. 1–2.

65. London, EL to LL, July 10, 1913, ELP; and "Indian Architecture," p. 20; Balmoral, MS to RC, September 12, 1912, CMP, I/10 (2); editorial, "Delhi," *Town Planning Review*, p. 168; editorial, "The New Delhi," p. 429; and Baker, "Architectural Design," *Times* (London), February 18, 1930, p. xviii.

66. Viceroy to Secretary of State, July 20, 1914, CHC, 112, pp. 304–5.

67. London, TH to Wells, May 29, 1913, and London, Wells to TH, June 23, 1913, enclosures nos. 1 and 2, to London, RC to GGIC, July 25, 1913, despatch no. 38-P.W., IOR, L/PWD/6/904, file 3144; Delhi, CH to JD, September 3, 1913, CHC, 112, pp. 96–7; "Delhi: Second Report of H. V. Lanchester," CMP, I/10 (1); and Brown, "Note on Proposed Employment," October 10, 1912, CHC, 111, pp. 104–5, in Effingham, Surrey, Brown to Colonel Frank Maxwell, October 9, 1912, ibid., p. 103.

68. Delhi, WH to JD, May 11, 1914, CHC, 112, pp. 263–4.

69. Delhi, EL to LL, April 29, 1912, ELP; Camp Delhi, RO to CH, December 12, 1911, CHC, 110, p. 1; and note by RO in RO to JD, December 23, 1911, ibid., p. 26.

70. Simla, GGIC to RC, June 6, 1912, GOI despatch no. 15-P.W., and "Report on the Estimate," November 11, 1912, enclosure no. 4 to Simla, GGIC to RC, November 14, 1912, GOI despatch no. 34-P.W. of 1912, PWD, Buildings-Delhi, IOR, L/PWD/6/1183, file 3577; "Completion Report of Temporary Works," Part 1, drafted by Lieutenant-Colonel H. W. G. Cole, April 14, 1913, PWD, Buildings-Delhi, no. 31; Rouse, "New Delhi," p. 368; and "Summary of the Administration," CHC, 131, p. 62.

71. Note by GW, April 29, 1912, HDD Deposit, February 1913, no. 2; and note by Butler, April 30, 1912, ibid.

72. Curzon, *PDL*, 12 (June 24, 1912): 141; and Rees, *PDC*, 40 (July 11, 1912): 2237, 40 (August 1, 1912): 2238–9, and 41 (August 6, 1912): 2896.

73. "Extract from a telegram," CHC, 110, p. 216, and "Note by Lieutenant-Colonel H. W. G Cole," July 27, 1912, ibid., pp. 226–7.

74. Notes by GW, June 22 and August 14, 1911, CHC, 113, pp. 37, 89; and Simla, Craddock to CH, June 26, 1912, CHC, 110, p. 1726.

75. Curzon, *PDL*, 11 (February 21, 1912): 163, and 12 (June 17, 1912): 92.

76. Calcutta, CH to GW, March 21, 1912, CHC, 110, p. 127; Delhi, EL to LL, December 16, 1913, ELP; and note by GW, March 27, 1913, IOR, MSS. Eur. E. 224/16.

77. Memorandum by Gordon, in Calcutta, Gordon to JD, March 23, 1912, CHC, 110, pp. 128–9; "Preliminary Report and Estimate," GOI, October 1, 1912, annexed to note by GD, GOI, October 8, 1912, CEL; CHPD, October 2, 1912; Viceroy's Camp, CH to TS, December 7, 1912, CHPS.

78. Delhi, GD to JD, December 18, 1913, CHC, 112, pp.

138–9; note by CH in Delhi, CH to WM, February 16, 1914, ibid., pp. 180–1; and CH, *PLCI*, 52 (March 24, 1914): 1050–2.

79. Crewe, *PDL*, 12 (June 17, 1912): 119–22; Montagu, *PDC*, 41 (July 30, 1912): 1884; Delhi, CH to WM, February 28, 1914, CHC, 112, pp. 189–90; Delhi, WM to CH, February 28, 1914, ibid., pp. 186–9; Delhi, Butler to CH, March 13, 1914, ibid., pp. 196–7; memorandum by CH, June 30, 1914, in Simla, CH to WM, June 30, 1912, ibid., p. 299; Simla, WM to CH, July 7, 1914, ibid., p. 304; and "Minute by the Permanent Under-Secretary of State," July 24, 1914, CMP, I/10 (2).

80. Curzon, *PDL*, 16 (May 11, 1914): 145–52; and Simla, CH to TS, June 4, 1914, CHPS.

81. J. C. Shorrock and Norman McLeod, Annual General Meeting, Bengal Chamber of Commerce, February 27, 1914, in "The New Capital at Delhi," IOR, L/PWD/6/923, file 1037; and extract from the *Statesman* (Calcutta), March 6, 1914, in Delhi, JD to Brunyate, March 10, 1914, CHC, 112, pp. 206–8.

82. London, MS to RC, July 5, 1913, CMP, I/10 (2); and Delhi, EL to LL, December 22, 1913, January 15, 1914, and no date, ELP.

83. Chitnavis, *PLCI*, 52 (March 24, 1914): 988; Currimbhoy, ibid., p. 1005; Sardar Daljit Singh, ibid., p. 1010; Raja Kushal Pal Singh, ibid., p. 1013; Jafar of Pirpur, ibid., p. 1012; and Sir Ibrahim Rahimtoola, ibid., p. 1028. Sir Fazulbhoy Currimbhoy Ebrahim, J.P., active in government and in charitable causes, was the fourth son of the enormously wealthy Muslim merchant, industrialist, and patron of charity, Sir Currimbhoy Ebrahim, first Baronet, of Bombay. Sir Gangadhur Chitnavis was a Nagpur textile industrialist and the leading landholder in the Central Provinces.

84. Delhi, JJ to CH, December 18, 1911, CHC, 110, p. 10; and Calcutta, CH to JJ, December 20, 1911, ibid., p. 13.

85. Note by JJ, January 1, 1912, ibid., pp. 36–7; and demi-official from Du Boulay to HDD B, April 1912, nos. 90–4.

86. Calcutta, GW to JD, December 13, 1910, CHK, U297/Va 16; Calcutta, GW to CH, December 26, 1911, IOR, MSS. Eur. E. 224/4 B; and Calcutta, GW to WH, December 27, 1911 and January 7, 1912, IOR, MSS. Eur. E. 220/1 A.

87. Simla, Craddock to CH, July 25, 1912, CHC, 110, p. 223; Srinigar, Kashmir, JH to WH, October 2, 1912, IOR, MSS. Eur. E. 220/1 A; "Summary of the Administration," CHC, 131, p. 1; Viceroy's Camp, CH to GW, October 24, 1912, IOR, MSS. Eur. E. 224/5; and London, CH to WH, September 11, 1918, IOR, MSS. Eur. E. 220/1 C.

88. Simla, RO to CH, July 6, 1912, CHC, 110, p. 178; Delhi, WH to JD, March 23, 1913, demi-official, HDU A, July 1913, nos. 280–90; Delhi, Wheeler to JD, *c.* February 14, 1913, CHC, 111, pp. 205–6; Delhi, WH to JD, March 4, 1913, ibid., p. 237; and "Extract from a letter," CHC, 112, p. 37.

89. Calcutta, JJ to CH, January 4, 1912, CHC, 110, p. 45; Simla, CH to Lawrence, May 28, 1912, ibid., p. 157; Balmoral, MS to RC, September 12, 1912, CMP, I/10 (2); "Programme of Annual Expenditure," Appendix C,

Preliminary Report and Estimate, October 1, 1912, CEL. 90. HBD, January 1, 1914; Delhi, EL to LL, February 18, 1914, ELP; and HB, "Resume, 1913–1921," HBK. Francis Leonard Hodgson Fleming (1875–1950) joined Baker as an assistant in South Africa in 1904 and became his partner in 1910. "The New Delhi: Designs for Government Buildings," *Times* (London), May 4, 1914; Delhi, WH to JD, April 20, 1914, CHC, 112, pp. 251–2; and Simla, CH to WH, June 16, 1914, IOR, MSS. Eur. E. 220/1 B.

## Notes to Chapter 6

1. Simla, GGIC to RC, April 9, 1914, GOI despatch no. 8-P.W., IOR, L/PWD/6/1009, file 2145; note by Russell, "Project Estimate for the Construction of the New Imperial Capital at Delhi," PWD, Notes, C.W.-Buildings-A, May 1914, nos. 12–22; London, EL to HB, August 1, 14, 1913, HBK; and London, MS to RC, June 30, 1913, CMP, I/10 (2). Meyer was Secretary to the GOI, Finance Dept., 1905–9, and Member of the Viceroy's Council (Finance), 1913–18.

2. London, MS to RC, June 30, 1913, CMP, I/10 (2); note by Butler on memorandum by CH on the Constitution of the Delhi Committee, November 26, 1912, HDD A, February 1913, no. 31; and Curzon, *PDL*, 16 (May 11, 1914): 147.

3. Delhi, CH to WH, November 20, 1914, CHC, 112, pp. 340–1.

4. Delhi, WH to CH, December 2, 1914, ibid., p. 343; Delhi, CH to WH, December 4, 10, 1914, ibid., pp. 345, 350; Bharatpur, Bannerman to JD, December 9, 1914, ibid., pp. 347–50; Delhi, WH to JD, December 11/12, 1914, ibid., p. 351; and "Proceedings of the Sixty-fourth Meeting of the Imperial Delhi Committee," in Delhi, WH to JD, ibid., p. 358.

5. Simla, WM to TH, August 18, 1914, ibid., p. 321; Simla, CH to WH, June 26, 1915, IOR, MSS. Eur. E. 220/1 B; Delhi, EL to LL, February 18, 1915, ELP; and Simla, CH to EL, July 28, 1915, CHC, 112, p. 415.

6. "Summary of the Administration," CHC, 131, p. 63; Simla, GGIC to AC, May 12, 1916, GOI despatch no. 107-Finance, IOR, L/PWD/6/984, file 1528; Delhi, "Redistribution by Sub-Heads," letter no. 996, Delhi, SIDC to SPWD, September 12, 1916, pp. i–iv, CEL; Keeling, "Memorandum Dealing with the Redistribution," pp. 1–3, in ibid.; "The New Capital," *Madras Mail*, June 24, 1917; Simla, GGIC to AC, July 14, 1916, GOI despatch no. 14-P.W., pp. 3, 4, IOR, L/PWD/6/992, file 2913; and JD, memorandum to CH, October 16, 1914, CHC, 112, p. 325.

7. "Summary of the Administration," CHC, 131, p. 27; "A Visit to New Delhi," *Statesman* (Calcutta), December 6, 1916; and Hardinge, *PLCI*, 54 (March 24, 1916): 561–2.

8. Delhi, EL to LL, February 18 and March 8, 1915, ELP.

9. London, TH to WH, June 4, 1915, IOR, MSS. Eur. E. 220/1 B, and Delhi, EL to LL, March 8, 1915, ELP.

10. Note by Lord Islington appended to "East India: Accounts and Estimates, 1915–16," *PP*, 1915, Cd. 8034, IOR, MSS. Eur. F. 111/436; and London, JI to GC, January 24, 1916, IOR, MSS. Eur. F. 111/434 B. John Poynder Dickson-Poynder, first Baron Islington, was Chairman of

the Royal Commission on the Indian Public Services, 1912–14; Under-Secretary of State for the Colonies, 1914–15; and Parliamentary Under-Secretary for India, 1915–18. Joseph Austen Chamberlain (son of Joseph Chamberlain, Secretary of State for the Colonies, 1895–1903, and half-brother of Arthur Neville Chamberlain, Prime Minister, 1937–40), Secretary of State for India, 1915–17, had been Chancellor of the Exchequer, 1903–6, and Chairman of the Royal Commission on Indian Finance and Currency in 1913.

11. London, AC to RC, August 16, 1916, confidential, CMP, C/8 (1916); London, AC to JT, June 22 and December 18, 1916, IOR, MSS. Eur. E. 264/2. Frederic John Napier Thesiger, third Baron Chelmsford (created first Viscount, 1921), had been Governor of Queensland, 1905–9, and Governor of New South Wales, 1909–13. GC, "The New Capital at Delhi," in London, AC to JT, June 22, 1916, ibid.

12. Delhi, CH to WH, March 18, 1916, IOR, MSS. Eur. E. 220/1 C; London, CH to AC, in London, CH to JT, July 19, 1916, IOR, MSS. Eur. E. 264/15; and London, CH to JT, July 27 and September 14, 1916, ibid.

13. London, GC to JT, August 3, 1916, IOR, MSS. Eur. E. 264/15; London, CH to JT, September 14, 1916, ibid.; Windsor, MS to JT, August 22, 1916, IOR, MSS. Eur. E. 264/1.

14. London, EL to LL, August 8, 1916, ELP; and London, AC to RC, August 15, 1916, CMP, C/8 (1916).

15. London, MS to CH, October 23, 1916, in London, CH to WH, October 26 and December 8, 1916, IOR, MSS. Eur. E. 220/1 C; and London, MS to JT, November 9, 1916, IOR, MSS. Eur. E. 264/1.

16. London, JT to WH, IOR, MSS. Eur. E. 220/1 C; Simla, JT to WH, May 17, 1916, ibid.; and Dehra Dun, JT to King George, April 16, 1916, IOR, MSS. Eur. E. 264/1.

17. Simla, JT to AC, July 21 and November 24, 1916, IOR, MSS. Eur. E. 264/2; and Viceroy's Camp, JT to King George, October 23, 1916, IOR, MSS. Eur. E. 264/1.

18. London, AC to GGIC, August 18, 1916, confidential despatch no. 23-P.W., IOR, L/PWD/6/1183, file 3577; London, CH to WH, December 8, 1916, IOR, MSS. Eur. E. 220/1 C; and Delhi, GGIC to AC, November 17, 1916, confidential GOI despatch no. 23-P.W., IOR, L/PWD/6/1183, file 3577.

19. London, AC to GGIC, February 23, 1917, draft despatch no. 7-P.W., IOR, L/PWD/6/1183, file 3577; and Montagu, *An Indian Diary*, pp. 346, 364.

20. *The Morning Post* (Delhi), November 25, 1918.

21. Wilson, *PLCI*, 51 (March 1, 1913): 287; Chakravarti Vijiaraghavachariar, *PLCI* 51 (March 24, 1913): 629; and Babu Surendra Nath Banerjee, *PLCI*, ibid.

22. Spear, *A History of India*, 2: 182, 189; Chimanlal Harilal Setalvad, *PLCI*, 53 (March 25, 1915): 630; Sir Gangadhar Chitnavis, *PLCI*, 54 (March 24, 1916): 508; and Pandit Bishan Narayan Dar, *PLCI*, 53 (March 25, 1915): 610.

23. Simla, JT to King George, May 25, 1920, IOR, MSS. Eur. E. 264/1; Rao Bahadur B. N. Sarma, *PLCI*, 58 (February 11, 1920): 705, 706; and Chaudhuri Muhammad Ismail Khan, *PLCI*, 58 (February 18, 1920): 748.

24. Rao Bahadur B. Narasimheswara Sarma Garu, *PLCI*,

58 (February 11, 1920): 708, 709; Walter Erskine Crum, *PLCI*, 58 (February 18, 1920): 739; Surendra Nath Banerjee, ibid., p. 741; V. S. Srinivasa Sastri Avargal, ibid., p. 744; and Delhi, EL to LL, February 8, 1920, ELP.

25. Hill, *PLCI*, 58 (February 18, 1920): 759, 760, and Mir Asad Ali, Khan Bahadur, ibid., p. 753.

26. Sir Zulfikar Ali Khan, ibid., p. 756; Sir Dinshaw Wacha, ibid., p. 761; Sachchidananda Sinha, *PCLI*, 58 (February 11, 1920): 713; and Vincent, *PCLI*, 58 (February 18, 1920): 748.

27. London, MS to JT, June 23, 1920, IOR, MSS. Eur. E. 264/1; and Simla, JT to King George, May 25, 1920, ibid.

28. Chelmsford, *Speeches*, 2: 551, 567–69; and HBD, February 8, 9, 10, 12, 1921.

29. Rao Bahadur T. Rangachariar, *PLAI*, 1 (March 16, 1921): 1167–8; S. C. Shahani, ibid., p. 1170; Sir Jamsetjee Jeejeebhoy, ibid., pp. 1172–3; Chaudhuri Shahab-ud-Din, ibid., p. 1173; and Colonel Sir Sydney D'A. Crookshank, ibid., pp. 1177–79.

30. J. K. N. Kabraji, *PLAI*, 1 (March 23, 1921): 1504; Chaudhuri Wajid Hussain, ibid., pp. 1512–13; Delhi, EL to LL, January 7, 1921, ELP; Intraoffice Note, Montagu to Duke, May 10, 1921, IOR, L/E/E & O/1325 (1926); and Simla, WH to HB, July 31, 1921, HBD.

31. Crookshank, *PLAI*, 1 (March 16, 1921): 1179; Delhi, HB to CH, February 23, 1921, CHK, U 929/029, p. 60a; Delhi, EL to LL, February 20, 1920, ELP; and Madras, EL to LL, April 8, 1920, ibid.

32. Delhi, EL to LL, January 7, 17, 19, 26, 1921, ELP; and Delhi, HB to CH, February 23, 1921, CHK, U 929/029, p. 60a.

33. Keeling, "Revised Project Estimate," Memorandum no. 61-N.C.C., January 12, 1921, CEL.

34. Hailey, "Report of the New Capital Enquiry Committee, 1922, "November 24, 1922, in Delhi, SPWD to Under-Secretary of State for India, PWD, December 14, 1922, IOR, L/PWD/6/1124, file 43.

35. "Our Royal Guest: Delhi's Proud Record," *Eastern Mail* (Delhi), February 18, 1922.

36. HBD, February 19, 1922; and Delhi, EL to LL, February 20, 1922, ELP.

37. "New Delhi: Protest by Mr. Edmund Candler," *Madras Mail*, April 23, 1922; "Condemnation of New Delhi Scheme: 'A Costly Blunder,'" *Statesman* (Calcutta), April 30, 1922; "Imperial Capital at Delhi: Dr. Gour's Criticism," *Statesman* (Calcutta), May 3, 1922. The author of ten books, Candler had served as wartime correspondent of the *Times* (London) and *Daily Mail*; *Times* correspondent for the Middle East, 1918–19; and Director of Publicity for the Punjab Government, 1920–1. Sir Krishna Govinda Gupta, educated at Dacca College and Middle Temple, had passed through all grades of the Indian Civil Service in Bengal. Hari Singh Gour, knighted in 1925, was Leader of the Opposition in the Legislative Assembly of India, 1921–34, and was later Vice-Chancellor of Nagpur University and the University of Saugor.

38. HBD, February 9, 1922; Bolithlo, *James Lyle Mackay*, pp. 110–13, fn. 1 on 168–9, 180; Reading, *Rufus Isaacs*, 2: 178, 212–13; and CH, "Report of the New Capital Enquiry Committee, 1922," in Delhi, SPWD to the

Under-Secretary of State for India, PWD, December 14, 1922, IOR, L/PWD/6/1124, file 43.

39. Delhi, EL to LL, November 28 and 13, 1922, ELP.

40. London, Mackay to GC, April 16, 1923, IOR, MSS. Eur. F. 111/434 B; Bolithlo, *James Lyle Mackay*, p. 186; London, CH to HB, January 4, 1923, HBK; and "Report of the New Capital Enquiry Committee, 1922," in Delhi, Crookshank to Under-Secretary of State for India, P.W.D., December 14, 1922, IOR, L/PWD/6/1124, file 43. As early as February 1920, Lutyens had concluded that it was "too late" to abandon the Delhi Project. Delhi, EL to LL, February 13, 1920, ELP.

41. Singh, "The Two Delhis," Part 2; and Curzon, *PDL*, 12 (June 17, 1912): 96.

42. Note by R. P. Russell, March 3, 1914, PWD Notes. C.W.-Buildings-A, May 1914, nos. 12–22; "Annual Progress Report, 1913–14," annexure no. 1 to enclosure to Delhi, GGIC to RC, GOI despatch no. 40-P.W., C.W.-Misc., December 25, 1914, IOR, L/PWD/6/1183, file 3577; Simla, GGIC to AC, GOI despatch no. 14-P.W., C.W.-Misc., July 14, 1916, IOR, L/PWD/6/992, file 2913; F. C. Rose, PWD resolution no. 3-M.D., C.W.-Misc., February 5, 1917, ibid.; and Delhi, EL to LL, January 3 and March 13, 1917, ELP.

43. Note by T. C. S. Jayarathnam, January 18, 1926, OCC, file B-130/Home, 1926; and Crookshank, "New Capital Committee," memorandum, February 24, 1920, enclosure to Delhi, GGIC to Montagu, GOI despatch no. 3-P.W., C.W.-Misc., March 25, 1920, IOR, L/PWD/6/992, file 2913.

44. Delhi, EL to LL, December 31, 1919, ELP.

45. EL, lecture, February 2, 1933, ELP; WH, "Report of the New Capital Enquiry Committee, 1922," November 24, 1922, IOR, L/PWD/6/1124, file 43; and Singh, *Khushwant Singh's India*, p. 205.

46. Ibid., pp. 206–8.

47. Ibid., pp. 204–5; and Simla, Booth-Tucker to JD, July 12, 1913, CHC, 112, p. 40.

48. Keeling, contribution to discussion, *JRSA*, 74 (July 2, 1926): 790; Keeling, contribution to discussion, *JRSA*, 35 (December 10, 1927): 75; Singh, "The Two Delhis," Part 1, Interview with John Greaves (Lutyens's first architectural representative at New Delhi), Sandwich, Kent, December 13, 1970; and Shoosmith, "The Design of New Delhi," p. 433.

49. Singh, *Khushwant Singh's India*, p. 205; idem, "The Two Delhis," Part 1, December 3, 1968; Rouse, "New Delhi," p. 370; and Baker, *Architecture and Personalities*, p. 73.

50. Shoosmith and Medd in Brandon-Jones et al., "Reminiscences on Sir Edwin Lutyens," pp. 234–5; Delhi, EL to LL, January 31, February 7, 20, 31, and December 12, 18, 1929, ELP; and EL, lecture, February 2, 1933, ELP.

51. Rouse, "New Delhi," pp. 368, 370, and "Wonders of New Delhi," *Daily Telegraph* (London), February 9, 1931.

52. Rouse, "New Delhi," p. 370.

53. Ibid., p. 371; and Mrs. A. G. Shoosmith, "New Delhi," *Bombay, Baroda, and Central India Annual* (1931), n.p.

54. Rouse, "New Delhi," pp. 371–2; and Keeling, contribution to discussion, *RIBAJ*, 35 (December 10, 1927): 75.

55. "Farewell Entertainment at Delhi: Tribute to Sir Hugh Keeling," *Pioneer* (Allahabad), March 24, 1925; "The New Delhi: Departure of the Chief Engineer," *Pioneer* (Allahabad), April 9, 1925; and *Pioneer* (Allahabad), April 11, 1925.

56. "Joint Note by the Chief Engineer and the Accounts Officer," 1926, CEL; and Rouse, "New Delhi," p. 368.

57. Note by T. C. S. Jayarathnam, January 18, 1926, OCC, file B-130/1926-Home; "Demi-Official Letter from G. M. Young, No. F-697/25, dated the 27th May, 1926," ibid.; "Demi-Official Letter from the Hon'ble Mr. A. M. Stow, no. 5694-Home, dated Delhi, the 23rd September, 1926," ibid.; and "Review on the Working of the Raisina Municipal Committee during the Year 1925–6," in Delhi, Stow to Haig, September 23, 1926, no. 5694-Home, ibid. On July 30, 1930, with the virtual completion of the New Delhi project, the Government of India abolished the New Capital Committee and directed that further matters be referred directly to the pertinent Government of India Department. Simla, Ryan to the Chief Commissioner, Delhi, July 30, 1930, no. B-3, OCC, file B-119/1930-Home.

58. Stow, "Proceedings of a Conference regarding the future administration of Imperial Delhi," OCC, file B-130/1926-Home; Delhi, Stow to Dunnett, December 7, 1926, Demi-Official letter no. 7475-Education, ibid.; and Haig, notification, December 31, 1926, GOI, Home Dept., No. F-694/1926-Public, OCC, Part B, file no. F-17/1927-Home. The Imperial Delhi Municipal Committee adopted the name "New Delhi Municipal Committee" on February 22, 1927. Copy of Resolution No. 2 of the Seventy-seventh Meeting of the New Delhi Municipal Committee, New Delhi, February 22, 1927, OCC, Part B, file no. 4 (43)/1927-Education; and Delhi, Stow to the Deputy Commissioner, Delhi, March 16, 1927, No. 1975-Education, ibid.

59. Delhi, EL to LL, January 24 and 31, February 7 and 14, 1929, ELP.

60. Delhi, EL to LL, January 21, 1920, January 12, 1925, January 26, 1928, and February 14, 1929, ibid.

61. Delhi, EL to LL, February 4, 1927, January 26, February 2, and August 29, 1928, and January 17, 1929, ibid.; and CHPD, February 17, 1931.

62. Rouse, "New Delhi," p. 378, and Delhi, EL to LL, January 26, 1928 and January 17, 1929, ELP.

## NOTES TO CHAPTER 7

1. London, EL to HB, February 29 and March 19, 1912, HBK; en route, EL to HB, November 1, 1912, ibid.; en route, EL to HB, April 6, 1912, ibid.; and Delhi, EL to HB, May 8, 1912, ibid.

2. En route, EL to HB, November 30, 1912, ibid.; and Delhi, EL to LL, February 8, 18, 1913, ELP.

3. HB, memorandum, February–March, 1931, HBK; HB, "Resume, 1913–20," ibid.; London, EL to HB, July 4, 1922, ibid.; and Delhi, EL and HB to CH, March 8, 1913, ibid.

4. Simla, CH to HB, August 30, 1913, ibid.; Delhi, CH to WH, March 13, 1916, IOR, MSS. Eur. E. 220/1 C; and

"Proceedings of the One Hundred and First Meeting," in Delhi, WH to JD, February 25, 1916, CHC, 112, pp. 474–9. Lutyens did not see a copy of Nicholls's perspective until 1916. Delhi, EL to CH, March 4, 1916, CHC, 112, p. 480.

5. Delhi, EL to LL, February 18, 1913, ELP; and EL to CH, March 21, 1913, CHC, 111, pp. 335–7.

6. Delhi, EL and HB to Chairman, Imperial Delhi Committee, March 11, 1913, HDU B, May 1913, no. 169; HBD, March 17, 24, 1913; HB, memorandum, February–March, 1931, ibid.; and HB, "Resume 1913–20," ibid.

7. London, Keeling to HB, February 6, 1915, ibid.; and "The New Capital City at Delhi," p. 187.

8. "Proceedings of the One Hundred and First Meeting," in Delhi, WH to JD, February 25, 1916, CHC, 112, p. 478; Bombay, EL to JT, March 20, 1916, HBK; and "E. L. Lutyens's Note on Mr. Baker's second letter to H. E. Lord Chelmsford," March 27, 1916, in EL to Maffey, March 27, 1916, ibid. Reproductions of Walcot's perspective from the Great Court appeared in the *Times* (London) on May 4, 1914 and the *Times of India* (Bombay) on May 7, 1914.

9. HB, memorandum, February–March, 1931, HBK; and Baker, *Architecture and Personalities*, p. 64.

10. Delhi, EL to HB, December 29, 1912, HBK; HB, "Resume, 1913–20," ibid.; and HB, memorandum, February–March, 1931, ibid.

11. HBD, November 11, 12, 13, 18, and December 23, 1913; HB, "Resume, 1913–20," ibid.; HB, February–March, 1931, ibid.; en route, EL to LL, November 13, 1913, ELP; and en route, EL to LL, November 14 and 17, 1913, ibid.

12. HBD, November 13, 1913; and HB, "Resume, 1913–20," HBK.

13. Delhi, EL to LL, March 17, 1915, ELP; London, GS to CH, November 13 and December 5, 1913, CHC, 112, pp. 129, 135–6; Viceroy's Camp, CH to GS, December 1, 1913, ibid., p. 130b; en route, EL to LL, November 13, 14, 17, 1913, ELP; HBD, December 23, 1913; and Hussey, *The Life of Sir Edwin Lutyens*, p. 310.

14. Delhi, EL to LL, December 8, 1913, January 27, February 12, and March 14, 1914, ELP; and Benares, EL to LL, December 28, 1913, ibid.

15. Delhi, HB to Mrs. Herbert Baker, December 20, 1919, HBK; and HB, memorandum, February–March, 1931, ibid.

16. HBD, November 28, 1913, January 20, 21, and March 16, 17, 18, 1918; HB, speech, June 23, 1921, ibid.; idem, "Resume, 1913–20," ibid.; idem, memorandum, February–March, 1931, ibid.; Baker, *Architecture and Personalities*, p. 66; copy of a letter from SIDC to HB and EL, no. 567, dated Delhi, the 16th March 1914, in Delhi, WH to JD, March 21, 1914, CHC, 112, p. 221.

17. HBD, December 18, 1913, and January 17, 18, 1914; "Proceedings of the Thirty-third Meeting of the Imperial Delhi Committee," in Delhi, WH to JD, January 24, 1914, CHC, 112, p. 162; and "Proceedings of the Thirty-fourth Meeting of the Imperial Delhi Committee," in GD to JD, January 29, 1914, ibid., pp. 167, 168.

18. Ibid., p. 167; "Proceedings of the One Hundred and First Meeting of the Imperial Delhi Committee," in Delhi, WH to JD, February 25, 1916, CHC, 112, p. 478; "The

New Delhi: Designs for Government Buildings," *Times* (London), May 4, 1914; *Times of India Illustrated Weekly*, May 6, 1914; and *Times of India*, May 7, 1914.

19. HB, memorandum, February–March, 1931, HBK; HB, "Resume, 1913–20," ibid.; and London, HB to C. P. Walgate, June 21, 1933, ibid.

20. HBD, December 18, 1913; and Delhi, EL to LL, March 2, 4, 1914, ELP.

21. Benares, EL to LL, December 28, 1913, ibid.; Delhi, EL to LL, December 6, 1913, February 12, 19, and March 4, 1914, ibid.; and HBD, February 10, 1914.

22. EL to CH, March 21, 1913, CHC, 112, p. 336; London, RB to CH, January 19, 1914, ibid., p. 159; copy of letter from EL and HB to SIDC and copy of a letter from SIDC to EL and HB, in "Proceedings of the Fortieth Meeting of the Imperial Delhi Committee," in Delhi, WH to JD, March 27, 1914, ibid., pp. 233–4; "Proceedings of the Thirty-ninth Meeting of the Imperial Delhi Committee," in Delhi, WH to JD, ibid., p. 221; Hussey, *The Life of Sir Edwin Lutyens*, pp. 326–8, 333–4; and Delhi, CH to WH, March 5, 1914, CHC, 112, pp. 203–4.

23. "Proceedings of the One Hundred and First Meeting of the Imperial Delhi Committee," in Delhi, WH to JD, February 25, 1916, ibid., p. 478, and Delhi, EL to CH, March 4, 1916, ibid., p. 480.

24. Delhi, EL to HB, January 27, 1916, typescript with notes and postscript by Baker, HBK; HB, "Resume 1913–20," ibid.; HB, memorandum, February–March, 1931, ibid.; London, HB to TH, October 24, 1917, ibid.; and Bombay, EL to JT, March 20, 1916, ibid.

25. Delhi, EL to LL, January 17 and March 18, 1915, ELP.

26. Copy of a note dated January 27, 1916, EL to HB, HBK; Longfield, Kent, HB to EL, May 3, 1916, ibid.; and Delhi, EL to LL, January 27 and February 4, 1916, ELP. Baker twice explained in 1916 that he understood his colleague's requests for a section drawing to refer to the raised platform's east walls, which Lutyens had proposed replacing with steps and terraces to widen the vista of Government House. Because he had shown Lutyens by sketches that the resultant injury to Government Court made such a scheme unacceptable, Baker thought no sections were necessary.

27. Postscript to HB, notes on copy of a note dated January 27, 1916, EL to HB, HBK.

28. Delhi, EL to LL, February 4, 1916, ELP; Delhi, EL to SIDC, February 10, 1916, copy, HBK; HBD, February 11, 1916, ibid.; Delhi, EL to GD, February 14, 1916, copy, ibid.; and "Proceedings of the One Hundred and First Meeting of the Imperial Delhi Committee," in Delhi, WH to JD, February 25, 1916, CHC, 112, pp. 476–7.

29. Ibid., pp. 477–9.

30. Delhi, EL to LL, February 1 and 4, 1916, ELP.

31. Delhi, EL to CH, March 4, 1916, CHC, 112, pp. 480–1; copy of a letter from HB in Delhi, WH to JD, March 28, 1914, ibid., p. 239; and Delhi, HB to CH, March 6, 1916, ibid., pp. 483–4.

32. Delhi, EL to LL, March 10, 1916, ELP; EL, note on interview with Hardinge on March 10, 1916, HBK; HBD, March 13, 1916, ibid.; and Delhi, CH to WH, March 13, 1916, CHC, 112, pp. 484–7.

33. Delhi, EL to LL, February 4, 1916, ELP; HBD, March 17 and 18, 1916; Delhi, HB to CH, March 18, 1916, CHC, 112, pp. 492–3; and en route, HB to WH, March 18, 1916, copy, HBK. Claude Hamilton Archer Hill, Member of the Viceroy's Council from 1915 to 1920, was responsible for the Department of Public Works as well as of Revenue and Agriculture.

34. CH, note, March 21, 1916, on Delhi, HB to CH, March 18, 1916, CHC, 112, p. 493.

35. HBD, March 26, 1916.

36. HBD, March 24, 25, 26, 1916; EL to JT, March 20, 1916, ibid.; en route, EL to Maffey, March 27, 1916, copy, ibid.; and en route, EL to JT, March 27, 1916, copy, ibid.

37. En route, HB to JT, March 24, 1916, copy, ibid.; and en route, HB to JT, March 26, 1916, copy, ibid. In defence of his designs for Raisina, Baker suggested the analogy with the Athenian acropolis as early as January 24, 1916. Copy of a note dated January 27, 1916, EL to HB, ibid.

38. *DNB, 1931–1940*, s.v. "Thesiger, Frederic John Napier, third Baron and first Viscount Chelmsford"; Mersey, *The Viceroys and Governors-General of India*, pp. 127–9; "The Viceregal Mystery," *India* (London), reprinted from *World* (London), undated clipping, *c.* February 1916; Delhi, JT to AC, April 7 and May 12, 1916, IOR, MSS. Eur. E. 264/2; and Delhi, Zombaste (Government of India) to HB, May 13, 1916, HBK.

39. Simla, Hill to EL, May 18, 1916, ibid.; Simla, Hill to HB, May 18, 1916, ibid.; and Delhi, EL to LL, December 13, 1916, ELP.

40. London, AC to JT, June 13, 1916, IOR, MSS. Eur. E. 264/2; London, EL to LL, August 8 and 15, 1916, ELP; "New Delhi Advisory Committee: Minutes of the Third Meeting," and Annexure B, "Memorandum by Mr. Lutyens," IOR, L/PWD/6/1156, file 4165; and London, EL to LL, September 11, 1912, ELP.

41. London, AC to JT, December 27, 1916, IOR, MSS. Eur. E. 264/2, and London, AC to JT, February 14 and 23, 1917, IOR, MSS. Eur. E. 264/3.

42. London, CH to WH, December 8, 1916, March 20 and May 7, 1917, IOR, MSS. Eur. E. 220/1 C.

43. Balmoral, MS to RC, September 12, 1912, private, CMP, I/10 (2); London, RC to MS, September 28, 1912, July 1, 1913, copy, ibid.; London, MS to RC, June 30, 1913, ibid.; London, Montagu to MS, July 1, 1913, copy, ibid.

44. "Home Committee on the Furnishing and Decoration of Government House, Delhi: Minutes of the First Meeting," in Delhi, EL to JD, January 13, 1915, CHC, 112, pp. 364–8.

45. Delhi, SIDC to SPWD, January 23, 1915, HDU B, March 1915, no. 45; Delhi, EL to LL, January 31, 1916, ELP; London, AC to RC, August 15, 1916, CMP, C/8 (1916); London, RC to AC, August 16, 1916, ibid.; London, AC to JT, February 23, 1917, IOR, MSS. Eur. E. 264/3; Delhi, CH to WH, February 7, 1916, IOR, MSS. Eur. E. 220/1 C; and London, EL to HB, August 1, 1913, HBD.

46. London, AC to RC, August 15, 1916, CMP, C/8 (1916); London, AC to JT, February 23, 1917, IOR, MSS. Eur. E. 264/3; "The New Delhi Advisory Committee,"

memorandum enclosed in ibid.; Delhi, JT to AC, September 15, 1916, IOR, MSS. Eur. E. 264/2; London, RC to AC, February 24, 1917; and "New Delhi Advisory Committee: Minutes of the First Meeting of the Committee," IOR, L/PWD/6/1156, file 4165.

47. "New Delhi Advisory Committee: Minutes of the Third Meeting of the Committee," ibid.; Annexure B, memorandum by EL, appended to ibid.; London, CH to WH, October 21, 1917, IOR, MSS. Eur. E. 220/1 C; HB, memorandum on interview with Hardinge, October 24, 1917, HBK; London, TH to Secretary of State, August 6, 1917, IOR, L/PWD/6/1186, file 3584; London, Secretary of State to Under-Secretary of State, August 14, 1917, ibid.; "New Delhi Advisory Committee: Minutes of the Fourth Meeting of the Committee, Minutes of the Fifth Meeting of the Committee, and Minutes of the Sixth Meeting of the Committee," IOR, L/PWD/6/1156, file 4165; and "Report by the New Delhi Advisory Committee on the Gradient of the Approach to Government House," January 31, 1918, ibid.

48. Montagu, *An Indian Diary*, p. 32; Simla, GGIC to Montagu, GOI despatch no. 14-P.W., May 17, 1918, IOR, L/PO/439; and London, TH to HB, March 7, 1918, HBK.

49. "New Delhi Advisory Committee: Minutes of the Eleventh Meeting of the Committee," with Appendix, IOR, L/PWD/6/1156, file 4165; Delhi, EL to LL, January 29 and February 25, 1920, ELP; and "HB memorandum of Meeting at the India Office, of Delhi Committee, Nov. 19th, 1920: Processional Way," HBK.

50. London, WS to Parsons, June 23, 1921, IOR, L/PO/439; London, HB to Reading, June 9, 1921, with notations by Lutyens, ibid.; Simla, WH to HB, July 31, 1921, HBK; and Crookshank, "Government House, New Delhi: Summary," printed April 26, 1922, IOR, L/PWD/6/1186, file 3584.

51. Delhi, EL to LL, February 28 and March 4, 1922, ELP; HBD, March 3, 1922; "Memorandum of Committee Meeting, Delhi, March 3rd, 1922," ibid.; and Crookshank, "Government House, New Delhi: Summary," printed April 26, 1922, IOR, L/PWD/6/1186, file 3584.

52. Delhi, EL to LL, March 4, 8, and 11, 1922, ELP; London, Carmichael to RC, December 13, 1920, private, CMP, M/13 (1); and London, RC to Carmichael, December 13, 1920, ibid.

53. Crookshank, "Government House, New Delhi: Summary," printed April 26, 1922, IOR, L/PWD/6/1186, file 3584; Delhi, EL to LL, November 13, 1922, ELP; HBD, February 21, 1926, HBK; London, Keeling to HB, February 6, 1945, ibid.; London, Stantiall to EL, June 16, 1922, copy, ibid.; London, WS to HB, June 16, 1922, ibid.; and London, CH to HB, January 4, 1923, ibid.

54. London, HB to EL, June 22, 1922, copy, ibid.; London, EL to HB, July 4 and 20, 1922, ibid.; Delhi, EL to LL, October 22, 1922, ELP; HBD, October 23, 1922; HB, "Resume, 1913–20," ibid.; HB, memorandum, February–March, 1931, ibid.; Medd in Brandon-Jones et al., "Reminiscences on Sir Edwin Lutyens," p. 235, and Baker, *Architecture and Personalities*, p. 207.

55. Delhi, LL to Viscountess Ridley, January 27, 1931, LEL; "Report by the New Delhi Advisory Committee on

the Gradient of the Approach to Government House," January 31, 1918, IOR, L/PWD/6/1156, file 4165; Delhi, CH to WH, March 13, 1916, CHC, 112, p. 485–6; London, EL to HB, July 4, 1922, HBK; Baker, *Architecture and Personalities*, p. 67; Governor's Camp, Punjab, WH to HB, July 31, 1926, HBK; and London, Keeling to HB, February 6, 1945, ibid.

56. En route, HB to JT, March 24, 1916, ibid.

57. Delhi, EL to CH, March 4, 1916, CHC, 112, p. 481; EL, note on Delhi, CH to WH, March 13, 1916, HBK; Bombay, EL to JT, March 20, 1916, ibid.; and London, EL to Montagu, June 21, 1921, IOR, L/PO/439.

58. London, HB to TH, October 24, 1917, HBD; "Proceedings of the One Hundred and First Meeting of the Imperial Delhi Committee," CHC, 112, pp. 476, 478–9; Delhi, CH to WH, March 13, 1916, ibid., p. 486; Delhi, EL to CH, March 4, 1916, ibid., p. 481; and en route, HB to JT, March 24, 1916, HBK.

59. Delhi, CH to WH March 13, 1916, and note by EL, CHC, 112, p. 486; en route, HB to JT, March 24, 1916, ibid.; Longfield, Kent, HB to EL, May 3, 1916, ibid.; CHC, 112, p. 486.

60. "Proceedings of the One Hundred and First Meeting of the Imperial Delhi Committee," in Delhi, WH to JD, February 25, 1916, ibid., p. 477; en route, HB to JT, March 24, 1916, HBK; Byron, "New Delhi," p. 13; Delhi, CH to WH, March 13, 1916, CHC, 112, p. 487; Cullen, *Townscape*, pp. 9, 17–20; and Chipkin, "New Delhi," p. 23.

61. En route, HB to JT, March 26, 1916, HBK; Longfield, Kent, HB to EL, May 3, 1916, ibid.; Governor's Camp, Punjab, WH to HB, July 31, 1926, ibid.

62. En route, HB to WH, March 18, 1916, ibid.; London, Carmichael to RC, December 13, 1920, CMP, M/13 (1); London, RC to Carmichael, December 15, 1920, ibid.; and Delhi, EL to LL, March 4, 8, 1922, ELP.

### NOTES TO CHAPTER 8

1. London, EL to LL, November 28, 1912, ELP; and Baker, *Architecture and Personalities*, p. 64.

2. Hussey, *Life of Sir Edwin Lutyens*, pp. 4–6, 9, 10, 17; R. Lutyens, *Six Great Architects*, pp. 164–5; Lutyens, "Foreword" to Voysey, p. 91; Baker, *Architecture and Personalities*, pp. 15–17; Owletts, Cobham, Kent, HB to Hussey, December 7, 1944, HBK; Slindon, Sussex, AS to Mrs. Richardson, August 22, 1968, ASD; and London, EL to LL, August 22, 1913, ELP.

3. London, EL to HB, February 15, 1903, HBK.

4. "Sir Edwin Lutyens at the A.A.," p. 66.

5. London, EL to CH, May 1, 1913 and September 20, 1912, CHC, 111, pp. 382, 391; and Delhi, EL to LL, undated, *c.* February 1916, ELP.

6. Temple Dinsley, Hitchin, EL to LL, September 27, 1914, ELP; Delhi, EL to HB, undated, between December 24 and 28, 1912, HBK; Baker, *Architecture and Personalities*, pp. 71–2; Cobham, HB to EL, September 26, 1913, HBK; Delhi, EL to HB, December 29, 1912, ibid.

7. Butler et al., *The Architecture of Sir Edwin Lutyens*, 2: 30.

8. Hussey, "An Early Lutyens Castle in the Air," pp. 148–9; and Pevsner, "Building With Wit," p. 219.

9. "Sir Edwin Lutyens at the A.A.," p. 64; and "Sir Edwin Lutyens's Plans for the New Delhi: How the Indian Sun Makes Building Difficult," *Indian Daily News* (Calcutta), December 5, 1920.

10. Byron, "New Delhi," p. 24.

11. Havell, *Indian Architecture*, pp. 15–16, 100; and R. Lutyens, *Sir Edwin Lutyens*, p. 76.

12. Byron, "New Delhi," p. 24; HBD, March 12, 1913; Delhi, EL to CH, March 21, 1913, CHC, 111, p. 336; London, RB to CH, January 19, 1914, CHC, 112, p. 159; London, EL to CH, September 13, 1912, CHC, 111, p. 75; and Viceroy's Camp, Dehra Dun, CH to EL, March 28, 1913, CHC, 112, p. 349.

13. En route, EL to HB, October 19, 1909, ELP.

14. London, EL to LL, September 20, 1920, ELP.

15. Delhi, EL to LI, December 26, 1929, OCC, Industries Dept., Part B, file no. 7/1930-I & L; and London, EL to CH, July 30, 1915, CHC, 112, p. 416.

16. Delhi, EL to LL, January 3 and 7, 1916, ELP; Andrews, "Brief Preliminary Note on the Proposal to Revive and Develop Indian Crafts," in Simla, Crookshank to WS, May 6, 1920, Annexure B to New Delhi Advisory Committee, "Minutes of the Tenth Meeting of the Committee," IOR, L/PWD/6/1156; Sarma, *PCSI*, 3 (March 21, 1923): 1333; Muddiman, *PCSI*, 4 (February 11, 1924): 148; Delhi, Keeling to EL, March 26, 1925, IOR, P/PWD/6/1161, file 1718; "Paragraph of Private Letter to the Viceroy," London, Birkenhead to Lytton, May 14, 1925, ibid.; "Extract from Private and Personal Letter from Lord Lytton to Lord Birkenhead, Dated 25th June 1925," ibid.; "Extract from Private Letter from Lord Lytton to Lord Birkenhead, Dated 16th July 1925," ibid.; note by Lytton, July 14, 1925, ibid.; Mitra, *PLAI*, 4 (August 30, 1927): 3631; McWatters, *PCSI*, 7 (September 12, 1927): 1101; en route, EL to LL, December 9, 1929, ELP; Delhi, EL to LI, December 26, 1929, OCC, Industries Dept., Part B, file no. 7/1930-I & L; Irwin, *Speeches*, 2: 135; "Notification," January 16, 1930, OCC, Industries Dept., Part B, file no. 7/1930-I & L; Irwin, *Speeches*, 2: 135; "Notification", January 16, 1930, OCC Industries Dept., Part B, file no. 7/1930-I & L; and Byron, "New Delhi," p. 29.

17. Simla, LI to EL, May 31, 1930, IOR, L/PO/440; and Brown, "The Mural Paintings at New Delhi," p. 399. Percy Brown (1872–1955) was Principal of the Government School of Art, Calcutta, 1909–27, and Secretary and Curator of the Victoria Memorial Hall, Calcutta, 1927–47.

18. MacDonald, *The Pantheon*, pp. 89–92; Brown, *Roman Architecture*, pp. 35–6; and Palladio, *The Four Books of Architecture*, p. 99.

19. Davidson, *Self's the Man*, p. 136.

20. Greenberg, "Lutyens' Architecture Restudied," pp. 130–1.

21. "Sir Edwin Lutyens at the A.A.," p. 65; Butler in Brandon-Jones et al., "Reminiscences on Sir Edwin Lutyens," p. 236; and Delhi, EL to CH, March 21, 1913, CHC, 111, p. 337.

22. Greenberg, "Lutyens' Architecture Restudied," pp. 129–30.

23. Murray, *PDC*, 41 (August 7, 1912): 3311–12; and Montagu, ibid., 3313.

24. London, EL to RC, July 4, 1922, IOR, L/PWD/6/1186.

25. Evelyn, *Diary*, 5: 237.

26. Delhi, EL to LL, January 24, 1929, ELP; Baker, "Architectural Design: Symbolism in Stone and Marble," *Times* (London), February 18, 1930; London, New Delhi Advisory Committee to Secretary of State for India, August 11, 1924, annexed to New Delhi Advisory Committee, "Minutes of the Thirteenth Meeting of the Committee," IOR, L/PWD/6/1156, file 4165; Viceroy's Camp, Reading to Birkenhead, November 1924, ibid.; and London, Birkenhead to CH, August 12, 1925, ibid.

27. Howes, *Viceregal Establishments in India*, pp. 3, 5–8.

28. James, "An English New Year," in *English Hours*, p. 170.

29. Delhi, EL to LL, January 24, 1929, ELP.

30. Delhi, LI to Benn, December 26, 1929, IOR, MSS. Eur. C. 152/5, p. 186; and Halifax, *Fulness of Days*, p. 144.

31. "Report by the New Delhi Advisory Committee," August 23, 1918, IOR, L/PWD/6/1156, file 4165; Villiers-Stuart, "Indian Water Gardens," p. 448; and idem, *Gardens of the Great Mogals*, pp. 96, 99–102, 164, 167.

32. Glendevon, *The Viceroy at Bay*, p. 83; Delhi, EL to LL, January 24, 1929, ELP; and Halifax, *Fulness of Days*, p. 144.

33. Davidson, *Self's the Man*, p. 136.

34. "Note dated 10th July 1913, by Chief Engineer, Delhi," HDUB, August 1913, nos. 91–7; Howes, *Viceregal Establishments in India*, pp. 2–8; Romsey, Hampshire, Mountbatten to Howes, March 2, 1976, BLM; and Romsey, Mrs. Travis to Howes, March 24, 1976, ibid.

35. "Project Estimate for the Construction of the New Imperial Capital at Delhi," section D(I)-Buildings, PWD, C.W.-Buildings-A, May 1914, nos. 12–22; Delhi, GD to SPWD, October 17, 1914, enclosure no. 1 to Delhi, GGIC to RC, December 10, 1914, GOI, despatch no. 39-P.W. of 1914, IOR, L/PWD/6/1182, file 3576; Delhi, Chief Engineer, Delhi, to SIDC, October 3, 1914, PWD, C.W.-B., March 1915, no. 37; "Proceedings of the Thirty-sixth Meeting of the Imperial Delhi Committee," in Delhi, WH to JD, March 2, 1914, CHC, 112, p. 195; "Proceedings of the Sixty-seventh Meeting of the Imperial Delhi Committee," in Delhi, WH to JD, January 14, 1915, ibid., p. 370; Delhi, SIDC to SPWD, February 3, 1915, HDUB, April 1915, no. 115; Delhi, Maxwell to WH, February 22–3, 1915, CHC, 112, p. 379; "Report by the New Delhi Advisory Committee on Sir E. Lutyens' Proposals for a Moghal Garden at the back of Government House," August 23, 1918, IOR, L/PWD/6/1156, file 4165; minute by WS, on EL, "Memo on the Relationship of Govt. House to its subsidiary buildings," ibid., L/PWD/6/1186, file 3584; Howes, *Viceregal Establishments in India*, pp. 15–17; and "The New Delhi: The Work of Sir Edwin Lutyens and Sir Herbert Baker," p. 220.

36. EL, memorandum to JT, January 1917, Annexure B to Minutes of the Home Advisory Committee, July 20, 1917, IOR, L/PWD/6/1156, file 4165; Delhi, EL to LL, March 19, 1917, ELP; Medd, "The Building of New Delhi," March 19, 1954, HMP; Delhi, EL to LL, *c.* February 9, 1914, January 17, February 4, 1915, January 19, 31, 1916, March 19, 1917, ELP; Delhi, EL to JD, March 1, 1915, CHC, 112, p. 383.

37. Delhi, SIDC to DPWD, January 23, 1915, HDUB, March 1915, no. 38; Nicholls, note for the Imperial Delhi Committee, December 14, 1914, in Delhi, Keeling to SIDC, December 15, 1914, ibid.; Kipling, "The Origin of the Bungalow," pp. 308–10; Nilsson, *European Architecture in India, 1750–1850*, pp. 176–85; Balfour, *Note on Housing in the Tropics*; and Wildeblood, *Note on the Problem of Roofs in the Plains of India*.

38. Delhi, JD to Maxwell, February 22, 1915, CHC, 112, p. 378; "Empty Delhi," *Statesman* (Calcutta), April 11, 1924; Editorial, *Simla Times*, July 30, 1925; London, HB to WH, June 22, 1922, HBK; and London, HB to WH, July 4, 1922, ibid.

39. Sir John Thompson, "New Delhi," IOR, MSS. Eur. F. 137/56, pp. 25–6.

40. Delhi, EL to LL, *c.* January 1, 1921 and December 31, 1929, ELP; Emily Lutyens, *Candles in the Sun*, pp. 95–6, 157; Elisabeth Lutyens, *A Goldfish Bowl*, p. 34; and M. Lutyens, *To Be Young: Some Chapters of Autobiography*, pp. 102–3, 138–9.

41. Medd, "The Building of New Delhi," HMP, p. 11.

42. Jaipur, Maharaja of Jaipur to JD, March 5, 1915, CHC, 112, pp. 385–6; and Sale, "Contingency in the Construction of New Delhi," JSP, pp. 2–3.

43. [Marjorie Cartwright Shoosmith], "The Many Wonders of New Delhi," *Pioneer* (Allahabad), December 23, 1929.

44. Brown, *Indian Architecture: Buddhist and Hindu Period*, pp. 9, 50; idem, *Indian Architecture: Islamic Period*, p. 11; London, EL to HB, June 1, 1915, ELP; London, EL to CH, June 30, 1915, ibid.; and London, WL to JD, January 12, 1913, CHC, 111, p. 154.

45. London, EL to CH, June 30, 1915, CHC, 112, pp. 407–8; "Copy of a letter from Maharaja of Jaipur to the Viceroy," in Viceroy's Camp, CH to WH, December 24, 1915, IOR, MSS. Eur. E. 220/1 B; Delhi, EL to LL, January 3, 1916, ELP; EL, memorandum to JT, January 1917, Annexure B to Minutes of the Home Advisory Committee, July 20, 1917, IOR, L/PWD/6/1156, file 4165; Delhi, Abbott to Rai Bahadur Lala Sultan Singh, February 1, 1926, OCC, file B-51/1926-Home; Delhi, Secretary, New Capital Committee, Delhi, to Chief Commissioner, Delhi, April 8, 1926, ibid.; Delhi, EL to LL, February 7 and 14, 1929, ELP; and Halifax, *Fulness of Days*, p. 144.

46. Viceroy's Camp, LI to EL, March 27/29, 1927, IOR, MSS. Eur. C. 152/17, pp. 223–4; and London, EL to LI, April 28, 1927, ibid., pp. 337–8.

47. Baker, *Architecture and Personalities*, p. 70; and Byron, "New Delhi," p. 6.

48. Pellenc, *Diamonds and Dust*, p. 108, and Kipling, *Verse*, p. 195.

49. Delhi, EL to LL, November 18, 1938, ELP; Medd, "New Delhi," HMP, p. 8; and Chandrasekhara, "The Central Vista: Effective Use for Recreation," Institute of Town Planners, India, DOC/ITP/DLI/TP-27, pp. 1–2.

50. *PP*, "Final Report of the Delhi Town Planning Committee," Cd. 6889, p. 6; Delhi, EL to LL, December 24, 1919, ELP; and "Architecture at the Royal Academy," p. 718.

51. "Project Estimate for the Construction of the New

Imperial Capital at Delhi," vol. 1, PWD, C.W.-Buildings-A, May 1914, nos. 12–22; and Delhi, EL to LL, March 9, 1917, and undated, *c.* March 1917, ELP.

52. London, EL to CH, September 2, 1915, CHC, 112, p. 431; "The New Indian Capital: Suggested War Memorial," *Madras Times*, June 22, 1916; Shoosmith, "The Design of New Delhi," p. 425; [Marjorie Cartwright Shoosmith], "The Many Wonders of New Delhi," *Pioneer* (Allahabad), December 23, 1929; and Delhi, EL to LL, *c.* March 1917, March 23, 1917, March 20, 1920, ELP. The foundation stone of the War Memorial Arch, like that of the Council House, was incorrectly placed and had to be relaid.

53. *Annual Progress Report, 1931–2,* CEL; Reed, *The India I Knew,* p. 97; and "India War Memorial: Dedication in New Delhi," *Times* (London), February 13, 1931. Sir Stanley Reed was editor of the *Times of India* from 1907 to 1923.

54. Baker, *Architecture and Personalities,* p. 208; Butler, *The Architecture of Sir Edwin Lutyens,* 3: 40–1; and Smith, *Architectural Symbolism of Imperial Rome and the Middle Ages,* pp. 26n, 28–9n, 30n.

55. Speer, *Inside the Third Reich,* pp. 74–6.

56. Smith, *Architectural Symbolism of Imperial Rome and the Middle Ages,* pp. 30–1, 69, 181, 184–5; Chelmsford, *Speeches,* 2: 562–5; "India War Memorial: Lord Irwin's Speech," *Times* (London), February 13, 1931; Delhi, EL to LL, March 23, 1917 and March 20, 1920, ELP; and London, EL to LL, July 7, 1919, ibid.

57. Chelmsford, *Speeches,* 2: 565.

58. Reed, *The India I Knew,* p. 168.

59. Smith, *Architectural Symbolism of Imperial Rome and the Middle Ages,* p. 30, fn. 76.

60. Thompson, "Delhi as Capital," p. 136; Rouse, "New Delhi," p. 366; Delhi, HB to Mrs. Baker, February 27, 1913, HBK; Baker, *Architecture and Personalities,* p. 75; Delhi, SIDC to SPWD, December 29, 1913, pp. 4, 6, enclosure no. 1 to Simla, GGIC to RC, April 19, 1914, GOI despatch no. 8-P.W., IOR, L/PWD/6/1182, file 3576; Delhi, Chief Engineer, New Delhi, GOI, PWD, to Secretary to GOI, Industries and Labour, April 29, 1929, Note on the Supplementary Project Estimate, OCC, Financial Dept., Part B, file no. 49/1929-Financial; "Project Estimate for the Construction of the New Imperial Capital at Delhi," vol. 1, p. 29, para. 41, PWD, C.W.-Buildings-A, May 1914, nos. 12–22; "Revised Project Estimate for the Construction of the New Capital," memorandum by Keeling, no. 61-N.C.C., January 12, 1921, CEL; "Joint Note by the Chief Engineer and the Accounts Officer, Central Accounts Office," ibid.; Thompson, "New Delhi," IOR, MSS. Eur. F. 137/56; GOI, *Annual Progress Report, 1931–33,* CEL; Delhi, Thompson to EL, May 12, 1931, and Simla, Thompson to EL, July 9, 1931, OCC, B. 39/1931-Industries; and interview by author on December 11, 1970, with Robert Tor Russell, Chief Architect to the GOI, 1919–39.

61. Windsor, *A King's Story,* p. 174.

62. Pope-Hennessy, *Lord Crewe,* p. 87; Rumbold, *Watershed in India,* p. 11; Eustis and Zaidi, "King, Viceroy and Cabinet," p. 171; Nicolson, *King George the Fifth,* pp. 88–9,

166; Chelmsford, *Speeches,* 2: 527–40; and Birkenhead, *Halifax,* p. 186.

63. "Lord Hardinge in India: A Great Record," *Habbel Matin* (Calcutta), June 7, 1916; Simla, CH to GB, August 18, 1913, CHC, 112, p. 78; London, GB to CH, August 1 and September 19, 1913, ibid., pp. 67, 100a–100b.

64. "Question Regarding the Grant of Lands," note by de Montmorency, March 18, 1912, HDD Deposit, April 1912, no. 10; note by Russell on "Project Estimate for the Construction of the new Imperial Capital at Delhi," PWD, Notes, C.W.-Buildings-A, May 1914, nos. 12–22; Delhi, JT to AC, January 19, 1917, IOR, MSS. Eur. E. 264/3, p. 8; Viceroy to Secretary of State for India, March 12, 1915, CHC, 112, p. 389; "Proceedings of the Ninety-sixth Meeting of the Imperial Delhi Committee," in Delhi, WH to JD, January 19, 1916, ibid., p. 461; Delhi, Secretary, I.D.C., to Secretary to GOI, Dept. of Revenue and Agriculture, December 24, 1914, in Simla, GGIC to AC, July 16, 1915, GOI, despatch no. 10-Land Revenue, GOI, Dept. of Revenue and Agriculture, IOR, L/PWD/6/966, file 2430; and "List of Ruling Princes and Chiefs to Whom Residential Building Sites Have Been Allotted in New Delhi," in Delhi, Chief Engineer, C.P.W.D., to Chief Commissioner, Delhi, November 3, 1931, OCC, Foreign Dept., Part B, file 17/1931-Foreign.

65. Mitter, *Much Maligned Monsters,* pp. 256, 270–2; and Havell, "The Message of Hope for India," p. 1274.

66. Windsor, *A King's Story,* p. 175; Collins and Lapierre, *Freedom at Midnight,* pp. 169–70; Lord, *The Maharajahs,* pp. 81–2; and Reilly, "The Progress of New Delhi," *Morning Post* (London), April 4, 1928.

67. Franklin, "Edwardian Butterfly Houses," pp. 220–5.

68. CHPD, February 15, 1931.

69. Lord, *The Maharajahs,* pp. 140–5.

70. Lutyens, "Persian Brickwork, II," p. 120; HB, Speech to the Art Workers Guild, London, June 23, 1921, HBK; London, H. A. N. Medd to author, February 11, 1976; Harvey, "Some Minor Problems, p. 44; Baker, contribution to discussion, *RIBAJ,* 35 (December 10, 1927): 77; and Byron, "New Delhi," pp. 20, 26.

71. Thompson, "New Delhi," IOR, MSS. Eur. F. 137/57, p. 24; "Social Life in the Capital," pp. 382–3; Pellenc, *Diamonds and Dust,* pp. 109–11; and Kincaid, *British Social Life in India,* p. 314.

72. Reed, *The India I Knew,* pp. 258–62; New Delhi Municipal Committee, *New Delhi Municipality: Annual Report for 1939–40,* 1: 33; Mosley, *The Last Days of the British Raj,* p. 176; and Trevelyan, *The India We Left,* p. 236.

73. Ealing, GB to CH, August 8, 1913, CHC, 112, p. 72b; and Simla, CH to the Lord Bishop of Lahore, July 13, 1912, in idem, July 12, 1912, CHC, 110, pp. 191–2.

74. Medd, "The Cathedral Church of the Redemption, New Delhi," December 17, 1953, HML; and Simla, EL to LL, June 9, 18, 1912, ELP.

75. Massingham, *Miss Jekyll,* p. 164; and Delhi, EL to LL, March 6, 1917, ELP.

76. Shoosmith, "The Design of New Delhi," p. 427.

77. Lutyens, *Six Great Architects,* p. 177.

78. London, EL to CH, May 1, 1913, CHC, 111, p. 391;

Lutyens, "What I Think of Modern Architecture," pp. 775–7; Hussey, *Life of Sir Edwin Lutyens*, p. 494; and Dar Tal-Ghar, Fawwara, Malta, Sir Basil Spence to author, May 20, 1974.

79. "Edwin Landseer Lutyens," p. 4; Slindon, Sussex, AS to Mrs. Richardson, August 22, 1968, ASD; Shoosmith, "Present-Day Architecture in India," p. 208; and Baker, *Architecture and Personalities*, p. 208.

80. Delhi, EL to LL, January 24, 1929, ELP.

81. Nehru, *The Discovery of India*, pp. 220, 576, 579.

## NOTES TO CHAPTER 9

1. "New Delhi: State Opening To-Morrow," *Times* (London), January 17, 1927; "Opening of New Delhi: Stately Ceremony," ibid., January 19, 1927; "Viceroy Opens Council House," *Pioneer* (Allahabad), January 20, 1927; Whyte, "The New Delhi," *Radio Times*, March 11, 1927; and Lady Haig, "Opening of New Council House, New Delhi," extract dated June 1967 from diary entry of January 18, 1927, HSAS.

2. Reilly, *Representative British Architects of the Present Day*, p. 52; Malcolm, "Sir Herbert Baker (1862–1946)," *DNB 1941–1950*, p. 41; Baker, *Architecture and Personalities*, pp. 1–19; HB, "South African Architecture," HBK; and H. E. Baker, "Sir Herbert Baker and the Crafts," address, May 30, 1974, ibid.

3. HBD, January 4, 1914; [Medd], "Makers of New Delhi: Sir Herbert Baker," *Statesman* (Delhi), February 18, 1931; and Wheeler, *High Relief*, pp. 53, 58, 61.

4. Baker, *Cecil Rhodes by His Architect*, p. 172.

5. Baker, "Cecil Rhodes: The Ideals Inspiring His Imperialism," letter reprinted in idem, *Architecture and Personalities*, Appendix C, pp. 223–4.

6. Baker, "New Delhi: The Problem of Style," *Times* (London), October 3, 1912, reprinted in idem, *Architecture and Personalities*, Appendix B, pp. 218–22.

7. Baker, "Architecture of Empire," HBK.

8. Baker, *Architecture and Personalities*, pp. 57–62, 162; and idem, "The Story of the Union Buildings," pp. 122–3.

9. Delhi, HB to Mrs. Baker, February 26 and March 4, 1913, HBK; and Baker, "The Government Offices of Pretoria and the New Delhi," p. 73.

10. Baker, *Architecture and Personalities*, p. 67; and idem, "Architectural Design: Symbolism in Stone and Marble," *Times* (London), February 18, 1930.

11. Reed, *The India I Knew*, p. 61; Baker, *Architecture and Personalities*, p. 67; and Governor's Camp, Punjab, WH to HB, July 31, 1926, HBK.

12. Baker, "The New Delhi," p. 784; idem, "Architectural Design: Symbolism in Stone and Marble," *Times* (London), February 18, 1930; HB, lecture, February 12, 1932, HBK; Johannesburg, HB to CH, July 25, 1913, CHC, 112, p. 59; and Baker, contribution to discussion, *RIBAJ*, 30 (March 24, 1923): 304.

13. Baker, *Architecture and Personalities*, p. 71; and Medd, "New Delhi," lecture, March 15th 1597, HMP.

14. Delhi, HB to CH, March 21, 1913, CHC, 111, p. 338; Baker, "The Architectural Needs of South Africa," p. 512; Delhi, HB to Mrs. Baker, February 26, 1913, HBK; and

Delhi, HB to C. P. Walgate, January 21, 1920, ibid.

15. Johannesburg, HB to EL, December 23, 1909, ELP; Johannesburg, HB to CH, July 25, 1913, CHC, 112, pp. 59–60; Allen, *Raj*, pp. 15, 45; and Baker, *Architecture and Personalities*, pp. 68–9.

16. Reilly, *Representative British Architects of the Present Day*, pp. 40, 52; and Baker, "Architecture and Education," lecture, July 1902, HBK.

17. "Delhi, New and Old: The Future Capital," *Times* (London), February 18, 1930; Byron, "New Delhi," p. 20; HBD, November 18 and December 2, 1922, with memorandum of December 3, 1922; Baker, *Architecture and Personalities*, p. 69; and Delhi, EL to LL, December 9, 1913, ELP. An engraving of J. M. W. Turner's painting of 1804 in the Tate Gallery, "London from Greenwich," in which the Royal Hospital features prominently, hung in Baker's office until the firm of Sir Herbert Baker and Scott was dissolved in 1972, twenty-six years after his death.

18. Northcliffe, *My Journey round the World*, p. 240; Delhi, HB to SIDC, December 18, 1913, CHC, 112, p. 154; and Baker, "The Architectural Needs of South Africa," pp. 512–24.

19. Mosley, *The Last Days of the British Raj*, p. 92, and Delhi, HB to CH, March 21, 1913, CHC, 111, p. 339.

20. Baker, "New Delhi: The Problem of Style," *Times* (London), October 3, 1912; Furst, "Mr. Fyzee Rahamin's Decorations at Delhi," pp. 11–16; and "Modern Indian Art Reviving Old Traditions: Mural Paintings in the Imperial Secretariat at New Delhi," pp. 410–11.

21. Brown, "The Mural Decorations at New Delhi," pp. 392–400; and Shoosmith, "Present-Day Architecture in India," pp. 204–13.

22. Baker, remarks, *RIBAJ*, 34 (July 16, 1927): 597; and HB, "New Delhi Inscriptions," March 9, 1931, HBK.

23. London, MS to CH, July 19, 1912, CHK, U927/Va 19, p. 1127; Simla, CH to MS, August 4, 1912, ibid., p. 1128; Delhi, WH to JD, January 7, 1915, CHC, 112, p. 360; Delhi, JD to WH, January 9, 1915, ibid., p. 361; Simla, CH to WH, June 26, 1915, ibid., p. 406; Dehra Dun, CH to WH, August 3, 1915, IOR, MSS. Eur. E. 220/1 B; and Delhi, EL to LL, January 17, 1915, ELP.

24. London, HM to author, February 11, 1976; HB, memorandum, February–March 1931, HBK; HB, memorandum, January 22, 1927, ibid.; HB, "Resume, 1913–20," ibid.; Grigg to HB, July 5, 1921, ibid.; London, HB to LI, May 20, 1926, ibid.; Delhi, EL to LL, January 17, 1929, ELP; HBD, February 9 and 24, 1929; and Delhi, HB to LI, February 21, 1929, HBK.

25. Baker, *Architecture and Personalities*, p. 74; "Extract from a private letter from the Secretary of State to H.E. the Viceroy dated 7th February, 1929," HBK; Delhi, George Cunningham to Sir B. N. Mitra, December 25, 1929, ibid.; and Delhi, Private Secretary to the Viceroy to HB, March 28, 1930, ibid.

26. Simla, GGIC to AC, June 22, 1917, confidential GOI despatch no. 17-P.W., C.W.-Buildings, IOR, L/PWD/6/1183, file 3577; and London, Long to GGIC, December 14, 1917, confidential despatch no. 58-P.W., IOR, ibid.

27. "The New Capital City at Delhi," p. 187; Delhi, EL to SIDC, February 10, 1916, HBK; HB, "Resume, 1913–20,"

ibid.; Medd, "The Building of New Delhi," paper read March 19, 1954, HMP; "New Delhi in the Making: Sir Edwin Lutyens' Survey," *Englishman* (Calcutta), March 4, 1925; CHPD, February 6, 1931; and "Wonders of New Delhi," *Daily Telegraph* (London), February 9, 1931.

28. HB, memorandum, February–March 1931, HBK; Baker, *Architecture and Personalities*, p. 75; and Delhi, EL to LL, December 17, 24, 28, 1919 and January 13, 1920, ELP.

29. HBD, January 5, 6, 8, 9, 10, 16, 23, 31, and February 6, 8, 10, 20, 22, 23, 25, 1920, HBK; and Delhi, HB to Walgate, January 21 and February 13, 1920, ibid.

30. Delhi, Marris to HB, February 22, 1920, ibid.

31. "Raisina Progress: The New Parliament House," *Times of India* (Bombay), March 13, 1926; London, Goodhart-Rendel to AS, November 28, 1927, ASA; Keeling, contribution to discussion, *RIBAJ*, 74 (July 2, 1926): 792; Cocke, *PLAI*, 1 (February 7, 1927): 519; and WH, "Report of the New Capital Enquiry Committee, 1922," in Delhi, Crookshank to Under-Secretary of State for India, PWD, December 14, 1922, IOR, L/PWD/6/1124, file 43.

32. London, HB to GD, June 14, 1922, HBK; London, HB to Under-Secretary of State for India, Economic and Overseas Dept., October 18, 1927, IOR, L/E/7/1480, file 6795/26; and Baker, "Legislative Chambers at Delhi," *Times* (London), January 24, 1922.

33. London, HB to Keeling, August 22, 1922, HBK; Burchard and Bush-Brown, *The Architecture of America*, pp. 487–8; Speer, *Inside the Third Reich*, chap. 6, n. 5, p. 529; Frampton, *Modern Architecture*, pp. 210–19; Baker, *Architecture and Personalities*, p. 75; Byron, "New Delhi," pp. 8, 18; Swinton, "New Delhi," pp. 441–8; "The Many Wonders of New Delhi," *Pioneer* (Allahabad), December 23, 1929; and GOI, *Annual Progress Report, 1928–29*, p. iii.

34. Mosley, *The Last Days of the British Raj*, p. 92.

35. Baker, *Architecture and Personalities*, p. 75; and Byrt, "The Council House," p. 386.

36. "The New Delhi," p. 470; Bagenal, "The Acoustics of the New Legislative Chamber at Delhi," pp. 851–2; Baker, *Architecture and Personalities*, p. 76; and CHPD, February 6, 1931.

37. Sale, "Contingency in the Construction of New Delhi," JSP, p. 16; and "Bombs in the Legislative Assembly," extract from Lady Haig diary, April 8, 1929, HSAS.

38. "Marvels of New Delhi," *Statesman* (Calcutta), February 8, 1931; Menon, *The Story of the Integration of the Indian States*, p. 17; and Pellenc, *Diamonds and Dust*, p. 118.

39. Baker, *Architecture and Personalities*, p. 76.

40. Byrt, "The Council House," p. 386; "Raisina Progress: The New Parliament House," *Times of India* (Bombay), March 13, 1926; and "Recent Lighting Installations," *Electrical Review* (London), 100 (June 17, 1927): 964.

41. Baker, *Architecture and Personalities*, pp. 73–4; Delhi, HB to Wood, March 1920, WSG; and Delhi, George to Blomfield, December 11, 1956, ibid.

42. Coatman, *Years of Destiny*, pp. 183–4.

43. Delhi, EL to LL, December 17, 1919, ELP; CHPD, February 6, 1931; and "Opening of New Delhi: Stately Ceremony," *Times* (London), January 19, 1927.

44. *PP*, "Final Report of the Delhi Town Planning Committee," Cd. 6889, p. 13; Delhi, SIDC to SPWD, December 29, 1913, IOR, L/PWD/6/1182, file 3576; Keeling, "New Imperial Capital, Delhi: Project Estimates for Works," vol. 1: "Report and Abstract of Expenditure," 1913, pp. 27–8, CEL; and note dated March 3, 1914, by R. P. Russell, Secretary to the GOI, P.W.D., on ibid., PWD, Notes, C.W.-Buildings-A, May 1914, nos. 12–22.

45. Rouse, "New Delhi," p. 366; GOI, *Annual Progress Report, 1924–25*, IOR, L/E/3/224, file 1961; idem, *Annual Progress Report, 1926–27*, IOR, T.7. xxi; idem, *Annual Progress Report, 1931–32*, CEL; New Delhi Municipal Committee (hereafter N.D.M.C.), *New Delhi Municipality: Annual Report for 1932–33*, N.D.M.C. Library.

46. Cullen, *The Ninth Delhi*, p. 43, and S. K. Kulshrestha, "Image of Delhi, Capital of India," Institute of Town Planners, India, DOC/ITP/DLI/TP-10.

47. Medd, "Robert Tor Russell, C.I.E., D.S.O., F.R.I.B.A., M.T.P.I., 1888–1972," obituary, HMP; idem, "What India Meant to Me," *Illustrated Weekly of India* (Bombay), April 11, 1971; and William Henry Nicholls, "Reminiscences," manuscript, WNP.

48. An Onlooker, "Architecture at the Royal Academy," p. 718.

49. "Mr. Henry Medd: A Lutyens Disciple in India," *Times* (London), October 31, 1977; Medd, "What India Meant to Me," *Illustrated Weekly of India* (Bombay), April 11, 1971; idem, "Walter Sykes George," p. 102; "Mr. Walter George," *Times* (London), January 8, 1962; "Walter George," *Statesman* (Delhi), January 8, 1962; Singh and George, "The Architecture of Walter George," p. 28; George, autobiographical manuscript notes, WSG; London, Medd to AS, January 23, 1962, ASA; Bexhill-on-Sea, Sussex, John Greaves to Medd, January 17, 1962, HML.

50. Medd, "The Cathedral Church of the Redemption, New Delhi," December 17, 1953, HML; "Our Cathedral," in *Cathedral Fete Brochure*, n.p.; on tour at Delhi, Bishop of Lahore to Chief Commissioner, Delhi, January 25, 1923, copy, IOR, L/PWD/6/1186, file 3584; Delhi, Keeling to EL, March 8, 1923, copy, ibid.; London, EL to CH, April 4, 1923, ibid.; London, CH to WS, April 5, 1923, ibid.; London, intra-office notes by WS, Sir Malcolm Seton, and Sir Arthur Hirtzel, India Office, April 7, 10, 11, 1923, ibid.; London, WS to CH, April 17, 1923, ibid.; and "Church Buildings at Delhi: The Funds Available," *Pioneer* (Allahabad), January 28, 1924.

51. Halifax, *Fulness of Days*, p. 145; and Medd, "The Cathedral Church of the Redemption," HML.

52. Ibid.; London, Medd to Byron, May 20, 1973, HML; Stamp, "Indian Summer," p. 368; and idem and Llewellyn Smith, *Henry Alexander Nesbitt Medd*, p. 6.

53. "Our Cathedral," in *Cathedral Fete Brochure*; Halifax, *Fulness of Days*, pp. 145–6; Delhi, HB to LI, February 17, 1931, HBK; and London, Medd to Stamp, January 20, 1976, property of Gavin Stamp, London.

54. Delhi, EL to LL, January 17, 1929, ELP; Halifax, *Fulness of Days*, p. 145; Medd, "The Cathedral Church of the Redemption," HML; and London, Medd to Byron, May 20, 1973, ibid.

55. Stamp, "Indian Summer," p. 368.

56. Ibid.

57. Singh and George, "The Architecture of Walter George," pp. 22–3.

58. "Arthur Gordon Shoosmith," in Royal Institute of British Architects, *Catalogue of the Drawings Collection*, 13: 62; Slindon, M. C. Shoosmith to Stamp, March 22, 1976, property of Gavin Stamp; and Stamp, "Indian Summer," p. 370.

59. "Mr. John Begg," p. 162; and CHPD, February 14, 1931.

60. En route, EL to AS, February 13, 1927, ELP.

61. Slindon, M. C. Shoosmith to Stamp, March 22, 1976, property of Gavin Stamp.

62. "The Garrison Church, New Delhi," pp. 293–4; and "Examples of Recent Architecture," p. 674.

63. Ibid.; "An Age of Imitations in Architecture," *Evening News* (London), January 9, 1957; Slindon, M. C. Shoosmith to author, March 18, 1975; Byron to AS, May 4, 1931, ASA; Hussey, "Recent Architecture," p. 582.

64. Rev. William Whewell, quoted in *PP* (Commons), "Report of the Select Committee on Aboriginees (British Settlements)" (no. 425), 1837, 7: 76.

65. Knapp-Fisher, "Sir Herbert Baker," p. 260; Greig, *Herbert Baker in South Africa*, pp. 193, 223; Baker, remarks, *RIBAJ*, 34 (July 16, 1927): 597; and Hardinge, memorandum in Simla, CH to WH, August 30, 1915, IOR, MSS. Eur. E. 220/1 A.

66. Baker, remarks, *RIBAJ*, 34 (July 16, 1927): 598; Churchill, *PDC*, 393 (October 28, 1943): 403; Irwin, *PLAI*, 1 (January 24, 1927): 43; HBD, January 24, 1927; and Irwin, *Speeches*, 2: 196.

67. Sir Arnold Wilson, quoted in Morris, *Pax Britannica*, p. 27; and Vitruvius Pollio, *On Architecture*, 1: 3, 5.

NOTES TO CHAPTER 10

1. "New Delhi: Preparations for Inauguration," *Times* (London), February 9, 1931; "New Delhi," *Yorkshire Post*, February 11, 1931; and Hardinge, "The Cost of New Delhi," *Times* (London), March 23, 1931.

2. Windsor, *A King's Story*, pp. 176–7; "Beauty of the New Delhi," *Observer*, February 8, 1931; and London, EL to LL, September 28, 1914, ELP.

3. "Beauty of the New Delhi," *Observer*, February 8, 1931; "New Delhi," *Manchester Guardian*, February 10, 1931; "The New Delhi," *Daily Telegraph*, February 9, 1931; and "New Delhi," *Yorkshire Post*, February 11, 1931.

4. M. Shoosmith, "New Delhi," *Bombay, Baroda, and Central India* (1931), n.p.

5. "A Shelter for Poor Travellers," *Pioneer* (Allahabad), February 6, 1931.

6. CHPD, February 1, 1931; and Delhi, LL to Viscountess Ridley, January 27 and February 9, 1931, LEL.

7. Hodgson, *Lord Halifax*, pp. 79–80; Birkenhead, *Halifax*, p. 189; CHPD, December 23, 1930 and February, 9, 1931.

8. Bernays, "*Naked Faquir*," p. 42; and Hodgson, *Lord Halifax*, p. 80.

9. "The Four Pillars of Fellowship," *Statesman* (Delhi), February 11, 1931; "The New Capital of India," *Daily Telegraph*, February 11, 1931; Irwin, *Speeches*, 2:326; and

CHPD, February 10, 1931.

10. "The Inauguration of New Delhi: People's Fete, Delhi Fort, 11th Feb. 1931," official program, ASA; "Festivities in Delhi," *Times* (London), February 12, 1931; and "Ancient Delhi Pageant," *Daily Mail*, February 12, 1931.

11. "India's Arch of Memory," *Statesman* (Delhi), February 13, 1931; "India War Memorial," *Times* (London), February 13, 1931; "War Memorial for India," *Morning Post*, February 13, 1931; "All-India War Memorial," *Manchester Guardian*, February 13, 1931; "War Dead of India," *Daily Telegraph*, February 13, 1931; "India's War Dead," *Daily Mail*, February 13, 1931; CHPD, February 12, 1931; Baker, *Architecture and Personalities*, p. 77; and Thompson, "New Delhi," IOR, MSS. Eur. F. 137/56, p. 46.

12. Rev. E. A. Storrs Fox to Mrs. Storrs Fox, February 15, 1931, IOR, MSS. Eur. E. 343; "English Church in New Delhi," *Times* (London), February 16, 1931; CHPD, February 7, 1931; Delhi, LI to Halifax, January 27 and February 15, 1931, IOR, MSS. Eur. C. 152/27, pp. 340, 343–4; and "The Form and Order of the Consecration of the Church of the Redemption, New Delhi," HML.

13. "The Viceroy's Message," *ISRM*, 4 (February 1931): 361; and Phillips, "India's New Capital," *Daily Mail*, February 10, 1931.

14. Bernays, "*Naked Faquir*," pp. 37, 50; CHPD, December 23, 1930; Delhi, EL to LL, December 31, 1929, ELP; Halifax, *Fulness of Days*, pp. 142–3; and Delhi, LI to Halifax, December 24, 1929, IOR, MSS. Eur. C. 152/27, p. 269.

15. Delhi, LL to Viscountess Ridley, February 1, 1931, LEL; "New Delhi," *Times* (London), February 11, 1931; and Bernays, "*Naked Faquir*," p. 37.

16. Phillips, "India's New Capital," *Daily Mail*, February 10, 1931; "Indian Princes and Delhi," ibid., February 14, 1931; "India's Change of Capital," *Manchester Guardian*, February 11, 1931; Phillips, "The Troubles of New Delhi," *Daily Mail*, January 16, 1925; Governor's Camp, Punjab, WH to HB, July 31, 1926, HBK; and Baker, *Architecture and Personalities*, pp. 76–7.

17. Nehru, *The Discovery of India*, pp. 458–9; and idem, *Toward Freedom*, Appendix C, p. 429.

18. Delhi, EL to LL, February 27, 1929, ELP; Bernays, "*Naked Faquir*," p. 87; and Tendulkar, *Mahatma*, vol. 3, *1930–1934*, p. 121.

19. "Gandhi & Lord Irwin," *Manchester Guardian*, February 16, 1931, and "Mr. Gandhi and the Viceroy," *Times* (London), February 16, 1931.

20. Johnson, *Viscount Halifax*, p. 296; Tomlinson, *The Indian National Congress and the Raj*, p. 35; and Payne, *The Life and Death of Mahatma Gandhi*, p. 600.

21. "A General View," January 30, 1931; and "Conservative Differences on India," February 23, 1931, in Churchill, *India: Speeches*, pp. 81, 94.

22. Srinivasa Sastri to T. R. V. Sastri, February 17, 1931, in Brown, *Gandhi and Civil Disobedience*, p. 178; Bernays, "*Naked Faquir*," pp. 146, 172; and London, MS to LI, February 20, 1931, IOR, MSS. Eur. C. 152/1, p. 67.

23. Viceroy's Camp, India, LI to King George, March 13, 1931, ibid., p. 153; Delhi, LI to Halifax, March 10, 1931, ibid., p. 348; Lady Haig, "Party to Meet Mahatma Gandhi,

Delhi," extract from diary entry of April 1931, HSAS; Sir Francis Humphrys in Birkenhead, *Halifax*, p. 299; and Bernays, *"Naked Faquir,"* p. 184.

24. Ibid., pp. 147, 183; C. R. Rajagopalachari in Birkenhead, *Halifax*, p. 307; and Gopal, *The Viceroyalty of Lord Irwin*, p. 106.

25. Grierson, *The Imperial Dream*, p. 211; Hodgson, *Lord Halifax*, p. 136; and *PP*, "Round Table Conference (1930–31): Proceedings during the second session, 7th September to 1st December, 1931," vol. 8 (East India: Accounts and Papers), Cmd. 3997, 1931–2.

26. Bernays, *"Naked Faquir,"* p. 280.

27. Ibid., pp. 290–1; and Irwin, *Speeches*, 2: 384–5.

28. Steegman, *India Ink*, p. 24; and Spear, "The Mughals and the British," in Basham, ed., *A Cultural History of India*, p. 357.

# SELECT BIBLIOGRAPHY

Unpublished materials

*Great Britain*

Birmingham. University Library, University of Birmingham.
 Papers of Chamberlain, Sir Austen.

Cambridge. University Library, University of Cambridge.
 Papers of:
 Crewe, Robert Offley Ashburton Crewe-Milnes, first Marquess of. Secretary of State for India, 1910–15.
 Hardinge of Penshurst, Charles Hardinge, first Baron. Viceroy of India, 1910–16.

Cambridge. Centre of South Asian Studies, University of Cambridge.
 Papers of:
 Haig, Sir Harry Graham. Private Secretary to the Viceroy of India, 1925, and Secretary, Home Department of India, 1926–30.
 Haig, Lady (née Violet May Deas). Wife of Sir Harry Graham Haig.
 Medd, Henry Alexander Nesbitt. Resident Architect in Delhi representing Sir Herbert Baker, 1919–31.
 Sale, John Lewis. Superintending Engineer, New Delhi, 1925–34.

Cobham, Kent. Owletts.
 Papers and drawings of Baker, Sir Herbert. Property of Henry Edmeades Baker.

London. Ashley Gardens.
 Papers of Medd, Henry Alexander Nesbitt. Property of Mrs. Marjorie Lloyd Medd.

London. India Office Records.
 Papers of:
 Butler, Sir Harcourt. Education Member of the Viceroy's Council, 1910–15.
 Chelmsford, Frederic John Napier Thesiger, first Viscount. Viceroy of India, 1916–21.
 Curzon of Kedleston, George Nathaniel Curzon, first Marquess. Viceroy of India, 1899–1905.
 Fleetwood Wilson, Sir Guy. Finance Member of the Viceroy's Council, 1908–13, and Acting Viceroy, 1912.
 Hailey, William Malcolm Hailey, first Baron. First Chief Commissioner of Delhi and President of the Imperial Delhi Committee, 1912–18.

Halifax, Edward Frederick Lindley Wood, first Earl of. Viceroy of India, 1926–31, as first Baron Irwin.
Laithwaite, Sir Gilbert. Private Secretary to the Viceroy of India, 1936–43.
Montagu, Edwin Samuel. Parliamentary Under-Secretary of State for India, 1910–14, and Secretary of State for India, 1917–22.
Public Works Department, India Office.
Reading, Rufus Daniel Isaacs, first Marquess of. Viceroy of India, 1921–6.
Storrs Fox, Reverend Edwin Aubrey. Chaplain of New Delhi and Vicar, Church of the Redemption, New Delhi, 1928–31.
Templewood, Samuel John Gurney Hoare, first Viscount. Secretary of State for India, 1931–5.
Thompson, Sir John Perronet. Chief Commissioner of Delhi, 1928–32.
Willingdon, Freeman Freeman-Thomas, first Marquess of. Viceroy of India, 1931–6.

London.
 Papers of Lutyens, Lady Emily. Property of Miss Jane Ridley.

London. Royal Institute of British Architects, The British Architectural Library, Drawings Collection, Portman Square.
 Drawings of:
 Lutyens, Sir Edwin Landseer.
 Medd, Henry Alexander Nesbitt. Resident Architect representing Sir Herbert Baker, New Delhi, 1919–31.
 Shoosmith, Arthur Gordon. Resident Architect representing Sir Edwin Lutyens, New Delhi, 1920–31.

London. Royal Institute of British Architects, Sir Banister Fletcher Library, Portland Place.
 Papers of Lutyens, Sir Edwin Landseer.
 Manuscript reminiscences of Nicholls, William Henry. Architect Member of the Imperial Delhi Committee, 1913–17.

Maidstone, Kent. Kent County Archives Office.
 Papers of Hardinge of Penshurst, Charles Hardinge, first Baron.

Penshurst, Kent. South Park.
 Papers of Hardinge of Penshurst, Charles Hardinge, first Baron. Property of the Dowager Lady Hardinge of Penshurst.

Romsey, Hampshire. Broadlands. Mountbatten Archives. Papers of Mountbatten of Burma, Louis Mountbatten, first Earl.

Slindon, West Sussex.
Papers of Shoosmith, Arthur Gordon. Property of Mrs. Marjorie Cartwright Reid Shoosmith.

### India

Delhi. Delhi Public Administration Record Office.
Papers of the Office of the Chief Commissioner, Delhi. Includes papers of Hailey, William Malcolm Hailey, first Baron, 1912–18.

New Delhi. British Council Library.
Papers of George, Walter Sykes. Resident Architect representing Sir Herbert Baker, 1915–24.

New Delhi. Central Public Works Department, Government of India, Drawings Archives, Nirman Bhavan.
Office drawings for New Delhi, 1913– .

New Delhi. National Archives of India, Government of India.
Papers of:
Government of India, Home Department: Delhi.
Government of India, Home Department: Political.
Government of India, Home Department: Public.
Government of India, Central Public Works Department.

### PUBLISHED MATERIALS

#### Government publications: Great Britain

London. India Office Library and Records.
*Native Newspaper Reports.*
Bengal, 1911–16.
Bombay, 1911–21.
Madras, 1911–21.
Northwestern Provinces and United Provinces, 1911–31.
Punjab, 1911–24.

*Parliamentary Debates*, House of Commons, 5th series, vols. 32–260, 1911–31.

*Parliamentary Debates*, House of Lords, 5th series, vols. 10–81, 1911–31.

*Parliamentary Papers.*
"Announcments by and on Behalf of His Majesty the King-Emperor at the Coronation Durbar, Held at Delhi on the 12th December 1911, with Correspondence Relating Thereto," vol. 55 (East India: Accounts and Papers), Cd. 5979, 1911.
"Correspondence Relating to the Attempt upon the Life of His Excellency the Viceroy and Governor General, on the occasion of the State Entry into Delhi, on 23rd December, 1912," vol. 61 (East India: Accounts and Papers), Cd. 6642, 1912–13.
"First Report of the Delhi Town Planning Committee on the Choice of a Site for the New Imperial Captial, with Two Maps," vol. 20 (East India: Reports of Commissioners), Cd. 6885, 1913.

"Second Report of the Delhi Town Planning Committee Regarding the North Site, with Medical Report and Two Maps," vol. 20 (East India: Reports of Commissioners), Cd. 6888, 1913.
"Final Report of the Delhi Town Planning Committee Regarding the Selected Site, with Plan and Two Maps," vol. 20 (East India: Reports of Commissioners), Cd. 6889, 1913.

#### Government publications: India

Delhi Province, Administration of the. *Report on the Administration of the Delhi Province.* Delhi: Government of India Press, 1913–32.

India, Government of. Council of State. *Proceedings*, vols. 1–9, 1921–7.

India, Government of. Legislative Assembly. *Proceedings*, vols. 1–8, 1921–7.

India, Government of. Legislative Council. *Proceedings*, vols. 49–58, 1910–20.

India, Government of. Consulting Architect. *Annual Report on Architectural Work in India*, 1907–18. Calcutta: Superintendent, Government Printing, India, 1908–19.

India, Government of. Department of Industries and Labour. Public Works Branch. *Review of Architectural Work in India, 1918–1921.* Calcutta: Superintendent, Government Printing, India, 1923.

India, Government of. Public Works Department. *Annual Progress Report for the New Capital Project at Delhi.* Delhi: Government of India Press, 1915–32.

### Books

Allen, Charles, ed. *Plain Tales from the Raj.* New York: St. Martin's, 1976.
———. *Raj: A Scrapbook of British India, 1877–1947.* Harmondsworth, Middlesex: Penguin, 1979.

Baker, Sir Herbert. *Architecture and Personalities.* London: Country Life, 1944.
———. *Cecil Rhodes by His Architect.* London: Oxford University Press, Humphrey Milford, 1934.

Balfour, Andrew. *Note on Housing in the Tropics.* Government of India, Public Works Department, Technical Publication no. 37. Calcutta: Superintendent, Government Printing, India, 1921.

Banerjea, Sir Surendranath. *A Nation in the Making: Being the Reminiscences of Fifty Years of Public Life.* London: Oxford University Press, Humphrey Milford, 1925.

Basham, Arthur Llewellyn, ed. *A Cultural History of India.* Oxford: Oxford University Press, Clarendon Press, 1975.

Beloff, Max. *Britain's Liberal Empire.* Imperial Sunset, vol. 1. London: Methuen, 1969.

Bence-Jones, Mark. *Palaces of the Raj: Magnificence and Misery of the Lord Sahibs.* London: George Allen & Unwin, 1973.

Benson, Arthur Christopher, and Weaver, Sir Lawrence, eds. *The Queen's Doll House*. London: Daily Telegraph and Methuen & Co., 1924.

Bernays, Robert. *"Naked Faquir."* New York: Henry Holt, 1932.

Bernier, François. *Travels in the Mogul Empire, A.D. 1656–1668*. Translated and annotated by Archibald Constable, 2nd. ed. rev. by Vincent A. Smith. London: Oxford University Press, Humphrey Milford, 1916.

Birkenhead, Frederick Winston Furneaux Smith, second Earl of. *Halifax: The Life of Lord Halifax*. Boston: Houghton Mifflin, 1966.

Birrell, James. *Walter Burley Griffin*. Brisbane: University of Queensland Press, 1964.

Blomfield, Sir Reginald. *Memoirs of an Architect*. London: Macmillan, 1932.

Bogle, James Main Linton. *Town Planning in India*. India of Today, vol. 9. Bombay: Oxford University Press, Humphrey Milford, 1929.

Bolitho, Hector. *James Lyle Mackay, First Earl of Inchcape*. London: John Murray, 1936.

Bopegamage, A. *Delhi: A Study in Urban Sociology*. Bombay: University of Bombay, 1957.

Breese, Gerald William. *Urban and Regional Planning for Delhi–New Delhi*. Princeton. N.J.: Princeton University Press, 1974.

Brown, Frank E. *Roman Architecture*. New York: George Braziller, 1961.

Brown, Glenn. *History of the United States Capitol*. 2 vols. Washington, D.C.: Government Printing Office, 1900–3.

Brown, Judith M. *Gandhi and Civil Disobedience: The Mahatma in Indian Politics, 1928–34*. Cambridge: Cambridge University Press, 1977.

———. *Gandhi's Rise to Power: Indian Politics, 1915–1922*. Cambridge: Cambridge University Press, 1972.

Brown, Percy. *Indian Architecture: Buddhist and Hindu Periods*. 5th ed. Bombay: D. B. Taraporevala Sons & Co., 1965.

———. *Indian Architecture: Islamic Period*. 5th ed. Bombay: D. B. Taraporevala Sons & Co., 1968.

Burchard, John Ely and Bush-Brown, Albert. *The Architecture of America: A Social and Cultural History*. Boston: Little, Brown, 1961.

Burnham, Daniel H., and Bennett, Edward H. *Plan of Chicago Prepared under the Direction of the Commercial Club during the Years MCMVI, MCMVII, and MCMVIII*. Edited by Charles Moore. Chicago: The Commercial Club, 1909.

Butler, Arthur Stanley George, with the collaboration of George Stewart and Christopher Hussey. *The Architecture of Sir Edwin Lutyens*. 3 vols. London: Country Life, 1950.

Butler, Iris. *The Viceroy's Wife: Letters of Alice, Countess of Reading, from India, 1921–25*. London: Hodder and Stoughton. 1969.

Campbell Johnson, Alan. *Viscount Halifax: A Biography*. London: R. Hale, 1941.

*Cathedral Fete Brochure*. New Delhi: Cathedral Church of the Redemption, 1969.

Chamberlain, Sir Austen. *Politics from the Inside: An Epistolary Chronicle, 1906–1914*. London: Cassell, 1936.

Chelmsford, Frederic John Napier Thesiger Chelmsford, first Viscount. *Speeches by Lord Chelmsford, Viceroy and Governor-General of India*. 2 vols. Simla: Government Monotype Press, 1919–21.

Chirol, Sir Valentine. *India Old and New*. London: Macmillan, 1921.

Choisy, Auguste. *L'art de bâtir chez les Byzantins*. Paris: La Société Anonyme de Publications Périodiques, 1883.

Churchill, Winston Spencer. *India: Speeches and an Introduction*. London: Thornton Butterworth, 1931.

Clarke, Basil Fulford Lowther. *Anglican Cathedrals outside the British Isles*. London: Society for the Propagation of Christian Knowledge, 1958.

Coatman, John. *Years of Destiny: India, 1926–1932*. London: Jonathan Cape, 1932.

Collins, Larry, and Lapierre, Dominique. *Freedom at Midnight*. New York: Avon, 1975.

Cooper, Duff, first Viscount Norwich. *Old Men Forget: The Autobiography of Duff Cooper*. London: Hart-Davis, 1953.

Creese, Walter Littlefield. *The Search for Environment: The Garden City, Before and After*. New Haven: Yale University Press, 1966.

Crowe, Sylvia; Haywood, Sheila; Jellicoe, Susan; and Patterson, Gordon. *The Gardens of Mughal India*. London: Thames and Hudson, 1977.

Cullen, Gordon. *Townscape*. New York: Van Nostrand Reinhold, 1971.

———. *The Ninth Delhi*, New Delhi: Government of India Press, 1961.

Curzon of Kedleston, George Nathaniel Curzon, first Marquess. *British Government in India: The Story of the Viceroys and Government Houses*. 2 vols. London: Cassell, 1925.

———. *Speeches by Lord Curzon of Kedleston, Viceroy and Governor-General of India*. 4 vols. Calcutta: Office of the Superintendent of Government Printing, India, 1900–6.

Davidson, John. *Self's the Man: A Tragi-Comedy*. London: Grant Richards, 1901.

Dunster, David, ed. *Edwin Lutyens*. Architectural Monographs, vol. 6. London: Academy Editions, 1979.

Earle, Sir Lionel. *Turn Over the Page*. London: Hutchinson, 1935.

Evelyn, John. *The Diary of John Evelyn*. Edited by E. S. de Beer. 6 vols. Oxford: Oxford University Press, 1955.

Fergusson, James. *History of Indian and Eastern Architecture*. 2 vols. New York: Dodd, Mead, 1891.

Ferrell, Donald W. "Delhi, 1911–22: Society and Politics in the New Imperial Capital of India." Ph.D. dissertation, Australian National University, Canberra, 1969.

Ferriday, Peter, ed. *Victorian Architecture*. London: Jonathan Cape, 1963.

Fitzroy, Yvonne. *Courts and Camps in India: Impressions of Viceregal Tours, 1921–1924*. London: Methuen, 1926.

Forbes, Rosita. *India of the Princes*. London: The Book Club, 1939.

Fortescue, Hon. John. *Narrative of the Visit to India of Their Majesties King George V and Queen Mary and of the Coronation Durbar Held at Delhi 12th December 1911*. London: Macmillan, 1912.

Frampton, Kenneth. *Modern Architecture: A Critical History*. New York: Oxford University Press, 1980.

Fraser, Lovat. *At Delhi*. Bombay: Times of India Press, Thacker, 1903.

––––––. *India under Curzon and After*. London: William Heinemann, 1911.

Glendevon, John Adrian Hope, first Baron. *The Viceroy at Bay: Lord Linlithgow in India, 1936–1943*. London: Collins, 1971.

Gokhale, Gopal Krishna. *Speeches and Writings of Gopal Krishna Gokhale*. Edited by R. P. Patwardhan and D. V. Ambeker. 3 vols. Bombay: Asia Publishing House, 1962–7.

Golant, William. *The Long Afternoon: British India, 1601–1947*. London: Hamish Hamilton, 1975.

Goodhart-Rendel, Harry Stuart. *English Architecture Since the Regency: An Interpretation*. London: Constable, 1953.

Gopal, Sarvepalli. *The Viceroyalty of Lord Irwin, 1926–1931*. Oxford: Oxford University Press, Clarendon Press, 1957.

Gordon, Leonard A. *Bengal: The Nationalistic Movement, 1876–1940*. New York: Columbia University Press, 1974.

Gore, John Francis. *King George V: A Personal Memoir*. New York: Scribner's, 1941.

Gowans, Alan. *Images of American Living: Four Centuries of Architecture and Furniture as Cultural Expression*. Philadelphia: Lippincott, 1964.

Gradidge, Roderick. "Edwin Lutyens: The Last High Victorian." In *Seven Victorian Architects*, edited by Jane Fawcett. London: Thames and Hudson, 1976.

Graham, Maria. *Journal of a Residence in India*. 2nd ed. Edinburgh: Constable, 1813.

Greig, Doreen E. *Herbert Baker in South Africa*. Cape Town: Purnell, 1970.

Griffin, Walter Burley. *The Federal Capital: Report Explanatory of the Preliminary General Plan*. Melbourne: Commonwealth of Australia, Dept of Home Affairs, 1913.

Halifax, Edward Frederick Lindley Wood, first Earl of. *Fulness of Days*. London: Collins, 1957.

––––––. *Speeches by Lord Irwin, 1926–1931*. 2 vols. Simla: Government of India Press, 1930–1.

Hambly, Gavin. *Cities of Mughal India: Delhi, Agra, and Fatehpur Sikri*. New York: Putnam, 1968.

Hardinge of Penshurst, Charles Hardinge, first Baron. *My Indian Years, 1910–1916: The Reminiscences of Lord Hardinge of Penshurst*. London: John Murray, 1948.

––––––. *Old Diplomacy: The Reminiscences of Lord Hardinge of Penshurst*. London: John Murray, 1947.

––––––. *Speeches by Lord Hardinge of Penshurst, Viceroy and Governor-General of India*. 3 vols. Calcutta: Superintendent of the Government Printing Office of India, 1913–16.

Havell, Ernest Binfield. *The Building of the New Delhi*. Guildford, Surrey: Billing & Sons, n.d., *c.* 1912.

––––––. *A Handbook of Indian Art*. London: John Murray, 1920.

––––––. *Indian Architecture: Its Psychology, Structure, and History from the First Muhammadan Invasion to the Present Day*. 2nd ed. London: John Murray, 1913.

Heber, Bishop Reginald. *Narrative of a Journey through the Upper Provinces of India from Calcutta to Bombay, 1824–25*. Edited by Amelia Heber. 5th ed. 2 vols. London: John Murray, 1844.

Hitchcock, Henry Russell. *Architecture: Nineteenth and Twentieth Centuries*. 3rd ed., reissued. Harmondsworth, Middlesex: Penguin, 1971.

Hodgson, Stuart. *Lord Halifax: An Appreciation*. London: Christophers, 1941.

Howard, Ebenezer. *Garden Cities of To-Morrow*. Edited, with a preface, by Frederick J. Osborn, and with an introductory essay by Lewis Mumford. 1902. Reprint. Cambridge, Mass.: M.I.T. Press, 1965.

Howes, Peter Norris. *Viceregal Establishments in India*. New Delhi: Governor-General's Press. 1949.

Hussey, Christopher. *The Life of Sir Edwin Lutyens*. London: Country Life, 1950.

Hyde, Harford Montgomery. *Lord Reading: The Life of Rufus Isaacs, First Marquess of Reading*. London: Heinemann, 1967.

India, Government of. *The Historical Record of the Imperial Visit to India, 1911, Compiled from the Official Records under the Orders of the Viceroy and Governor-General of India*. London: John Murray, for the Government of India, 1914.

Irving, Robert Grant. "Indian Summer: Imperial Delhi." Ph.D. dissertation, Yale University, 1978.

Ismay, Hastings Lionel Ismay, first Baron. *The Memoirs of General Lord Ismay*. New York: Viking, 1960.

James Henry. *English Hours*. Edited by Alma Louise Howe. London: Mercury, 1963.

Joly, Jean-Baptiste-Jules de. *Plans, coupes, élévations et détails de la restauration de la Chambre des Deputés, de sa nouvelle Salle des Séances, de la bibliotheque et de toutes ses dependances, suivis de la salle provisoire.* Paris: A. Le Clerc, 1840.

Kincaid, Dennis. *British Social Life in India, 1608–1937.* 2nd ed. London: Routledge and Kegan Paul, 1973.

King, Anthony D. *Colonial Urban Development: Culture, Social Power and Environment.* London: Routledge & Kegan Paul, 1976.

King, Joseph. *Empire and Craftsmanship.* Plymouth: William Brendon, 1913.

Kipling, Rudyard. *Rudyard Kipling's Verse, Inclusive Edition, 1885–1918.* Garden City, N.Y.: Doubleday, 1922.

Lanchester, Henry Vaughan. *The Art of Town Planning.* New York: Scribner's, 1925.

Lester, Alfred W. *Hampstead Garden Suburb: The Care and Appreciation of Its Architectural Heritage.* London: Hampstead Garden Suburb Design Study Group, 1977.

Lord, John. *The Maharajahs.* New York: Random House, 1971.

Lothian, Sir Arthur Cunningham. *Kingdoms of Yesterday.* London: John Murray, 1951.

Low, Donald Anthony, ed. *Soundings in Modern South Asian History.* Berkeley: University of California Press, 1968.

Lutyens, Sir Edwin Landseer. Foreword to *Gertrude Jekyll: A Memoir,* by Francis Jekyll. London: Jonathan Cape, 1934.

Lutyens, Elisabeth. *A Goldfish Bowl.* London: Cassell, 1972.

Lutyens, Lady Emily. *Candles in the Sun.* London: Rupert Hart-Davis, 1957.

———, and Elwin, Whitwell. *A Blessed Girl: Memoirs of a Victorian Childhood, Chronicled in an Exchange of Letters, 1887–1896.* London: Rupert Hart-Davis, 1953.

Lutyens, Mary. *Edwin Lutyens.* London: John Murray, 1980.

———. *To Be Young: Some Chapters of Autobiography.* London: Rupert Hart-Davis, 1959.

Lutyens, Robert. *Six Great Architects: Inigo Jones, Sir Christopher Wren, Sir John Vanbrugh, the Adam Brothers, John Nash, Sir Edwin Lutyens.* London: Hamish Hamilton, 1959.

———. *Sir Edwin Lutyens: An Appreciation in Perspective.* London: Country Life, 1942.

Lytton, Victor Alexander George Robert Bulwer-Lytton, second Earl of. *Pundits and Elephants: Being the Experiences of Five Years as Governor of an Indian Province.* London: Peter Davies, 1942.

MacDonald, William Lloyd. *The Architecture of the Roman Empire, I: An Introductory Study.* New Haven: Yale University Press, 1965.

———. *The Pantheon: Design, Meaning, and Progeny.* Cambridge, Mass.: Harvard University Press, 1976.

MacLeod, Robert. *Style and Society: Architectural Ideology in Britain, 1835–1914.* London: RIBA Publications, 1971.

Mason, Philip [Woodruff, Philip]. *The Men Who Ruled India.* 2 vols. London: Jonathan Cape, 1953–4.

Massingham, Betty. *Miss Jekyll: Portrait of a Great Gardener.* London: Country Life, 1966.

Masson, Madeleine. *Edwina: The Biography of the Countess Mountbatten of Burma.* 1960. Reprint. London: White Lion, 1975.

Mehrotra, S. R. *India and the Commonwealth, 1885–1929.* New York: Praeger, 1965.

Menon, Vapal Pangunni. *The Story of the Integration of the Indian States.* Calcutta: Orient Longmans, 1956.

Mersey, Charles Clive Bigham, second Viscount. *The Viceroys and Governors-General of India, 1757–1947.* London: John Murray, 1949.

Minto, Mary Caroline Elliott-Murray-Kynynmound, Countess of. *India, Minto and Morley, 1905–1910.* London: Macmillan, 1934.

Mitra, Asok. *Delhi: Capital City.* New Delhi: Thomson Press (India), 1970.

Mitter, Partha. *Much Maligned Monsters: History of European Reactions to Indian Art,* Oxford: Oxford University Press, Clarendon Press, 1977.

Montagu, Edwin Samuel. *An Indian Diary.* Edited by Venetia Montagu. London: Heinemann, 1930.

Moore, Charles. *Daniel H. Burnham: Architect, Planner of Cities.* 2 vols. Boston: Houghton Mifflin, 1921.

Moore, Robin James. *Liberalism and Indian Politics: 1872–1922.* London: Edward Arnold, 1966.

Morris, James. *Pax Britannica: The Climax of an Empire.* London: Faber and Faber, 1968.

Mosley, Leonard Oswald. *The Last Days of the British Raj.* London: Weidenfeld and Nicolson. 1961.

Mountbatten of Burma, Louis Mountbatten, first Earl. *Time Only to Look Forward: Speeches of Rear Admiral the Earl Mountbatten of Burma as Viceroy of India and Governor-General of the Dominion of India, 1947–48.* London: Nicholas Kaye, 1949.

Moynihan, Elizabeth B. *Paradise as a Garden in Persia and Mughal India.* New York: Braziller, 1979.

Nehru, Jawaharlal. *The Discovery of India.* New York: John Day, 1946.

———. *Toward Freedom: The Autobiography of Jawaharlal Nehru.* New York: John Day, 1941.

Nicolson, Hon. Sir Harold George. *King George the Fifth: His Life and Reign.* London: Constable, 1952.

Nilsson, Sten. *European Architecture in India, 1750–1850.* London: Faber and Faber, 1968.

————. *The New Capitals of India, Pakistan and Bangladesh.* Scandinavian Institute of Asian Studies Monograph Series, no. 12. Lund, Sweden: Studentlitteratur, 1973.

Northcliffe, Alfred Northcliffe, first Baron. *My Journey Round the World (16 July 1921–26 Feb. 1922).* Edited by Cecil and St. John Harmsworth. Philadelphia: Lippincott, 1923.

O'Neill, Daniel. *Sir Edwin Lutyens: Country Houses.* London: Lund Humphries, 1980.

Padover, Saul K., ed. *Thomas Jefferson and the National Capital, Containing Notes and Correspondence Exchanged Between Jefferson, Washington, L'Enfant, Ellicott, Hallett, Thornton, Latrobe, and Commissioners, and Others, Relating to the Founding, Surveying, Planning, Designing, Constructing, and Administering of the City of Washington, 1783–1818.* Washington, D.C.: United States Government Printing Office, 1946.

Palladio, Andrea. *The Four Books of Architecture.* Trans. Isaac Ware, 1738. Reprint. New York: Dover Publications, 1965.

Parkinson, Cyril Northcote. *Parkinson's Law and Other Studies in Administration.* Boston: Houghton Mifflin, 1957.

Parvate, Trimbak Vishnu. *Gopal Krishna Gokhale: A Narrative and Interpretative Review of His Life, Career and Contemporary Events.* Ahmedabad: Navajivan Press, 1959.

Patte, Pierre. *Mémoires sur les objets les plus importans de l'architecture.* Paris: Rozet, 1769.

————. *Monumens érigés en France à la gloire de Louis XV, précédés d'un tableau du progrès des arts et des sciences sous ce règne, ainsi que d'une description des honneurs et des monumens de gloire accordés aux grande hommes, tant chez les anciens que chez les modernes; et suivis d'un choix des principaux projets qui ont été proposés, pour placer la statue du roi dans les differens quartiers de Paris: par M. Patte.* Paris: A. Guerinet, 1765.

Payne, Robert. *The Life and Death of Mahatma Gandhi.* New York: Dutton, 1969.

Pellenc, Baron Jean. *Diamonds and Dust: India Through French Eyes.* Trans. Stuart Gilbert. London: John Murray, 1936.

Petrie, Sir Charles. *The Life and Letters of the Rt. Hon. Sir Austen Chamberlain.* 2 vols. London: Cassell, 1939–40.

Pevsner, Nikolaus. *A History of Building Types.* Princeton, N.J.: Princeton University Press, Bollingen Series, 1976.

Philips, Cyril Henry, ed. *Politics and Society in India.* New York: Praeger, 1962.

————. with Singh, H. L. and Pandey, B. N. *The Evolution of India and Pakistan, 1858 to 1947: Select Documents.* London: Oxford University Press, 1962.

Pope-Hennessy, James. *Lord Crewe, 1858–1945: The Likeness of a Liberal.* London: Constable, 1955.

Pott, Janet. *Old Bungalows in Bangalore, South India.* London: Janet Pott, 1977.

Pound, Reginald and Harmsworth, Geoffrey. *Northcliffe.* New York: Praeger, 1959.

Rao, Vijendra Kasturi Ranga Varadaraja and Desai, P. B. *Greater Delhi: A Study in Urbanisation, 1940–1957.* Bombay: Asia Publishing House, 1965.

Reading, Eva Isaacs, Marchioness of. *For the Record: The Memoirs of Eva, Marchioness of Reading.* London: Hutchinson, 1973.

Reading, Gerald Rufus Isaacs, second Marquess of. *Rufus Isaacs, First Marquess of Reading.* 2 vols. London: Hutchinson, 1942–5.

Reading, Rufus Daniel Isaacs, first Marquess of. *Speeches of the Earl of Reading, 1921–1926.* Simla: Government of India Press, 1924–6.

Reed, Stanley. *The India I Knew, 1897–1947.* London: Odham's, 1952.

Reilly, Sir Charles Herbert. *Representative British Architects of the Present Day.* London: B. T. Batsford, 1931.

————. *Scaffolding in the Sky: A Semi-architectural Autobiography.* London: George Routledge, 1938.

Reps, John William. *The Making of Urban America: A History of City Planning in the United States.* Princeton, N.J.: Princeton University Press, 1965.

Robertson, John Henry [John Connell]. *Auchinleck: A Biography of Field-Marshall Sir Claude Auchinleck.* 2nd ed. London: Cassell, 1959.

Rosenau, Helen. *The Ideal City: Its Architectural Evolution.* New York: Harper & Row, Icon Editions, 1972.

Royal Institute of British Architects. *Catalogue of the Drawings Collection of the Royal Institute of British Architects.* Vols. 9, 13. Edited by Margaret Richardson. Farnborough, Hampshire: Gregg International, 1973, 1976.

Rudra, Abani Bhushan. *The Viceroy and Governor-General of India.* London: Oxford University Press, Humphrey Milford, 1940.

Rumbold, Sir Algernon. *Watershed in India, 1914–1922.* London: Athlone Press, 1979.

Saint, Andrew. *Richard Norman Shaw.* London: Yale University Press, 1976.

Sanderson, Gordon. *Report on Modern Indian Architecture.* Allahabad: Government of India Press, 1913.

Sandison, Alan. *The Wheel of Empire: A Study of the Imperial Idea in Some Late Nineteenth and Early Twentieth-Century Fiction.* London: Macmillan, 1967.

Sarkar, Jadunath. *Studies in Mughal India.* Calcutta: M. C. Sarker, 1919.

Scholfield, Peter Hugh. *The Theory of Proportion in Architecture.* Cambridge: At the University Press, 1958.

Sekler, Eduard. *Wren and His Place in European Architecture.* New York: Macmillan, 1956.

Service, Alastair. *Edwardian Architecture: A Handbook to Building Design in Britain, 1890–1914.* New York: Oxford University Press, 1977.

———. *Edwardian Architecture and Its Origins.* London: Architectural Press, 1975.

Sharp, Sir Henry. *Good-Bye India.* London: Oxford University Press, 1946.

Sharp, Thomas. *Town and Countryside: Some Aspects of Urban and Rural Development.* London: Oxford University Press, 1932.

Singh, Khushwant. *Khushwant Singh's India: A Mirror for its Monsters and Monstrosities.* Edited by Rahul Singh. Bombay: IBH, 1969.

Smith, Earl Baldwin. *Architectural Symbolism of Imperial Rome and the Middle Ages.* Princeton, N.J.: Princeton University Press, 1956.

———. *The Dome: A Study in the History of Ideas.* Princeton, N.J.: Princeton University Press, 1950.

Smith, Vincent Arthur. *The Oxford History of India.* Edited by Percival Spear. 3rd ed. Oxford: Clarendon Press, 1958.

Spear, Thomas George Percival. *A History of India.* Harmondsworth, Middlesex: Penguin, 1965.

———. *Delhi: A Historical Sketch.* Bombay: Oxford University Press, Humphrey Milford, 1937.

———. *Delhi: Its Monuments and History.* Bombay: Oxford University Press, Humphrey Milford, 1945.

———. "Mughal Delhi and Agra." In *Cities of Destiny,* edited by Arnold Toynbee. New York: McGraw-Hill, 1967.

———. *Twilight of the Mughals: Studies in Late Mughal Delhi.* Cambridge: At the University Press, 1951.

Speer, Albert. *Inside the Third Reich.* Translated by Richard and Clara Winston. New York: Macmillan, 1970.

Stamp, Gavin and Llewellyn Smith, Arthur. *Henry Alexander Nesbitt Medd.* London: Art Workers Guild, 1977.

Stanhope, Philip Henry Stanhope, fifth Earl. *Notes of Conversations with the Duke of Wellington, 1831–1851.* New York: Longmans, Green, 1888.

Steegman, Philip. *India Ink.* New York: William Morrow, 1940.

Tavernier, Jean-Baptiste, Baron of Aubonne. *Travels in India.* Translated by V. Ball, and edited by William Crooke. 2nd ed. 2 vols. London: Oxford University Press, Humphrey Milford, 1925.

Tendulkar, Dinapath Gopal. *Mahatma: Life of Mohandas Karamchand Gandhi.* New ed., rev. 8 vols. Delhi: Publications Division, Ministry of Information and Broadcasting, Government of India, 1960–3.

Thakore, M. P. "Aspects of the Urban Geography of New Delhi." Ph.D. dissertation, University of London, 1962.

Thévenot, Jean de. *The Travels of Monsieur de Thévenot into the Levant.* Translated by A. Lovell. London: Henry Clark, 1687.

Thompson, Edward J. *The Making of the Indian Princes.* London: Oxford University Press, Humphrey Milford, 1943.

Tomlinson, B. R. *The Indian National Congress and the Raj, 1929–1942: The Penultimate Phase.* London: Macmillan, 1976.

Trevelyan, Humphrey Trevelyan, first Baron. *The India We Left.* London: Macmillan, 1972.

Unwin, Raymond. "On the Building of Houses in the Garden City." In *The Garden City Conference at Bournville.* London: Garden City Association, 1901.

———. *Town Planning in Practice: An Introduction to the Art of Designing Cities and Suburbs.* 2nd ed. London: T. Fisher Unwin, 1911.

Valentia, George Annesley, ninth Viscount (later second Earl of Mountnorris). *Voyages and Travels to India, Ceylon, the Red Sea, Abyssinia, and Egypt in the Years 1802, 1803, 1804, 1805 and 1806.* 3 vols. London: William Miller, 1809.

Venturi, Robert. *Complexity and Contradiction in Architecture.* 2nd ed. New York: Museum of Modern Art, 1977.

Villiers-Stuart, Constance. *Gardens of the Great Mogals.* London: Adam and Charles Black, 1913.

Vitruvius Pollio. *On Architecture,* 2 vols. Translated by Frank Granger. London: Heinemann, 1962.

Waley, Sir Sigismund David. *Edwin Montagu: A Memoir and an Account of His Visit to India.* London: Asia Publishing House, 1964.

Weaver, Sir Lawrence. *Houses and Gardens by E. L. Lutyens.* London: Country Life, 1913.

———. *Lutyens Houses and Gardens.* 2nd ed. London: Country Life, 1921.

———. *Lutyens Houses and Gardens.* 3rd ed. London: Country Life, 1925.

Wheeler, Sir Charles. *High Relief: The Autobiography of Sir Charles Wheeler, Sculptor.* Feltham, Middlesex: Country Life, 1968.

Wheeler, Sir Mortimer. *Roman Art and Architecture.* New York: Praeger, 1964.

———. "The Vision Turns Inward: The Art and Architecture of a World Empire." In *The Birth of Western Civilization: Greece and Rome,* edited by Michael Grant. New York: McGraw-Hill, 1964.

Wigmore, Lionel. *The Long View: A History of Australia's National Capital.* Melbourne: F. W. Cheshire, 1963.

Wilber, Donald Newton. *Persian Gardens and Garden Pavilions.* Rutland, Vermont: Charles E. Tuttle, 1962.

Wildeblood, H. S. *Note on the Problem of Roofs in the Plains of India.* Government of India, Public Works Department, Technical Publication no. 1. Calcutta: Superintendent, Government Printing, India, 1906.

Windsor, H.R.H. Prince Edward, Duke of. *A King's Story: The Memoirs of the Duke of Windsor.* New York: Putnam's, 1947.

Wolpert, Stanley A. *Tilak and Gokhale: Revolution and Reform in the Making of Modern India.* Berkeley: University of California Press, 1961.

Wortley, Violet Stuart. _Grow Old Along With Me._ London: Secker & Warburg, 1952.

Wren, Christopher (1675–1747), comp. _Parentalia: or, Memoirs of the Family of the Wrens; viz. of Matthew, Bishop of Ely, Christopher, Dean of Windsor, etc. but Chiefly of Sir Christopher Wren, Late Surveyor-General of the Royal Buildings, President of the Royal Society, etc., etc._ London: Printed for T. Osborn & R. Dodsley, 1750.

Zetland, Lawrence John Lumley Dundas, second Marquess of. _Essayez: Memoirs._ London: John Murray, 1956.

Zucker, Paul. _Town and Square: From the Agora to the Village Green._ New York: Colombia University Press, 1959.

## Periodical Articles

"A.A. Ordinary General Meeting." _Architectural Association Journal_ 36 (November 1920): 56.

Adshead, Stanley Davenport. "The Architecture of Delhi." _Architects' & Builders' Journal_ 36 (December 11, 1912): 617–18.

———. "The Town Planning Conference of the Royal Institute of British Architects." _Town Planning Review_ 1 (October 1910): 181.

"Architecture at the Royal Academy." _Builder_ 122 (May 12, 1922): 718–19.

Bagenal, Philip Hope Edward. "The Acoustics of the New Legislative Chamber at Delhi." _Architect and Building News_ 121 (June 28, 1929): 851–2.

Baker, Sir Herbert. "Architectural Design: Symbolism in Stone and Marble." _Times_ (London), "India Number," February 18, 1930.

———. "The Architectural Needs of South África." _State_ (Johannesburg) 1 (May 1909): 512–24.

———. "The Government Offices of Pretoria and the New Delhi." _Journal of the Royal Institute of British Architects_ 35 (December 10, 1927): 63–77.

———. "The New Delhi." _Journal of the Royal Society of Arts_ 74 (July 2, 1926): 772–93.

———. "The Story of the Union Buildings." _South Africa_ (London) 207 (August 23, 1941): 122–3.

———. Symbolic Constellation of the Empire," _United Empire_ 28 (October 1937): 561–4.

Betjeman, Sir John. "Memorial to a Great Architect, Sir Edwin Lutyens." _Country Life_ 109 (February 2, 1951): 324–5.

Binney, Marcus. "An Architecture of Law and Order: The Lutyens Centenary Exhibition at the RIBA." _Country Life_ 145 (April 10, 1969): 867–77.

Brandon-Jones, John; Hussey, Christopher; Bagenal, Hope; Furneaux Jordan, Robert; Farquharson, Horace; Milne, Oswald Partridge; Hannen, Nicholas; Worthington. Sir Hubert; Green, W. Curtis; Shoosmith, Arthur Gordon; Medd, Henry Alexander Nesbitt; Hall, H. Austen; and Butler, A.S.G. "Memories of Sir Edwin Lutyens: Nostalgia at the AA." _Builder_ 116 (February 13, 1959): 318–19.

———. "Reminiscences on Sir Edwin Lutyens." _Architectural Association Journal_ 74 (March 1959): 226–36.

Brett, Lionel, fourth Viscount Esher. "The Cyma and the Hollyhock." _Architectural Review_ 93 (March 1943): 80–1.

———. "The New Haussmann." _Architectural Review_ 93 (January 1943): 24–5.

Briggs, Cecil C. "The 'Pantheon' of Ostia (and Its Immediate Surroundings)." _Memoirs of the American Academy in Rome_ 8 (1930): 161–9.

"British Architects' Conference, London, 20 to 25 June 1927: The Annual Banquet, Presentation of the Royal Gold Medal to Sir Herbert Baker, A.R.A." _Journal of the Royal Institute of British Architects_ 34 (July 16, 1927): 591–600.

Brown, Percy. "The Mural Paintings at New Delhi." _Indian State Railways Magazine_ 4 (February 1931): 392–400.

Byron, Robert. "New Delhi." _Architectural Review_ 69 (January 1931): 1–30.

———. "New Delhi, I: The Architecture of the Viceroy's House." _Country Life_ 69 (June 6, 1931): 708–16.

———. "New Delhi, II: The Interior of the Viceroy's House." _Country Life_ 69 (June 13, 1931): 754–61.

———. "New Delhi, III: The Decoration of the Viceroy's House." _Country Life_ 69 (June 20, 1931): 782–9.

———. "New Delhi, IV: The Settings of the Viceroy's House." _Country Life_ 69 (June 27, 1931): 808–15.

———. "New Delhi, V: The Architecture of Sir Herbert Baker." _Country Life_ 70 (July 4, 1931): 12–19.

Byrt, A. H. "The Council House." _Indian State Railways Magazine_ 4 (February 1931): 385–91.

Chipkin, Clive M. "Lutyens and Imperialism," letter to the editor. _Journal of the Royal Institute of British Architects_ 76 (July 1969): 263.

———. "New Delhi." _South African Architectural Record_ 43 (November 1958): 21–8.

Davies, C. Collin. "Calcutta as Capital: The Objections of Warren Hastings." _Journal of the East India Association_ n.s. 24 (April 1933): 139–44.

"Delhi." _Builder_ 140 (February 13, 1931): 310–11, 319–21.

"Delhi." _Town Planning Review_ 3 (October 1912): 167–8.

"Edwin Landseer Lutyens (1869–1944)." _Architects' Journal_ 99 (January 6, 1944): 2–4.

Eustis, F. A. II and Zaidi, Z. H. "King, Viceroy and Cabinet: The Modification of the Partition of Bengal, 1911." _History_ n.s. 49 (June 1964): 171–84.

"Examples of Recent Architecture." _Country Life_ 70 (December 12, 1931): 674.

Falkner, Harold. "The Late Sir Edwin Lutyens." _Builder_ 166 (January 14, 1944): 31–2.

Franklin, Jill. "Edwardian Butterfly Houses." _Architectural Review_ 157 (March 1975): 220–5.

Furst, Herbert Ernest Augustus. "Mr. Fyzee Rahamin's Decorations at Delhi." _Apollo_ 10 (July 29): 11–16.

"The Future of Hull: THe Lutyens–Abercrombie Planning Report." *Builder* 171 (November 1, 1946): 448–51.

"The Garrison Church, New Delhi." *Architect and Building News* 127 (September 11, 1931): 293–5.

Gebhard, David. "The Viceroy's House in New Delhi." *Sunday Times Magazine* (London), May 14, 1972, pp. 18–30.

Goodhart-Rendel, Harry Stuart. "Lutyens and His Work." *Builder* 168 (February 16, 1945): 127–31.

———. "Sir Edwin Lutyens, O.M., P.R.A." *Journal of the Royal Institute of British Architects* 51 (January 1944): 51–2.

———. "The Work of the Late Sir Edwin Lutyens, O.M." *Architect and Building News* 181 (February 16, 1945): 107–13.

———. "The Work of the Late Sir Edwin Lutyens, O.M., lecture, with discussion. R.I.B.A., February 13, 1945." *Journal of the Royal Institute of British Architects* 52 (March 1945): 123–9.

"Government House, Delhi." *Builder* 116 (May 9, 1919): 454.

"The Government Offices of Pretoria and the New Delhi." *Builder* 133 (November 25, 1927): 809–10.

Green, W. Curtis. "Sir Edwin Lutyens, O.M., P.R.A." *Journal of the Royal Institute of British Architects* 51 (January 1944): 52–3.

Greenberg, Allan. "Lutyens' Architecture Restudied." *Perspecta* 12 (1969): 129–52.

Gupta, Narayani. "Military Security and Urban Development: A Case Study of Delhi, 1857–1912." *Modern Asian Studies* 5 (January 1971): 61–77.

Harvey, William. "Some Minor Problems of a Great Building: Imperial Delhi Secretariats." *Builder* 122 (January 6, 1922): 43–4.

Havell, Ernest Binfield. "The Message of Hope for India." *Nineteenth Century and After* 72 (December 1912): 1274–82.

Heal, R. G. "Edwin Lutyens: A Centenary Assessment." *Building* 216 (March 28, 1969): 73–4, 93–4.

Hill, Oliver. "Edwin Landseer Lutyens: 1869–1944." *Builder* 181 (October 26, 1951): 546–50.

———. "The Genius of Sir Edwin Lutyens." *Country Life* 145 (March 27, 1969): 710–12.

Howling, G. J. "Lutyens: Some Reflections." *Builder* 196 (February 13, 1959): 313.

Hussey, Christopher. "An Early Lutyens Castle in the Air." *Country Life* 125 (January 22, 1959): 148–9.

———. "Government House, Delhi." *Country Life* 70 (July 25, 1931): 388–94.

———. "More London Plans from the Royal Academy Planning Committee's Exhibition." *Country Life* 92 (November 6, 1942): 897.

———. "The Personality of Sir Edwin Lutyens." *Journal of the Royal Institute of British Architects* 76 (April 1969): 142–5.

———. "Recent Architecture." *Country Life* 69 (May 9, 1931): 581–3.

———. "Sir Edwin Lutyens, O.M., K.C.I.E., P.R.A." *Country Life* 95 (January 14, 1944): 68–71.

———. "A Vision of the New London: Plans by Sir Edwin Lutyens's Committee Exhibited at the Royal Academy." *Country Life* 92 (October 9, 1942): 692–6.

"Indian Architecture." *British Architect* 80 (July 11, 1913): 19–20.

King, Anthony D. "The Bungalow." *Architectural Association Quarterly* 5 (July–September 1973): 4–26.

"Kingston-upon-Hull: A Plan for the City and County." *Architects' Journal* 104 (October 31, 1946): 313–18.

Kipling, John Lockwood. "The Origin of the Bungalow." *Country Life in America* 19 (February 15, 1911): 308–10.

Knapp-Fisher, Arthur Bedford. "Sir Herbert Baker." *Architects' Journal* 65 (February 16, 1927): 251–62.

Lanchester, Henry Vaughan. "Architecture and Architects in India," lecture, with discussion. *Journal of the Royal Institute of British Architects* 30 (March 24, 1923): 293–308.

———. "The Architecture of the Empire: India." *Architectural Review* 55 (June 1924): 230–5.

———. "The Future of Hull: The Lutyens–Abercrombie Planning Report." *Builder* 171 (November 1946): 448–51.

———. "The Late Sir Edwin Lutyens, O.M., P.R.A." *Builder* 166 (January 7, 1944): 7–8.

Leslie, Sir Bradford. "Delhi, the Metropolis of India," lecture, with discussion. *Journal of the Royal Society of Arts* 61 (December 27, 1912): 133–48.

Lutyens, Sir Edwin Landseer. Foreword to "1874 and After," by Charles Francis Annesley Voysey. *Architectural Review* 70 (October 1931): 91.

———. "Persian Brickwork, II." *Country Life* 73 (February 4, 1933): 118–23.

———. "The Robotism of Architecture." *Observer* (London), January 29, 1928.

———. "What I Think of Modern Architecture." *Country Life* 69 (June 20, 1931): 775–7.

———. "The Work of the Late Philip Webb." *Country Life* 37 (May 8, 1915): 619.

Lutyens, Robert. "The Genesis of Sir Edwin Lutyens." *Country Life* 112 (November 28, 1952): 1726–8.

[Marris, Sir William.] "India and the English." *The Round Table* 1 (November 1910): 41–57.

McIntyre, Mary Lee. "The Gardens of Delhi." *News Circle* (Delhi) 14 (February 1969): 36–9.

Mehta, Vasuedo B. "Mural Paintings at Delhi." *Builder* 137 (December 13, 1929): 996, 1002.

"Modern Indian Art Reviving Old Traditions." *Illustrated London News* 175 (September 7, 1929): 410–11.

"Mr. John Begg." *Building News* 119 (October 1, 1920): 161–2.

"The Necessity for Lutyens." *Architects' Journal* 97 (February 18, 1943): 119–20.

"The New Capital City at Delhi." *Town Planning Review* 4 (October 1913): 187.

"The New Delhi." *Architect & Building News* 115 (May 21, 1926): 464–70.

"The New Delhi." *Builder* 103 (October 18, 1912): 429.

"The New Delhi: The Work of Sir Edwin Lutyens and Sir Herbert Baker." *Architectural Review* 58 (December 1926): 216–25.

"New Government Buildings, Delhi." *Builder* 107 (September 25, 1914): 296.

Nicolson, Sir Harold George. "Marginal Comment." *Spectator* 180 (May 28, 1948): 644.

Pevsner, Nikolaus. "Building With Wit: The Architecture of Sir Edwin Lutyens." *Architectural Review* 109 (April 1951): 216–23.

———. "Richard Norman Shaw, 1831–1912." *Architectural Review* 89 (March 1941): 41–6.

"Plan for London: The Exhibition at the Royal Academy of the Work of the R.A. Planning Committee." *Architect and Building News* 172 (October 16, 1942): 39–45.

Pollen, Hon. Francis. "The Genius of Sir Edwin Lutyens, II: The Last of the Classicists." *Country Life* 145 (April 3, 1969): 794–6.

Pollen, Hon. Mrs. Arthur. "Sir Edwin Lutyens," letter to the editor. *Country Life* 95 (February 4, 1944): 208.

"Recent Lighting Installations." *Electrical Review* (London) 100 (June 17, 1927): 964.

Reilly, Sir Charles Herbert. "Eminent Living Architects and Their Work: Sir Edwin L. Lutyens, R.A." *Building* 4 (May 1929): 200–7.

Reiss, R. L. Review of *Plan for Kingston upon Hull* by Professor Sir Patrick Abercrombie and Sir Edwin Lutyens. *Town and Country Planning* 14 (Winter 1946–7): 170–5.

Richardson, Sir Albert. "The Influence of Lutyens." *Building* 19 (February 1944): 32–4.

———. The Late Sir Edwin Lutyens, O.M., P.R.A." *Builder* 166 (January 7, 1944): 6–7.

———. "Obituary: Sir Herbert Baker." *Journal of the Royal Institute of British Architects* 53 (March 1946): 189–90.

Rouse, Sir Alexander. "New Delhi." *Indian State Railways Magazine* 4 (February 1931): 363–77.

Sahai, Viren. "Lessons from Tradition." *Journal of the Royal Institute of British Architects* 74 (March 1967): 103–10.

Shoosmith, Arthur Gordon. "The Design of New Delhi." *Indian State Railways Magazine* 4 (February 1931): 423–33.

———. "Present-Day Architecture in India." *Nineteenth Century and After* 123 (February 1938): 204–13.

Shoosmith, Mrs. Arthur Gordon. "New Delhi." *Bombay, Baroda, and Central India Annual* (1931); unpaginated.

Singh, Khushwant. "The Two Delhis." 2 parts. Delivered on All-India Radio, December 3, 10, 1968.

Singh, Patwant and George, Walter. "The Architecture of Walter George." *Design* (Bombay) 4 (September 1960): 16–28.

"Sir Edwin Lutyens at the A.A.: Informal Meeting, Thursday, June 2nd, 1932." *Architectural Association Journal* 48 (August 1932): 64–6.

"Sir Edwin Lutyens, O.M., K.I.C.E., P.R.A." *Journal of the Royal Society of Arts* 92 (February 4, 1944): 121–2.

"Sir Edwin Lutyens, O.M., P.R.A.: The Born Artist as Architect." *Times* (London), January 3, 1944.

"Sir Herbert Baker: A Memoir by a Friend." *Builder* 170 (February 15, 1946): 158–9.

Smithson, Alison. "The Responsibility of Lutyens." *Journal of the Royal Institute of Indian Studies* 76 (April 1969): 146–51.

Smithson, Peter. "The Viceroy's House in Imperial Delhi." *Royal Institute of British Architects Journal* 76 (April 1969): 153–4.

"Social Life in the Capital." *Indian State Railways Magazine* 4 (February 1931): 381–3.

Spear, Thomas George Percival. "The Cities of Delhi." *Indian State Railways Magazine* 4 (February 1931): 404–22.

Spence, Sir Basil. "Royal Institute of British Architects: The President's Address." *Builder* 96 (February 6, 1959): 273–4.

Stamp, Gavin. "Indian Summer." *Architectural Review* 159 (June 1976): 365–72.

Summerson, Sir John. "The Lutyens Memorial Volumes." *Journal of the Royal Institute of British Architects* 58 (August 1951): 390–1.

Swinton, George Sitwell Campbell. "New Delhi." *Empire Review* 53 (May 1931): 441–8.

Thompson, Sir John. "Delhi as Capital," lecture, with discussion. *Journal of the East India Association* n.s. 24 (April 1933): 109–38.

"The Town Planning Conference." *Journal of the Royal Institute of British Architects* 3rd ser. 17 (October 22, 1910): 783–97.

Venturi, Robert, and Brown, Denise Scott. "Learning from Lutyens." *Royal Institute of British Architects Journal* 76 (August 1969): 353–4.

Villiers-Stuart, Mrs. Patrick. "Indian Water Gardens," lecture with discussion. *Journal of the Royal Society of Arts* 62 (April 10, 1914): 447–67.

Wedderburn, William. "King George and India." *Contemporary Review* 101 (February 1912): 163–4.

Williams-Ellis, Clough. Review of *Sir Edwin Lutyens: An Appreciation in Perspective*, by Robert Lutyens. *Town and Country Planning* 11 (Spring 1943): 30–1.

Wright, Arthur F. "Symbolism and Function: Reflections on Changan and Other Great Cities." *Journal of Asian Studies* 24 (August 1965): 667–79.

# INDEX

Numbers in italics refer to pages with illustrations.